EXPERIENCING THE TWENTIETH CENTURY

EXPERIENCING THE TWENTIETH CENTURY

Edited by
NOBUTOSHI HAGIHARA
AKIRA IRIYE
GEORGES NIVAT
PHILIP WINDSOR

UNIVERSITY OF TOKYO PRESS

909.82
E

CONTENTS

PREFACE

This book is the outcome of a symposium held at Karuizawa, Japan, in September 1983, under the auspices of The Japan Foundation. Having encouraged intellectual interchange on a variety of specific questions in many parts of the world for the last ten years, the Foundation wished to provide a framework for discussion of the relationship between some of the central themes of the twentieth century. To this end, it invited a number of scholars from Western Europe, the United States, and Japan, drawn primarily from the fields of history, philosophy, and politics. Inevitably, the themes were selective, and the approach was not historical. The discussions were an attempt to confront and relate interpretations of some of the major transformations of the world in this century and their implications for our understanding of the future.

The papers presented at the symposium are reproduced here in full. The discussions have been edited by the steering committee of the symposium, and for that the responsibility is ours.

HAGIHARA Nobutoshi
Akira IRIYE
Georges NIVAT
Philip WINDSOR

March 1984
Divonne-les-Bains, France

CONTRIBUTORS

Saul FRIEDLÄNDER	Professor of History, Tel Aviv University, and Professor, Graduate Institute of International Studies, Geneva
HAGIHARA Nobutoshi	Writer and Historian
Jeanne HERSCH	Formerly Professor of Philosophy, University of Geneva
Akira IRIYE	Professor of History, University of Chicago
James JOLL	Emeritus Professor of International History, University of London
Barry D. KARL	Professor of History, University of Chicago
Leszek KOLAKOWSKI	Senior Research Fellow, All Souls College, Oxford, and Professor of Social Thought, University of Chicago
KYOGOKU Jun-ichi	Professor of Political Science, The University of Chiba, Japan
Charles S. MAIER	Professor of History, Harvard University
MARUYAMA Masao	Formerly Professor of Political Thought, University of Tokyo
Wolfgang J. MOMMSEN	Director, German Historical Institute, London, and Professor of History, University of Düsseldorf

Georges NIVAT — Professor of Russian Language and Literature, University of Geneva

Benjamin I. SCHWARTZ — Professor of History and Government, Harvard University

UMESAO Tadao — Director-General, National Museum of Ethnology, Senri, Japan; formerly Professor of Social Anthropology, Kyoto University

Philip WINDSOR — Reader in International Relations, London School of Economics and Political Science

YAMADA Keiji — Professor of the History of Science, Kyoto University

EXPERIENCING THE TWENTIETH CENTURY

INTRODUCTION: SOME REFLECTIONS ON THE TWENTIETH CENTURY

JAMES JOLL

History does not move at an even speed. There are decades in which it appears to stand still and in which the changes are gradual and, so to speak, underground. But there are other periods, of which the twentieth century is one, when, to quote a phrase used in the 1920s, "History is galloping like a frightened horse." Historians and, perhaps more important, statesmen as different as Bismarck, Lenin, and Harold Macmillan have often seen history in terms of similar metaphors: it is like a river, a railway train, a great wind which carries us along with it. The optimists think they know where they are going and that they can choose their destination; the pessimists see themselves as being carried on inexorably toward an unknown future that lies outside their control. And indeed if we think of history as a river—the river of time—we can divide mankind into three groups: those who swim against the current, those who allow themselves to be carried along with it, and those who believe they can use the force of the current to help them navigate toward their chosen destination.

Every century in every part of the world for which we have any recorded history has experienced crises, whether man-made, such as wars and revolutions, or resulting from natural forces— tempests, earthquakes, floods, famines. Yet many people have the feeling that the crisis of the twentieth century (a phrase we hear all the time) is even deeper and of a different kind from that of any previous epoch. Is this true? Or, rather, why do we think this? There are many reasons, and most derive from two principal features of our century. It has been a century of wars on an unprecedented scale, and it has been a period of technological change of a more rapid and a more fundamental kind than ever before. Two world wars not only caused an exceptional degree of human suffering and economic disruption; they also changed fundamentally the map of the world, since they led directly or indirectly to the creation of many new national states. They changed our ideological attitudes, since they produced in the real world political and social revolutions which previously had existed only in the minds of utopian dreamers or fanatics. They contributed widely, since only a centralized state can effectively conduct a total war, to the extension of the power of the state. The two wars also speeded up technological development, not only—though this was of course the main purpose at the time— by producing new methods of large-scale destruction or of defense against it, but also by developing many techniques that could subsequently be used for peaceful purposes, such as electronic devices or new surgical methods for dealing with injuries.

The application of technology to war, and above all the development of the atomic bomb and its use at Hiroshima and Nagasaki, has left hanging over us a cloud of fear from which we have never escaped and which has in many cases changed fundamentally our attitude to life and to the world around us. Whereas other forms of annihilation that have been predicted—a new ice age or the exhaustion of the world's energy and food supplies—have been situated centuries or at least decades away, the threat of nuclear destruction hangs over us from one moment to the next. There is no need to dwell on this central element in our twentieth-century experience, except perhaps to say that fortunately human beings do carry on with their ordinary lives and occupations as if they were going to live their allotted span of years. Even if we are intellectually convinced of the probability of sudden and total destruction, it is a notable feature of the psychology of the majority of human beings that we continue to act as if we did not believe it. In spite of recurrent eruptions and the permanent threat that these pose to the people who live on the slopes of volcanoes, they persist in returning and carrying on as if nothing had happened and no danger exists. Some people see in these reactions simply a sign of the incorrigible short-sightedness, folly, and frivolity of humankind, but one can perhaps also see in this tenacity a sign of human resilience and capacity to survive.

The threat of nuclear war is obviously so central a feature of our political and international life that it may in fact lead us to overlook some of the other developments resulting from the two world wars which are still profoundly affecting the world. World War I destroyed the Austro-Hungarian and Ottoman empires, as well as creating the conditions for the success of the revolution in Russia. The result was the replacement of these large, multinational states by a number of small, national ones. The peacemakers of 1919, and especially the American President Woodrow Wilson, believed that the triumph of the principle of "national self-determination" would lead to a new and more stable international order. The reverse was the case; and the national tensions that had produced the final crisis in Austria-Hungary and Turkey were now transferred to the international plane. Indeed, one of the most tragic disappointments for the hopes of nineteenth-century liberals has been the sad realization in the twentieth that the creation of national states is not automatically followed by the development of democratic institutions and the growth of international harmony.

World War II was followed by a similar multiplication of national states. Directly or indirectly, it led to the end of the old European empires—British, French, Dutch, Belgian, Portuguese. This process owed much, for better or worse, to the Japanese advance into Southeast Asia. It shattered the belief in the inevitability of European supremacy, as the Japanese victory over Russia nearly forty years earlier had also done. With the Japanese defeat, it also left a vacuum which the old imperial powers, however hard they tried, were unable to fill. The end of European rule in Asia and Africa resulted in yet another proliferation of new states. Some of these, especially in Africa but also in the Middle East, had frontiers that had been drawn to serve the administrative, strategic, or diplomatic convenience of the colonizing powers, rather than following ethnic or physical boundaries. But this has not prevented them from rapidly developing their own strongly felt nationalisms and their own feelings of hostility and rivalry toward their neighbors. Thus over much of the world the two world wars produced a multiplicity of states that were neither democratic, as liberals had hoped they would be, nor living at peace with one another, so that their existence added a new dimension to the international instability of the twentieth century.

This century has been a century of wars. The two world wars, and especially the second, were followed by many smaller wars. There were those involving great powers, as in Korea, Vietnam, Afghanistan, and the South Atlantic, and also those between smaller states—Israel, Syria, Egypt, Iraq, Iran—as well as long drawn-out civil and guerrilla wars providing a constant problem for the great powers as they tried to exploit these conflicts or at least fit them into the overall model of rivalry between the United States and the Soviet Union. The result has been, as Iriye has pointed out, that our century has become one in which the distinction between peace and war has become increasingly blurred. Even if we have so far escaped the "hot war" that may well destroy all life and social organization in many parts of the world, we have a cold war in which an arms race is accompanied by a propaganda campaign that tends increasingly to make people feel that war is inevitable. And at the same time smaller wars and local national tensions constantly tempt the great powers to use them for their own advantage and thus increase the danger that a small war may escalate into a large one. (It is also worth remembering that some of these "small" wars, in the Middle East for example, are after all themselves not so small in terms of the armaments involved or the human suffering caused.)

The two world wars led to a multiplication of the number of national states and this in turn led to a new international instability, contributing to the blurring of the distinction between a world at peace and a world at war. But the two world wars also led to profound social and ideological changes in the internal life of many states: the Russian revolution and Communist hopes of an international revolution, the Fascist regime in Italy and the Nazi regime in Germany, insofar as these were at least in part the product of defeat, and perhaps also the militarization of Japan in the attempt to win and attain a place among the world's great powers. Both the Russian regime established by Lenin and developed by Stalin into a totalitarian dictatorship and the National Socialist system of Adolf Hitler demonstrated new and frightening features which distinguish the twentieth century from previous eras. Earlier dictatorships had attempted to establish all-embracing tyrannies either in the interests of the personal rule of an autocrat or, as in the brief Jacobin phase of the French Revolution, to impose ideological conformity by the use of terror. There had been earlier examples of the hounding to death of heretics and of the enforced confessions of those whom it was intended to execute anyway, as in the Inquisition of the Roman Catholic Church. But never before had the control of every aspect of human life been carried so far or the scale of imprisonment and murder in the name of the state's ideology been so great. This was in part at least the result of the technological means now available—means of mass propaganda, means of police control and espionage, or, most horrifying of all, means of cold-blooded scientific elimination of 6 million European Jews. But this total control was also achieved by ideological indoctrination, so that people came to accept the Nazi ideas of racial superiority and the all-seeing wisdom of the Führer, and this succeeded in masking the reality of dictatorhip and terror, just as the dictatorship of Stalin and his successors is masked by the language of a debased and often meaningless form of Marxist ideology.

One of the effects of this use of ideology for the purpose of totalitarian mass control has been, especially among some members of the intelligentsia of the advanced nations, to make people suspicious of ideology as such or at least critical of the utopian ideologies of the Left which seem to some bound to lead to a Stalinist dictatorship and a Stalinist terror. On the Left, this has led to a reinterpretation of Marx to emphasize the humane and pluralistic elements in his thought and to the revival of those twentieth-century Marxist thinkers who seem, rightly or wrongly, to allow a dialogue with traditional liberal beliefs. On the Right, the experience and observation of Soviet totalitarianism has confirmed a belief that any form of state control carries with it the risk of tyranny, and has produced what is in fact a return to a version of nineteenth-century liberalism, with its emphasis on the freedom of the market and the need for giving scope to individual initiative without interference from the state, regardless, it seems to some, of the injustices to which this gives rise. The reaction against socialist theory and practice as a result of the belief that it leads at worst to a Communist tyranny and at best to the crippling of the economy by an expensive and inefficient bureaucracy has been accompanied by a reaction against a theory of a different kind, that of the economist John Maynard Keynes, who believed—to put it very crudely—that the chief economic problem was that of unemployment and that it could be solved by an increase in consumption brought about by an increase in government spending, and that this course could prolong the life of the capitalist system. The result of the reaction against collectivism and against Keynesianism is that many of the advanced industrial societies seem to be left without an adequate social and economic theory to deal with their problems.

War, nationalism, totalitarian dictatorships: these have undoubtedly been characteristic features of the twentieth century. War accelerated the pace of technological change; the dictatorships showed how technology could be used in the service of tyranny; the breakup of the old global empires and the emergence of a large number of new national states only served to emphasize the gap between the rich nations and the poor ones, between those states which had access to advanced technology and those which did not. This has had many consequences: people from former colonies come to the cities of their former imperial rulers in search of jobs and the amenities of life which they feel only an advanced technology can provide. Often disappointed and frustrated in their hopes, they form a discontented minority that poses a constant social and political problem. The elites of some of the new states, eager for access to the products of modern technology for themselves, if not always for their fellow citizens, are in a position to bargain for technical assistance from the rival great powers, and in the process sometimes overlook the real problems of their countries or the real purposes of those who are offering assistance; and this in turn contributes to international instability.

One of the many paradoxes of the present decade of our century is that, at a moment when the underprivileged of the world dream, however vainly, of attaining some of the benefits of modern technology, some of the intellectuals in the advanced countries are expressing doubts about those benefits. These doubts have taken two forms. First, it seems to many people that some of the by-products and side effects of modern technology are intolerable: the air, the rivers, lakes, and seas are being polluted, the forests are dying, the whole balance of the ecology is being upset. Thus in some advanced countries the desire to attack the symbols of advanced technology, especially nuclear power stations, has led to the development of a significant political movement which wants, it seems, to opt out of the twentieth century and return to a utopian, preindustrial past that in fact never really existed. Second, there are also people who, without joining what has come to be called the "Green" movement, are worried that technology seems to have taken on a momentum of its own which no one can stop, especially in fields involving the construction of artificial intelligences and even the creation of life itself. Man, it is felt, is taking on himself the function of God and, like Icarus in the Greek myth, who made wings and ventured too near the sun and in so doing destroyed himself, will pay a fearful penalty, or, like Goethe's sorcerer's apprentice who made a robot he was unable to stop, will lose control of his own creations. (It is striking, as has often been observed, how these archetypal myths still have relevance.)

It is possible that this view is more common in Europe and North America than among the Japanese, who have been so successful in solving technological problems; and indeed there seems no reason why technology should not be able to solve the problems it itself has created as long as technologists are constantly reminded that it is their duty to do so—by, for example, solving the problem of the disposal of atomic waste by the construction of improved reactors, since otherwise we should have to renounce all uses of nuclear power. What is certain, however, is that any effective action to deal with the side effects of technological advance such as the pollution of cities or rivers must involve government action, and that a neo-conservatism bent on dismantling the powers of the state will find itself powerless in the face of those vested interests which put immediate personal profit before long-term public loss, and so be unable to prevent the destruction of the environment.

For the past hundred years at least, Western intellectuals, and especially those in reasonably secure economic positions, have suffered from recurrent fits of what the Germans call *Kulturpes-*

simismus, a despair about the future of our culture. It is easy to make fun of this and to point, for example, to the paradox of people brought from all over the world by jet aircraft to a symposium in Japan, listening in air-conditioned rooms to a simultaneous translation of speeches deploring the advance of technology. Yet these feelings of cultural despair do represent an important feature of the intellectual and emotional life of the advanced countries of today. In the nineteenth century science weakened the hold of religion, especially of Christianity, while at the same time the prevailing optimistic liberal philosophy seemed to promise a future in which all problems could be solved by rational and scientific means. The world would become one in which, to quote Herbert Spencer: "Progress is not an accident but a necessity. Surely must evil and immorality disappear; surely must men become perfect." When this did not happen and when human efforts to control society and the environment did not work out as we had hoped, and indeed sometimes had horrifying results, so that a positivist faith in science and social planning had to be abandoned, we were left without many traditional beliefs and without, it seemed, anything to put in their place. Just as Nietzsche had proclaimed, God was dead, while at the same time the utopian visions of a man-made future had failed. (It is true that the so-called death of God mattered less to those of us who had never believed that he existed and was perhaps not so critical for those people who grew up in non-Christian or at least non-monotheistic societies. Does it mean much in the Japanese "cosmos of meaning" in which, in Kyogoku's words, "there is no personal god who has dialogue directly with human beings" but rather "the eternal being inheres ... in everything in the cosmos"?)

While we can understand and sympathize with those who see in a revival of a personal religious faith the only hope for humankind, we must also sometimes wonder whether there is not too much belief around in the twentieth century. The terrorists who kill ruthlessly and often indiscriminately and are willing to sacrifice themselves in the process do not lack conviction or belief in their nationalist or revolutionary goals. The present regime in Iran justifies its tyranny in terms of a return to the Islamic faith and Islamic law.

The twentieth century has seen horrors at least as great and perhaps, because of the technical means at our disposal, greater than those of any previous century. It has also seen achievements which provide means to save, improve, and enrich human life as great or greater than those in any other century. The two are intimately connected, and in the perpetual struggle in history between good and evil it is too soon to say which will triumph. The belief that everything is possible can be a source of hope or of despair, and which we choose is often as much a matter of temperament or even perhaps of physical constitution as of rational decision. Our fate is perhaps, as Leszek Kolakowski has said, bound to be a clumsy compromise. The French writer Romain Rolland once wrote that we must be "pessimists of the intellect and optimists of the will." The discussion recorded in this volume has not been without some intellectual pessimism, but the tone of the argument, the rational analysis of a wide range of fundamental problems, has given ground for optimism. It has helped us to look directly, without hypocrisy and without the obfuscations of the language of rival propaganda systems, at the problems of our troubled and dramatic century. It has done all that any intellectual discussion can be expected to do—that is, to show us, in the words of the eighteenth-century British philosopher Bishop Berkeley, that "things are what they are and the consequences of them what they may be. Why then should we seek to be deceived?"

WAR AND PEACE

WHAT JAPAN MEANS TO
THE TWENTIETH CENTURY

HAGIHARA NOBUTOSHI

I

The theme that I am proposing to treat in this paper will be approached in a somewhat crab-like manner. I am really concerned with the question of the responsibility a nation has, or should have, to itself and to common standards of human decency. There is an immediate paradox here: A nation's responsibility to itself could take the form of nationalism, which might completely disregard more general criteria for all humanity. Equally, a sense of obligation to humanity, such as that commonly expressed in the various "peace movements" in the world at present, could take the form of an abrogation by a nation of its own spirit of independence, even that of a state's renouncing its obligations toward its own citizens. The crux of the paradox lies in the fact that the sovereign state is still the only framework we possess for the perpetuation of a culture which allows and enjoins us to behave toward each other as civilized and responsible human beings (culture might be negatively defined as that without which we are merely the most savage of animals), but it is also the framework within which, and conscious of our culture as we are, we can commit the most barbarous acts (all wars are ultimately justified by the need to defend cultural values). In my view, Japan has experienced the consequences of this paradox in a particularly vivid way, and I think that the nature of the Japanese experience should be of some interest to a group examining the twentieth century.

At the same time, however—and this accounts for my crab-

15

like approach—the Japanese experience between the years of the
Meiji Restoration in 1868 and the drafting of the present constitution in 1946 has been unique. I therefore think this experience both helps to throw into relief some of the central problems
we might consider and also must be understood in its own terms.
What I wish to do is to consider these terms first: the characteristics of the Japanese experience, in which I shall touch upon
the men of 1868, the men of 1919, and the men of 1945. I shall
also consider Japan's position in terms of the center vs. the periphery, and the question of whether it created or only responded
to history. Thereafter, I shall look at the problems Japan must
confront today. In examining these, I shall treat the idea of the
spirit of independence, that of responsibility, and that of an
Orwellian decency as if they were one and the same. I am aware
that they are not, but that is meant to state a paradox, not resolve it, and perhaps to provide a basis for discussion. This paper
is in consequence deliberately inconclusive.

Now, to some aspects of the Japanese experience, in other
words to history—which in the case of twentieth-century Japan
begins in the nineteenth century. Almost everything in modern
Japan can be traced back to the Meiji Restoration of 1868 and
its background, so that it would not be inappropriate to discuss
that briefly, before going on to the twentieth century. It is also
worth examining why the fate of China was so different from that
of Japan, when the two countries were forcibly dragged by the
Western powers into an international society under their command and on their terms. Why was Japan more fortunate than
its neighbor?

In the first place, Japan had already been accustomed to using
an outside model for over a thousand years, so much so that, in a
sense, the Japanese were "professionals" in this respect. All that
was required was to change the model or the goal value, from
China to the West. It had long been a Japanese tradition to take
a "low," or even "resigned" posture and to place itself on the
periphery while imbibing from the center. For this reason, if the
eminent American scholar had entitled his book *Japan as No. 2*
instead of *Japan as No. 1*, it would have been more telling. This
relationship between the center and the periphery also helps to
explain the typical Japanese attitude of responding to history

rather than creating it. Such an approach can degenerate into irresponsible opportunism, but can also produce a people fundamentally pluralistic rather than monistic—yet bearing the burden of an inner tension and moral and intellectual uncertainty. The case of the center, the self-contained Middle Kingdom of China, was very different.

I will not dwell on a further consideration, the obvious political and military advantages of Japan's geographical position, but it might be worth pointing out that these helped to save Japan from the fundamentalist approach of Korea, which was much more wholehearted in accepting such Chinese doctrines as Confucianism. In consequence, Japan was able to continue learning from outside, even from the West, throughout its semi-secluded period of nearly two hundred years (semi-secluded because it was never entirely closed to the Chinese, the Koreans, and the Dutch, however small their number was). This certainly contributed to cultural maturity—for example the spread of literacy well below the ruling *samurai* classes.

Finally, China also provided an anti-model for Japan. Its humiliating defeats in the Opium War of 1840–42 and in the war against the combined Anglo-French forces in 1856–60 spelled out unforgettable lessons which were learned thoroughly by the Japanese.

One can see therefore that the Japanese were ready to switch their model from China to the West. But this does not mean that it was easy. Japan had to undergo a "baptism of fire" several times, in bombardments by Western warships and in civil wars, the last of which was the Satsuma Rebellion of 1877.

Throughout these turbulent years of the 1860s and 1870s, however, the strength of national sentiment, shared by all sides, was so impressive that one foreign observer, the British diplomat Ernest Satow, had already remarked in 1870: "The (British) Legation (in Tokyo) must be terribly shorthanded. I quite share your feeling of disgust with Japan. For at least a year before I left, I had ceased to take any interest in the work. The natives may be making progress there, but we foreigners only fall back, I think."[1]

This remark is doubly interesting, first because Satow was one of the best-informed foreigners on Japan, and had already spent seven years there, but also because he had been deeply involved in Japanese politics and had sided with the anti-Tokugawa forces. The Meiji Restoration two years earlier should have been a triumphant moment for him. But the letter quoted here seems to convey a sense of alienation and even a sense of failure. Perhaps, in addition to the strength of nationalism, Satow had the experienced cool-headed calculation of gains and losses in the intrigues preceding the Meiji Restoration that would later become the basis of mature political skills.

The Meiji Restoration can be regarded as the first successful national revolution outside the West. Western imperialism had often been founded upon willing or unwilling collaboration, but in the case of Japan in the 1860s it was unable to find what one might call a Japanese political "comprador."

II

After the Meiji Restoration, Japan accepted the nineteenth century wholeheartedly, and the new model became the West. Taking full advantage of its position as the late-comer, Japan made serious efforts to choose and select "teachers" in the different spheres of Western civilization—the British navy, German army, French police system, and so on. The German constitution and its practice provide the most prominent example, but that is partly because the British system was too subtle to imitate quickly, apart from the lack of a written constitution. But on the whole, Britain, or the British Empire, long remained the center of the model, and "Britain in the Far East" was both an emotional aspiration and a catchword. This will explain the symbolic meaning of the Anglo-Japanese alliance of 1902 (and its ending in 1921 under American pressure), which was far greater than that of mere diplomatic and military usefulness, especially for the men of 1868 and their successors.

Japan encountered the twentieth century in the midst of heightened Western imperialist activity in East Asia, the battle of concessions in China between 1895 and 1904. In the process, Japan followed suit and cast itself as a full-fledged imperialist power, though as early as 1876, eight years after the Restoration, Japan had already experienced the first taste of imperialist power in a minor degree in Korea. That is, Japan forcibly opened the gate of the more secluded and the more fundamentalist Korea and imposed "unequal" treaties, even though Japan itself was suffering from them and was trying to revise them into more equal ones.

The battle of concessions was in turn the result of Japan's victory over China, which amply disclosed the weakness of the Middle Kingdom. It started with the Triple Intervention by Russia, Germany, and France against Japan's gains, immediately after the peace treaty in April 1895. Satow returned to Japan as the new British minister and asked Salisbury, the prime minister, for instructions in view of the probable Russian advance southward, and also of the fact that the British attitude on the occasion of the Triple Intervention had caused considerable disappointment among the Japanese leaders. Salisbury replied: "I am quite sure their conduct will not be biased, when the time for decision arrives, by any recollection of what we or Russia or France may have done for them or against them in the past."[2] Salisbury had recognized the political maturity and shrewdness of the Japanese leaders.

In fact, Japan managed to live through the strains of the imperialist era in East Asia and emerged successfully from it. The climax of its success was the victory in the Russo-Japanese War of 1904–5. "Until the enormous impact of the Japanese victory over Russia in 1904 [sic], no non-European people presented itself to the gaze of Western social or political theorists as a nation in the full sense of the word."[3] The victory frustrated Russia's ambitions in East Asia and turned its attention back to Europe, especially to the Balkans, so helping to bring about World War I. It also inspired the first revolution in Russia itself. And it encouraged the awakening of the political consciousness of non-Western peoples, for example, in India.

Its impact upon the Japanese themselves was, needless to say, also enormous, and the memories of the victory rather than the war itself became the basic frame of reference for the subsequent Japanese mentality. The war was the last war conducted by the men of 1868, and after the victory, Japan's goal was to become what might be called a "respectable imperialist" in the eyes of the West, the center. The trouble was that the center would itself be diversified as time went on, especially after World War I. Herein lies a major contrast between the experience of Japan and that of the West.

Japan did not really experience World War I, and this is fundamental to any understanding of its later conduct. The Japanese were unable to cope with the ideas and forces released by the war. If the Great War opened the twentieth century, Japan remained outside until 1945—a nineteenth-century state or a pre-1914 imperialist state, at least as far as the Japanese military and political leaders were concerned. With fading memories of the Russo-Japanese War, they continued nineteenth-century imperialist practices, even when confronted with a new situation in East Asia which combined Chinese nationalism, American idealistic internationalism, and Soviet communism.

It is true that in 1919, Japan tried to have inserted in the covenant of the League of Nations a declaration of the principle of racial equality, and its rejection by Wilson came as a shock. But it was accompanied by another proposal, to take over the German concessions in the Shantung peninsula (which was accepted), so Japan's resentment over the former proposal can hardly be justified easily. China, of course, refused to sign the Treaty of Versailles because of the latter.

The effects of the ending of the Anglo-Japanese alliance can perhaps be overestimated. But its symbolic meaning was the diversification of the center, in itself a result of the disintegration of the West after World War I. Even then, Britain appeared as a power in East Asia with which Japan could talk on the old terms; but the growing British preoccupation with Europe, especially after Hitler's rise to power, closed this possibility. Japan was isolated not only diplomatically but also mentally from the twentieth century.

Chinese nationalists often remarked wistfully that the spirit of the Meiji Restoration was the model for their aspirations. They questioned the inability of the children of the Meiji Restoration to appreciate Chinese nationalist ideas. Perhaps the men of 1868 might have been able to respond more sympathetically or more wisely, but between the makers of the Restoration and their children, between those who created history and those who responded to it, there was a qualitative difference.

The old "center" for Japan was certainly the British Empire, but its disappearance, as the center was diversified, left Japan without a sense of direction. Japan became, or had to become, a "quasi-center" itself and continued to impose its own imperialist designs on Korea and China, partly because imperialism could sustain itself only through further imperialist advances, partly because of the fear of Soviet communism, partly because of the sheer unintelligibility of American idealistic obstinacy.

The chain of events between the Manchurian incident of 1931 and 1941 is well known and can hardly be called other than a succession of imperialist aggressions. They were not inevitable because alternative courses were open at each stage of the process. But they are also partly to be accounted for by the fact that Japan was the least affected among the victorious powers of World War I in that Japan had only gained and had not lost anything. Thereby, it lost a great deal.

III

The contrast between the men of 1868 and the men of 1941 is that Japan drifted through the 1930s with a basically pre-1914 mentality, one which only responded to history rather than making it. Maruyama Masao has summarized the mental process of the political and military leaders as that of "submission to *faits accomplis*."[4] Mentally and diplomatically isolated, Japan was anxious to seek a partner in the West. Thus, the anti-Comintern pact with Nazi Germany was concluded in 1936 on the assumption that Nazi Germany was still the old imperialist Germany. There was perhaps some truth in that, but still the pact showed the lack of understanding of Nazism, a major twentieth-century phenomenon. When the Nazi-Soviet Pact was signed in 1939, the cabinet resigned, saying that "the European situation was too complicated and too strange to be intelligible"—an extraordinary confession of intellectual isolation from what was happening in the center of the twentieth century. Even worse was Japan's alliance with Nazi Germany in September 1940, despite the "betrayal" of the previous year, by which Japan almost cut off with its own hands any possibility of negotiation with the Anglo-Saxons. The chief background to this alliance was Japan's fascination with German blitzkrieg tactics and its easy triumph over France a few months earlier.

On November 26, 1941, three days after he had presented the Japanese ambassador with a high-handed note (which in Japanese eyes at least was certainly an ultimatum), U.S. Secretary of State Cordell Hull expressed to Lord Halifax, then the British Ambassador in Washington, "the view that the diplomatic part of our relations with Japan was virtually over and the matter will now go to the officials of the Army and the Navy." Then, he went on, "A calm, deliberate Japanese government would more than ever desire to wait another thirty days to see whether the German Army is driven out of Russia by winter," but added that the Japanese government "would probably take no serious notice of the Russian-German situation but would go forward in this desperate undertaking which they have advocated for some time."[5] The shrewdness of the Japanese politicians on which Salisbury had relied in 1895 had now disappeared.

The disregard for the European situation was further emphasized by the fact that it was the very day after the successful attack on Pearl Harbor that Hitler abandoned the idea of capturing Moscow and ordered the German Army to change to a defensive posture because of the "unusually cold weather."[6] This is only an incidental example, but it shows how irrational Japan's decision-making had become by this time.

Hitler's attack on Russia had "revolutionized" the "whole outlook of the war,"[7] but this was not grasped by the Japanese leaders. Indeed, it only hastened their advance into the southern part of French Indo-China, to which the United States retaliated with an oil embargo—a fatal blow to the Japanese war economy. Meanwhile, all the reports on the Russian front from the Japanese embassy in Berlin, a key listening post, merely conveyed the public statements from Hitler's headquarters. Even though it was told through the German embassy in Washington that the Americans had broken its diplomatic code, the Japanese foreign ministry did not react seriously.[8]

In many ways one can see that the Japanese decisions were being made without regard to the rapidly changing situation outside the country. Japanese leaders made decisions as if they were simply rejecting the "disturbing intervention" of the latest intelligence. Finally, at the beginning of November, the Japanese government decided to go to war with the United States if the American-Japanese negotiations, which had been going on (and off) in Washington since April, had not reached a satisfactory conclusion (to Japan of course) by the end of the month. In this decision, the question of oil was taken seriously, but not that of the Russian front.

At any rate, Japan's irrationality in this context indicates the irrelevance to Japan, and the Japanese ignorance, of the situation in America and in Europe. If we confine our consideration only to the high-handed Hull Note of November 26, the ensuing war might be described as inevitable. But if we extend our view a little further back to the chain of events from the moment of the German attack on Russia in June, the myth of inevitability begins to collapse. If we extend the view further back to the Axis alliance of 1940, the undeclared war with China of 1937, the Manchurian incident of 1931, and so on, we are bound to ask how we could possibly call Japan's chain of follies and misdeeds inevitable.

Before the Hull Note, there was a slight possibility of reaching a *modus vivendi* between Japan and America, on the basis of returning to the situation before Japan's advance into southern French Indo-China in July. According to Hull, that was destroyed by Chiang Kai-shek, with the support of Churchill.[9] Certainly, any American-Japanese rapprochement, however temporary, could have been made only at the expense of the Chinese. This takes us back once again to the chain of Japanese actions in China in the 1930s.

In the process of the war, the twentieth century was forced on Japan in its totality from above and from outside, as symbolized by "unconditional surrender" and the dropping of the atomic bombs. Japan was finally and forcibly dragged into the heart of the twentieth century in the form of total destruction. In a sense, World War II was for Japan, its World War I, which helps to explain what subsequently happened after its defeat.

IV

After 1945, the Japanese may have been catapulted into a post-twentieth century, jumping over the realities of the twentieth century; and thus Japan may no longer be inside this century. I am referring to the Japanese constitution of 1946, including Article 9.[10]

In this connection, I am interested in two remarks made recently by Miyazawa Kiichi, a Liberal-Democratic politician. First, he says that though he does not deny that he often wonders how long the present political system could be effective hereafter in general terms, he still believes that it does work effectively. The nucleus of this political system is clearly the Japanese constitution, including Article 9; and both the belief and the doubt on the part of Miyazawa involve the problems of social memories and of the men of 1945. Second, Miyazawa says that when he was asked what he thought was the "undesirable" by-product of that system, he replied: "If Fukuzawa Yukichi were alive, he would probably reply that what was lost was 'the spirit of independence.' "[11] But he also invites a consideration of the problem of Japan's responsibility which, in my view, is closely related to the further question of how Japan can be decent as a nation if it wishes to offer something to the twentieth century.

The Japanese constitution is clearly based on American drafts (the "occupying" American drafts) which were presented to the Japanese government in February 1946 after the American general headquarters had rejected earlier Japanese proposals. The "undignified" context of its birth has always been quoted since by those who disapprove of the constitution.

On the occasion of the debates in the Upper House of the Diet, the government invited a group of distinguished professors of law and political science to offer their opinions. The group as a whole was strongly critical of Article 9, which in turn was passionately defended by the government. Nambara Shigeru, professor at the University of Tokyo, and later president of that university, expressed his criticism in these words: "The higher our ideal is, the more realistically we should see the actual state of affairs at our feet. Otherwise, it will become a mere fantasy. When the drafts of this constitution were made public, a part of the American press described it as nothing more than a mere utopia, which in my opinion we should listen to. War should not exist—this is certainly a principle of political morality of universal validity. But the fact is, however regrettable, that as long as human beings exist, wars will also continue to exist. That is the reality of history. When we look squarely at this reality of history, it is absolutely natural to think that our country should have the right of self-defense at least, and should possess armed forces with the minimum capacity to sustain the right of self-defense. In the Lower House of the Diet, Prime Minister Yoshida Shigeru explained, so I hear, that many aggressive wars have been waged in the past in the name of the right of self-defense, and that therefore it would be better to abandon the right of self-defense itself. Does this mean that he is proposing to abandon the right of self-defense even if or even when its execution is regarded as objectively valid and correct? I am sure that the government hopes and expects that Japan will be admitted to the United Nations someday in the future. Having this in mind, does the government still think that the constitution will not conflict with the duty that the members of the United Nations should observe? The United Nations certainly recognizes that each state should have the right of self-defense, and I ask whether the government is proposing that when we are admitted into the United Nations in the future, Japan should abandon both its right and duty under the United Nations. If such a situation should arise, I am seriously concerned that Japan might be in danger of permanently becoming a nation of Oriental resignation or defeatism, relying for its existence and survival only on the good will and the good faith of other nations. If such things were to occur, I am seriously concerned that our positive ideal of defending freedom and justice, without hesitating to accept the sacrifice of our blood and sweat alongside those who share the same ideal, so as to establish a lasting peace in the world, would have to be abandoned."[12]

How did the government respond to Nambara? Yoshida's reaction was twofold. In one way he referred to the past, as Nambara had already mentioned. But he also declared that by this unprecedented act and clause in the constitution, Japan desired to show the world its determination to contribute to peace in the future. Shidehara Kijūrō, the former prime minister, was more emphatic than Yoshida about the future role of Japan in the vanguard of the peace-loving forces.[13]

The Japanese constitution was born in this manner. It was based on common memories of the recent past, and seriously debated by the men of 1945. And Nambara's questions almost forestalled all the subsequent criticisms leveled by the anti-constitutional voices, except in one respect, namely the "undignified" nature of its birth.

I am trying to be provocative here for the sake of argument because I feel that otherwise there is little point in having this kind of symposium. I am also aware that this is not an occasion to concentrate exclusively on Japan but one on which to consider problems common to "advanced" industrial societies in the twentieth century. But I am trying to suggest how Japan illustrates some of these twentieth-century themes.

I had also better make clear my position toward the constitution. I think that it has worked very well and that the ideals embodied in it are really worth defending. But it is undeniable that the common memories which are the basis of the constitution are naturally weakening as the years go by, and that the men of 1945, shrinking in number, are being replaced by new men who "don't know the defeat, the war, and the preceding events." In fact, Miyazawa, too, is a man of 1945.

And I do share his misgivings in the remark in which he quotes Fukuzawa. Indeed Nambara had already touched upon them in his speech. An "independent" nation without the "spirit of independence," to put it crudely, seems to have been their basis. Nambara's questions have been seriously discussed, but the answers are not convincing. They are either to renounce armed forces, or else to be armed at a lower level in the name of greater security. There is some merit to these partial answers, but they do not carry much conviction in terms of the "ordinary man" within ourselves. Or, one might put it in another way by quoting George Orwell's memorable words, in which he refers to "left-wing intellectuals who are so 'enlightened' that they cannot understand the most ordinary emotions."[14]

But what of the spirit of independence? Under this constitution and its application by successive conservative governments, rationalism, the cool-headed calculation of profit and loss, has realized itself almost completely. Its contribution to Japan's economic recovery has been enormous.

But the spirit of independence requires something more than a rational calculation of profit and loss. It requires self-sacrifice rather than self-interest or self-preservation. A preoccupation with security, which is not necessarily the product of the constitution but which has certainly been strengthened by it, could go to the other extreme from the spirit of independence. And such a highly idealistic clause could sometime lead to a desolate state of mind.

In this deadlock, I would even propose that those who wish to defend the constitution and its ideals, including myself, should go a step further and take the initiative in putting the constitution to a test by a national referendum. It will naturally help to clear up the problem of its "undignified" birth. It will help to clarify the ideals of the Preamble and Article 9. It will help to revitalize Japanese politics. It will help awaken a sense of responsibility. It will help to open serious discussion on Japan's positive role to the outside world, which will lead to the question of what Japan means to the twentieth century. And it will help create new memories of the constitution which can morally sustain the new men of the coming generation, when the men of 1945 have all departed. In such a context, the outcome of discussion lies beyond rational calculation. After all, we would need a symbolic act to confront the paradox mentioned at the beginning of this paper, if we are to make the constitution a challenge for the future.

This year is the eve of Orwell's 1984, but for the postwar Japanese it is also the 38th year after the defeat of 1945—just as Japan's victory over Russia took place in the 38th year of the Meiji period. This could inspire some comparative association of ideas on Japan's different forms of success, but they might be better related to each other in terms of memories. A major industry of Orwell's Oceania is the gradual destruction of social memory. But even without such deliberate action from above, social memories can metamorphose or simply evaporate in modern society—as indicated by those of the Russo-Japanese War. In this sense we should be alert, as it were, in treating our memories of the defeat of 1945, which have so far provided moral assets for the postwar Japanese.

Of course, there are two other alternatives for Japan. The first is to refrain consciously from meaning anything positive to the twentieth century while Japan places itself in a modest position on the periphery, always keeping some distance from the center. This posture accords with Japan's traditional role; but sometimes it is also accompanied by serious reflections on Japan's performance in the 1930s. That is, when Japan played the role of "quasi-center," it imposed its designs only on its neighbors at their expense. The morality of this alternative is that of *Japan as No. 2*, a state of "divided soul." But this modest posture, too, might be difficult to sustain without the memories of the defeat of 1945, especially if the country begins to feel like *Japan as No. 1* or an emerging superstate, encouraged and flattered to do so from outside.

The other alternative is simply that of responding to history rather than creating it. More crudely, just drifting. Sticking to the enjoyment of the present without reflections or regrets about the past, and without any longing for the future. Remaining basically conservative in disposition, but trying only to maximize the utility of the present.

But these two alternatives cannot create the social basis or the background for a sense of decency, which is morally related to Fukuzawa's "spirit of independence." Nor can they hope to foster a sense of responsibility. Are we entitled to urge a sense of decency on the collective body of a nation? By definition, a sense of decency is spontaneous in nature and does not provide a platform for the coercion of others, including "ordinary people."

So my paper is bound to be inconclusive, but I hope it does provide a basis for discussion.

Notes

[1] Satow to W. G. Aston, London, 14 June 1870, Satow Papers, PRO 30/33/11/2, Public Record Office, London.

[2] Salisbury to Satow, Private, 3 October 1895, Salisbury Papers, Christ Church, Oxford.

[3] Isaiah Berlin, "Nationalism," in his *Against the Current* (London, 1979), p. 354.

[4] Masao Maruyama, "Thought and Behaviour Patterns of Japan's Wartime Leaders," in his *Thought and Behaviour in Modern Japanese Politics*, ed. Ivan Morris (Oxford, 1969), p. 103ff.

[5] Memorandum of Conversation, by the Secretary of State, 29 November 1941, *Foreign Relations of the United States*, 1941, vol. 4, The Far East (Washington, 1956), pp. 685–87.

[6] *Hitler's War Directives, 1939–1945*, ed. H. R. Trevor-Roper (London, 1966), pp. 165–70.

[7] B. H. Liddell Hart, *History of the Second World War* (London, 1970), p. 141.

[8] German chargé d'affaires (Washington) to the Foreign Ministry (Berlin), 28 April

1941, *Documents on German Foreign Policy*, Series D, vol. 12, no. 418. The Japanese ambassador in Berlin, Ōshima Hiroshi, relayed this information to Tokyo shortly afterward.

9 *The Memoirs of Cordell Hull* (London, 1948), vol. 2, p. 1077ff.

10 Article 9 reads as follows: "Aspiring sincerely to an international peace based on justice and order, the Japanese people forever renounce war as a sovereign right of the nation and the threat or use of force as a means of settling international disputes. In order to accomplish the aim of the preceding paragraph, land, sea, and air forces, as well as other war potential, will never be maintained. The right of belligerency of the state will not be recognized."

The relevant part of the Preamble reads as follows: "We, the Japanese people, desire peace for all time and are deeply conscious of the high ideals controlling human relationship, and we have determined to preserve our security and existence, trusting in the justice and faith of the peace-loving peoples of the world. . . ." Also, see an important observation by Maruyama on Article 9, "Some Reflections on Article IX of the Constitution," in *Thought and Behaviour*, pp. 290–320.

11 Quoted in Gotō Motoo, Uchida Kenzō, and Ishikawa Masumi, *Sengo Hoshu Seiji no Kiseki* [Records of conservative governments in postwar Japan] (Tokyo, 1982), pp. 324–25. Fukuzawa (1835–1901) was an important and influential philosopher and educator of the first half of the Meiji period (1868–1912).

12 Nambara expressed this view in the Upper House on 27 August 1946. Proceedings of the 90th Session of the Imperial Diet, House of Peers, vol. 24. Author's translation.

13 Yoshida, for example, made a remark to this effect in the Upper House on 5 September 1946. Proceedings of the 90th Session of the Imperial Diet, House of Peers, Select Committee on Revision of the Imperial Constitution, vol. 5.

14 "My Country Right or Left," *The Collected Essays, Journalism, and Letters of George Orwell* (London, 1969), vol. 1, p. 540.

WAR AS PEACE, PEACE AS WAR

AKIRA IRIYE

"Is there a way to liberate mankind from the doom of war?"
asked Albert Einstein in a letter he wrote to Sigmund Freud in
September 1932.[1] The same question has been asked by virtually
every living human being in the twentieth century. It is, to be
sure, not exclusively a twentieth-century problem; neither war nor
concern about war can be considered unique to this century. At
the same time, never before has the whole of mankind been more
preoccupied by visions of total destruction through war—or more
powerless in preventing calamitous mass murder. No discussion
of the present century would be complete without recognition of
these facts. And yet it is difficult to see in what ways the century
has produced novel ideas about war and peace. It may be that
about the only significant contribution the twentieth century has
made to theories of war and peace is the Orwellian dictum that
"war is peace."

Einstein's letter posed war and peace as opposites. It had been
written on behalf of the International Institute of Intellectual
Cooperation, an organ of the League of Nations. The institute
had been anxious to have prominent thinkers of the time exchange
letters on matters "calculated to serve the common interest of the
League of Nations and of the intellectual life of mankind." Such
a mandate in itself is interesting, reflecting a widely shared view
in the 1920s that "intellectual cooperation" was one sure way of
promoting peace. I shall come back to this point later. In his
letter to Freud, Einstein noted that "because of technological
progress, a threat to our very existence" had to be considered a
real possibility. The only way to prevent war would be "the unconditional renunciation by all nations of part of their freedom

31

of action and sovereignty." Here the eminent physicist was expressing a typically interwar view that the existence of modern states was in itself a condition that bred wars. He also shared the growing pessimism that not much could be done about restricting national sovereignty. The "desire for power" on the part of nations had never been curtailed, and within each society the ruling class, "in possession of the schools, the church, and the press," had succeeded in obtaining mass compliance with the drive for national power. The masses, too, despite the fact that they "stand only to lose and to suffer" by war, had frequently been aroused "to the point of insanity," exhibiting a "mass psychosis . . . of hate and destruction." The intelligentsia, on its part, had only too readily succumbed to "disastrous collective suggestion." Given such a condition of modern existence, Einstein wondered if it would ever be possible to "guide the psychological development of man" in such a way that he would overcome "the need to hate and to destroy."

In this brief letter one can readily see several prevailing ideas about war and peace. War was seen as an agent of destruction, an anticivilizational force. The paradox, of course, was that it was also a product of modern civilization; Einstein particularly stressed technological development and mass indoctrination as two important aspects of modern warfare. He was also interested in the psychological dimension. Reflecting the growing fascination of intellectuals with the primeval and the irrational, he wondered if "the need to hate and to destroy" was not inherent in human nature and, if so, how man could be made to resist such psychosis. Finally, Einstein was concerned with the role of intellectuals. They, he assumed, should be the agents of peace, and he had advocated the creation of "an association of intellectuals . . . in the fight against war." But too often they had betrayed their role as potential peacemakers and instead made use of their privileged status to inflame the masses with visions of national glory.

Because, for Einstein, modern war made no sense but was a product of irrationality, he eagerly sought Freud's insights. The latter's response accepted the dichotomy of war and peace. The psychologist agreed that while the "prevention of war is only possible if men agree upon the establishment of a central body to which legal powers are given to resolve all conflicts of interest," the "dominant national ideals of today" ran counter to the institution of such a body. Freud also shared Einstein's view that because of "highly developed weapons of destruction," a future war would "probably mean the eradication of one or perhaps both adversaries." However, Freud was hopeful that this very possibility would persuade nations and peoples not to resort to war. More fundamentally, he believed that modern man was the product of a cultural process that had created "psychological attitudes" which conflicted with and rebelled against war, aggression, and destructiveness. According to him, just as "readiness to go to war represents the discharge of the destructive instinct," it could be checked by "the other instinct, Eros," which created "emotional ties between human beings and must inevitably counteract war." Man's cultural development had been accompanied by the "strengthening of the intellect which is beginning to dominate the instincts, and internalization of the aggressive instinct." In this sense, war "conflicts with the psychological attitude which results from the cultural process." In other words, while war might appear to be "a natural occurrence, biologically well founded, and evidently scarcely avoidable," it must also be seen as counter to human instincts of self-preservation. Modern man, at least, had come to recognize that "war destroys hopeful lives, puts the individual into situations which degrade him, forces him to murder others, and destroys precious things created by human hands." The fact that war nevertheless occurred had to be attributed to insufficient recognition of these facts. For this reason, Freud emphasized the need for "an elite of independent thinkers" to provide leadership to the masses and to continue their struggle for truth against intimidation and irrationality. Unlike Einstein, he was confident that "everything that serves to promote cultural development works against war," and that the intellectuals were agents of this process.

In analyzing war in these terms, Freud too was reflecting the contemporary fascination with the relationship between modern civilization and destructive warfare—or, in his words, between "cultural development" and aggression. He was eloquent in asserting that as man reached a certain stage of cultural development, his interests and preoccupations turned more toward matters that created emotional ties and intellectual identifications with other humans. That was why he agreed with Einstein in calling for an association of cultural elites in various countries to speak for and maintain peace. This was a vision of peace defined as intellectual understanding.

Between the two of them, Einstein and Freud summed up most of the ideas about war and peace that had emerged by the fourth decade of the century. Some of them went back to the nineteenth century. To begin with, as Raymond Aron reminds us in his recent book, *Pensez la guerre, Clausewitz*, there was the Clausewitzian legacy. In the classical formulation of Karl von Clausewitz, war was a means to a specific end, and it was to be conducted as expeditiously as possible so as to bring about the annihilation of the enemy's will to fight. As Aron himself admits, this view of war was not universally shared or practiced. World War I certainly ran counter to this view, as the goals of war kept changing while contending armies dug in for a long period of trench warfare. That war, once started, would go beyond all bounds of rationality had been recognized by writers prior to 1914, and in fact the predominant view in the West had been to equate war with irrationality, primitiveness, and emotionalism. Not a few, to be sure, welcomed the prospect of fighting for this very reason. For them, war would provide an emotional release from the frustrations of mechanistic modern living. Robert Wohl's study of "the generation of 1914" reveals the considerable hold such a view had on young European intellectuals at the turn of the century. For them, the coming of war was "a moment of fulfillment," when spirit would finally overcome matter, and life would be reconfirmed through willingness to face death.[2]

It would seem that both the "rational" and "irrational" conceptions of war were opposed at that time by a single view of peace. The late nineteenth-century formulation, represented by Spencerian sociology, of war as the main feature of man's premodern state of existence was further refined but essentially confirmed by writers such as John A. Hobson, Joseph Schumpeter, and Norman Angell. They popularized the view that as a society reached a higher stage of industrial development, it no longer needed to satisfy its needs through military conquest. It stood to gain more from a peaceful pursuit of interests, which was defined primarily in economic terms. Wealth, in other words, could be increased without war and without augmented military power. On the contrary, war wasted a nation's resources and only served the interests of armament manufacturers, military bureaucracies, and colonial administrators. The assumption here was that the more advanced a country became economically, the less reason there was for it to engage in war (except in self-defense). Economic development was equated with peace, while peace was viewed as creating a necessary condition for prosperity. By the same token, less developed societies, or less modern sectors in a developed society, were likely to be driven to war, to exalting the martial spirit and finding glory in physical violence. As these premodern societies and classes were replaced by a more advanced variety, war would become obsolete, both as a rational means of obtaining an end and as an irrational emotional release.

Of course, peace defined as economic development could also be viewed as a world order established and sustained by a handful of developed nations. They would impose their economic power upon the world and call it peace. That might be a rational way of ordering affairs among developed nations, but it would look like imperial domination from the standpoint of the less developed. As Reinhold Niebuhr wrote in 1930, "The civilized world is fairly well disciplined and permits its life to be ordered and its social and political relationships to be adjusted by the use of economic force without recourse to the more dramatic display of military power. . . . Our imperialism reveals ancient motives, but the technique is new. . . . We are able to dispense with the soldier almost completely; we use him only in a few underdeveloped nations."[3] War in the sense of keeping undeveloped areas under control was still a possibility, an integral part of this definition of peace. To eradicate that kind of war, it would be necessary to do away with imperialism. Whether this could be done without war was, of course, a hotly debated issue that split Marxist writers in the first two decades of the century. The Leninist conception that eventually triumphed may be seen, in this context, as a counterpart to the Spencerian notion of peace; if peace was to be achieved through economic maturation, this latter stage was also calculated to bring about imperialism, and the only way to establish a more universal peace was through anti-imperialist wars. Although, as Aron has shown, Lenin was an avid reader of Clausewitz, it would seem that he turned to the Prussian officer more for learning about strategy than about warfare. The Bolsheviks sought peace with Germany in 1918 to enable them to achieve their revolutionary aims at home. But they believed no lasting peace would obtain so long as there remained capitalist nations with their overseas empires.

The significance of Leninist ideas for our discussion lies in the fact that they tended to relativize peace and war. These were no longer clear-cut opposites, one rational and the other irrational, one more civilized and the other less developed. On the contrary, capitalist nations, Lenin argued, sought peace in order to perpetuate their imperialist domination, which in turn enhanced chances of war. Opponents of imperialism, on their part, were going to wage war in the name of a future peace. Leninism, no less than eighteenth-century progressivism, held to a notion of historical development. Both envisioned world peace as an ultimate achievement of that process, and war as something that characterized prior stages of development. But whereas for one school of thought war was destined to become less and less frequent, for the other it was always inherent in a given peace, and vice versa, until the utopian age of universal peace was reached. In thus blurring the distinction between war and peace, Leninism may be said to have introduced a typically twentieth-century idea.

So too did the proposals of Woodrow Wilson, Lenin's counterpart in the global drama of American-Soviet confrontation that has defined an aspect of world affairs in this century. When the United States declared war on Germany in 1917, President Wilson asserted: "Our object . . . is to vindicate the principles of peace and justice . . . against selfish and autocratic power. . . . We are glad to fight thus for the ultimate peace of the world."[4] The idea that a war was being fought for peace, if narrowly constructed, could be taken as a paraphrasing of the Clausewitzian dictim about war being an extension of politics by other means. However, the Wilsonian formulation went much beyond defining specific objectives for which the nation went to war, and rationalized the use of military force on the grounds of far-reaching universalistic goals. The United States was fighting a war, Wilson insisted, not for its own selfish objectives, but for the peace and happiness of the entire world. In thus blurring the distinction between war and peace, Wilson was joining Lenin as a characteristically twentieth-century figure. In Wilson's case, to be sure, the peace that was to come after the war was to be a durable one; there would not again be another such conflict. Still, in calling his war a crusade for peace, he was setting an important precedent for future leaders. For it was not clear where war ended and peace began; peace was contained in the act of war, and future war was a possibility until "the war to end all wars" had been successfully followed by a just peace.

It may be that in bringing war and peace closer together, both Lenin and Wilson were reflecting the orientations of their respective states. Although both were messianic thinkers, depicting visions of a future world, in reality those visions were intimately connected to the present: America's liberal democracy or Russian socialism. William Appleman Williams has argued that the American Revolution had succeeded in burying the notion of time so that henceforth the new nation would seek to preserve the present and, by extension, transform other societies in the image of itself.[5] Something similar may be said about the Bolshevik revolution; the overriding issue was that of preserving the new system, and other countries became relevant primarily as potential adversaries or else as possible, if temporary, allies. In such a situation, both war and peace were means for meeting the needs of the present.

Put this way, a paradox emerges. Although both Bolshevik Russia and Wilsonian America espoused universalistic principles and upheld internationalist visions, they remained passionately committed to nationalism. Because the Soviet Union and the United States emerged as two rising powers after the war, the postwar peace was inevitably affected by their behavior. On one hand, it was characterized by the internationalism of a League of Nations; as Aristide Briand declared at a meeting of the League assembly: "No special circumstances, no individual aspirations, however justifiable, can be allowed to transcend the interests of peace. Peace must prevail, must come before all."[6] On the other hand, by staying out of the League, Russia and America symbolized the persistent force of nationalism. The two, to be sure, continued to embody internationalist aspirations, the former ideologically and the latter economically, and espoused ideas of peace grounded on them. At the same time, these very ideas contained nationalistic components, notably Joseph Stalin's "socialism in one country" and Herbert Hoover's "independent internationalism." In other words, nationalism was reinforced through internationalist rhetoric. Whether it—in Russia, America, or elsewhere—would create a situation where a Clausewitzian war might recur, or generate atavistic pressures for an irrational war, was not clear in the 1920s. What was evident was that with nationalism remaining as strong as ever, war had still to be thought of as a possibility. This was the basis of Einstein's and Freud's fear of war in 1932.

It was for this reason that efforts were redoubled during the 1920s to find new bases for peace. The pre-1914 emphasis on human progress and the idea of peace as economic development remained, but something more was needed, expecially since neither progress nor development had prevented the Great War. One contribution postwar thinkers made in this connection may have been their espousal of intellectual freedom and cross-cultural understanding as preconditions for lasting peace. The Einstein-Freud exchange pointed to these ideas. Earlier, right after the war, Romain Rolland's "declaration of intellectual independence" had called on intellectuals throughout the world to free themselves from the service of their respective states and to address themselves to "the whole of Humanity." They must dedicate themselves to generating a sense of the universal brotherhood of man and to raising above "blind battles the Ark of the Covenant—the unshackled Mind, one and manifold, eternal."[7] No doubt the League of Nations Committee on Intellectual Cooperation took inspiration from such thought. And Einstein, who declared himself "free of national feelings," identified with such a movement, as did others who sought to give the postwar peace movement direction by establishing an international solidarity of intellectual elites.

How were the masses, as distinct from the elites, to contribute to peace? One popular idea in the 1920s was that people everywhere were becoming more cosmopolitan, subject to transnational influences, and that their cosmopolitanism could become a solid foundation for a more peaceful world. No transnational influences were more pervasive than America's popular culture— the radio, movies, jazz—and so it was not surprising that "Americanization" came to be seen as a universalizing, and therefore peacemaking, force. With Europeans as well as Asians flocking to American movies and listening to American music, there was a widespread perception that "the American way of life" was obliterating differences among cultures and peoples. Many resented such "cultural colonization," but at least some writers in Europe and Japan were viewing the phenomenon at the end of the 1920s as perhaps an inevitable phase on the road to mutual understanding and peace. This view, of course, was in sharp contrast to that which emphasized mass irrationality and hysteria—as witnessed even in the United States by Ku Klux Klan activities or the Sacco-Vanzetti executions. Nevertheless, the spread of America's popular and material culture, even to the Soviet Union, the Middle East, and Africa, was an undeniable fact that impressed observers as a more effective agent for breaching psychological barriers among nations than the League of Nations or disarmament treaties.

Unfortunately, neither intellectual exchange nor mass culture proved effective in preventing war in the 1930s. The new decade's paramount contribution to the vocabulary of war and peace was made by Fascist states. However one views fascism, its principal feature was certainly militarization of society. Representatives of the Nazi revolution, declared Franz von Papen, "are men and soldiers who are physically and morally warriors." "If our intellectual upper class," wrote Adolf Hitler, "had not been brought up in an atmosphere of culture but had been trained in boxing we should never have had the disgrace of 1918." The embodiment of physical power was the armed forces. "When one asks what the Army did for Germany, the answer is, everything. . . . The Army fostered personal courage in a cowardly world; revolution in a vacillating world; idealism, readiness to sacrifice, and unity in a class-divided State."[8] The glorification of the soldier, the ecstasy of death, emphasis on strong physique and character— these served to direct the state and people toward a constant struggle for survival and for power. Peace was not a virtue or a distinct value in itself. To the extent that it represented sedate civilization, culture for its own sake, or the enhancement of intellect, it must be rejected in favor of a more whole view of national life in which there could be no distinction between peacetime and war-related pursuits. War "is the national ideal and the end of all political and social aspirations," not a possible evil to be avoided, a contemporary observer noted. War "is no longer conceived as a measure for the protection of the state; it is the end of statecraft itself."[9] The conception of Italian fascism was little different. As Benito Mussolini declared, "Fascism believes neither in the possibility nor the utility of perpetual peace. . . . War alone brings up to its highest tension all human energy and puts the stamp of nobility upon the peoples who have the courage to meet it."[10]

These expressions belied the expectations of cultural internationalists like Rolland and Einstein that culture, because it implied intellectual freedom, was ultimately conducive to liberation, progress, and peace. Culture in that sense was now to be rejected in favor of a state-defined cult. Fascism, Leon Trotsky wrote in 1933, had become "the instrument of the destruction of [Europe's] economic and cultural acquisitions."[11] The new totalitarian state signaled a revolt against the cultural heritage, and war was an integral part of this revolt. As Igor Stravinsky remarked in his 1936 autobiography, "The openly irreligious masses in their degradation of spiritual values and debasement of human thought necessarily lead us to utter brutalization."[12] Although the cult worshippers romanticized their national pasts, these were manufactured pasts, not pasts freely remembered. In that sense, they were being true to the totalitarian dictum as summed up by Orwell: "Who controls the past controls the future. Who controls the present controls the past." Culture defined as memory no longer had autonomous existence, because memory too became controlled. This was again part of the Orwellian universe. As the novelist so graphically put it: "The control of the past depends above all on the training of memory. . . . And if it is necessary to rearrange one's memories or to tamper with written records, then it is necessary to *forget* that one has done so."

Ironically, the Western democracies found it necessary to respond to Fascist belligerence and denial of culture through their own physical strengthening and preparation for war. I. A. R. Wylie, an English writer, insisted in 1933 that culture must be defended through "intellectual moral heroism," not physical power. The ideal should be, she said, the moral hero, not the fighter.[13] But how could the "highly civilized Western nations . . . composed of many diverse elements with conflicting ideals, critical, doubting, individualistic, valuing the things of the mind rather than the 'brutal fist,' " defend themselves against a power that boasted unity and physical prowess? How could the moral hero struggle with the fighter when the latter stressed physical struggle and determination, whereas the former was dedicated to peace and brotherhood among men? Was not war inevitable between two such conflicting ideals? And in any war, was not the decisive factor military power and strategy, regardless of the cultural bases from which these were derived? However, would not another war prove "suicidal to the whole of Western culture," as Niebuhr wrote in 1934?[14]

These questions seriously divided European and American thinkers. On one side were those who equated peace with civilization and war with denial of culture, no matter who was fighting against whom. As Aldous Huxley wrote in a letter to Leonard Woolf in 1936, "The worst way of dealing with one evil is to do another evil, or to threaten another evil." Results of war, however justified, "are always identical . . . : people are slaughtered and a passionate sense of wrong and desire for vengeance are created in the survivors—feelings which make yet further wars inevitable." This proposition, reflecting a widely shared view of the Versailles peace, would be heard less and less as German action went beyond rectifying the wrongs of the peace settlement. But Huxley contributed a more persuasive argument when he added: "In the war industry technological progress is being made at the rate of ten per cent per annum. In these circumstances can we possibly afford to go on using war-like means to preserve peace?" To defend democracy by military means, he wrote, "one must be militarily efficient, and one cannot become militarily efficient without centralising powers, setting up a tyranny, imposing some form of conscription or slavery on the state. In other words, the military defence of democracy in the contemporary circumstances entails the abolition of democracy even before war starts."[15]

These fears were widely shared, and provided the intellectual and emotional foundations of the peace movement of the 1930s. It is to be noted, however, that the peace which was visualized here no longer entailed earlier notions of global economic interdependence or cultural interchange. Rather, it was a mere absence of war between democracies and totalitarianism. Advocates of such a peace—called "appeasement"—had essentially only two concrete proposals. One was for an international conference of all nations to which revisionist powers would be invited to express their grievances. Presumably, such a conference might lead to the reestablishment of international order.

When in reality all international conferences—whether regarding armament, territorial, or economic questions—only made "dissatisfied nations" even more dissatisfied and belligerent, some pacifists, especially in the United States, fell back on a nationalistic isolationism that would sever all ties with the outside world. The result was not so much peace as neutrality, a determination to absent oneself from international affairs. One irony of this position, as far as the United States was concerned, was that it led to a "fortress America" idea—militarily strengthening the nation so that it would be impregnable no matter what happened elsewhere. America's military preparedness in the end proved no more successful in avoiding war than calls for international conferences. In both instances, one again sees the continued blurring of the distinction between war and peace. If the totalitarian states were glorifying war, the democracies, in order to avoid war, were taking measures that made peace a more and more remote possibility.

For this reason, there came an argument that called for frankly recognizing the need to go to war against the dictatorships. The two sets of nations, it was argued, were so irreconcilable as to make even a truce, let alone durable peace between them, impossible. In 1934, Reinhold Niebuhr, in a book entitled *Reflections on the End of an Era*, reversed his earlier optimism and admitted that "the anarchic, the demonic and the primeval in man's collective behavior" had not been eliminated in modern states, where power still "seems to be the only protector against extinction." There was a lasting opposition between "the ethical and the imperial force in life," and unless this fact was recognized, Western civilization was doomed to disintegration. This would be its fate so long as the "spirit of liberalism" dominated Western culture.

The dilemma, of course, was that the liberal emphasis on harmony, rationality, and peace among nations was the very foundation of modern culture, and as such it was incapable of coping with the "imperial force in life." If the challenge were to be met, the West would have to be willing to fight, and in the process emphasize the very qualities—physical courage, discipline, dedication—that were being emphasized in totalitarian states. By the late 1930s, many erstwhile liberals were willing to accept this solution, however repugnant it might be to their intellectual sensibilities. Norman Angell, a symbol of liberal pacifism, was now arguing, as he said just after the British and French declarations of war against Germany, that the "principle on behalf of which Britain has declared war is in truth the fundamental principle of all organized society and of orderly civilization. . . . If in the midst of man's appalling agonies we get the feeling that despite the rhetoric it will not make much difference in the long run whether we or the enemy is victorious, the feeling that both will be engulfed in a common ruin anyhow . . . then we shall lose this war."[16] This would surely be the end of civilization. Likewise, Niebuhr declared in 1940, "Whatever may be the moral ambiguities of the so-called democratic nations, and however serious may be their failure to conform perfectly to their democratic ideals, it is sheer moral perversity to equate the inconsistencies of a democratic civilization with the brutalities which modern tyrannical States practice."[17] The fate of civilization turned on making the distinction, and peace between two such divergent systems must be rejected. These ideas provided the intellectual underpinnings for the democracies' war against Germany, Italy, and Japan. The alternative to war was no longer peace, but tyranny; the price of avoiding war was more war.

"When the most fundamental values of life are at stake," wrote an American historian in 1941, "there is only one thing to do about it, and that is to do something about it." A calm indifference in such a situation was morally reprehensible. There were values involved in the war that was going on, for the simple reason that "it is better to live today in the United States or in

England than in Germany." He went on to say, reflecting emerging views of the war, that "the most fundamental thing at issue is not the present . . . but the future contained in the present—in the freedom of the people to plan boldly and to act democratically in the realization of their plans."[18] In such a conception of the war, it was being fought for the past ("values") and for the future ("plans"). Both were contained in the present. It was in that sense that the anti-Fascist conflict was a total war enveloping past, present, and future. Put another way, war and peace were comprehended as simultaneous occurrences; war was necessary to enjoy the fruits of peace, and visions of peace were part of the war effort.

The blurring of distinction between war and peace continued to characterize World War II after Japan and the United States entered it. It would seem that Japanese thought and behavior, insofar as war and peace were concerned, fitted into the overall pattern thus far sketched. Unlike Nazi Germany or Fascist Italy, the Japanese militarists and their civilian apologists did not repudiate culture as a universalistic perversion or the antithesis of the warrior ethic. As the famous 1937 booklet, *Kokutai no hongi* (Essentials of the Nation), an official statement for school-level indoctrination, took pains to point out, Japan's warrior ethic had aimed not at killing but at living; the fighter struggled not for destruction but for regeneration, development, and harmony. War, according to this doctrine, never aimed at destroying, overwhelming, or conquering others, but at creating a world of peace.[19]

This sort of ideology revealed the reluctance of the Japanese leaders to embrace a more explicit theory of militarism and war. Even when they engaged in aggressive wars and committed atrocities, they couched their actions in the name of peace and harmony, the best example of this being the rhetoric of "eight corners of the world under one roof," a vision of universal peace in the name of which war against Europe, America, and Asia was waged. Likewise, although officially Japanese propagandists called on the nation to repudiate modern culture and found a new cult fit for the age, much as Germans and Italians were doing, this never led to a total rejection of Western civilization, for the simple reason that Japan would not be able to wage war without learning from Western technology, science, and even its "rational spirit," as a commentator noted on the eve of Pearl Harbor.[20] Japanese society was no less Western in 1941 than it had been ten years earlier.

The key here, however, was that in Japan, perhaps to a greater extent than elsewhere, war and peace were becoming increasingly blurred. For ten years, starting with the Manchurian war of 1931, the nation had been involved in military action on the continent of Asia, even though no formal war had been declared—an indication in itself that war and peace were no longer clearly separable. If the country was not actually engaged in fighting, it was making preparations for war. The military would mobilize national resources and seek to influence mass opinion through manipulation of information and suppression of dissident intellectuals. At the same time, however, they would never completely control national politics and economy. These would mostly remain in the hands of civilians, who would seek their own survival by offering cooperation with the military.

A state of war preparedness (called "peacetime war" in Japan) served both interests well, and under the circumstances it was a rare writer who publicly questioned this state of affairs and urged the nation to return to a genuinely peacetime footing. Even among those who had earlier identified with Western liberal perspectives on international affairs, considering peace to be a normal condition of world affairs, there was now readiness to accept war and war preparedness not for their own sakes but, as one of them declared, for the sake of a more peaceful Asia.[21] How Japan, the most westernized of Asian countries, could lead them in the utopian crusade for a new Asia was never clear, but at least such an idea served to confirm the illusion that war was peace.

In a sense war *was* peace during the war years 1941–1945. In all countries engaged in fighting, soldiers and civilians were provided with visions of what would come after it was all over. World War I had already established a precedent when President Wilson enunciated his Fourteen Points, but during World War II there were far more numerous enunciations of this kind. Moreover, compared with Wilson's fourteen conditions for peace, the declarations from 1941 to 1945 were much vaguer and more grandiose, perhaps indicating the difficulty in foreseeing precisely the shape of the postwar world, or even lack of confidence in achieving a durable peace. At least the experiences of the interwar years seemed to indicate that it was a mistake to stress the value of peace as a given. It would be more realistic to consider it a relative phenomenon, no more permanent than rates of exchange or trade balances. Such a view—the school of "realism"—provided an intellectual and psychological transition into the postwar world.

In the influential *Conditions of Peace* published during the war, for instance, E. H. Carr argued that "the supreme importance of peace" on which the capitalist, democratic countries had insisted had itself doomed the peace. By stressing fear of war, political and intellectual leaders in the West had been blind to the "revolutionary frame of mind" in totalitarian states that sought to repudiate the status quo. The democratic nations had at last awakened to the challenge, but their struggle against dictatorships would never be assured so long as they maintained their preference for peace over change and revolution.[22] "The political, social, and economic problems of the postwar world must be approached with the desire not to stabilise, but to revolutionise." Peace, Carr was saying, should not be built upon a nostalgia for the past, but grasped as an aspect of constantly changing world conditions. A rigid dichotomy between war and peace was no longer relevant. War, whether for preserving Western civilization or as an instrument for its transformation, must be accepted as preferable to peace, if peace meant inaction, status quo, and rejection of change.

In some such thinking, one sees the grounds being prepared for post-1945 conceptions of war and peace. Admittedly it is easy to exaggerate, but at least it may be noted that the onset of the Cold War did not create a difficult intellectual problem, but rather fitted into existing ideas. Those who had grown up during the 1930s had in fact experienced a "cold war" of one kind or another between Germany and England or between Japan and the United States, and were quite ready to accept the state of "neither peace nor war" with the Soviet Union. They had learned to view peace as fragile, war as always a possibility, and change rather than stability as the norm in world affairs.

Precisely because this was the case, however, the postwar years also gave rise to a serious peace movement, and the often furious debate between realists and pacifists has persisted to this day. The debate was, from the outset, given impetus by two new developments after 1945: nuclear armament and Third World nationalism. There had been different kinds of war and peace in the past, but none had involved the prospect of nuclear annihilation of the entire world, or nationalistic "people's wars" against organized armed forces of the modern states. Ironically, the introduction of these new forces has only served to confirm the twentieth-century phenomenon of blurring the distinction between war and peace.

That in the atomic age there could never be a peace without the ever-present danger of war, or a war that led to a real peace, was recognized as soon as the first atomic bombs were dropped. Although they ended the Japanese war, the event immediately gave rise to speculation about the next war, most likely to be waged between the United States and the Soviet Union, both armed with the new weapon. Neither the American nor the Russian people, nor anyone else, enjoyed even a brief period of respite; on the contrary, they had immediately to brace themselves for another war. Some even argued that they were already in a war. The Cold War, as official American documents frankly stated, was "in fact a real war," to be waged until victory was achieved.[23] In such a situation, war preparedness became a cardinal necessity. In supporting the buildup of atomic weaponry, an American scientist wrote in 1947: "So long as it is the policy of our nation to prepare for war, I shall certainly not attempt to impede such preparations," including technical improvements in weapons, which were a "relatively insignificant matter," whether they led to nuclear profusion or not. It was "deplorable but understandable that this country, desiring and working toward peace, feels it necessary to be strong in a military sense."[24] This summed up the prevailing view in the Western democracies at the outset of the Cold War: military preparedness was necessary for peace.

Such thinking was clearly a product of the experiences of the interwar years, which seemed to teach the lesson that peace could never be preserved by goodwill, disarmament, or other nonpower means. In *War and Civilization* (1950), Arnold J. Toynbee stated: "By rising to the Warrior's level in the world wars of A.D. 1914– 18 and A.D. 1939–45, unaggressive peoples did exercise the cardinal virtues in War to such good effect that they twice defeated a militarist empire's long-prepared attempt to conquer the World; and, in winning these successive victories at a fearful cost in blood and tears, they twice bought for our society an opportunity to get rid of War by a better way than submission to a world-conquerer's forcibly imposed *Pax Oecumenica*."[25] The war had been necessary for the kind of peace the democracies could accept; for otherwise the only peace they knew would have been a world empire of evil forces.

The idea that peace at any price was to be repudiated, and that war could be removed only by a refusal to compromise with evil, underlay Cold War thinking. The framework now was "peace with justice." The West would seek both peace and justice, and the waging of a cold war against the Soviet Union was the means for that end. While it was wrong to engage in an open warfare with Russia to destroy communism, it was equally unacceptable to maintain a peaceful relationship with it at the expense of cherished values. As Niebuhr put it in 1953: "We face two problems in our generation rather than one: the avoidance of war and resistance to tyranny. The 'pure' idealists are always tempted to war against communism in the name of justice or to come to terms with it in the name of peace." Both alternatives must be rejected in terms of "a wisdom which is more relevant to our two-pronged predicament." The wise stance would take note of "the endless complexities in the moral issues in politics" and try to alleviate tensions with Communist states while at the same time building up "our defenses even though the peril of conflict always confronts us."[26]

The coming of the nuclear age did not immediately challenge such Cold War orthodoxy. Toynbee lightheartedly predicted in 1951 that "America would win a third world war hands down," while Niebuhr justified continued production of nuclear arms on the grounds that peace "is preserved by the fear of these atomic weapons."[27] "Freedom was won for us by men who valued it above life," declared an American scientist who opposed any step toward nuclear arms control; "we should preserve it even at

the cost of lives."[28] The outbreak of World War III was "ultimately inevitable," a commentator noted in 1954, and the United
States was justified in doing everything possible to prepare for it,
for "American survival as a sovereign power is the sole hope of
freedom in the world for generations to come."[29] Whether there
would be such a thing as freedom at the end of a nuclear war
was not seriously questioned. As Toynbee himself admitted, in a
global atomic war the only survivors might be "Negrito Pygmies
of Central Africa" who might have to "salvage some fraction of
the present heritage of mankind."[30] Such pessimism, however,
was rare, and the majority of writers, ranging from Pentagon
officials drawing up war plans to popular writers, assumed that
somehow an atomic war would be "over so quickly" (as Vannevar
Bush put it as early as August 1945) that war preparations must
include planning for the postwar world.[31] Such a view should
not necessarily be attributed to ignorance or naiveté, but to a
habit of mind in which war and peace were simultaneous propositions. It was impossible to think of peace without war, or of
war without peace. Both amounted to the same thing, and
themes such as justice, humanity, or freedom joined the two.

Because war and peace thus became confused, it was not surprising that advocates of peace—those Niebuhr called "purists"—
should have launched a massive counteroffensive against the
whole body of assumptions of Cold War orthodoxy. To take one
example from early writings in this genre, Cord Meyer, a retired
marine officer, published an article in the June 1947 issue of the
Atlantic entitled "What Price Preparedness?" and elaborated on
what was involved in the strategy of "peace through preparedness
for war." According to him, the United States would, under
this program, have to "maintain the world's largest arsenal of
atomic bombs, radioactive poisons, disease-producing germs, and
long-range rockets and bombers." Moreover, industrial and
population centers would have to be dispersed and underground
shelters built, so that in the event of an atomic war, "the country
may be able to fight on though its cities lie in ruins and the
majority of its people are maimed, dying, or dead." It would also
be necessary to guard against "atomic or biological sabotage"
by creating "the most efficient intelligence system in the world"
and "a very large security police armed with sweeping powers to

search and arrest." The irony then would be that in preparing for their showdown, the United States and the Soviet Union would become alike: both would be regimented states. But their leaders would have to "exaggerate the points of difference in the two societies as a means of persuading their respective populations of the moral value of their sacrifices." The conclusion, for Meyer, was inescapable: "Total preparedness means totalitarianism for American citizens. . . . they will become mere instruments of the state." Freedom would no longer be what they had known, but an empty propaganda slogan to disguise "an amoral competition for brute force."

The idea that the Cold War confrontation could transform America in such a way that the nation might come to resemble its opponent was expanded by Lewis Mumford, the consistent opponent of state power, when he asserted that in order to fight Hilter's war machine, the United States and Britain had had to create their own. "So far . . . from the megamachine's being utterly discredited by the colossal errors of its ruling 'elite,' the opposite actually happened: it was rebuilt by the Western allies on advanced scientific lines, with its defective human parts replaced by mechanical and electronic and chemical substitutes. . . . [In] the very act of dying the Nazis transmitted the germs of their disease to their American opponents: not only the methods of compulsive organization or physical destruction, but the moral corruption that made it feasible to employ these methods without stirring opposition." While this was an extreme argument, Mumford posed a question that concerned many others: "how to prevent the human race from being destroyed by its demoralized but reputedly sane leaders."[32] Here, peace was equated with human survival and given a special value superior to all other factors.

While most were asserting, as Archibald MacLeish did, that they must try "to avoid world war on the one hand and Communist domination of the earth on the other," Mumford was implying that avoidance of war should take precedence over all other objectives, for the simple reason that war created "unparalleled wastes" and was worse for the earth than Communist domination.[33] Western thinking was divided on the matter, but the problem became vastly more complex because of the second postwar phenomenon: self-consciousness on the part of under-developed countries. They, after all, comprised the majority of mankind and occupied vast spaces on the earth, and their awakening inevitably had an impact on discussions of war and peace. First, they were far less concerned with the ongoing struggle between capitalism and communism, or between democracy and totalitarianism, than with their own nation-building. Because, as Jawaharlal Nehru said, this goal could not be accomplished unless there were peace, they took the initiative in trying to persuade the superpowers to end their arms race and the division of the world into two military blocs.

This sort of neutralism provided ideological unity for Asian and African countries when they met for the first time as a bloc at Bandung in 1955. There they adopted their own definition of peace along the lines of Chou En-lai's "five principles of peace," which the Chinese leader had enunciated a year earlier: respect for sovereignty, noninterference in internal affairs, nonviolation of territorial integrity, equality, and peaceful coexistence. These principles were rather vague and redundant, and some of the Bandung nations themselves were prone to violate them. Nevertheless, the emergence of self-consciousness on the part of developing countries certainly added a new dimension to the problem of war and peace. At the least, their argument that they should not have to suffer from the pernicious effects of radioactive fallout as a result of the atmospheric testing of nuclear weapons was sufficiently powerful to play a role in American-Soviet negotiations for a test ban treaty.

Second, for many of these countries "justice" meant liberation from colonial and semi-colonial conditions. What this amounted to in practice was not always clear. Presumably it implied support for the independence of colonial areas, but it was not always easy to determine how the goal was to be obtained, or what form independence should take. Advocates of "wars of liberation" belied the Bandung principles of peace by openly calling for guerrilla warfare against colonial regimes and turning anti-colonial struggles into revolutionary movements. They added to the vocabulary of war and peace the conception of the "people's war" which, as Raymond Aron has noted, made no distinction between civilian and military activities, or between civil and external wars.[34] This concept too confirmed the twentieth century's blurring of the distinction between war and peace.

Third, even when they were not engaged in wars of national liberation, Third World countries' conceptions of international order conflicted with the idea of peace as a mere interlude in the Cold War. They viewed such a peace as involving the freezing of the status quo, which would keep them in a state of dependency. "Peace with justice" for them must involve a global redistribution of wealth so that the anomaly of three-fourths of mankind enjoying only one-quarter of the world's income could be rectified. In the meantime, they would assert their sovereign rights over national resources—subsoil, coastal, and atmospheric, as well as above ground. They would demand preferential access for their primary products, which comprised close to 90 percent of their exports in 1955, into markets of advanced nations, both capitalist and socialist.

Fourth, the advent of non-Western countries into the world arena broadened the perimeters of cross-cultural relations. Cultural "understanding" as a foundation of peace would no longer be simply among Western nations, or between Americans and Russians. It would be more global and multidimensional. Whether this could be comprehended in the older, simplistic framework of "East and West" relations, or in the newer formula of "North and South" problems—or whether far more ambitious schemes might have to be worked out—remained a central issue for the second half of the century. What was unquestionable was the relevance of this issue for peace. As early as 1946, the United Nations Educational, Scientific, and Cultural Organization had adopted a "declaration on human rights," in which it was asserted that "Peace must be founded upon the intellectual and moral solidarity of mankind." Clearly, here was a broadened definition of peace, one that harked back to the Einstein-Freud exchange but now embraced the whole of humanity.

As the twentieth century approaches its end, it will bequeath to the twenty-first—if there is to be a twenty-first century—an array of ideas about war and peace, evidence that they have constituted one important core of the century's intellectual history. Ideas about war and peace are, after all, ways of representing the world as it is—and as it has been, could have been, and could yet be. The fact that the boundaries between war and peace have become increasingly ill-defined may indicate the blurring of the distinction between what is and what could be, or between what has been and what could have been. If so, it also indicates a confusion among past, present, and future. This is a truly Orwellian universe; one either submits to it or seeks to be liberated from it. For Orwell, liberation would mean historical consciousness, for human memory is the guarantor of freedom. Equally important would be a consciousness of the future. To have an articulate vision of the future—not as blindly determined by the present but with a life of its own—may rescue mankind from intellectual slavery and defeatism. And what else would one rather envision for the future than peace, understanding, and brotherhood among peoples of all countries? "Today, when the danger of global conflict has diminished," wrote Henry Kissinger in 1973, "we face the more profound problem of defining what we mean by peace."[35] The danger of war may not have diminished since then, but the task of defining peace remains as urgent as ever. One could begin by recognizing that no matter what one means by peace, it is a value one must clearly distinguish from war.

Notes

[1] "Why War?" Reprinted as a pamphlet of the Chicago Institute for Psychoanalysis, n.d.; also in Otto Nathan and Heinz Norden, *Einstein on Peace* (New York, 1960), pp. 186–202.

[2] Robert Wohl, *The Generation of 1914* (Cambridge, MA, 1979), p. 27.

[3] Reinhold Niebuhr, "Awkward Imperialists," *Atlantic*, 145 (June 1930), p. 670.

[4] Robert Dallek, *The American Style of Foreign Policy* (New York, 1983), p. 85.

[5] William Appleman Williams, *America Confronts the Revolutionary World* (New York, 1976).

[6] E. H. Carr, *Conditions of Peace* (New York, 1944), p. xvi.

[7] Daniel Aaron, *Writers on the Left* (New York, 1961), p. 51.

[8] Ludwig Lewisohn, "The German Revolt against Civilization," *Harper's*, 167 (August 1933), p. 277; Alice Hamilton, "The Plight of the German Intellectuals," *Harper's*, 168 (January 1934), pp. 159–63.

[9] Ludwig Lore, "How Germany Arms," *Harper's*, 168 (January 1934), p. 157.

[10] Sigmund Neumann, *Permanent Revolution* (New York, 1942), p. 41.

[11] Leon Trotsky, "What Hitler Wants," *Harper's*, 167 (August 1933), p. 393.

[12] Igor Stravinsky, *Autobiography* (New York, 1936), p. 40.

[13] I. A. R. Wylie, "Our Pernicious Virtues," *Harper's*, 167 August 1933, p. 519.

[14] Hamilton, "Plight," p. 168; Niebuhr, *Reflections on the End of an Era* (New York, 1934), p. 23.

[15] *Letters of Aldous Huxley*, ed. Grover Smith (London, 1969), pp. 401, 407, 411.

[16] Norman Angell, *For What Do We Fight?* (London, 1939), pp. 1, 89.

[17] Reinhold Niebuhr, *Christianity and World Politics* (New York, 1940), pp. 16–17.

[18] G. T. Robinson in *New Republic*, 105, 5 (August 4, 1941), p. 153.

[19] Ministry of Education, *Kokutai no hongi* [Essentials of the Nation] (Tokyo, 1937), part 1, chap. 4.

[20] Morito Tatsuo, in *Chūōkōron*, 56, 11 (November 1941), p. 15.

[21] Miles Fletcher, *The Search for a New Order* (Chapel Hill, 1982), p. 102.

[22] Carr, *Conditions*, pp. xv, xvi, xxiii.

[23] Thomas H. Etzold and John L. Gaddis, eds., *Containment* (New York, 1978), p. 442.

[24] Louis N. Ridenour, "The Scientist Fights for Peace," *Atlantic*, 179, 5 (May 1947), pp. 80–82.

[25] Arnold J. Toynbee, *War and Civilization* (New York, 1950), p. xi.

[26] Niebuhr, "Christianity and the Moral Law," *Christian Century*, 70, 48 (December 2, 1953), pp. 1386–88.

[27] Toynbee, "Can We Live in Peace?" *New Republic*, 125, 27 (1961), p. 15; Niebuhr, "Coexistence or Total War?" *Christian Century*, 71, 33 (August 18, 1954), pp. 971–73.

[28] Robert Divine, *Blowing on the Wind* (New York, 1978), p. 128.

[29] J. B. Matthews, "America Is Losing the War against Communism," *American Mercury*, 78 (January 1954), pp. 4–5.

[30] Toynbee, "Civilization on Trial," *Atlantic*, 179, 6 (June 1947), pp. 34–38.

[31] James F. Schnabel, *The History of the Joint Chiefs of Staff*, vol. 1 (Wilmington, 1979), p. 139.

[32] Lewis Mumford, *The Pentagon of Power* (New York, 1964), pp. 242, 251, 253.

[33] Archibald MacLeish, "The Power of Choice," *Atlantic*, 188, 2 (August 1951), p. 42.

[34] Raymond Aron, *Pensez la guerre, Clausewitz*, vol. 2 (Paris, 1976), pp. 103–16; see also Wolfgang W. Mommsen, *Theories of Imperialism* (New York, 1980), pp. 59–61.

[35] Henry A. Kissinger, *American Foreign Policy*, 3d ed. (New York, 1977), p. 118.

Discussion: Hagihara Paper

Hagihara: My paper is centered on two major Japanese experiences: the Meiji Restoration of 1868 and the Japanese constitution of 1946. I maintain that we have yet to make this constitution a truly Japanese constitution. Let me come to the conclusion first. We should put this constitution to a test by a national referendum. I suspect we have not experienced enough trials and tribulations to come up with our own constitution. Unless we go through this process, we will not really come to feel that this is our constitution.

Mommsen: I found one particular aspect of the paper very interesting; namely, the argument that Japan in some ways did not experience World War I fully and therefore did not undergo the sorts of changes other countries in the West did. To some degree, I would not agree. The situation of Germany in the interwar period offers certain parallels, inasmuch as Germany also in some ways remained part of a pre-1914 state, and the social changes after 1918 were incomplete. In a way the traditional ruling classes, while not maintaining full control over the political system, still exercised a substantial influence, and this clearly contributed to the development of national socialism. The parallel between these two systems goes further than is suggested.

But I would like to ask one question in this context. This description of the nature of Japanese politics and in particular Japanese imperialism in the interwar period would imply—if I understand it correctly—an interpretation of imperialism in terms that showed the driving force coming primarily from the traditional elites and from the military establishment. I see in this a Schumpeter-like interpretation of imperialism and I would like to learn whether I read that rightly. I am a little doubtful whether in fact the Japanese drive to establish an East Asian empire can be ascribed to the traditional elites only. Accepting basically the sharp distinction between the Japanese system in the 1930s and the Fascist systems in Europe, I nonetheless think that it is not quite as sharp as the paper would have it.

55

Joll: There are two very interesting points here. One is how far the Japanese experience is a unique experience and not comparable with that of other countries. The other is the question of a national referendum on the constitution, and how far a nation makes a constitution its own by institutional methods.

Maier: What I found especially interesting was the way in which different generations of Japanese statesmen in the twentieth century found their points of orientation in earlier experiences. But the paper should really be entitled, "What the Twentieth Century Means to Japan," in that it is a presentation of these points of conjuncture in twentieth-century history as they have impinged upon Japanese development and as they have been interpreted by successive generations of Japanese statesmen. But is there a universalizable experience in the Japanese national development? Hagihara raises the question tangentially toward the end of his paper when he talks about emulation. Japan in some ways has been an amazing success story, and yet it may not be a replicable success story for other countries outside the Anglo-American or European-American center. But the problem could be turned around more in the conclusion by some reflection on the Japanese role, which for Americans has become so preoccupying in many ways.

Friedländer: I would like to push the question even a little further, and relate it to the problem of center and periphery, which is very tantalizing. Hagihara seems to assume that Japan could choose its historical order: stay at the periphery or become one of the main actors at the center. But this is not a matter of choice. This is a matter of structural developments that do not depend on the choice of this or that government. And I am a little puzzled by the rather eighteenth-century approach to twentieth-century history. Japan is being pushed into the center of world history by its economic development, by its own dynamics. It has to assume that position not of its own choice, but as the result of internal and external developments. It cannot choose to stay at the periphery—or could you explain how one makes that choice when one is practically the second power in the world in terms of economy?

Joll: That links up very much with what Hagihara was saying earlier about the national referendum on the constitution. Perhaps one of the reasons why the Japanese people feel they can remain on the periphery is that, because of the historical circumstances in which their constitution was drafted, the passive role was forced upon them. Does Hagihara feel that conducting a national referendum that would make the Japanese people feel the constitution is their own is linked with the idea of Japan's playing a more positive political, as well as economic, role in the world outside?

Hagihara: Yes, I do mean that. Japanese economic power makes it necessary for Japan not to remain on the periphery, whether politically or psychologically. But then, what kind of role is it to play? I feel we need to establish a public consensus on the constitution so that we may assume the role we are convinced best fits our position. Article 9 is particularly relevant to the question of a positive political role.

Windsor: There are two arguments. The first is that the Japanese constitution does not yet truly belong to Japan because, in the language of the paper, no memories are attached to it except the memory of the defeat of 1945. That memory is linked precisely to the economic success and the social development of Japan. But at the same time, these are confined by the memory of the defeat and prevent Japan from being acted upon in the way that Friedländer was suggesting. There is no dynamic at present to force Japan into a more prominent political or indeed a strategic role. Japan, after all, has for many years been under considerable pressure, notably from the United States, to take a more prominent part in international affairs, to pursue a more active foreign policy, and to make a bigger contribution to what the United States regards as a common defense effort.

Japan has generally exercised a negative choice by refusing to accept these pressures and to assume that role. So the question of the acceptability of the constitution and the ability to choose a more prominent role in world affairs are indeed linked in the paper. In that sense, the symbolic importance of Article 9 may be what is most important in the review.

Iriye: Hagihara puts Japanese developments in the context of our discussion of the meaning of the twentieth century. One of the points he makes is that Japan had not experienced the twentieth century until 1945. Up to that point, Japan had emulated other countries—their behavior, their ideas. Most of those were of nineteenth-century vintage. Then he argues that only in 1945, through defeat, was Japan forced to join the twentieth century. Does the paper view the new constitution as a symbol of Japan's having joined the twentieth century? If so, what is Japan's way of representing the twentieth century in terms of the constitution? Or would one say that much of this is an eighteenth-century rationalist idea? Article 9—renouncing war—could be viewed as eighteenth-century idealism or nineteenth-century liberalism, not exactly a twentieth-century response. One could argue that Japan has joined the twentieth century by going back to the eighteenth century; or that by renouncing war in the context of the twentieth century, Japan may in fact be making a unique contribution. Japan's experience has not been unique, because what it has done is to emulate other countries in terms of the nineteenth-century background. But if Japan is in fact going to define its role in the twentieth century at least partially in terms of the new constitution, that may in fact be, for the first time, a unique contribution to the twentieth-century definition of itself.

Hagihara: In the Japanese constitution there is an element of passivity. That, in my view, brings about the lack of a spirit of independence. Article 9 of the constitution was undeniably produced in response to an external force. That fact continues to plague us. Unless we are able to feel, or to convince ourselves, that we "created" this constitution, we will have difficulty in really defining not just our political role, but our moral responsibility as well.

Schwartz: What does "joining the twentieth century" mean? I would argue that the twentieth century is an outgrowth of the nineteenth century, and that there is a great deal of continuity between the two. But that aside, I wonder whether Japan did not in 1945 make a kind of societal decision to turn away from making a national destiny in the world, toward almost a full concentration on economic development. Now maybe the time has come when Japan feels that it wants to rethink this sort of total concentration on economics—*fukoku* (rich nation) rather than *kyōhei* (strong army). But I wonder if it is correct to say that after 1945 Japan just became a passive actor in the world.

Mommsen: In some ways Germany had the same experience. In a sense, the West German constitution was made by the Germans themselves, though under very heavy conditions imposed by the Allies; and one could well argue that we have to some degree lived since 1948 under a system which has been dictated to us. Nonetheless, the present situation is such that no German would ever raise this kind of question. They would all say that Germans have come to acknowledge the system, that it has acquired a quality in itself. I would argue that tradition-established legitimacy has worked in the West German case. And I really wonder whether this is not true, to some degree at least, for the Japanese. Of course, we in the West always assume that the consensus in Japan is very high as compared with many other states; it does seem an amazingly stable system, and not only because of economic success.

Hagihara: If I understand correctly, the West German constitution has no clause corresponding to our Article 9, so the situation is quite different. As Schwartz pointed out, we certainly made "a kind of societal decision" in 1945, and I have no intention of suggesting that we go back to *kyōhei* rather than *fukoku*. My question is what can Japan contribute to the world, outside the economic sphere.

Joll: Perhaps it might clarify the discussion if I were to ask Hagihara whether he feels that the national referendum on the constitution is intended primarily to enable Japan to have a more positive and active foreign policy than at present, or whether he has some other sociopolitical ideas in mind when he wants to internalize the constitution in the Japanese people so that they feel that it is their own.

Hagihara: I could say both, but my main concern is that the very spirit of the constitution may be lost as the memories of defeat are eroded. The ideals may become merely platitudes.

Kyogoku: The role assigned to Japan in the international political arena has changed. In 1945 Japan was defeated and occupied. At that time it had to be overhauled to make it into a democratic and non-belligerent state. This "angelicism" (to borrow Hersch's word) is being denied today because of Japan's changing role. This is quite a traumatic experience. Under the present constitution, we do have the right to self-defense. We have rearmed without much inconvenience. But we have overdone the economic recovery, and trade frictions have sprung up.

We have created these frictions; they were not forced upon us. But we find this passive image rather convenient. Economically we are trading peacefully with all nations of the world, and militarily we are playing a rather obscure role. We have established a self-deceptive way of thinking.

Today, in Japan one group has been trying to prevent rearmament or a military buildup. Its members are mainly Leftists, Socialists, Communists. And though the Liberal Democratic party remains in power, the fact that there is an opposition has been convenient for the government in resisting American requests for a more rapid buildup. But, are we really passive in the objective sense, or do we simply prefer to act as if we were passive in order to integrate the populace and pacify domestic opinion?

Maier: The real constitutional debate, it might be argued, took place in Germany in the early 1950s when rearmament was debated. That was the issue that invoked the public to a much greater degree than the formation of the 1949 basic law. And it might also be said that if the peace movement in Germany becomes a major force, this would reopen constitutional issues in a major way.

So that constitutional discussion here, the opening of the fundamental issues, does seem to relate to the question of a nation-state in the international arena. But it is striking that this is still a rather traditional notion of the world we live in, which remains a world of nation-states, as it was in the nineteenth century. And I would suggest that the problem raised by the paper is revealing in that much of what we are going into represents traditional problems. Each nation must undergo these debates. America undergoes them not as constitutional debates, but they are certainly— with the one exception of the racial issue—the most divisive debates that America has ever engaged in. This presses home the point that in a world of nation-states, to make a constitution, to become active in history, really must mean acceptance of a type of national decision.

Hersch: Why limit yourselves to the constitution? I believe there is much more. I believe that to state facts is in a way passive, and to digest facts is in a way active. It is the digestion of facts that gives to those facts a certain meaning. We have spoken of two fundamental facts: military defeat on the one hand, and victory in economics on the other. These are two facts. I would like to ask what meaning the Japanese people give to these two facts. After so many years they have probably digested these facts in some way, given them some finality, some aim. If this has not happened, then you can have a referendum, but it will be an empty referendum. In order to have real content, you must have actively digested the given facts. And I would like to know if, in Japan, defeat is simply defeat—a fact—or if there is meaning in this defeat. And if the extraordinary success in economics is simply a fact, or if the Japanese people give it a meaning?

Hagihara: What I am suggesting is that we should reassess these meanings or even find these meanings by the symbolic act of putting the constitution through a kind of rescreening process.

Maruyama: The points raised in the Hagihara paper might be better understood had he made clearer why he contrasted the case of the Meiji innovations (Restoration) with that of postwar reforms, including the new constitution. After 1868, Japan was the first non-Western modern state in the world to emerge without losing its independence. It is undeniable that this paved the way for the independence of the hitherto colonized nations of the Third World, whose national liberations so characterize the twentieth century.

But what of the implication of the new Japan that emerged in 1945, after defeat? Hagihara emphasizes, on the one hand, that the rebirth of Japan from an imperialist state to a peace-loving nation was symbolized by the new constitution; on the other hand he is concerned whether the Japanese people understand the significance of their present constitution. Do they accept it passively as an unavoidable consequence of military defeat and subsequent American occupation? I suppose it is in such a context that Hagihara cited a speech given by Nambara Shigeru in the Imperial Diet, a speech stressing the spirit of independence and autonomy, which Nambara feared was lacking even among the Japanese political leaders of the day.

It is, of course, possible to compare postwar Japan with the Meiji innovations within the context of modern *Japanese* history, but as has already been suggested by several participants, the question more central to *this* symposium is: does Japan's new constitution have any *universal* significance comparable with the Meiji innovations? In this sense, I do not think the national referendum issue raised in the discussion of this paper is of primary importance, not only because it is a domestic affair, but also because Japan has already held a national election for the House Representatives in 1955, in which the main issue was whether the parties supporting the constitution could secure enough seats to prevent a revision of the constitution. And after the election, the governing party has refrained intentionally from raising—at least openly as a party policy—the question of constitutional reform lest it should provoke the electorate. The outcome of a national referendum is self-evident, considering the results of repeated public opinion polls.

Still, the problem underlying Hagihara's paper remains unsolved. How is it possible for Japanese people to evaluate the constitution in terms of *universal* significance? I would say it is very difficult so long as we take for granted the traditional sovereign state as a unit of world order. Clearly renouncing the right of belligerency as a fundamental right of the state tampers with the basic dogma of sovereignty as hitherto understood. Thus among Japanese, particularly among intellectuals, there have appeared, though still small in number, people who ask: is present-day Japan still a sovereign state? Only when we try to reexamine the very nature of national sovereignty, only when we begin by doubting the validity of a world order consisting of sovereign (if only self-styled) states, now more than 160 in number, only then can we discuss the universal significance of Article 9 without limiting ourselves to Japan.

Instead of giving my personal view on such a broad subject, allow me to quote the words of an eminent figure: "Convention after convention has been entered into, designed to humanize war. Yet, each war becomes increasingly savage as the means for mass killing are further developed. You cannot control war. You can only abolish it. Those who shrug it off as idealistic are the real enemies of peace, the real warmongers." This is from a speech made neither by Philip Noel Baker nor by Bertrand Russell but by General Douglas MacArthur. It was given after the Korean War broke out, by the time the American occupation policy had made almost a 180-degree turn from its initial liberal stance of the immediate postwar period. And yet the general made this speech. Not that MacArthur based his ideas on the *Problematik* I have mentioned above. But this remark could only have been made by someone who had served twice as a military commander in total wars. And it is in this context that I would like to regard Article 9 as a meaningful challenge to the traditional concept of state sovereignty, although this may seem too bold a challenge.

Discussion: Iriye Paper

Iriye: My paper tries to raise some questions about ideas of war and peace in the twentieth century. Obviously, because there would be no such thing as war unless there were nation-states, one cannot avoid dealing with the issue of the nation-state. The nation-state means, among other things, war, warfare, war preparedness. When you talk about warfare or twentieth-century ideas about war, obviously there is a tradition based on Clausewitz's ideas. There are definitions of national interest, *Realpolitik*, balance of power, that go back to the nineteenth century and even to the seventeenth century. To this extent, the twentieth century has made no significant contribution to ideas about war or strategy. Also, there is a nineteenth-century idea counter to that, the idea that war is outmoded or primitive: the atavistic definition of war.

Now what I have tried to point out is that in addition to these more classical formulations of war, the twentieth century has made some notable contributions. One is the Leninist idea. Again one could argue, as James Joll has pointed out in many of his writings, most recently in an article he wrote about socialist ideas of war and peace, that this idea of war as a product of imperialism or capitalism at a certain stage of development goes back to the nineteenth century. But it has become much more common in the twentieth century, particularly since 1916. And on the American side there is the idea of war as a catalyst for reform; that is, not necessarily as a conflict among nation-states as such, nor necessarily as a product of a certain stage of capital-

istic development, but as a catalyst for domestic reform, which
I view as Wilsonian: the idea of war for democracy; the idea of
war for freedom. That Wilsonian, American contribution I think
has been quite notable in the twentieth century. These two—the
Leninist formulation of warfare and what I view as the Wilsonian
formulation—seem to have in common the fact that both view
war as inherent in peace, or war and peace as not necessarily
distinct entities, but interrelated, indistinguishable.

And I argue in my paper that one thing that has happened in
the twentieth century is the blurring of the boundary, the distinction between war and peace. This, it seems to me, was particularly
notable in the 1930s, whether we talk about Germany or Italy
or Japan or indeed their democratic enemies. One could not
discuss war without talking about peace, and vice versa. And
when one talked about peace, one also had to discuss how to
defend the peace, how to preserve the peace—which, of course,
raised questions about preparedness and the domestic context in
which that would take place. After 1945, there is the Cold War,
which is defined as a state of neither peace nor war. The Cold
War was war, but it was also peace. This phenomenon of neither
peace nor war, or peace and war simultaneously, does seem to
have characterized the century.

If the twentieth century may be characterized by the breaching
of the boundaries between war and peace, can we still point to
areas where peace as such can be defined in its own terms? Not
in terms of war, not in terms of war preparedness, but in its own
terms. Has the twentieth century contributed anything to ideas
about peace? Well, here I make two suggestions. One is that one
of the things the twentieth century has contributed is the idea
of intellectual or cultural exchange as a basis for human understanding, which in turn is viewed as a basis for peace. I think
one could say that things like The Japan Foundation as well as
other organizations that are dedicated to intellectual exchange
would be a rather important twentieth-century innovation in
terms of the effort to define peace.

Secondly, apropos of remarks by Maruyama and others, the
twentieth century has also brought efforts at transcending the nation-state, nationalism, or national interest as narrowly defined,
in a discussion of war and peace. I refer to such things as a global

concern with the protection of the environment, or the preservation of the whale (the Greenpeace movement), or the antinuclear movement. These efforts, even though they have just begun and have not been terribly successful, do indicate to me that this century may yet be making some kind of effort to transcend the old framework of the nation-state as the only one in which one could discuss peace or war.

Finally, if I may come back to Japan's postwar constitution. I am in agreement with Maruyama that to the extent that Japan's new constitution, Article 9 in particular, may be said to be making a contribution to twentieth-century history, it may be in renouncing national sovereignty as the framework for discussing questions of war and peace.

Kolakowski: It is indeed ironic that such concepts as war and peace, which seem to be very clear, have become in fact, as Iriye pointed out, obscured in our century. You have mentioned, certainly quite rightly in this context, Lenin's contribution to this Orwellian language in which we do not know any longer what is war and what is peace. Lenin often quoted Clausewitz during World War I, so much so that Clausewitz even became the author of the main statement of the dialectics on war. But Lenin went further by arguing that the very distinction between aggressive and defensive war was no longer tenable. The point is not who is attacking and who is defending; the point is which class is waging war. If it is the progressive class which wages war against a reactionary class, the war is just, by definition. The Soviet Union, by definition, the embodiment of the progressive class on a world scale, is by definition right in any war in which it might be involved, no matter who is attacking whom.

This strange theory became extremely convenient politically for the Soviet Union. As you may know, one of the fundamental principles of Soviet education in this particular area is the quotation from "the great humanist" Gorky, who said: "If the enemy doesn't surrender, one should destroy him." And the point is that the enemy is not just an enemy in war. The enemy is the class enemy. There is no moral distinction between war and other forms of class struggle.

On the other hand, no country would now accept the notion that it might ever become an aggressor. Hitler and Mussolini were not afraid of expressing their policies in terms of conquest. They extolled the military virtues and the idea of conquest clearly and unambiguously. But who is against peace now? Absolutely nobody. There is nothing but defense all over the world. Sixty-five years have elapsed since the end of World War I, and the world has known innumerable wars since then. However, in all those years there has never been a war waged between two democratic countries. This is a simple fact which is very much worth remembering. It is despotism that engenders wars. We probably cannot overcome the Orwellian language concerning war and peace without strengthening the democratic institutions all over the world.

Nivat: One small comment. War and peace have been blurred in the twentieth century. But the idea of the nation is perhaps also blurred. At one point you indicate a paradox in Bolshevik Russia and Wilsonian America—namely, that both were global and also in a way nationalistic. But at the beginning of the revolution the Bolsheviks were not nationalists; they did much to destroy the Russian nation in words and deed. It was proclaimed that Russian nationalism must be destroyed. Gorky came in handy because he despised the Russian peasant, and his contempt helped destroy that great part of the Russian nation which was peasant Russia. What is now left of the Russian nation? If the Soviet Union is supposed to do this and that, it does not mean the Russian nation. Some Russian emigré sociologists, historians, and philosophers even argue that there is no longer a Russian nation.

The general problem of the idea of the nation being blurred is important. Hagihara raised the problem, as I understand it, of a nation which decides, or is compelled to decide, to renounce the nation's basis—self-defense. Self-defense is the core of everyday Soviet discourse, but that discourse does not represent nationalism. There was, of course, a revival of nationalistic values after 1935 and during the war, through the Party's alliance with the church it had previously crushed. But I think in the Brezhnev era all this disappeared. One might argue that today, certain aspects of Russian nationalism reappear in official circles, in the military literature, and in the resistance literature, but as the expression of a nation, they are very questionable.

Schwartz: I would like to differ a little with this business of what is a nation. What we tend to define as nation is what comes under the jurisdiction of a territorial state. In Africa there are nations whose boundaries were established by the imperial system. They were not nations, but if you go to Ghana now, you can find a nationalist history of Ghana. So it is still the territorial state that defines what we mean by the nation. In the twentieth century this is reinforced by universalistic doctrines. Universalistic doctrines with transnational claims have been captured by territorial states. I draw no symmetry between democratic and despotic states, but in fact the United States represents capitalist liberalism, and the Soviet Union, at least to many, still represents Marxism-Leninism. If such universalistic doctrines had not become embodied in territorial states, we might be better off. I think if we still had an older and simpler utilitarian conflict of interests, perhaps in the face of a nuclear holocaust agreement based sheerly on interest considerations might be possible. But ideology reinforcing nationalism resists compromise.

Mommsen: I would like to go further. The premise that in the eighteenth or perhaps in the nineteenth century there was a clear-cut distinction between war and peace is questionable. It is to some degree necessary to assume an autonomous nation-state—actually it does not need to be a nation—which in the old traditional sense has a right to go to war in order to implement policies if it cares to do so. A system of states then decides whether there is peace or war. But this overlooks the fact that many conflicts inside these states were not considered war. As a rule, wars on the periphery were not called wars. Most colonial conflicts were punitive actions; they did not come under the heading of war. So in some ways, the nineteenth-century situation is much more blurred on the periphery than at the center of the power system. That of course would mean that now the twentieth century just brings things into the open. I do not think the twentieth century is so much worse; it is perhaps more honest about these things than the nineteenth century.

Friedländer: I found the typology suggested by Iriye very interesting, but I want him to clarify some points. First of all, is it really a twentieth-century phenomenon, this blurring? The French Revolution is obviously a classical case of a mixture of war and peace. Universalist ideologies, by definition, blur war and peace. And there are also other reasons for blurring which start in the nineteenth century; the global impact of imperialist powers had already created a mixed situation of war and peace then.

A third point not yet raised would complete our typology: the technological aspect. You cannot differentiate between war and peace when you reach the level of total destruction because its very nature creates this confusion. Where are we? The Cold War is not war, but not peace either, because of the nature of the weapons. And at the guerrilla level, which is a phenomenon mostly of the twentieth century but also has earlier roots, war and peace are again mixed. So universalist ideologies, globalism, and the level of technology add to the blurring; any hope of distinction is very difficult to visualize, given developments at all those levels.

Karl: One other element: The removal of some of the mechanisms for maintaining the distinction has been important. Racial definitions of culture in the nineteenth century—elsewhere in the world but also in the United States—helped justify wars against Indians precisely because they were wars against Indians. Racial groups defined as inferior were not worthy of the definition of war. In the twentieth century, and certainly since World War II, many of the fundamental justifications for defining war, among which race certainly was central, have been removed.

Windsor: There is a distinction perhaps between the question of blurring and the ambiguities Iriye has suggested: the war as peace and the peace as war, which is more fundamentally a twentieth-century phenomenon. It provides a global context within which we conduct other forms of state activity. That condition also reinforces the state and weakens the nation in the sense that the nation confronted with this ambiguity, confronted with a threat to its survival, has to debate its own values in relation to peace and war in an unprecedented way. A safe and well-defined war can reinforce nationalism. The ambiguity weakens nationalism, yet precisely because of the need to control the ultimate weapons of destruction, it does strengthen the power of the state. And the difficulty is that states, by definition, have a vested interest against internationalist movements which are out to challenge their power. The state, therefore, maintains its position as the ultimate guardian of this ambiguity, and as such operates both against the nation internally and against the emergence of some kind of world community. In turn, this reinforces the guerrillas, who find irregular war the only way to cope with what in many ways is the guardian power of the Platonic state.

Maier: It is natural that, given the levels of violence which the world wars introduced and given the possibilities for destruction which a World War III would mean, we have constantly to find more and more sweeping justifications. This type of double-think seems reasonably logical and predictable, however dismal. But I think we should look at the question of organized violence between peoples, rather than just war and peace. Here, I agree that the continuity of organized violence is striking: In a sense, World War I and World War II, although they are the searing events of our history, may yet be exceptional events. Since World War II we have had a reversion to a pattern of peripheral violence. Perhaps there is continuity there, but why did the peripheries break somewhere in the early twentieth century, and why has it been possible to reestablish them? I would suggest that the typology of war and peace should isolate the period of hyperbolic war in the world wars, and then we might be able to see the links before and after that period.

Iriye: I have focused on ideas about war and peace. The implication of this for discussion of the twentieth century lies in the fact that war has tended to be thought of as a constant, if not as a normal, state of affairs, at least something that all nation-states, peoples, and societies have to be concerned with. This has tended to result in a poverty of ideas about peace. Peace as a mere absence of war is clear: the neutrality idea, isolationism, peace as a movement against something, against nuclear armament, peace as an anti-something. But by presenting discussions about war in this fashion, there has been a failure to look at the problem of how to define peace, which has been unfortunate. In trying to visualize what the rest of the century or the twenty-first century might be like, we may need to be more prescriptive than descriptive. How does one try to define peace in the changing world of the twentieth century, in terms of technological changes, globalism, imperialism? Would it still be possible to have a peace that can be relevant to large countries as well as small countries, democratic as well as nondemocratic states? That is the central question I tried to raise.

Hersch: I had a strange experience reading this paper. I found several ideas that were quite close to things I had thought. For instance, the confusion between the adversaries in war, who are becoming very similar to each other. And the reflection about the distinction of the dimension of time at the end is very important. I believe that the confusion here belongs in the conduct of people in the face of war and peace rather than in the definition of war and peace. It is not so much war and peace that cannot be differentiated, but that the way people behave in the service of peace becomes the same as in the service of war. But then I do not understand the last sentence: "One could begin by recognizing that no matter what one means by peace, it is a value one must clearly distinguish from war." If I understand the paper, that is impossible. It is part of the human condition that we cannot do just that. Perhaps we should try to see why we cannot achieve this distinction. Why do we have to live without this distinction, or with a clear understanding of the impossibility of clear knowledge? It is an illusion that tomorrow we will make this distinction clear. One last remark. I have the feeling that, in most cases, when speaking about war in a general, abstract way, it is fake— because you never have war for the sake of war; you always have war because something else is at stake. The problem to take into consideration—what is at stake—is not an accident, but belongs to the essence of the thing. Speaking about war as something separate makes clear thinking as something impossible.

Joll: This might point to the need not so much for redefining the distinction between war and peace in order to try to return to a state where they are quite distinct from each other, but for a redefinition of what we mean by war. In the twentieth century we have experienced wars of such different kinds, both in their scope and in their effect, that it can be confusing to describe them all as if they were the same thing. Perhaps people are horrified by the concept of a nuclear war because this kind of war, in which the means are bound to destroy any of the ends for which war is being fought, does suggest a war of a different kind—not just on a different *scale* from World Wars I and II, but a different *kind*.

Iriye: War could be defined, I think, as organized violence; since organizations very in size and scope, there have been different kinds of war. But they have had this in common: They have all been justified in the name of peace or human rights or democracy or some universalistic principle. The fact that there has been, particularly in the twentieth century, a large variety of conflicts has to be kept in mind when we talk about peace too, because it might be that just as there are different kinds of war, there will have to be different kinds of peace. And one kind of peace may be preferred to another. It is sometimes argued that certain kinds of peace are less desirable than war. This has been used as a justification for going to war. Here the point about the human condition is quite fundamental. Given human organizations as well as human proclivities, is it really impossible to make a sharp distinction? Here one goes back to the question, what is at stake? That is prior to discussions of relations among states or relations among different organized groups. It does seem that one problem about the century has been the disrepute into which the concept of peace has fallen because it has tended to be defensive. Peace advocates have tended to react to the view that war is more inherent in the human condition, or that, given the realities of the world, war or proto-war is always a strong possibility. They have tended to view peace in the context of war. I wonder if it might not also be possible to talk about war and peace by having a clear idea of what is meant by peace.

Kyogoku: Much depends on what is at stake and also on the quality of war. The argument of "Better dead than Red" is relevant here.

Iriye: One still has to cope with this. Can one be free from it? I think the slogan in the 1950s in the United States, as Reinhold Niebuhr said, was the question of peace with justice, or peace and justice. That is, one had to have both peace and justice. If one could not have justice, one must be prepared to give up peace. But these problems have become globalized. It would not be enough simply to think in terms of the survival of freedom in one country and going to war against another country in the name of that freedom, because one does have to think in terms of the implications for the rest of humanity. That is why phenomena like the antinuclear movement can be an important breakthrough; they force us to think in global terms. While the questions of Red versus dead and freedom versus peace are very important, they have to be put in the context of transnational and global considerations.

Umesao: War to me is a product of freedom. Without freedom, I do not think war can happen. In the past, the Pax Britannica existed. In the case of Japan, for over 250 years we had the Pax Tokugawa—the regime of Tokugawa Japan kept under a very tight rein—and war did not occur. When the Pax Tokugawa collapsed, war broke out. Thus we gained freedom. We gained freedom to fight war, albeit within a nation. Even today I think this can be seen all over the world. Various types of constraints have been done away with, and new nations, one after another, have been born. Only the twentieth century is characterized by this abundance in the number of nations. Minuscule nations have emerged and obtained freedom. And when they advocate freedom and are fragmented, they have an increased possibility of conflict. Perhaps in the twenty-first century this tendency may be accentuated. A race, or *minzoku*, may now be considered a unit for freedom. In such terms, the whole human race can probably be broken down into some two thousand ethnic groups. Hence the possible fragmentation of the world into minuscule nations. They might fight wars to assure their freedom, to earn freedom from war. And we have found no principle, no mechanism, to restrain them. Can we really constrain all these movements in the framework of peace when everybody wants to have peace by war? What is a valid way to keep some two thousand different ethnic groups in an organized, disciplined framework?

Nivat: When I read the sentence, "In a sense, war was peace between 1941 and 1945," I think I understood the meaning. It may have been peace in the heart of a soldier who thought he was fighting for a just cause. I think peace is a personal notion. War is not; war is collective. And when it is said that war is peace and peace is war, I wonder whether those two terms can be treated equivalently. There is little dispute about wars once they have begun. About peace, there are not disputes but really different convictions. The paper gives the sociologist's viewpoint. There are others—for example, the personal, religious point of view. If you discuss with somebody who from a very religious point of view repeats *besser rot als tot*, you cannot find an argument against it. It is a question of personal conviction, and we are—thank God—in the position where we can have our personal conviction about peace, and it is an ethical and religious notion.

THE TWENTIETH-CENTURY STATE

THE SLOW DEATH OF IMPERIALISM

WOLFGANG J. MOMMSEN

Nowadays we pride ourselves on having put the age of imperialism behind us. We believe that a completely new era has dawned in the relations between Western industrial societies and the countries of the so-called Third World. Any overt use of power to maintain or reestablish imperial rule over peoples beyond one's national territory is not regarded as legitimate. Whenever it happens, it must be presented in such a way as to appear legitimized by those being dominated—whether a client regime calls for "assistance," or aid is given within a more or less fictitious alliance system. Overt imperialist rule cannot be reconciled with the principles of Western democracy, or indeed Eastern "people's democracy." Imperialism, once thrown into the political arena as a term of abuse and later cheerfully used as a battle cry by the proponents of an expansive *Weltpolitik*, has today fallen into disrepute.

Seen from the perspective of history, the decline and ultimate collapse of the great colonial empires that developed from the eighteenth century onward, often built upon much older foundations, could be regarded as the most significant event of this century. In this context it is even more momentous than the rise of the Soviet Union or the suppression of the Fascist systems, which in some respects can themselves be seen as anachronistic manifestations of imperialist rule. And yet the term imperialism, sometimes replaced by the slogan neocolonialism, has by no means disappeared from our vocabulary. On the contrary, disputes about the various forms of imperialism in the past and their survival into the present haunt current political discussion to a remarkable degree, and not only where relations between the West and the so-called Third World are at issue. In the political language of orthodox Marxism-Leninism, which in the Soviet bloc still claims an ideological monopoly, imperialism is synonymous with the capitalist system.

Despite the fact that the Soviet bloc has recognized the possibility of a limited peaceful coexistence between the two great world systems, it accuses the Western capitalist societies of pursuing imperialist policies—policies aimed at the exploitation of other nations and, at the same time, at expanding their sphere of power (with the long-term objective of imposing upon the world their own ideas of social order, a purpose that is said to derive from the nature of capitalism in its monopolistic stage). Conversely, Soviet policy seems to many Western observers to be basically geared toward expansion and aggrandizement, and therefore to be imperialist in a new and more extreme sense. For some time, China has joined in the condemnation of Soviet imperialism. China itself, heir to a great empire, is endowed with enormous political and military potential, which although largely underdeveloped could provide the basis for regional imperialism. In the countries of the so-called Third World, condemnation of imperialism provides the backbone of their own, often still embryonic, national identity. Many of these nations are inclined to blame all their national problems, and above all their economic difficulties, on the consequences of yesterday's imperialism or, more particularly, on the forms of imperialism that supposedly or actually still exist today. Finally, the radical anti-imperialist ideology, as exemplified rather than expressed by Che Guevara in the 1950s, provides legitimation for radical terrorist movements, which believe they are taking the struggle for emancipation of the Third World into the industrial heartlands of the West. The growing gap between the advanced industrial societies of the Western world, including Japan, and the developing countries offers a somber foil to these considerations.

What really is happening? Have we reached the end of imperialism? Or are we merely in a new, admittedly less obvious and therefore all the more effective, phase of control of the earth by a few economically advanced nations led by the United States, while the Eastern bloc takes up a sort of intermediate position between verbal anti-imperialism and parasitic participation in Western neocolonialism? Not only Marxist-Leninist and Western Marxists, but also many liberal thinkers in the West would subscribe to the second answer. The influence of the *dependencia* theorists has declined in recent years, but their claim that capitalist penetration of the Third World, with a few exceptions, led at best to the emergence of a "peripheral capitalism" which did not allow genuine economic development in those countries cannot simply be rejected.

A whole school of theorists of neocolonialism, from Paul A. Baran to Johan Galtung, have put forward one key argument in many variations—namely, that the end of formal colonial rule in the wake of decolonization was in reality only the transition to a new phase in which the periphery was far more dependent on the industrial metropolises. The continuation of imperialist control by more effective means made the comparatively crude forms of military intervention and formal colonial rule largely redundant. The emergence of collaborationist regimes in former colonies with a vested interest in maintaining relations with the former mother country, and the emergence of comprador classes whose economic interests are closely related to those of the former colonial rulers overseas (even though they are at variance with the interests of the indigenous population), transferred dependence to a less conspicuous but far more efficient plane. Henceforth, so the argument runs, the imperialist metropolises no longer needed the old-fashioned instruments of formal control.[1]

The way things have developed has made these arguments seem rather thin, in some respects. For some time now, many of the developing countries have revealed a degree of independence in their relationship with the West that is not reconcilable with these assumptions. And the terms of trade have not always changed to the disadvantage of the developing countries, as many of the *dependencia* theorists believed would happen. On the other hand, the expectations of Western politicians and development theorists have not been fulfilled either. They had assumed that the less developed countries would in due course follow the example of the West in gradually modernizing their societies by introducing Western models of government and administration and by taking over Western technology. The 1940s and 1950s were dominated by the idea that it was the duty of the colonial powers to lead the peoples of the Third World to independence step by step and provide them with the political institutions that would enable them to take their fate into their own hands. It was more or less assumed that the political, cultural, and economic ties which connected territories to former mother countries would be maintained for a long time to come.

In the 1950s and 1960s Great Britain and France were remarkably successful in conducting the process of decolonization in an orderly fashion; they largely succeeded in establishing European-style governmental systems. Furthermore, the new states, with but a few exceptions, were willing to join the Union Française and the Commonwealth of Nations, organizations in which the former colonies maintained distinct political ties. But there were catastrophes too. The dramatic collapse of internal order in the Congo after the end of Belgian rule in 1960 and the bloody civil war in Nigeria shortly afterward foreshadowed later troubles. These days little is said about the efforts of an entire generation of colonial reformers to implant the traditions of Western parliamentary democracy in the former colonial territories. We are thankful if the regimes in the Third World do not become too oppressive, as they did in Idi Amin's Uganda or in Pinochet's Chile. But this is perhaps unfair to those who worked with determination and conviction to help these countries establish Western-style administrations in the first place.

Worse still, the confident expectation of Western development theorists that the countries of the Third World, having achieved independence, would by and large follow the same path of gradual modernization and industrial development which the West had trod a century earlier turned out to be a disappointment. In the majority of cases, the modernization strategies recommended by the West have failed, or at best succeeded in a limited way. In only a few cases has there been continuous development toward an industrial economy that would have been able gradually to conquer the massive poverty in many regions of the under-developed world. The number of countries that have in fact managed to emulate the industrial development of the West and Japan is still small. In the specialized language of the development theoreticians, they have earned the epithet newly developed countries (NDCs). With the exception of some highly specialized sectors, their overall contribution to international trade is still limited. Yet complaints have already been heard in the West that these countries, thanks to cheap labor, are providing unfair competition for the old industrial economies! In fact—apart from the white dominions of the British Commonwealth and the special case of Japan, which was never subjected to colonial rule— there are only two groups of countries that have actually experienced a breakthrough. The first is a group of geographically advantaged countries in the Far East, such as Korea, Singapore, Hong Kong, and Taiwan; the second is the oil-producing countries in the Middle East. And even here it is questionable whether the wealth created by oil provides a solid basis for healthy, long-term economic development.

The present sobriety in the Western world after the great period of growth following World War II has increasingly affected the economic climate of Third World regions. These are hit far more seriously by worldwide economic recession than the developed countries. Above all, the collapse of the Keynesian strategies of the 1950s and 1960s has largely shattered belief in the possibility of coming to grips with the problems of underdevelopment by means of a consistent policy of government support for the economy, with the active participation of international institutions such as the World Bank. In most Third World countries, little hope can be placed in the self-regulating forces of the world market, for these seem rather to exacerbate the polarization of rich and poor nations. Even the modest successes achieved in the sphere of developmental aid, which the countries of the Western world have undertaken to varying degrees, have recently come under fire because, either supposedly or in fact, such aid merely distorts the economic structure of the countries affected and favors the indigenous ruling elites.

The crisis of belief in the superiority of the Western path toward the modern capitalist consumer society is nowhere more apparent than in the case of Iran. The collapse of Reza Shah's regime, which to some degree took Western observers by surprise, provides perhaps the most dramatic example of the disenchantment of Third World countries with Western concepts of modernization. Reza Shah was highly regarded in the Western world precisely because of his vigorous policy of modernization, which seemed to be leading Iran toward a new and better future by leaps and bounds. Close economic collaboration with Western nations, not least the Federal Republic of Germany, seemed to be further proof that Iran was well on the way to catching up. The fundamentalist revolt led by Khomeini swept away this regime by appealing to the independent traditions of Islam. It achieved power thanks to a deep dissatisfaction with the Western model of modernization in parts of the Islamic world. It would not be altogether surprising if this example were to be followed elsewhere. On the African continent things may be somewhat better at the moment, insofar as radical movements against the Western tradition have found only scattered support, often under the flag of communism (without, however, having much in common with Marxism-Leninism of the Soviet variety). All in all, the West's philosophy of gradual emancipation and moderni-zation is no longer unquestionably accepted by the peoples in the Third World.

This makes it possible to take a more sensible view than usual of the relationship between the West and the countries of the Third World, as it has developed since the beginning of the twentieth century. One can admit today that the European powers adopted a policy of decolonization relatively late and with great reluctance. Indeed, as Jean Surêt-Canale pointed out recently, it is even questionable whether the notion of "decolonization" is not itself an ideological distortion of the process of gradual emancipation of the Third World countries. The concept may have suggested to the former colonial rulers their active and leading role in that process, whereas in reality they were compelled to give up their imperial positions under the pressure of emancipa-tion movements and in view of crucial changes in the international system. Indeed, it is doubtful whether even in the case of Great Britain it is justifiable to speak of a consistent policy of gradually leading the colonial territories to independence, as suggested by the formula "from British Empire to Commonwealth of Nations." On the whole, the Western powers were overtaken by events at the periphery, however much planning there had been for a gradual development toward self-determination, and eventually they found themselves pushed ahead by a sudden upsurge of nationalist feelings.

The survival of colonial empires had been called into question as early as 1917 with the Russian October Revolution and Woodrow Wilson's Fourteen Points. Lenin explicitly appealed to the nations subjected to imperialist domination to throw away their colonialist yoke, and Woodrow Wilson let it be known clearly that the United States did not wish to be a partner in any policies designed to maintain empire. In 1918 even the British Foreign Office found that imperialism was dead when Italy suggested that the German claim to parts of the Portuguese colonies, as stipulated in the Anglo-German Angola Treaty of 1913, be transferred to Italy.[2] In the negotiations on the Paris peace treaties, the transfer of the formerly German colonies and the Arab territories of the Ottoman Empire to Western imperialist rule was considered unacceptable by the United States. Only with considerable difficulty did the Allied and associated powers agree upon mandatory rule of these territories by Britain and France. The mandate system served as a means of reconciling the actual continuation of imperial rule in the Middle East and South Africa with the idea of the democratic right to self-determination. The idea of government in trust in favor of the indigenous population became an important ideological formula for justifying the continuation of control under the political conditions that developed after the end of World War I.

But the reality of rule in the colonial territories was somewhat different. Admittedly the idea was generally accepted that independence would eventually be granted, albeit under conditions that guaranteed close liaison with the mother country. But hardly anyone thought that colonial rule would virtually come to an end within his own lifetime. It was generally assumed that the process of gradually preparing the colonies for independence would extend over several generations. In many respects it was only after 1918 that the colonial powers began to commit themselves to systematic economic development of their possessions and, with the aid of public investment, to creating the infrastructure that was the precondition of an economic upswing. Before 1914 the maxim that the colonies should pay their own way had been generally accepted, although the expenses for policing them did at times far exceed the sums which could be exacted from them. Apart from a few exceptions, the metropolises had shown no willingness at all to make infrastructural or economic investments from public funds. This, at least, began to change.

In addition, an end was finally put to the rule that the economic interests of the colonial territories must always be subordinate to those of the mother country. In the 1920s, the British government for the first time allowed the introduction, albeit on a moderate scale, of protective tariffs in British India in order to protect indigenous production against powerful competition from third countries. This measure, incidentally, was as much directed against Japanese competition as against trade with the motherland itself. But it was the Government of India Act of 1935 that first provided the legal precondition for a policy of promoting the Indian economy and of expanding the Indian welfare system with the aid of public funds from the mother country.

All in all, the interwar period brought a considerable economic upswing at the periphery. The policy of *mis au valeur*, which had already been propagated in the last decades of classical imperialism, now at last seemed to be bearing fruit. Many territories finally began to repay the taxpayers of the mother countries. The extent to which the indigenous population profited from this remains a hotly debated question. Undoubtedly most of the colonial territories remained economically under the guidance of the ruling nations. For example, in the area of currency policy, the colonizers used their position to the disadvantage of the indigenous economies. But on the whole the conclusion has to be tentatively positive. For the first time progress was being made, even if it was only by small steps.

The modest economic progress many overseas territories experienced after World War I, however, initiated processes of social change that at first were not favorable to the unrestricted maintenance of imperial rule. The newly emerging bourgeoisie in colonial societies, and with it the indigenous intelligentsia, gained political weight and on occasion called into question the informal compromise with the traditional elites on which rested the stability of British colonial rule and in most territories also that of the French. It became progressively more difficult to neutralize nationalist movements politically, as the British had tried in vain to do with Gandhi's Congress Party by extending the right to vote to the rural population on a local, provincial, and ultimately national level. Conversely, it became less and less possible to resort to force, in view of the general political climate and the disinclination of the home populations to make the financial sacrifices necessary for military operations overseas. All in all, in many regions of the Third World and especially in Asia, indigenous nationalist movements made considerable headway during the 1930s, although for the time being, with the possible exception of the Indian national movement, they obtained only modest concessions in the political sphere. In the majority of cases the colonial powers, such as the Dutch in Indonesia or the French in Indochina, managed to keep the nationalist movements at bay.[3]

Without the great crisis of World War II, an "accelerating process" in Jakob Burckhardt's sense, decolonization would certainly not have progressed as rapidly as it did. The massive claims made on the resources of the colonial territories for the conduct of war, as well as the various sorts of aid the Allied Powers received from their colonies, made far-reaching concessions to national liberation movements unavoidable. An even more important factor was that in 1943 the Japanese army conquered large areas in Southeast Asia and encouraged anticolonial groups and movements to demand independence from Western domination—even if it was within the context of an emerging Japanese empire that had anything but emancipation in mind. Colonial rule was restored in East Asian territories after the collapse of Japan, but the magic spell of the West's claim to superiority was broken. Mao Tse-tung's victory over Chiang Kai-shek in China and China's subsequent retreat from the West changed Asia's political map. Especially from the point of view of the United States, this proved to be a traumatic experience.

The United States had already made it unequivocally clear during World War II that it was not at all interested in restoring the colonial empires of the European allies to their former splendor. The stronger the American position in the Allied camp became, the less conceivable it was simply to continue the strategies of imperialist rule prevalent in the prewar period. It became a practical necessity to legitimize colonial rule as "trusteeship" on behalf of the indigenous population, and to act accordingly, at least to some degree. The strategies of imperial rule were subjected to fundamental changes. It was no longer possible to maintain long-term imperial control in alliance with traditional collaborating elites or other groups willing to work with the colonial authorities and thereby withstand the nationalist movements, which could now count on considerable support from the masses. The crucial question now was which indigenous national groups to cooperate with. The superior military force or moral prestige of the colonial power would no longer suffice. Political solutions were needed, and eventually found, by bargaining with the nationalist movements for compromise solutions by which the mother country's paramountcy could be stabilized on a lower level. The policy of gradually preparing the colonial territories for political independence pursued as one of its primary objectives the creation of a constellation in which political and economic ties with the mother country would be secured for the foreseeable future, if only in an informal way. This feature of decolonization policy coincided with American ideas. As Tony Smith has suggested: "In short, American anti-colonialism presupposed the establishment, in Asia and elsewhere, of stable regimes capable of being dependable allies."[4]

However, the degree of willingness on the part of the colonial powers to tread the path of compromise with national liberation movements varied considerably from region to region. With the Indian Independence Act of 1947, Britain unquestionably laid a foundation stone that became the focal point for national movements not only in the rest of Asia, but also in Africa. France, on the other hand, was little inclined to give up its imperial positions and clung determinedly to them wherever possible. Even though by 1960 it had granted independence to the majority of its former territories, it insisted upon unconditional superiority within the newly created Union Française. This was designed to provide the framework for informal French control even after independence. In Vietnam and Algeria, France clung to the remnants of its imperial position to the bitter end. This was to have serious consequences for the political system of the mother country. Furthermore, the French defeat in Indochina provoked the United States into action, which eventually resulted in the bitter and long-drawn-out Vietnam war. The Dutch were persuaded only by massive international pressure, especially from the United States, to give up their colonial empire, which from an economic point of view had developed brilliantly, and to give Sukarno a free hand.

The "release into independence" was associated with the expectation that the new sovereign states would stick to the rules of the game and maintain close ties with their former colonial masters, especially with regard to respecting the rights of those white residents who decided to stay in the country. For the time being at least, the idea of a possible military intervention if these principles were not adhered to was not completely dropped from the arsenal of international politics. When, in 1956, Nasser nationalized the Suez Canal Company in accordance with international law, Great Britain, otherwise the main protagonist of an evolutionary course toward the postimperial era, felt obliged to resort to military intervention, coldbloodedly exploiting the Soviet intervention in Hungary, while Israel took the opportunity to launch an offensive against Egypt.

The failure of this last, unreservedly imperialist intervention, undertaken against the protest of the United States and the USSR, marked a historical turning point. Henceforth it was no longer possible to maintain imperial rule, even for a short time, against the manifest opposition of indigenous nationalist liberation movements. The Western powers also lost all interest in stemming the tide. Even so, decolonization did not proceed without serious conflicts, in particular in those cases where it was difficult to sort out the interests of European settlers from those of the indigenous population. The white settler communities eventually became the last desperate force clinging to imperial power, frequently let down by the mother country itself, as the white farming community in Kenya was to experience to its dismay. South Africa, whose Boer population had been in the country for a long time, is a particularly critical borderline case. The Vietnam war too must be seen primarily as a consequence of delayed decolonization which allowed a colonial conflict to be interpreted in terms of the East-West antagonism. This interpretation led to military intervention by the United States.

Nowadays an overt imperialist policy of the classical type cannot usually be conducted, if only because the two superpowers, the United States and the USSR, no longer allow it, as it might trigger a nuclear confrontation between them. On the basis of very different ideological premises, both the United States and the USSR regard themselves as anti-imperialist powers, at any rate in the traditional meaning of this notion. For this reason, neither can condone imperialist action of the classical type, quite apart from reasons relative to the balance of power. It is this global situation that makes direct military intervention in Third World countries by the Western powers, and also by the Soviet Union, an extremely risky business.

Only limited "police actions" under an international flag, or "proxy wars," which are conducted with limited means and without too-obvious participation by the powers in question, remain possible. In recent decades there has been no shortage of the latter type of conflict. On the other hand, the relative stalemate between the superpowers has made it possible for second- and even third-rate powers, which were previously subjected to imperialist control themselves, to conduct an imperialist policy on a regional level in the wake of the territorial disputes that accompanied the end of decolonization. Notorious in this regard is South Africa. While formally proclaiming the right to self-determination of those colored peoples living within its domain, the white population actually conducts a massive repression despite all the protests by the Western world. The present conflict between Iran and Iraq can be viewed from the same perspective; here, too, it is basically a question of exploiting the relative power vacuum in the Middle East to establish a hegemonial position within the Arab-Islamic world.

The world is full of conflicts that can be regarded as the legacy of former imperial conflicts. This is particularly true in the Middle East. For over a century, the European powers had considered it in their interests to keep the Ottoman Empire alive against the opposition of the majority of its subject Arab populations, even though it allowed a gradual erosion of the sultan's power on the periphery of the empire, in particular in North Africa. The present bitter nationalist struggles within the Arab camp only reached their current fever pitch as a result of a century of repressing Arab national aspirations in the interests of Europe. And historically it is quite inappropriate to regard the founding of the state of Israel as a byproduct of British imperialism in the Middle

East, as has repeatedly been pointed out by the Arab side. It is all the more paradoxical that the dispute over the future of Israel has been conducted in the form of two types of subimperialisms in bitter competition with one another. Regrettably, the classic methods of "preventative annexation" and "war of pacification" have been resuscitated by a country whose traditions should have committed it unreservedly to the anti-imperialist ideals of liberal democracy.

Imperialism, as a policy for establishing global systems of territorial or even mere hegemonial rule over vast regions of the Third World, belongs, it would seem, to the past. But this has not really put a stop to imperialist rule in a regional context, precisely in regions of the Third World. Vietnam, for example, itself the victor in a war with the United States that was in many respects imperialist, did not hesitate to use its position in Southeast Asia to subject Cambodia to its control. It has become increasingly difficult for the superpowers to tame and control such secondary forms of imperialism, especially when they have initially covertly encouraged them.

But what is the position of the superpowers themselves? Both the United States and the USSR saw themselves from the very beginning as anti-imperialist powers. Thanks essentially to the war efforts of the United States and the USSR, the Fascist empires were eventually defeated in 1945. Through military operations on a grand scale the United States succeeded in reversing the war in East Asia and in bringing down the Japanese empire which, as late as 1944, ruled the whole Pacific and had effectively invaded the British Empire on the Indian subcontinent enough to unleash strong anti-British tendencies in India. It now became clear that the Fascist empires and the Japanese empire (which in some ways can be put on the same level, although the Japanese empire had been both far more efficient and far more successful) had actually been anachronistic ventures. They had tried to base their rule on the predominance of what they themselves considered master races, while at the same time reverting to the time-honored methods of direct rule and formal territorial control. But by 1930 it had become obvious that the methods of indirect or informal rule in collaboration with indigenous elites had proved to be far more effective than old-fashioned colonialism. Even so, the collapse of the Fascist empires also heralded the end of the older colonial empires. Colonial rule was no longer justifiable and could certainly no longer be maintained in the face of strong indigenous opposition.

The United States played a decisive role in this development, inasmuch as it actively discouraged the restoration of the Western powers' colonial empires. Old-style imperialist rule was incompatible with the American notion of a free world order characterized by unrestricted free trade and free access to all markets by all nations. Seen from this point of view, the dismantling of colonial rule was an essential element in the American policy of creating a new world order, based upon the political principle of democracy and the economic principle of competitive capitalism. From the beginning, the United States made considerable efforts to reconstruct Western Europe and Japan in accordance with these principles. The restoration of democratic governments and the reestablishment of free enterprise were closely linked. The United States was prepared to make considerable sacrifices in order to achieve this end, as is shown by the Marshall Plan, which poured considerable sums of money into the European economies in order to get them going again.

On the other hand, it would be shortsighted not to realize that the United States would benefit greatly from this policy, at least in the near term since its economic predominance in the West was thereby secured for the foreseeable future. Today the enormous investments of the United States in various regions of the world, including the advanced economies of Western Europe, are a factor of great importance; the present economic position of the United States in the world would not be possible without them. In a way, the restoration of the capitalist system in the West after World War II, along with the reestablishment of democratic regimes, could be described as a new variety of informal imperialism. For although other powers like Great Britain had some share in all this, it took place under the undisputed paramountcy of the United States.

This development must also be seen, however, against the background of the USSR's endeavors after 1945 to extend as far as possible its control over those parts of the globe amenable to Russian influence. The USSR appealed to the peoples of the

Third World to join forces against the Western "imperialist" powers in order to throw off their yoke once and for all. For the intellectual elites in the Third World, the idea of socialism—that is to say, economic development by means of a centrally directed economic system—had understandable advantages, given their situation. The Soviet path toward modernization seemed to some of them more appropriate than the Western one. Even so, the hope that an alliance with the liberation movements of the Third World would bring the USSR nearer its ideological goal of replacing the capitalist world system by a socialist one did not materialize. The time-honored Leninist prognosis that imperialism heralded the end of capitalism again proved to be unfounded.

In fact, from the beginning the USSR was not in a position effectively to challenge the position of the United States in the West as well as in vast regions of the Third World, and not only because for the time being only the United States possessed the nuclear bomb. In 1945 the USSR was not in any economic position to pursue an effective forward policy. It is all too simple to blame the USSR for being expansionist in the decade after World War II. Ideologically, the Soviet Union indeed harbored the idea that as capitalism decayed, the socialist system might gradually be extended over the rest of the world. Indeed, Soviet theoreticians never tired of forecasting the collapse of capitalism in the not too distant future, however little evidence they could muster. Reality, however, was different. In fact, the USSR was not thinking of a continuous extension of its own sphere of domination, by either revolutionary or military means. Rather, its policies were motivated by defensive instincts. The Soviets always reckoned with the possibility of a joint endeavor by the capitalist powers to wipe out socialism altogether, given the historical precedent in the years immediately after World War I. In the main this fear was, in fact, of Russia's own making, a reflection of its own ideology. But it did contribute to the endeavor to build a solidified Soviet empire in east-central Europe.

As a result of World War II, in the course of which the USSR had sustained huge losses in terms of both men and material goods of all sorts, in 1945 the USSR found itself in control of a large part of east-central Europe, almost without opposition from the Western powers. The gradual Sovietization of the newly established "people's democracies" in these European countries was essentially designed to secure this sphere of domination; only as a corollary was the extension of the sphere of Marxist-Leninist rule welcomed. This was not the result of a master plan, but of very skillful manipulative policies. There is some justification for the assumption that the Soviet Union would have preferred a unified Germany outside its own imperial system, but permanently checked by the joint control of the four powers, to a partition of Germany and the integration of what was to become the GDR into its sphere. Direct participation in decisions on the future of the whole of Germany and access to the industrial resources of West Germany seemed more valuable than Soviet control over East Germany, given the Soviet Union's economic requirements and its preoccupation with security.

The dialectic of the relations between the superpowers during the Cold War, and a growing awareness in both Great Britain and the United States that the western zones in Germany could not be kept permanently at the level of a mere subsistence economy, which would have been the precondition for a possible agreement with the USSR on the future of the whole of Germany, accelerated the process by which two systems directly opposed to each other emerged. In east-central Europe a bloc of formally sovereign states developed. In fact, however, they are largely dependent on the Soviet Union. They are all under the leadership of Communist parties; all belong to a common, largely integrated economic system and are allied to each other in a close military alliance clearly directed against the West. The degree of independence of individual states in the Eastern bloc varies, but it is obvious that certain basic rules of Communist domination cannot be transgressed. The GDR experienced this in 1953; the Hungarian uprising of 1956 was suppressed, as was the "Prague Spring" in 1968. In the case of Poland things are still fluid, but all the actors on the political stage in this deeply unhappy country behave in accordance with the rule that direct provocation which could lead to military intervention by the Soviet Union and possibly other states of the Eastern bloc should be avoided.

The Soviet bloc, established in the two decades following World War II, must be considered an imperialist system of a new type, but with much the same features as the older empires.

Indeed, the Soviet system can be described very well in terms of the classic model of imperialist rule with the assistance of indigenous collaborative regimes. In all the countries belonging to the Soviet camp, political power is wielded by relatively small Communist ruling elites, composed partly of ideologues, partly of pragmatic politicians who are interested only in maintaining power, and partly of civil servants and technocrats who have a manifest interest in preserving the status quo. They secure this by relying on a network of Communist cadres strictly controlled from the top. These stifle individual initiative and enforce conformity to the existing state of affairs. It is not only for ideological reasons, feigned or real, that these ruling elites are interested in cooperation with the USSR; their power and their entire material existence are dependent upon the continuation of this system. Under a democratic system, they would not last a day. This explains the conspicuously conservative posture of these regimes; it is no coincidence that Realpolitik is their holiest principle. Under these circumstances, the respective ruling elites accept that in the economic system of the Eastern bloc there will always be a sizable discrepancy in favor of the USSR, which in per capita national product is far behind the GDR, Hungary, and Czechoslovakia. It would lag even further behind were it not for the constant transfer of resources to the advantage of this monolithic colossus, which is not capable of running its economy efficiently.

The fact that even after more than thirty years the governments of the Soviet bloc still take every opportunity to profess with great display their "friendship with the great Socialist Soviet Union" proves that there is an Achilles' heel in the system. As long as the collaborating Communist elites are firmly in the saddle and their right to select the people to fill key positions in state and society remains unchallenged, the system functions fairly smoothly, with little direct intervention by the USSR. It is only when these collaborating regimes are put under pressure, and unexpected popular unrest threatens their removal, that things become dangerous. Then intervention to restore "tolerable" conditions becomes necessary, unless the threat alone is enough to restore the situation.

The Soviet intervention in Afghanistan followed the pattern of

Russian imperialism established in the early nineteenth century. Withdrawal of Soviet forces can be expected when, and only when, the existing collaborating regime, whose crisis has been resolved by Russian intervention, is firmly back in the saddle. There were comparable phenomena in the days of classic imperialism; the British intervention in Egypt became necessary only when the collaborating regime under Taufiq, which allowed control of Egyptian state finances by two European controllers in the interests of European creditors, was removed. Similarly, it was not until 1911, when the regime of the collaborating sultan of Morocco was endangered by a nationalist uprising, that France considered open intervention and eventually the establishment of formal rule necessary.

Thus, the system of the Soviet bloc can be considered a new manifestation of the classic type of imperialism, albeit in a new garb and under new auspices. An additional aspect is that the territorial aspirations of Soviet imperialism are largely identical with those of tsarist imperialism and at times, for example in Afghanistan, directly take up its objectives again. The Marxist-Leninist ideology commonly professed by the ruling elites provides an additional link, since the official ideology provides the moral legitimation of their privileged positions within their society. This state of affairs requires, of course, that the free expression of opinion be suppressed, so that the collaborating elites' claim to power can be secured in the long run. In the meantime, of course, the fact that the "people's democracies" are now well established, with huge bureaucracies which develop a drive to maintain themselves, whatever the social costs, provides them with an additional source of stability and relative legitimacy. From the point of view of the techniques of rule employed here, one cannot but admire this system; it operates with the Soviet Union having only limited recourse to direct force, although of late the "crises at the periphery" have mounted, requiring the USSR to rely on military superiority more than ever. Its ideological prestige is gradually withering away and the signs of decay of empire are unmistakable, although the eventual collapse still appears to be far off.

The USSR can rightly be considered the center of an empire which, however indirectly it is run, is forced to conform to Soviet ideas and principles to a very large degree, and finds itself effectively under Soviet military control. Although the United States exercises a good deal of influence and informal control over the West, including most West European states, it cannot be considered an imperialist power in the same way as the USSR. Nonetheless, it is not unjustified to speak of an American empire, albeit of an informal sort, in the two decades after the end of World War II if we accept the notion that imperialist rule may mean many things. It may involve a broad spectrum of means of control, extending from mere paramountcy (as the British call it) to various forms of indirect control, by economic means or otherwise, and as a rule making use of indigenous collaborating regimes, to formal territorial control. The paramountcy of the United States after the end of World War II in the West indeed in many ways displayed the features of an informal empire, particularly since the reconstruction of Europe depended very largely on the United States. As has already been pointed out, the reestablishment of democratic government and the restoration of capitalist economies in the West undoubtedly corresponded not only to American wishes, but also to American economic interests.

Although all the partners profited from the new economic order that slowly came into being in the 1950s, the main beneficiary was, at least initially, the American economy, which had been practically untouched by the immediate impact of the war. But apart from that, for more than a quarter of a century an American hegemony emerged in many areas of life, including the relatively sublime sphere of culture and scholarship. Surely the period from 1945 to 1960 can be designated from the vantage point of universal history as a time of American paramountcy over the Western world. In the 1960s it became common to speak of an American empire, although in rather loose terms. Although the ultimate criterion of imperialist control—namely, the ability to use force—was almost entirely lacking even during this period, the overwhelming might of the United States made itself felt in many ways, direct or indirect.

But the postwar system in the West developed very much on the basis of voluntary cooperation by the peoples concerned, even the Japanese, although they had many reasons to be resentful.

The economic, military, and political potential of the United States in this period was so great that it could largely win out without any direct pressure. To be sure, the Marshall Plan was not simply an instrument of American informal imperialism, as has been polemically maintained, but helped to guide the reconstruction of Europe in the desired direction—that is, toward the establishment of a new order on democratic and capitalist lines. Whenever other Western powers, like the British, had different ideas—for instance, on the issue of the socialization of heavy industry in West Germany—they had to give way to the American preference for a free enterprise economy because they were dependent upon American assistance and financial aid.

In addition, the unfolding Cold War forced the United States to take up the role of protector of the West against what was believed to be Soviet aggression. The policy of containment upon which the United States embarked in the 1950s indeed added a new imperialist quality to the informal American empire in the West. Raymond Aron tried to escape the dilemma by calling the United States an imperial, not an imperialist, power, but in his analysis the American policy of containment nonetheless developed imperialist features. He argued: "The concept of containment was in fact expanded into a doctrine of international order, and this doctrine was calculated to lead to imperial or even to imperialist intervention, or to put it another way, intervention in order to uphold a government favorable to the institutions and ideologies of the United States, even against its people's aspirations."[5]

The United States considered it a duty to erect barriers against the further spread of Communist ideology and of Communist power not only in Europe, but also in the Third World. In Europe this was on the whole remarkably successful, even though it resulted in a rigid division of Europe into two power systems. In the Third World, however, the United States entered into a number of dubious partnerships, since the repulsion of communism often appeared possible only by seeking the cooperation of traditional elites or authoritarian regimes that had come to power during the final phase of Western imperialism. In a number of cases, notably in Indochina, the nationalist emancipation movements were driven totally into the camp of Marxist-Leninist communism. Indeed, in many of these nations, communism came to be seen as the only political movement that really stood for the emancipation of the peoples of the Third World from colonial domination. It took the Americans some years to realize that there had not been just one Communist world movement, but a variety of movements that proclaimed to be Communist in one sense or another. The failure to realize this was one of the factors responsible for getting the United States entangled in the Vietnam conflict, even though it was in fact a leftover from the period of formal imperialism. The Americans' own anti-imperialist philosophy should have persuaded them not to intervene after Dienbienphu.

The trauma of the lost Vietnam war, and the concomitant view that the American policy of containment of the world Communist movement had been pursued partly on the basis of false premises, led the United States for a time to practice a certain self-restraint in its role as the leading power in the West. But even if it had really wanted to give up this role, it could not realistically be expected to do so. It could be observed—somewhat disquietingly—that the United States has still not given up the Monroe Doctrine, and feels it should continue the old policy of dollar diplomacy in Latin America by different methods—primarily direct and indirect military aid. This is seen as necessary to prevent further penetration of this region by the Marxist-Leninist forces.

Today the conditions for an unrestricted system of informal hegemony by the United States in the Western world and in large sections of the Third World are no longer present to the same degree. This is partly because the Soviet threat to the stability of the world order no longer seems as serious as it did in the 1950s and 1960s, although at this point opinions have again deviated sharply as regards the deployment of missiles in Europe. Unlike the first decades after World War II, now the relative economic and military strength of the Western European states has increased considerably, and the system of alliances is perhaps no longer so strongly tipped in favor of the United States. A system of partnership has emerged instead. Although continually subject to controversy, particularly as regards assessment of the real intentions of the USSR, essentially a consensus exists. Still, the present situation can be conceived of as a recently intensified rivalry between two world systems that fear each other. On balance, the USSR would appear to be more inclined than the United States to make up for economic and moral deficits in the event of a crisis by recourse to military force. This, it would seem, constitutes a grave danger. Decaying empires have always been potential danger spots for the development of wars, and this is still valid today.

Rivalry between the two world systems headed by the super-powers helped the former colonial countries to emancipate themselves. Indeed, the necessity of fending off any political influence by either the USSR or more recently China contributed a great deal to speeding up the process of decolonization. But the question still remains whether imperialism has really come to an end with the formal ending of all direct colonial control by the Western powers over Third World countries.

Without doubt, the process of decolonization has been a gradual one. It did not end with the formal granting of political independence to the former colonial territories, which initially was meant to stabilize the existing economic and cultural relationships by informal means. The countries of the Third World have now freed themselves from the direct tutelage of their former colonial masters, sometimes by exploiting rivalries between the USSR and the United States. The composition of the ruling elites has also changed so much that they can no longer be considered collaborating elites or comprador classes, functioning as bulwarks of the "mother countries" on an informal basis. Nonetheless, the heritage of the imperialist age is still alive. Classic imperialism tended to support the traditional ethnic groups in indigenous societies, rather than those that could have become effective leaders in the new nation-states, thereby strengthening the peripheral forces which later tore many of the new nation-states apart. The lopsided integration of many of these countries into the international economy during the age of imperialism also created structural disadvantages that are proving difficult to overcome. In many countries, a "peripheral" rather than a well-balanced capitalist system developed which is still predominantly oriented toward export markets in the former mother countries, while indigenous markets receive but little attention. Other regions have been only marginally integrated into the world economy, if at all, and have little chance of changing their position of economic pariah by their own devices.

Yesterday's imperialism rather than today's exploitation contributes to this situation, but this does not reduce the responsibility of the West. Today it would seem that the real problem is not the progressive "exploitation" of undeveloped countries in the interests of capitalist metropolises, as maintained by the *dependencia* school, but rather the fact that the underdeveloped countries are slipping into the fringe areas of the world economy. There is not enough productive investment at the periphery, regardless of the political and economic framework, because the respective internal markets are regarded as uninteresting and the political situation as unstable. This syndrome could be called "negative imperialism" if it were not simultaneously supported by mechanisms that are themselves embedded in the Western economic system. The phase of expansion of the Western economic system in the nineteenth and early twentieth centuries seems to have been followed by a phase of contraction. And in both cases, the peoples of the Third World have lost out.

From this perspective, the collapse of the colonial empires of the nineteenth and twentieth centuries seems not to have been an unqualified blessing for the peoples of the Third World. Rather, it has been an ambiguous affair. It formally relieved the Western states of responsibility for the fate of these regions, while at the same time making it permissible to cultivate only those economic relations with undeveloped countries that best suit the world market. In terms of the rules of the market, in the dispensing of credits and development aid, in the channeling of trade by tariffs and other measures of government intervention, these countries still lag behind as hopelessly as ever.

In view of all this, it has to be admitted that there is a growing imbalance in the international system as regards the advanced industrial countries on the one hand and the underdeveloped countries on the other, with a few happy NDCs in between. The advanced industrial countries in the West, notably the United States, can largely determine the rules of the game. The Third World countries have little chance to influence the financial and trade policies of the advanced industrialized countries upon which their own well-being largely depends. The international organizations established to help the Third World, such as the World Bank or Unesco, are dependent on the Western countries that put up most of the funds. The United States especially often puts informal pressure on these organizations to see that its interests are taken care of. The international monetary system undoubtedly works to the disadvantage of the poorer countries, and the same is true of the terms of trade. While it would be futile to call this state of affairs a new form of imperialism deliberately contrived by the West, it undoubtedly displays some of the features of imperial control, though with little political responsibility. Surely classic imperialism is dead, and while to some degree new political imperialisms have taken its place, the patterns of informal economic imperialism that emerged during the nineteenth and early twentieth centuries have proved to be tenacious.

Notes

1 For an overview of this continuing debate see, among others, Roger Owen and Bob Suttcliffe, *Studies in the Theory of Imperialism* (London, 1972; Anthony Brewer, *Marxist Theories of Imperialism: A Critical Survey* (London, 1980); Wolfgang J. Mommsen, *Theories of Imperialism: A Critical Assessment of the Various Interpretations of Modern Imperialism* (London, 1980); P. W. Preston, *Theories of Development* (London, 1982).
2 W. Roger Louis, *Great Britain and Germany's Lost Colonies, 1914–1919* (Oxford, 1967), p. 153.
3 We are indebted here to D. A. Low's masterful analysis, "The Asian Mirror to Tropical Africa's Independence," in Prosser Gifford and W. M. Roger Louis, *The Transfer of Power in Africa: Decolonization 1940–1960* (New Haven, CT, 1982).
4 T. Smith, "Patterns in the Transfer of Power: A Comparative Study of French and British Decolonization," in Gifford and Louis, *The Transfer of Power*, p. 94.
5 Raymond Aron, *The Imperial Republic: The United States and the World, 1945–1973* (London, 1973), p. 304.

THE STATE AND ECONOMIC ORGANIZATION IN THE TWENTIETH CENTURY

CHARLES S. MAIER

If we ask "What was the twentieth century?" or "What is the meaning of the twentieth century?" then surely we must think about the relationship of the political sphere to the economic. Except for problems of war and peace, no public issue arouses more continuing concern than the state of the economy. Perhaps this is not new; society has always had to think about its underlying material welfare. What does seem new—that is, new in the twentieth century—is that government has been assigned responsibility for maintaining a continuing level of economic activity. Citizens look to the state as the guarantor of employment, relative price stability, and growth. If parties or regimes cannot deliver these goods, they certainly lose popularity, and, ultimately, they sacrifice legitimacy as well. If we want to reflect on the meaning of the twentieth century, we must ask how this condition came about.

But we must also try to be more precise than many historical accounts that merely chronicle the progress of state intervention as if it were a continuing and progressive tendency. Certainly the twentieth century has witnessed an intense degree of interaction between the state and civil society, or the political sphere and that of the market or economy. But this interaction is only one of several in which politics has been invoked. Family policy, education, the maintenance of religion, the obligations of wartime, the guarantees of environmental health, the sanctioning of sexual relations have all been subjects for "legislation" or policy. In some of these spheres—the environment, for example—the state has intervened more massively. In some spheres, such as sexual behavior, political action has been required to loosen

101

state control. The fact that an issue area becomes more a subject of political controversy does not mean that state intervention is necessarily increasing; it is probably changing in some important way. Here I want to consider the changes without implying that they mean more or less intervention. And I hope to consider the interaction of the state and the economy against the whole backdrop of the *recourse to politics* that has characterized twentieth-century history.

For British and American commentators, at least, the traditional view of the role of the state in economic activity during the twentieth century has been one of significantly increasing intervention. In 1913, A. V. Dicey declared that a new collectivist era had supplanted the previous century's predominant laissez-faire.[1] And while subsequent scholars have criticized the notion that the nineteenth century was a period in which the state stayed out of economic regulation, most historians still insist that the degree of state intervention was of such a greater degree that there is more break than continuity. The liberal era, with its separation of government from the "market," gave way in the twentieth century to the age of regulation, then to the "mixed economy" and the welfare state.

My purpose in this essay is neither to confirm nor to contest this general view of the twentieth-century relationship between politics and economics. One can accept the rough distinction between an age of laissez-faire and an age of state intervention, if we make clear what sorts of regulation laissez-faire presupposed (guarantees of property rights, after all), and what sorts of liberty regulation actually advanced (more independence from employer arbitrariness, or from the costs of unemployment and sickness). The question must be this: What sorts of collective control over the economic realm have twentieth-century societies sought to impose? Since most of the contributions to this conference focus on intellectual developments, I will focus as much on major ideas concerning political economy as on actual economic changes.

Since finally all the major economies of the non-Socialist world have faced a decade of relative difficulty following a quarter-century of unparalleled real growth, I wish to reflect upon the lessons of the current "crisis." A period of crisis or turbulence usually illuminates the historical premises, the implicit foundations of achievements that had earlier been unquestioned: The owl of Minerva flies at dusk. Having our earlier accomplishments placed in jeopardy should help us discern what have been the significant changes of the twentieth-century political economy.

The Arcadia of the Market

It required more than a century to develop the notion of an autonomous economic sphere. Writers in France and Britain in the early seventeenth century, such as Thomas Mun and Edward Misselden, were groping for such a concept when they separated the prosperity of their people from the wealth of the sovereign. In a sense later mercantilist theory represented a step backward; it sought to define the conditions of national prosperity without conceding that people and government might have different criteria of welfare. Nonetheless, by the time of Locke, who differentiated civil society (which sanctioned the creation of money and unequal accumulation of property) from political society (which established a sovereign to protect this property), theorists could safeguard the notion of an autonomous economic sphere. Whig writers such as Defoe celebrated entrepreneurial pluck and the social conventions underlying money and credit, which allowed Walpole's Britain to prosper. The French Physiocrats formalized the concepts of an economic cycle that generated surplus, while Adam Smith clarified the process by which independent motives linked interdependently through the market produced optimal outcomes for welfare.[2]

By the end of the eighteenth century, therefore, Enlightenment writers had developed a criterion of public economic welfare (the "wealth of nations") distinguished from the wealth of the sovereign. They had also described the system of autonomous interactions (the market) that let it flourish. Finally, they had provided a set of recommended policies for achieving the best economic outcomes. These included guaranteeing property rights on the one hand and suppressing conspiratorial monopolies on the other. For Adam Smith, such policies also included some infrastructural investment by the state in education and other forms of social capital that no individual entrepreneur would find it profitable to undertake, but from which all would benefit.[3]

There is no need here to trace how the classical school in England, aided by sympathizers abroad, such as Jean Baptiste Say, elaborated the laws of the market. Nineteenth-century theorists sought to demonstrate not only that the market guaranteed the best outcomes, but that state efforts to alter those outcomes were useless and counterproductive. As Karl Polanyi later argued, the crucial issue became that of labor: If economic progress were to rely on the decentralized market, then labor power had also to be thrown into the crucible of transactions. This meant dissolving the paternalistic village-based system of subsidizing wages that the British had tried to revive at Speenhamland in 1795 and supporting only the unalterably destitute, not the working poor. Polanyi exaggerated the extent of the Speenhamland system and the rupture with the past that the New Poor Law of 1834 actually entailed. Still, he powerfully exposed the intellectual implications of a market society. He also insisted that reliance on the market was only one path to arranging for material welfare in the spectrum of world economic arrangements.[4]

Of course this market arcadia aroused bitter opponents. We can cite two who presented radically different critiques. Friedrich List argued that its assumptions fitted only the technologically most advanced society of the day (Britain). For a country that lagged economically, to establish the free trade that the Smithian system demanded would be to accept permanent economic inferiority, to become, in today's terms, only a peripheral nation producing primary products for the benefit of the core nation transforming these products in its own industries. Without industrialization, a country was consigned to permanent inferiority in political terms as well. List's ideas have been echoed down to the present *dependencia* critics and remain the basis for the major intellectual argument against free trade. If comparative advantage, as preached by Smith and Ricardo, yields the highest *current* aggregate welfare, it does not necessarily yield the highest long-term welfare. It allows for no concept of development and recognizes no dimension of politics. The "wealth of nations" hardly allows for the competitive realities of a world of nations.[5]

The other major critique was, of course, that of Karl Marx, who recognized the power of the classical school of economics and the bourgeois achievement it accompanied. But for Marx these doctrines rested on an ideological masking of reality. Labor could be made a market commodity only within a certain matrix of social and political relationships, because labor power actually underlay all commodity values. Labor could be assigned an exchange value only in a system of social relationships that denied its primacy. Once labor organized itself politically, it would do away with the fiction of an autonomous economic sphere and abolish the private control of capital that had made such a market vision plausible.[6]

Marx's doctrines became the ideological basis of the opponents of liberal capitalism within the advancing industrial societies. But in effect, outside of Britain Listian views became more important for policy. In Germany and Italy, for example, the liberal leaders and bureaucrats who rose to power in the 1850s and 1860s moved to establish liberal politics and liberal markets internally. But they also accepted a vision of state intervention for economic growth that was more in the spirit of List, as was the Meiji-sponsored development of Japan. European continental liberalism, it might be said, involved a passionate belief in a free press, a secular society, and the social importance of railroads.

It was no mere coincidence that the period of political upheaval and state building in the 1850s and 1860s (in Germany, Italy, Austria-Hungary, France, Canada, Russia, the United States, and Japan) brought to the fore new coalitions of liberals and state bureaucrats. In each case it involved a mixture of economic promotion by public officials, insistence on national unity against opponents without and against aristocratic ("feudal") dissenters within. Economic development within Prussian Germany, Italy, and Japan relied on encouraging a new class of entrepreneurs and venturesome capitalists. But it also meant nurturing these capitalists (some of whom were older aristocrats who saw where new opportunities lay) by state contracts, tariffs, infrastructural investment, and the encouragement of education. In short, the state incubated the liberal market, and a symbiosis of shared objectives and personnel emerged.

Modifying the Market: "Organized Capitalism" and Hilferding, Keynes, and the Welfare State

By the late 1870s the arcadia of the liberal market began to run into serious trouble. Although it was not really abandoned in the industrial countries outside of Russia, important modifications were to be generated—some as the result of conscious policy, others by the momentum of economic developments themselves. The first set of modifications involved those from the 1880s into the 1920s that one can label with the admittedly imprecise but still useful concept of "organized capitalism."[7] The theorists who would draw the most extensive implications from these developments derived from the German social democratic tradition, and I will briefly discuss the analysis of Rudolf Hilferding. The second set of modifications (in part arising out of the problems that led to the first set, but triggered in larger part by the great crisis of the 1930s) were the provisions for intervention that we associate with the welfare state. Naturally the theorist of most interest here remains Keynes. In effect, Hilferding and Keynes both remained advocates of the evolutionary transformation of the market arcadia. Hilferding would have denied that he envisaged a system remaining within the parameters of capitalism, but I think the case can be made. In contrast, Keynes would have insisted that his vision remained consistent with a functioning capitalism, but his opponents would have denied this. (Both interpretations can be justified, I believe.)

Very briefly, what constituted the "organized capitalism" that set in by the late 1870s? As the vigor of the 1850s and 1860s gave way to sharp credit contraction, bankruptcies in new industries, and agricultural price declines in North America and Europe during the 1870s, liberal prescriptions seemed less persuasive. Liberals lost their political influence in Central Europe and Britain during the same period. Governments yielded to a new clamor for protective tariffs which the growing international rivalries, imperialist competition, and Darwinian attitudes could only reinforce. By the 1890s tariff protection was instituted in Germany, Austria, France, Italy, the United States, and most countries outside Britain. At the same time, industrial producers organized pressure-group associations to influence legislators as well as cartel-like marketing organizations or "trusts" to allocate production quotas and sales percentages. On the other side of the class divide, between the 1890s and World War I labor unions and social democratic parties began to challenge employer prerogatives and bourgeois control of the market, although with only limited effect before 1914.

Hence in the generation before World War I economic structures and organization changed significantly even if within the formal ground rules of liberal capitalism: Cartels and monopolies sought to limit the sway of unregulated competition; nations attempted to buffer their own producers from cheaper imports by means of protective tariffs; and an organized working class began to reverse the earlier liberal concept of treating labor as just another commodity. At the same time, national governments undertook significant measures to protect labor against the vicissitudes of sickness, accident, and old age. Social insurance emerged as part of a conservative stabilization strategy, as in the case of Bismarck, and as part of a liberal design for assimilation of the new working classes in a broad political coalition, as in the case of the Liberal government in Britain (1906–14) and more fragmented reformist initiatives elsewhere.

It was these encroaching developments in Britain that Dicey feared as the advent of collectivism. Seeing them from the Austrian and German perspective, where cartelization was relatively advanced and the working class most solidly organized under a nominally Marxist banner, Rudolf Hilferding identified them as "organized capitalism" by 1915. For this social democratic reformist, these developments would facilitate the transition to socialism. The web of capitalist organization would continue to grow ever denser, so that finally a workers' majority might simply collectivize the networks that the economy and state had already generated without violence and upheaval. For the moment, labor representatives might work within the system, confident that their reformist measures would help prepare for the superseding of capitalism. (Hilferding did not fear that this strategy might just help rationalize and entrench capitalist hierarchies; indeed, the same excessive optimism characterized his confidence in the power of the SPD within the Weimar Republic.)[8]

If Hilferding was somewhat deluded to believe himself still a socialist, Keynes may have been under an equivalent illusion when he insisted that he was not. To be sure, Keynes asserted that collectivization was irrelevant for the economic problems of depression, and he clearly affiliated with the Liberal party. Individualism, he insisted, "is the best safeguard of personal liberty in the sense that, compared with any other system, it greatly widens the field for the exercise of personal choice."[9] But the preservation of individualism required intelligent intervention by the state. Government spending would restore the aggregate demand that would let capitalism recover full employment. Despite the commitment to individualism, the longer-term Keynesian vision was perhaps more revolutionary than Keynes conceded.

By and large, the *General Theory* of 1936 turned Adam Smith on his head. Smith had argued that "parsimony" or saving was the foundation of economic growth. Keynes proposed that excessive saving was responsible for the depression: "The growth of wealth, so far from being dependent on the abstinence of the rich, as is commonly supposed, is more likely to be impeded by it."[10] The whole Victorian ethos of accumulation and deferred consumption had led to the miseries of the interwar economy, and the answer was to emphasize consumption. "The love of money as a possession—as distinguished from the love of money as a means to the enjoyments and realities of life—will be recognised for what it is, a somewhat disgusting morbidity, one of those semi-criminal, semi-pathological propensities which one hands over with a shudder to the specialists in mental disease."[11]

In the long run, Keynes seems to have envisaged a sort of technological threshold setting in, such that capital investment would become less necessary. "I feel sure that the demand for capital is strictly limited in the sense that it would not be difficult to increase the stock of capital up to a point where its marginal efficiency had fallen to a very low figure."[12] In effect, Keynes's concepts implied the transformation to an economy of services from that of industrial manufacture: the coming preponderance of the tertiary sector. Adam Smith, we might argue, had a "hardware" vision, and he assigned value only to "vendable" goods, denying it specifically to services. Keynes predicated the "economic prospects for our grandchildren" on a "software" perception of economic value. This was probably insightful; nonetheless, Keynes underestimated the amount of continuing investment that a service economy would demand.

Restraint from current consumption was not just the imperative for turning out steel and concrete, but for producing knowledge, health care, mental therapy, and amusements as well. Keynes's optimistic scenario for the decreasing rigors of accumulation was implicit in his theory of interest. If there was any area ripe for state control it was that of credit, and Keynes envisioned an increasing socialization of investment. Keynes's theory of interest argued essentially that interest was analogous to Ricardo's rent on land, a function not of its inherent fruitfulness, but only of its scarcity. There should be no reward for the ability to hoard a resource that required neither inventiveness nor virtue to acquire. But with this concept of interest—the vision not merely of "a euthanasia of the rentier,"[13] but of capital formation in general— did not Keynes really strike at the ground rules of nineteenth-century liberal capitalism? Had not Marx been more to the point when he described its maxim as "Accumulate, accumulate! That is Moses and the prophets"?[14]

We have tended to recall the anti-accumulationist aspects of Keynes only in the wake of the 1970s, when economic problems seem to center on the difficulties of capital formation and invest-ment rather than on conventional unemployment. If Keynes lived through a surfeit of unemployment, we have lived through a surfeit of inflation. And insofar as unemployment has reemerged on the economic agenda, Keynesian remedies do not appear applicable, for today's unemployment seems to be "structural" rather than "cyclical," the product of not getting our workforce fast enough from steel to silicon. As of the 1930s and 1940s, Keynes could be read primarily as an accommodationist of capitalism, a theorist who demonstrated that to preserve one must reform. The reforms he proposed—the resort to government not merely to establish the ground rules of property and competition, but to serve as the consumer of last resort—were largely instituted. World War II demonstrated that states need not go bankrupt through massive public expenditure and that in fact they might make their societies more prosperous than they were before. At least that was the lesson for the United States and Great Britain.

And coming out of World War II, the European working classes were strong enough politically to demand extension of Keynesian full-employment commitments and extension of the provisions for social insurance and related welfare measures.

The prosperity the industrialized countries enjoyed from the end of the 1940s through the 1960s probably did *not* spring from the application of Keynesian prescriptions. Other massive, epochal causes can be specified if we wish to write an economic history of the postwar era. But certainly the consensus on Keynesian welfare policies as a backup in the case of hard times (ironically, a recourse that hardly had to be invoked and then was partially abandoned once it was seriously tested!) helped assure working-class adhesion to postwar capitalism. The Keynesian consensus at home (along with the Cold War internationally) formed part of the political presupposition of postwar growth.

A century has passed since the death of Marx and the birth of Keynes, events that occurred within a few months of each other in 1883. The structural modifications of capitalism that Hilferding felt would lead to the advent of socialism certainly have blurred the separation of state and economy. In societies where a MITI helps coordinate industrial strategies or *polytechniciens* allocate credits for investment or an IRI holds massive stock shares, it is clear that the autonomy of the market from the state hardly exists. But such state intervention characterized Japanese, German, and Italian development in the nineteenth century, and indeed most countries outside Britain and the United States. Moreover, a meshing of state and capital does not mean socialism in any traditional sense.

Hilferding discerned the developments of the present but did not correctly decipher the trajectory of the future. On the other hand, Keynes was correct to insist that the state could intervene to determine the level of economic activity without having to alter its structures *directly*. The Keynesian revolution did not depend upon changing the institutional or organizational aspects of capitalism: Cartels, unions, welfare funds were not key variables (tariff protection was a different matter). The level of spending and investment was crucial, and the state could manipulate these without any transformation of institutions. But did Keynes adequately see the implications of these allegedly minimal interventions? Schumpeter suggested that the very guarantees of prosperity a high-performance capitalism would provide could subtly alter the mentalities, the entrepreneurial vigor, and "animal spirits" on which the system ultimately rested.[15] What Schumpeter evidently regretted, however, Keynes was probably happy to see come about.

The point is that the structural changes Hilferding felt were so subversive probably were not really so. If capitalism remains defined as private control of investment decisions, the changes of the late nineteenth and early twentieth centuries often made the system more resilient. They reinforced the power of economic elites by intertwining them more closely with political managers. The nonstructural changes that Keynes counseled were probably more corrosive in the long run, although we are still in the middle of the long run and, as is well known, Keynes had little patience for the really long run. Both Hilferding and Keynes described modifications of the nineteenth-century market, Hilferding to change the system, Keynes allegedly to preserve it, but perhaps with an agenda of unavowed subversion. By the late twentieth century we seem to have arrived at a rather indeterminate mixture of systems.

The State and the Economy: Dimensions of Interaction

Contrasting Hilferding and Keynes alerts us to two major types of transformation that have come about since the late nineteenth century. Governmental agencies and economic organizations have, as Hilferding suggested, become more interwoven. The line between private and public control of economic activity has become far more porous than it was at the beginning of the century. Governments may then have owned arsenals and railroads; today they hold stock portfolios and banks and exert direct controls far beyond what they own.

Government has also become far more of a consumer, especially of services, than previously. Keynes, of course, counseled government consumption for periods of depression, but in fact state consumption has become a constant feature of economic activity. Nonetheless, it can be a misleading guide to the degree of transformation that has occurred in our economic systems.

There are other dimensions of transformation in the twentieth century that may be more historically momentous. For the moment, however, can we assign any quantitative or qualitative measures to the changes we can loosely associate with Hilferding and with Keynes?

The second is initially easier to quantify than the first, but still leaves us with conceptual problems. The usual measure chosen is public expenditure as a percentage of gross national product (or gross domestic product). Estimates for most societies before the postwar era are often deficient at best, but we do have statistical studies for Germany and Britain and the United States, and we can approximate the ratio for other societies. Most Western European societies seem to have been spending between 12 and 15 percent of gross national product through public agencies on the eve of World War I on military expenses, education, rudimentary welfare transfer payments, infrastructure (such as roads), and debt service. During the war public spending claimed up to 40 percent of GNP of the belligerent nations, but by the mid-1920s the new level of European public spending had probably stabilized at about 22 to 25 percent of GNP.

Public spending rose to meet the emergency of the Depression and again for purposes of rearmament by the late 1930s, such that on the eve of World War II major governments in Europe were probably spending about 30 to 33 percent of their output through government agencies. By and large European societies had public expenditure levels of 33 to 40 percent in the decades after the second world war until the late 1960s, when inflation set in and public spending rose toward the 50 percent level or even above (in Britain, Sweden, the Netherlands, and West Germany).[16]

Political coalitions seem to have played only a minor role in differentiating high and low spenders. The trend seemed to obey deeper causes: Social Democratic Sweden and Christian Democratic Germany ended up with very close levels of public expenditure by the late 1960s. Wealth and poverty apparently made some difference: Ireland and Italy, relatively poor countries, had lower public spending bills. And for reasons of long-term tradition and political culture, both the United States and especially Japan also maintained lower levels of public spending by assigning welfare tasks to private firms and associations. (In the case of the United States at least, the past decade has seen more convergence to the European model.)

In general, however, the tendency of public spending has been upward in the twentieth century, but not as a smoothly rising curve. Instead, public spending has tended to spurt from one plateau to another, with the major jumps occasioned by the two wars and the Great Depression of the 1930s. (Explaining the major jump of the late 1960s is more difficult. The United States recourse to inflationary finance with the Vietnam war, the impatience of European labor movements after two decades of relative wage restraint, the breakdown of the Bretton Woods system of fixed exchange rates, then the sharp increase in the price of petroleum, all played a role.)[17] Each of these jumps, moreover, was accompanied by a significant wave of world inflation, which testified to the difficulties of covering the new expenditures by taxation.

The question this pattern of jumping public spending raises for this essay is whether there is any particular level of public expenditure which necessarily changes the economic system in a qualitative manner. Is there a tax or expenditure threshhold beyond which capitalism can no longer function as capitalism? Critics of public spending have tended to claim that the threshhold was at hand each time government expenditure and taxation went up significantly. And indeed most societies have now stabilized their public spending from the maximum levels that marked the post-OPEC I recession in the mid-1970s. But logically there does not seem to be any particular point at which public expenditure must transform capitalism into something else. If we can pay 40 percent in taxes, why can we not pay 50 percent, or 60 percent, or even more? We may not like doing so, but our discomfort need not signify the death of capitalism.

Schumpeter recognized this in his essay "The Crisis of the Tax State," published toward the end of World War I. Despite the massive claims by the state to fight the war, the private economy and the state could both survive.[18] One reason that the overall figures of government spending are often brandished so alarmingly is that critics overlook the difference between government centralization of social consumption and government's own end-use consumption. Government spending—except perhaps for defense hardware (and total defense bills including salaries total no more than 3 to 6 percent of NATO-country GNPs and far less in Japan) —does not go for purposes that civil society would not spend for on its own. We can run transportation facilities publicly or privately, but all advanced societies must provide for the movement of people and goods. Retirement funds can be provided by families and corporations, or by government. (And government provision rests usually on payroll taxes that are largely passed on to consumers.) In either case, those who work in the society must support those considered too old to labor.

It is sometimes argued that once government channels social expenditure, it vastly expands the consumption of certain items, especially nonproductive services. This is far from clear. Americans must arrange to pay their medical care largely through private, albeit collective associations, but their medical bill as a percentage of GNP is as high as in any country that has "socialized medicine." Certainly some differences in end use will result once we make the decision for public channeling of consumption. We probably do spend more for medicine on the old (the United States does have public compensation for some of the medical bills of the elderly). Still, the effects of private and public consumption are far from clear. Is it a private housing market in America that leads to so many detached housing units? Or is it the result of public policy—extensive tax breaks for home ownership?

It would probably be foolish to deny that once societies decide for more spending on services, they usually choose government channeling of funds to carry it out. Higher education enrollments in France, Britain, and Germany multiplied (as a proportion of the eligible age cohort) in the period from 1950 to the late 1960s. This represented a major change in social priorities and spending that was facilitated through government taxation and spending. Likewise, government support of research in the United States was mobilized by public foundations as well as private ones. Government has been used to centralize the purchase of mental health therapy, social counseling, educational advisers outside the classroom, and the mental-massage services that have so proliferated in the West. (Or have we just replaced what we used to spend on religious ministration? The final consumption of services may be more static than we believe: Does twentieth-century Germany spend more proportionally as a society on music than did eighteenth- or nineteenth-century Germany?)

By and large, I think that the end-use patterns of social consumption will vary only marginally as government expenditure rises—or that both will respond to common underlying perceived needs. In fact, I would argue that one might envisage a system in which all income was taken by the government and all services provided in return and which was still capitalist in some sense. I think that Marx's instincts were correct when he focused on control of capital—the right to decide where and how much to invest—as the defining aspect of economic society during the era of industrial growth.

The next question then becomes whether the changes we associate with Hilferding's analysis have already transformed or are likely to transform the economic systems with which Western societies entered the century. I think that one can argue for transformation, but not for a qualitative rupture with an earlier socioeconomic system. Certainly one of the major twentieth-century developments has been the increasingly administered regulation of capitalism. Market mechanisms regulate only a small proportion of production and transactions. Some of this administration (pricing, planning of output, allocation of markets, perhaps one might count the influencing of public opinion) is carried out by private firms themselves and by what John Kenneth Galbraith termed the "technostructure."[19] Other administrative regulation is carried out by state agencies—government ministries, "technocrats," legislators. These processes have been described in great detail, but the question still persists wherein the source of initiative lies: with the public officials (who often later become corporation officers), or with the economic elite (who often furnish the personnel for government regulation)?

The point is that the new shape of Western economies tends more to dissolve the public-private line than to displace it in a clear manner.[20] But on reflection this is not so new either. When one recalls the role of Physiocrat officials in the *ancien régime* or of Prussian officials in the architecture of the Zollverein or the interventions of the Meiji state, only Britain and America appear to have moved unambiguously toward a more administered economy and toward restricting the power of those who control large economic units. (Perhaps France is on the way.) If we seek evidence for a qualitative change in the ideal type of capitalism as such, then I think that the twentieth century, despite all its upheavals along the way, provides as much evidence of continuity as of rupture.

The history of "planning" in twentieth-century capitalist societies reflects this continuity. To be sure, state planning is a hallmark of the socialist economies in Eastern Europe, although even in these societies, outside Russia the effort has been to reintroduce as many elements of the market as Communist officials can allow without undermining their political monopoly. But planning also appeared as a great hope for transforming the economies of the West. In the United States, Herbert Hoover and some of the social scientists sympathetic to government intervention in the 1920s and 1930s felt that engineers and experts could reduce the waste of resources that competition supposedly allowed. The massive unemployment of the 1930s, the rearmament efforts of the years before World War II, and finally the need to coordinate wartime economies also generated an enthusiasm for planning and coordination of scarce economic resources.

In Great Britain, Herbert Morrison, Evans Durbin, and other technocratically inclined intellectuals built upon the earlier Fabian enthusiasm for bureaucratic planning. In the United States, advocates of planning set their hopes on the National Resources Board—a minor New Deal agency that congressional conservatives finally deprived of funds during World War II. In France, the engineers and administrators of the Ecole Polytechnique formed a nucleus of would-be planners, and in Belgium, in Fascist Italy, sponsored by Giuseppe Bottai, and in Germany under the aegis of defense agencies, planners sought to steer national economic output. After World War II, Jean Monnet, who was in fact an enthusiast of American entrepreneurship, introduced national economic plans as an argument for retaining control of scarce credit. And finally, the vision of democratic planning remains a component of those who call for a national "reindustrialization" policy for the United States.[21]

But what remains remarkable about such efforts, I believe, is how gradually they have changed the contours of twentieth-century capitalism. (Here I am distinguishing planning as such from such changes as social insurance, which has meant a difference.) Certainly planning has comprised a major preoccupation of social thinkers and Western intellectuals in thinking about the economy. But economic success, as measured by high employment, rapid growth, or rapid technological transformation, has rested upon the vigor of firms and innovators more than upon government direction. This does not mean that capitalism has always functioned well. Far from it! But where planning has appeared successful, it has generally been in situations where it has helped the entrepreneurial forces in a society to revive. The good planner, such as Monnet, has known how to funnel funds to the vigorous industrialist.

Of course, there was another thrust to economic planning besides that of growth or efficiency. Planning was meant to provide some democratic control in an age of monopolies. It was meant to restore to the public sphere the determination of a society's major priorities, instead of just abandoning these to those who controlled large-scale capital. But where planners have functioned effectively, they have generally done so in close cooperation with businessmen and engineers. They have helped to dissolve the conceptual boundary between the public domain and the private sphere, not to reassert the primacy of the public.

What Has Changed?

It would be foolish, however, to argue that nothing major has changed in the relationship of the political to the economic realm. But the growing role of the state in channeling GNP will not capture the important transformations. Nor does the growing interpenetration of state and corporate decision makers resolve the issue of control. I would propose that we look elsewhere: to the shifting balance of class representation and ultimately to the erosion of an autonomous economic realm.

By the shifting balance of class representation I mean simply that working-class spokesmen have become an essential component of public policy in almost all industrial societies that are not ruled by repressive regimes. (Japan remains the major exception, and here we might argue for implicit consultation.) This does not imply that a working class as such has achieved parity of influence or is finally about to push through a program of "economic democracy" or total codetermination. My own feeling is that the working class as a category cannot really be grasped outside its political or economic representation. (In a sense there can be no proletariat *without* a workers' aristocracy.) And just as the major political transformation of the nineteenth century was to coopt bourgeois representatives alongside landed ones in the formation of public policy, so the major twentieth-century change has been to absorb the spokesmen for the nonrevolutionary working class into selected areas of decision making.

By and large many of the political conflicts of the twentieth century can be seen as an argument between those moderate middle-class forces who wagered on cooptation and those who resisted. The latter sometimes turned to fascism, only to discover that even Fascistic regimes had to construct corporatist structures to allow for at least a crypto representation of the working class. Since World War II, of course, integration of labor spokesmen has significantly increased. Incorporation of working-class representatives, however, has tended to involve a patchwork parceling out of jurisdictions, not a total power sharing. Ministries of labor and regional planning involve a voice for working-class delegates, but foreign offices and finance policies remain more restrictive preserves. Working-class organizations have likewise become significant property-holders, whether of real estate, banks, or pension funds, and their delegates sit on the boards of corporations in Germany and elsewhere. Taken together, these developments may have diluted the power of spokesmen for capital in the traditional sense; but they have not really superseded capitalism as such. Union spokesmen on the boards of private firms are still subjected to the basic rules of profitability and face the same tradeoffs between wages and investment. Indeed, the harsher and more unpromising the game, the more employers and governments like to share their responsibilities with labor representatives.

Because it has run into difficulty in recent years, we can construe the post-1945 settlement with the representatives of the working class as a sort of exchange. Business spokesmen, conservative parties, and government officials accepted the priorities of Keynesian intervention to preserve full employment. They also accepted significant extensions of the welfare state, or at least they removed social insurance from an area of intense controversy to one of consensus. In Britain, the stigma of the means test was abolished; on the Continent, social security systems were expanded in coverage. Only the United States was half-hearted about the new entitlements as conservative forces in Congress sought to retreat from the achievements of the New Deal, and the postwar labor movement remained weaker than in Europe (though not so constrained as in occupied Japan). In return for agreement on full employment and social welfare, labor movements and socialist parties largely dropped earlier notions of controlling production and investment. Public ownership still beckoned British Labour and a planned, collectivist economic democracy evoked support in Germany; by and large, however, the Left retreated on these more distant objectives. (The 1959 Bad Godesberg conference of the SPD provides a useful symbolic transition.) In short, a generation of postwar politics rested on an implicit welfare capitalist settlement.

What the economic difficulties since 1973, and most acutely since the post-OPEC II recession, suggest is that this social *Ausgleich* is now in question. The terms of the compromise no longer suffice, for the implicit promise of full employment has become too expensive for industries and conservative governments that perceive the need for massive investment in new industries and the shutdown of the old. So far labor has largely accepted renegotiation of the post-1945 settlement on disadvantageous terms, accepting large doses of unemployment and the rescinding of cost-of-living increases or even wage cuts.

But if the post-1945 Keynesian bargain is thrown open for renegotiation, it may not be long before labor too seeks new terms —that is, returns to its earlier objective of a voice in investment. Indeed, with the economic difficulties of the 1970s we may have come to the end of the postwar era (its recessional to be marked by, say, the United States' abandonment of Bretton Woods or the oil price increases). Government spending alone, we argued, did not force a decisive break from the economic systems of the earlier twentieth century. Nor did the progress of bureaucratic intervention really rupture the mixture of private investment and governmental supervision that characterized capitalism from the late nineteenth century. But if a more decisive form of union or social-ist party control over investment were once again to be placed on the agenda, a significant shift in economic power might result.

It would be foolish to predict outcomes. Nonetheless, one can suggest possible alternatives. Eventually economic recovery will strengthen the influence of labor representatives once again. At that point, labor spokesmen may seek to renegotiate the social compact and press for more control of investment and overall production decisions. Perhaps more likely, by then, the labor force will have been so restructured that a new leadership will represent only the survivors, so to speak, those affiliated with new industries and services and willing, once again, to make a compact for growth that renounces demands for investment control in return for a corporatist coziness and economic guarantees.

Twentieth-century history suggests that the second outcome is a plausible one; for despite the heroic moments of the working class, *grandes journées* have not yielded radical results. In Western Europe, 1917, 1936, and 1968 are memorable chapters in the history of *fraternité* but less significant in terms of institutional change. In effect, the twentieth-century capitalist nations man-aged to "solve" the social dilemmas of capitalism without having to make the particular transformations of the system that social-ists demanded. They did so by successive phases of cooptation and exclusion, negotiating compromise settlements with work-ing-class leaders on the basis of economic rewards for a renewed commitment to "productivity." Every move toward the integra-tion of classes earlier excluded has usually involved drawing a new perimeter as well and establishing, in effect, a new proletariat. (Pareto's *Systèmes Socialistes*, written at the dawn of the century, still retains its relevance, even if we reject its cynicism.)

I would argue further that in this process of cooptation and exclusion, more substantive social changes took place as a result of the prosperity of the post-1950 decades than as a consequence of earlier social conflict. Wealth allowed some gradual increase of equality (Lorenz curves reveal their real progress in this direc-tion especially by reducing the destitution associated with old age and unemployment). Hierarchies have probably become more meritocratic. On the other hand, we have often just shifted the boundaries of marginality without abolishing them. It has been easier to give political and economic voice to the spokesmen for indigenous industrial classes because low-skill occupations or those hard to organize have become the preserve of migrant groups.

Indeed, if we look ahead to the remaining years of the century, the *Problemstellung* that was left to us by the classical theorists about capitalism seems terribly limited. To be sure, some of the major conflicts they outlined remain, especially in a period of recession. The tradeoff between wages and profits, or between consumption and investment, is a real constraint, not to be wished away even by imagining an economy of services. (The economic debates of 1980–83 echo the issues and the rhetoric of the issues at the end of the 1920s.) Nonetheless, this antagonism will not consistently generate class divisions, since working-class organizations have become administrators of capitalism alongside entrepreneurs and public officials.

It is also unclear to what extent the new economic issues of the rest of the century can be usefully cast into the categories of accumulation—or, for that matter, into the Anglo-American/ Walrasian categories of marginal utility. Hilferding, Keynes, Schumpeter, Sraffa, et al. had a different agenda from today's. Issues of migration, of the scope for national or supranational policy in an economy of international dimensions, of demographic change (aging of populations), of the decline of manufacturing still require an adequate theoretical framework.

I would argue in conclusion that perhaps the whole concept of the economic is losing those illusorily sharp outlines it seemed to possess between Adam Smith and the Keynesians. The great theoretical thrust of economics from the seventeenth century on was to establish and describe the workings of the market: that arena of transactions which was not coerced by political power and did not rest on mere custom or moral sanction or kinship and affection. The liberal market was defined first by allegedly removing political intervention, then by its extending its jurisdiction to include, sequentially, land and labor. Obviously one of the major transformations of the twentieth century has been to narrow that arena, to minimize the scope for market transactions, to remove health and education and even once again, to a degree, labor and land from its purview. Since the market depended in turn upon property, which was the sanctioned right to sell a good or capacity that yielded income, it has become less autonomous as the right of property has itself been subject to limitation. Think only of the role of environmental impact requirements or local planning agencies. Market decisions are increasingly switched to administrative, legislative, or jurisprudential forums.

Some economists would argue that this process can and should be reversed. Administrative decisions or public choices can be subjected to a logic of economic analysis by determining the appropriate prices to compare. But therein lies a further difficulty. Each of the great transformations of economic awareness has been attended by a crisis in the concept of value and by the need to redefine what constitutes value and whence it derives. For Smith, value arose from the possibility of commodification—of land, labor, or capital being thrown into the market; he contested the Physiocrats' insistence that only the land could generate surplus value. Marx proposed overlapping definitions of value, but basically saw the source of economic value in labor power.

One indication of today's "crisis of economic theory"[22] consists of the fact that a major current concept of value—the global GNP that counts all increments of goods and services—is increasingly subject to question. Is a service that merely compensates for the negative effect of another activity really to be assigned a full value? Should we think of cleaning up our rivers as an addition to national income when we polluted them to begin with? The ramifications of this question cannot be treated here; the point is that we do face uncertainties as to appropriate concepts of value, and therefore difficulties in assigning the appropriate measures we would need to put economics on a sure footing once again.

The economic realm, the political realm, the private realm (including family, affect, and belief) no longer retain the separate integrity that liberalism ascribed to them. We have moved from trying to safeguard a sphere of economic transactions toward a more global administrative, legislative, or jurisprudential regulation. Family life, health, the use of land, access to leisure, create dilemmas that necessitate interventions by public authorities, even as these public authorities often seek to involve private groups in the relevant decision making. Why should the economic realm of allegedly nonconstrained choices (but scarce goods) be any more protected from the attrition of autonomy than sexuality or even definitions of life itself?

In actuality, issues of political choice and economic transactions are probably not more muddled than they ever really were. In the eighteenth and nineteenth centuries the state had active family and welfare policies, regulated labor relations and prices, and defined property. But the confidence that, despite some borderline interventions, the political and economic spheres of decision making could be separated no longer exists. The significance of the twentieth century in the economic domain, at least, may have been precisely the undermining of the economic domain.

Notes

¹ A. V. Dicey, *Lectures upon the Relation between Law and Public Opinion in England during the Nineteenth Century* (London, 1905).
² On Mun, Misselden, and Locke, see Joyce Oldham Appleby, *Economic Thought and Ideology in Seventeenth-Century England* (Princeton, NJ, 1980), chaps. 2 and 8; Louis Dumont, *From Mandeville to Marx: The Genesis and Triumph of Economic Ideology* (Chicago, 1977), pp. 33ff.; on the Whig writers and the growth of commerce, J. G. A. Pocock, *The Machiavellian Moment* (Princeton, NJ, 1975), chaps. 13–14; also Elizabeth Fox-Genovese, *The Origins of Physiocracy* (Ithaca, NY, 1976), and for general reference, Joseph A. Schumpeter, *History of Economic Analysis* (London, 1954).
³ Adam Smith, *An Inquiry into the Nature and Causes of the Wealth of Nations* (1776), book V, chap. I, part iii.
⁴ Karl Polanyi, *The Great Transformation: The Political and Economic Origins of Our Time* (Boston, 1957).
⁵ Friedrich List, *The National System of Political Economy* (New York, 1856).
⁶ Karl Marx, *Capital*, I, chaps. 6 and 19.
⁷ See Heinrich August Winkler, ed., *Organisierter Kapitalismus. Voraussetzungen und Anfänge* (Göttingen, 1974). The phrase was first used by Rudolf Hilferding in "Arbeitsgemeinschaft der Klassen?" *Der Kampf*, 8 (1915), p. 322.
⁸ See W. Gottschalch, *Strukturveränderungen der Gesellschaft und politisches Handeln in der Lehre von Rudolf Hilferding* (Berlin, 1962) and Winkler, "Einleitende Bermerkungen," in *Organisierter Kapitalismus*, pp. 9–18.
⁹ John Maynard Keynes, *The General Theory of Employment, Interest, and Money* (London, 1960 ed.), p. 380. For a useful brief introduction, see D. E. Moggridge, *John Maynard Keynes* (Harmondsworth and New York, 1976).
¹⁰ Keynes, *General Theory*, p. 373.
¹¹ John Maynard Keynes, "Economic Possibilities for our Grandchildren" (1930), in *Essays in Persuasion* (New York, 1963), p. 369.
¹² Keynes, *General Theory*, p. 375.
¹³ Keynes, *General Theory*, p. 376.
¹⁴ Karl Marx, *Capital*, I, chap. 24, sect. 3.
¹⁵ Joseph A. Schumpeter, *Capitalism, Socialism and Democracy* (London, 1943), pp. 121–63. For a recent discussion along some similar lines, see Daniel Bell, *The Cultural Contradictions of Capitalism* (New York, 1978), pp. 33–84.

[16] G. Warren Nutter, *Growth of Government in the West* (Washington, DC, 1978), has assembled some of these statistics. Cf. David Cameron, "Does Government Cause Inflation?" in Leon Lindberg and Charles S. Maier, eds., *The Politics of Inflation and Economic Stagnation* (Washington, DC, forthcoming).

[17] See Charles S. Maier, "Inflation and Stabilization in the Wake of Two World Wars: Comparative Strategies and Sacrifices," in Gerald Feldman et al., *Die Erfahrung der Inflation im internationalen Zusammenhang und Vergleich* [The Experience of Inflation: International and Comparative Studies] (Berlin and New York, 1983).

[18] Joseph A. Schumpeter, *Die Krise des Steuerstaates* (Vienna, 1918).

[19] The notion of the technostructure was elaborated by John Kenneth Galbraith in *The New Industrial State* (New York, 1967), chap. 6. For a useful survey of the modern firm as a bureaucratic regulator of economic activity, see Alfred D. Chandler, Jr., and Herman Daems, *Managerial Hierarchies: Comparative Perspectives on the Rise of the Modern Industrial Enterprise* (Cambridge, MA, 1980). This essay cannot consider the rise of socialist planned economies, but the reader might profitably consult David Granick, *Enterprise Guidance in Eastern Europe* (Princeton, NJ, 1975).

[20] For these developments, the treatise of Andrew Schonfeld, *Modern Capitalism: The Changing Balance of Public and Private Power* (London and New York, 1965) is still valuable. Trends a decade later were surveyed in Raymond Vernon, ed., *Big Business and the State: Changing Relations in Western Europe* (Cambridge, MA, 1974); and for a recent discussion, see John Zysman, *Governments, Markets, and Growth* (Ithaca, NY, 1983).

[21] See Barry Karl, *Charles E. Merriam and the Study of Politics* (Chicago, 1974); Ellis W. Hawley, "Herbert Hoover, the Commerce Secretariat, and the Vision of an Associative State, 1919–1928," *Journal of American History*, 61 (June 1974); Otis L. Graham, *Towards a Planned Society: From Roosevelt to Nixon* (New York, 1976); Richard F. Kuisel, *Capitalism and the State in Modern France* (Cambridge, England, and New York, 1981); Mario Telò, ed., *Crisi e Piano: Le alternative degli anni Trenta* (Bari, 1979). On planning ideas in British labor, see Ben Pimlott, *Labour and the Left in the 1930s* (Cambridge and New York, 1977). The important question of the role of the world wars in advancing government planning and intervention cannot be taken up in this brief essay. By and large, despite the fact that the state could claim supreme power to allocate raw materials, control labor, and limit profits, its interventions were in good part temporary. The wars tended to legitimate an interpenetration of political and economic decision making that was underway in any case.

[22] See Daniel Bell and Irving Kristol, eds., *The Crisis of Economic Theory* (New York, 1981). For two very different but intelligent and provocative reflections on the crises of value in today's economic/political domains, see Fred Hirsch, *Social Limits to Growth* (Cambridge, MA, 1978), and Albert O. Hirschman, *Shifting Involvements: Private Interests and Public Action* (Princeton, NJ, 1981).

Discussion: Mommsen Paper

Mommsen: In this paper the point of departure is the conceptualization of classic imperialism, which has undergone in the last thirty years a progressive widening. There is not only imperialism in the sense of establishing colonial control over particular territories or perhaps establishing a formal empire, but a variety of forms of imperialist control—from paramountcy to formal administrative control.

Now, are we justified in talking about the end of imperialism? Are we in a postimperial age? In a way, this is undoubtedly so. The process of decolonization that has been going on for the last three decades has resulted in giving at least formal political sovereignty to the great majority of all formal colonial dependencies. I do think that this in a way is a change of a far-reaching nature. And I dare say that possibly the collapse of imperialist systems is a greater event in the history of the twentieth century than even the rise of the Soviet system and the collapse of the Fascist systems. I would integrate the Fascist systems into the long-term interpretations of imperialism, because you could describe both Italian and German fascism as belated attempts to establish formal colonial control over huge areas beyond their own national borders, with the intent of economic exploitation and, of course, establishing what is called cultural or racial predominance.

There is, of course, a large school of dependency thinkers, who with much justification have argued that after formal decolonization the dependency of so-called Third World countries has survived, and I think at least to some degree that is true. It is true that the means to enforce imperialist control of however informal a nature are less and less at the disposal of the great powers, and therefore we see it as a receding phenomenon. But this again does not seem to be necessarily a positive thing, because the widening gap between the majority of former colonial dependencies and their mother countries is largely governed by an international economic system that is in some ways a heritage of

125

the era of formal colonialism. So we cannot simply ignore it, even though in terms of international law, the important powers can do so.

After World War II, both superpowers turned into what can be described as imperialist systems. With regard to the Soviet system, I think this is obvious. I have tried to apply the model of the collaborationist pattern of imperialist rule as developed by Robinson and Fieldhouse to the Russian example and think it fits surprisingly well. In the American case it is not that obvious, inasmuch as here clearly the attempts to use direct control are very, very limited indeed. But I do nonetheless think that in universal historical terms, it is perhaps fair to say that there developed a sort of informal or perhaps not quite formal imperialist system, which determines in some ways the present-day world. What of course adds to it is that the relative stalemate of the two great superpowers which will determine the destinies of the people of the twentieth century allows the development of secondary imperialisms in other regions of the world, with bloody conflicts and consequences that even the superpowers cannot control. So in some ways the situation is a very complicated one and not easy to describe clearly.

Kolakowski: I think you are very right in pointing out the indiscriminate use of the concept of imperialism which, by covering so many different social phenomena, has become as indistinct and as obscured as the concepts of war and peace analyzed in Iriye's paper. Indeed, if imperialism means a policy aiming either at the use of direct violence or the threat of the use of direct violence in order to gain the domination of some territories or peoples by one state or by one people, there is no point not to extend this concept far into antiquity.

However, we cannot assimilate under the same concept, say, an equal partnership between a power like the United States and a small and economically feeble country on the one hand, and direct political and military domination of other countries by the Soviet Union on the other. If you go to a country like Brazil, you invariably hear people say: "Look at our television; they show American films time and again. That is American imperialism." Now it is true that there are plenty of American films on Brazilian television. But it is not the case that the American president threatens Brazil with American troops if it refuses to take American films. In fact, the threat of force and violence in the relationships between the United States and its allies does not exist. After all, de Gaulle withdrew from the joint NATO command and so did Greece without any possibility of the use of violence by other NATO countries having been taken into account. But any attempt not even to withdraw from the Warsaw Pact, but to modify the internal system within the Soviet bloc, immediately raises the threat of direct violence by the Soviet Union. Therefore, I think we may speak of Soviet imperialism as the only active great imperialism of our period.

To be sure, one speaks of the use of covert American action in various countries. But again, let us look at our hypocrisy in such matters. When the CIA intervened in Chile in order to destabilize the country and to cause the fall of Allende's government, the action provoked an enormous outcry all over the world. But the CIA did something similar in the Dominican Republic, and I am still waiting for any show of moral indignation. This kind of interference is a rather peripheral phenomenon in the global policy of the United States.

I would also like to say that, speaking generally, the main wealth of any country in the twentieth century is not natural resources, not minerals, not oil, but technical skills. After all, Japan is a country that has no natural resources to speak of. If it has become a great economic power, it is because it managed to organize and produce a large class of highly skilled, very competent technicians and managers. Even within the Soviet bloc, the country that manages better than others economically is Hungary, which has no natural resources whatever and not even access to the sea. In other words, what is perhaps important in contrast to the nineteenth century is that the direct taking of ready-made goods does not help anybody any longer. The taking of technology, of technological skills, technological abilities, by contrast, is very important. The main problem of underdeveloped or developing countries is technical skills, not resources—whether or not they will be able to produce a sufficiently large class of skilled technicians and managers. Otherwise, they will be doomed to suffer one calamity after another and be tempted to put the responsibility for all their failures on the American imperialists.

Nivat: You do not mention one thing that seems to me important, which is the crisis of Europe and the developing of anti-European feelings, mainly in Europe. The developing of a crisis of its own identity by Europe played a great active and historic role at the same time as another ideology, active Marxism, lost its faith in Europe itself while developing on the periphery all the time. In fact it seems to me now that in questions of imperialisms, many revolutionaries in, say, Latin America and many people who are supporting them in Europe have come to a sort of tragic conclusion: that they cannot help this new kind of emancipation going through Marxist revolutions, and at the same time they know and everybody knows that Marxism will soon become a new yoke, a new imperialism.

Mommsen: I think that the Russian system qualifies as a system of imperialist control; the American one, less so. I think after World War II the Western world was, if not formally then informally, very much dependent on the United States. In a way, that process is slowing. But the policy of the United States with regard to South America is basically in continuity with its classic policies. With regard to the Soviet Union, the remarkable thing is that though there is the ultimate possibility of recourse to violence, it is seldom needed. The degree of violence Russia needs to maintain what is, in general, a decaying empire is still comparatively low. Our study of classic imperialist systems shows that in fact violence is much too costly and has repercussions. The astounding thing is that the Russian system can work as it does. And there you indeed need the collaborationist elites whose interests and destinies are tied up with the system.

I am a little bit doubtful about Nivat's point—the so-called crisis of the identity of Europe. One can, of course, say that World War I was the apogee of European dominance in the world system, and that from that date on, European imperialist control was doomed. I myself would take the rather more decidedly liberal point of view and say, "Thank heavens it was doomed." Even so, I do not think the collapse of imperialism has much to do with the crisis of identity in the sense that Europeans lost heart. Of course, it has very much to do with the success of liberal forces, which always thought imperialist rule was not possible for democratic systems.

Surely technical skills are important, but in many cases social conditions at the periphery are such that the rapid development of technical skills cannot be expected. There is a heritage of the imperialist age that we probably have not quite gotten hold of yet, and the temptation of the West, by and large, to leave those countries that are not doing very well mostly alone is high. There is the problem of benign neglect as the newest policy, which is the opposite of imperialism. And even though I have been brought up in and have written quite a few things on imperialism in a liberal, anti-imperialist mood, I sometimes think it may have been after all less bad than the benign neglect to which some countries are exposed today. One has to admit that the main factor why this is not quite as bad as it could be is the rivalry between the superpowers. If not for that, the situation would probably be even worse.

Iriye: Perhaps the end of formal empires has been a good thing for the former empires, but not necessarily for the former colonies.

Karl: American historians have considered the United States the first of the successful modern rebellions against a colonial empire. But it has been a peculiar kind of awareness for Americans, particularly as they have had to wade through the nineteenth century and cope with Western expansion as some kind of non-imperial, noncolonial system of expansion. I think there has been a lot of writing recently among critical historians about the ruthlessness with which that was done. There is a kind of internal hidden imperialism in American history that raises a number of issues and that might put the United States, particularly in the 1890s, into the odd position of having become an expanded nation that now needed to expand its own colonial interests, a newcomer to imperial expansion like Germany and Italy at the same point.

The development of an anti-imperialist movement in the United States was very closely associated—at least the intellectual side of it—with British anti-imperialism, which leads to a question of ethnic identity and the establishment of the independence of ethnic groups. The interest Louis Brandeis had in British imperialism, his interest in the development of a Palestinian state, was based on a belief that you really did have to define nations, you had to define communities by historical ethnicity of some kind, and that it was necessary to break empires down not because there was anything necessarily evil about imperialism, but because there was something essentially right about the development of ethnic unity, historical ethnic unity.

Hersch: Does the word *imperialism* nowadays really promote clarity in political thinking? I think it does not. We might do better to drop it altogether and to leave it for propaganda use. The relations between nations are so complicated today and of so many different kinds on so many different levels that if you take any situation of dependence as being imperialistic, you would have only imperialism in politics. And if you say that we should not speak of the imperialism of the Soviet Union because its military interventions are rare, it is because the pressure is so constant that it does not need to intervene most of the time. If the Soviets would leave the people alone, then they would have to intervene more often. They have an imperialistic presence which is such that they do not often need to send military expeditions.

Maier: I still think the word *imperialistic*, problematic though it might be, has important uses. One thing that strikes any observer about the classic British, French, and other empires is how small an occupying force was necessary in proportion to the huge numbers of people who were controlled. This testifies to different levels of organization, which I think is truly amazing, and the fact that that has collapsed is one of the momentous changes of this century. The part of the paper I find a little difficult is the inability to distinguish between uneven development and economic imperialism. I think this has always been a question. I have some sympathy with the Leninist view of imperialism as rooted in uneven development, but that would imply that we must erect a counterfactual type of inquiry. If the European metropolitan countries had not expanded with soldiers, to what extent would the unevenness of economic development have bequeathed a legacy of economic backwardness? I think that uneven development is a very important concept and really has to be distinguished from imperialism and probably would explain a great deal. Finally, one of the ironies of history is that the end of empire in the last twenty years has been accompanied by the sizable formation of Third World enclaves within the metropolises of the developed world. Anybody who follows questions of linguistic development in America, who follows the questions of growth of populations in the cities of London, Berlin, and elsewhere, must see that this has been a major change and that ultimately the balance sheet of imperialism should include this type of development.

Friedländer: Within the center, there is a radical difference between the imposition of direct control by force, which in my view is Soviet imperialism, and the attempts at political and economic influence used by the United States. South America is a good example. There are two different types of control here, and to mix them or to make them symmetrical is in my opinion very questionable.

Then there is an inverse imperialism within the periphery. Former colonies or ex-dependents, such as Saudi Arabia and the OPEC countries, now try to influence the economic stability of the West. This is certainly an attempt by the periphery to get back at the center.

There are also attempts by peripheral countries to destabilize other countries in the periphery—Syria, Libya—using all kinds of methods, training terrorists and so on, which is again a totally different attempt at controlling neighboring countries or even Western countries through very indirect means.

Mommsen: I would not talk about the reappearance of imperialism, but a sort of slow fading of the remnants of the classic forms of imperialism, which then give way to other forms. I would say that there is a declining line: at the end you have benign neglect. I would not say that there is a reappearance.

Joll: Historically, the classic imperialism, the rule of non-European territory by European powers, was undermined by the ideologies the imperial powers have brought with them to the colonies. That is to say, the language that the imperial powers of Europe—Britain, France, the Netherlands, Belgium, even to some extent Portugal—used to justify their imperialism was the language the inhabitants of the colonial territories used to justify their revolt. The liberal ideologies of the nineteenth century, whether political liberalism or intellectual liberalism, the idea of *mission civilisatrice*, the duty of the imperialist powers to raise the level of life of the colonies so that they would eventually achieve something comparable to that of the mother country—all these produced a built-in necessity that imperialism would carry with it the seeds of its own end. Now what happened increasingly after World War I, particularly in regard to the British Empire, was that opinion at home—and this may be what Nivat means by the European powers losing their nerve—became increasingly aware of the difference between the standards they were applying in their political life at home and the standards they were applying in the political life of the colonies. Once you get this awareness of the discrepancy between the standards you allege you are carrying to the colonies, of impartial justice, education, and so on, and the actual way in which the government of the colonies is being carried on, you are bound, I think inevitably, to get what we have seen in all the old empires—a situation leading to decolonization.

The second point I want to make is that the state of the colonies after independence is directly related to the speed of decolonization. Decolonization in the 1940s and 1950s occurred very much more quickly than anyone anticipated. Consequently, the preparation of cadres able to take over not only the administration but also the running of the economy—the creation, as Kolakowski said, of the class of technologists needed to make the former colonies into modern societies—was largely a matter of how long the preparation for decolonization had been going on. In many of these countries, the rapid withdrawal of the colonizing power meant that there was not just a political vacuum, but a vacuum at every level in the running of the institutions and the economy of the country. And into this vacuum, as always, come outside forces. Then you get the beginnings of a new imperialism based, in some cases, on the return of the old colonial power. The vacuum that was caused by the lack of preparation for decolonization very often conditioned the circumstances of the initial years of the new states.

Schwartz: There are parts of the world that have not had the kind of state or technical development that East Asia has. I do not necessarily deprecate the cultures of these parts of the world; some of the things that make them very unable to respond are very attractive. Nevertheless, it is a problem. Mommsen says that neglect in itself is a form of indirect imperialism. Should we go in there to help these cultures that are not very efficient? Would we bungle the help? Would it turn out not to be help? Do you favor a policy in these areas of departing from benign neglect and intervening directly?

Mommsen: The surprising thing is that the liberal ideology did take a long time to come home to those people who were responsible for running these territories. Initially, they had the interesting effect of making imperialist control more effective— more cost-effective and more effective in the sense of making these territories pay for themselves. Especially in the French case, one can see that in the interwar period the whole thing became, in many ways, more beneficial for all partners concerned. And that, of course, is in a way the first step toward a new departure. But by and large I would maintain that all this hard work of preparing these countries for independence operated from assumptions which to a great degree have become obsolete. And we have to face the fact that the concept of modernization on the periphery, with which, hopefully, the West moved into decolonization as far as it did it consciously, has by and large failed. I consider this a very, very great problem.

Discussion: Maier Paper

Maier: Let me revert in this statement to the theme of the blurring of lines: peace is war; war is peace. In a sense my paper is also concerned with the blurring of a line nineteenth-century civilization thought could be kept separate, that between political systems and economic activity. What strikes me about the nineteenth century is that so much of the effort of European civilization went into establishing clear boundaries and dualisms—for example, public versus private: the location of the family and the location of work are separated. Also, the separation of peace and war; the separation of what is white and civilized against what is backward. In a sense, nineteenth-century civilization can be construed as an exercise in perimeter-drawing—establishing boundaries. Clearly, the public-private distinction, that between politics and the market or the realm of economy, is one of the key aspects of these divisions. The distinction that Hegel established between state and civil society is a German expression of it. It preoccupied theorists of the nineteenth-century tradition, even the social democratic theorists emerging out of that tradition, such as Hilferding.

Now Hilferding, I suggest, outlined a certain kind of structural change that would overtake market capitalism. Keynes I take as symbolic of another type of change, and that is the growth of welfare systems, the melding of state and market in the provision of social services for the unemployed and in the general process of using the state to maintain a level of public spending that would keep up aggregate demand. Hilferding's changes—those of organized capitalism—were already under way and always existed in the market. And when they occur, they can be accommodated within the parameters of what we would call capitalism. Certainly the type of mixed capitalist regime we have in Western Europe today accommodates a type of development that Hilferding proposed without some qualitative or revolutionary transformation.

Keynes's implications are perhaps more interesting. Do the levels of public spending entail any type of qualitative systemic transformation? Certain conservative circles argue that they do, that there is a tax threshold, a public spending threshold beyond which capitalism somehow loses its vitality and ceases to exist as such. I do not believe this is necessarily the case. One reason is that, in fact, the end uses of public consumption do not change particularly, but remain remarkably constant. Keynes may be more subversive in his antiaccumulationist ideas, those he brought up at the end of *General Theory*. He envisaged that investment accumulation would be less necessary as an economy made the transition from the classic industrial hardware type of development—that based on iron and steel and even chemicals—to that based on services, to a software economy.

So I find that neither of these two major theorists is really adequate to explain the type of transition that may be occurring in the relationship between state and society. One of those transitions is the cooptation of the working class in Western Europe, or the enlistment, the absorption of at least half of the political representatives of the working class, much as the bourgeois aristocracy was absorbed into aristocratic state management in the nineteenth century. The other aspect is the fact that people do not have confidence any more in the cybernetic or self-regulating aspects of the market as an automatic system. Even technology and environment, the control of family and private relations, or in some cases the liberation of family and private relations, has required political intervention. In this sense, the state's intervention in the economy is one of many phenomena that reveal this type of blurring of outlines.

Finally, what will change? Where are the sources for change? Some of them are involved in moving toward a computer, silicon era. The principles of class stratification are probably changing, but I think we will probably have a different type of stratification, and the elimination of stratification. That is what we face perhaps: the emergence of people who are skilled, who acquire their skills through education, and those who even in a service economy will be performing the services of—as we say in the United States—pushing brooms and not pushing buttons. That seems to me one change in the principles of social stratification. The others are the questions of demographic movements, the growth of the number of aged in the society, and the growth of different ethnic groups coming into former metropolises and perhaps forming new subclasses.

Finally, I think that the whole concept of economic value developed in the nineteenth century, from Adam Smith, the Physiocrats, and through Keynes, is in some sense in an intellectual crisis. GNP, the measurement of national income statistics, was in a sense its highest expression. And it was predicated on the belief that you could just add up types of different goods and services and come out with a measure. How do we measure value when some of our goods and services are precisely designed to offset the negative effects of others? Any reflection on this indicates that we have come to a transition about economic thinking and perhaps about activity. But it is not a transition that is describable within the terms the theorists of the late nineteenth and early twentieth centuries left to us.

Windsor: On the one hand, you argue that Keynes predicated software economic growth, but underestimated the amount of investment that would be necessary to carry this through. On the other hand, when talking about the relatively high levels of unemployment which have come about in recent years, you suggest that we are slow in transferring workers from steel to silicon. But this transfer of skills presumably demands a very high level of investment. Would that be the case? And if so, can it be met out of the taxation patterns and public expenditure patterns that you also discuss?

Maier: The movement of people from steel to silicon will require investment. But the problem of what the social stratification would look like after that movement takes place is another question. I am not sure we are prepared yet for the type of social stratification the new employment will require. And how one deals with that in the political system is still up for grabs.

Karl: One of the consequences of the experience of World War I was an enormous interest among American governing groups in economic planning. The New Deal picked that up and elevated it to rather remarkable heights, despite all the rhetoric against Roosevelt in the business community. By the time you get to World War II, you have an altogether new business leadership developing in the United States: a leadership of younger people who are very willing now to look to government to support their interests. But one of the consequences of World War II is a rejection of planning and of the whole concept of planning, even of the use of the term. While close relationships between government and business are being developed in Japan and in other parts of the world, the United States retains this kind of hostility, although Keynes and Keynesianism remain a kind of constant throughout the period.

Mommsen: Of course, there was a time in which it was thought that the Western and the Eastern European systems would converge, because the West might slowly reach a state in which the degree of state control would be very high, while the East European systems might decelerate state control and introduce more market factors. I think that died down and I think rightly so.

Friedländer: The Galbraithian theory of growing interconnection between the executives of large companies and state officials certainly confirms Maier's case. But then he did not mention another level, that of the growth of multinational companies which have submitted less to state control than any economic domain and which add a new dimension—that is, a growing economization of politics.

Maier: I am not describing a system that actually existed, but rather conceptualization of an economic system that held sway, that was immensely persuasive, and that was ideologically hegemonic. And my question is, why was it so persuasive?

There are two dimensions of state intervention in the economy. One is what I called the Hilferdingian one, in which government tries to implant and encourage certain structural and organizational changes. That is what went on with Hoover, where industries bore the efforts of coordination. This was rejected after World War II, in part because of the ideological conjuncture with the competition with the Soviet Union.

The other dimension of the state's role in the economy is what I called the Keynesian one, and that is the role of the government not in steering an economy, but in stabilizing a certain level of economic activity. That has not really been given up. I think by and large most of the Western states accepted the premise of keeping a certain level of economic activity. In fact, one of the reasons there is confusion about this is that when American liberals talk about planning in World War II, they are often referring to the second type of aggregate demand stabilization, the Keynesian dimension, as economic planning.

The multinational corporations, the growing economization of politics, is a different sort of development. All I would argue is that insofar as the economy requires more politics, politics will become more economically conditioned—for example, the Common Market. My argument ultimately would be for the failure of the autonomy of an economic domain, not the fact that the action of intervention is always one way.

Schwartz: I think one of the advantages Japan may have had from the beginning of the Meiji Restoration is that it never really participated too much in the free market myth.

Windsor: One political phenomenon that puzzles me in all this is that, at least in many countries, the greater the involvement of the state—and here I mean state, a government, not public expenditures—in the direction of the economy, the greater the responsibilities of the state for a wide variety of private activities.

The more the state and the government become a sectoral interest in the society, the more trade unions or other bureaucracies will fight against the government itself as if the government represented one kind of interest among a number of others.

Maier: If you look at Weimar Germany or Italy right before the Fascists came to power, one of the right wing's critiques certainly is that the state has become less of a state because it has gone into too many areas. And the efforts to restore a strong state but in a limited area are a counterprogram to having what right-wing circles conceive of as a weak state that is overextended, a state that has become only one interest group among many. I think this is a perennial type of appeal in restorationist political symbolism. Let's get the state back where it belongs, but make it really decisive in that sphere.

Mommsen: It would appear as if the great difference between the 1920s or the war period and the period after 1945 has been that the conditions for the growth of international trade have been much better, and that international trade seems to have been the prime mover behind this astounding economic success. In this field, government control and intervention apparently are limited. I think that in some ways the structure of the international system of financial exchange and exchange in goods becomes increasingly difficult for governments to control directly. I myself have a feeling that we are in a situation of the relative helplessness of politics in these matters.

Karl: When you deal with the American situation, one has to recognize the fact that Americans have always, but now increasingly, made a very sharp distinction between a state that responds to their political demands, whatever they might be, and a bureaucracy that blocks their access to the state. And as the demands of technological society require expanded bureaucracies to manage these systems, the response of the American citizen to that bureaucracy is already set in opposition. It is a crisis, one I think will get worse.

Kolakowski: In the Marxist tradition there has always been a hesitation between two concepts, capitalism as a market or as private ownership of the means of production. Conceptually, they are not the same thing. You say at one point that one might envisage a system in which all income was taken by the government, all services were provided in return, and which was still capitalist in some sense. Now, in what sense might it still be capitalist?

The second question is about the role of inflation in politics. Inflation is redistribution of the national income. Classes that are the least affected by inflation are the richest and those who live from one week to another. The classes that are the most affected by inflation are middle classes, the saving classes. Is it therefore, in your opinion, likely that with the enlargement of the middle classes, Keynesian economic policies would tend to be rather less supported on a broad scale and that a more liberal politics would be supported, with the state acting on economic development by indirect means—taxation, monetary policy, influencing the interest rate, and so on?

Maier: The foreign trade of the Western world reattained the 1913 levels only some time during the 1960s. The growth of international trade depended on certain clear political guidelines being set to establish an international market, much as guidelines had been set to establish national markets in Adam Smith's England. One was that you had to have a convertible currency, and to establish a certain sort of order. The United States was critical in establishing these conditions after World War II. In a sense political power, and not power so crassly expressed, but political and economic power or influence, set the parameters for foreign trade. Some of this economic activity is hard to control, but it is not unrelated to a type of political setting of boundary conditions.

I am ambiguous about capitalism. I do think probably Marx had a point when he looked at the control of capital as such. Investment decisions in a society and the capacity to make them seem to me crucial for the sort of definitional minimum of what capitalism might be.

Now the question of the politics of inflation. Yes, I would generally agree that the middle classes lose by inflation, by and large to the lower and upper levels. But the question of inflation in the last fifteen years—an epoch that is now ending—and the question of inflation in the epoch from 1914 to 1924 are different, because our middle classes are far less *rentier* classes than they were then. They put far less of their wealth into money-denominated assets, and more into housing or education. It seems to me that the political uses of inflation are not particularly economically determined in advance—and neither are the political outcomes. It is harder to predict how inflation can be used. And you can mobilize resentments about inflation that cut all sorts of different ways.

FREEDOM AND COMMUNITY

THE TWENTIETH CENTURY:
INNOVATION AND IMMOBILITY

BENJAMIN I. SCHWARTZ

The twentieth century is, of course, the age of unremitting and relentless innovation. The triumph of natural science and of technology continue at an accelerated pace, and we are now told that the computer revolution will soon transform our lives in unimaginable ways.

I mention these by now banal observations because this vast tide of innovation has lent much encouragement to the view that twentieth-century Western thought has also been marked by an originality and creativity unprecedented in human history. I shall not presume to judge the various fields of natural science, but I would suggest at this point that in the fields of the human and social sciences, this view is much exaggerated. It is, of course, true that new vocabularies are constantly being spawned and that whole new sciences such as semiotics and communications continue to emerge. And yet the question of whether the "deep structures" that underlie these new creations are truly new is one which bears close scrutiny.

It may, of course, be urged that the question of "originality" is not in itself important. Yet the obsession with originality is so persistent that the claim cannot be ignored. If, in fact, a good deal of twentieth-century thought is basically continuous with nineteenth- and even eighteenth-century thought, the constant claim of originality simply may serve to disguise the essential immobility of some of our deeper assumptions at a time when our situation generally cries out for a reconsideration of our basic categories.

I have spoken here of modern Western thought, and I shall in these remarks confine my attention to modern Western thought.

For better or worse, the categories of nineteenth- and twentieth-century Western thought continue at least for the time being to dominate much of the intellectual discourse of the non-Western world. To be sure, the spectacular "modernization" of Japan and other East Asian societies has raised profound questions concerning many of our implicit assumptions concerning the nature of "modernity," and non-Western influences in the areas of esthetic and even religious life have begun to affect Western society. But at this point in time, the dominant categories of discourse continue to be Western.

I have referred above to the human and social sciences and yet one is, of course, aware of the claims that have been made for radical breakthroughs in the realm of philosophy. The names of Wittgenstein, Nietzsche, and Heidegger in particular—and others might be added to the list—have been mentioned as marking a radical break with the whole pre-Cartesian and even post-Cartesian philosophic heritage. It is often stated that we have not even begun to understand the implications of their thought for our age. As a layman in philosophy who has struggled with the writings of these most difficult thinkers, I would hardly presume to question these claims. Yet it does indeed appear that it has been difficult for most of us to grasp the concrete implications of their thought for our late twentieth-century experience. What I simply propose to do at this point is to pose certain questions concerning their work which have greatly puzzled me in particular.

Wittgenstein in many of his nonphilosophic utterances evinces a most critical—one might even say antipathetical—attitude toward the modern world and all its works. Yet it remains difficult for the ordinary person to spell out the links between these views and his strictly philosophic analyses. We all know that one of the main targets of his attack is the perversion of language in much philosophic and metaphysical discourse. There is, of course, nothing new in the attack on metaphysics. Not many twentieth-century intellectuals are prepared to identify themselves as metaphysicians. Yet Wittgenstein obviously uses the term in his own way and is prepared to attack even his own previous commitment to logical positivism as metaphysical. No doubt, in his view many of our social scientists are as involved in the pathological use of language as were the metaphysicians of the past. It is nevertheless extraordinarily difficut for us to understand how the reliance on unreflective ordinary language represents our hope for salvation within the conditions of modern life, or indeed how ordinary language can remain uncontaminated in the conditions of the modern world. Neither Wittgenstein nor his interpreters seem to have succeeded in making concrete the implications of his thought.

When we turn to Nietzsche we can, of course, quite readily appreciate his negative critiques of many aspects of modern life. Yet the thrust of his vision remains dark and difficult to grasp, and many of the efforts made to interpret him as a transvaluer of values turn him into a kind of Enlightenment figure or nineteenth-century romantic. One appreciates Heidegger's desperate effort to recapture a sense of being and his despair at its loss. One appreciates also his insistence on human limitations and the dilemmas he poses about the implications of technology for this sense of limits. Yet here again, the effort to make his message vivid and concrete for most late twentieth-century people remains elusive. All these figures may indeed represent a new turn in our ways of perceiving our world, yet most late twentieth-century people seem unprepared to comprehend or accept what may be truly new in their visions.

There are other twentieth-century modes of thought which make strident claims to represent "breakthroughs," and yet I would submit that these claims all deserve the most skeptical scrutiny. One might simply mention Freudianism, the various versions of structuralism, and some of the American "behavioral sciences." All drastically demote the role of human consciousness as a causative factor in human affairs, and all claim to have discovered the specific mechanisms that operate behind ordinary human consciousness. This insight into the impotence and super-ficiality of ordinary conscious life is almost uniformly put forth as one of the great revelations of our century. Again one is puzzled, since it seems quite clear that much nineteenth-century thought was already fully committed to this very project. The entire effort to use the methods of science to study man as well as the entire historicist enterprise of the nineteenth century necessarily presup-posed the elimination of the queer phenomenon of individual human consciousness as a determinant of human affairs.

Leaving aside the obvious case of Marx, can one really say that the great nineteenth-century evolutionary and historical systems lent any weight to individual human consciousness as factors in the study of man? To be sure, there were contradictions in all these modes of thought. We are now able to perceive in retrospect how Spencer, Marx, Comte, and Hegel were able to except their own thought from the sway of the genetic conditions which govern the conscious life of others. They were able to achieve a transcendental position by dint of their privileged access to the true scientific method or by dint of the fact that the historical process had, in their lifetimes, reached a point in human evolution which made it possible for certain spirits to achieve an unbeclouded clarity. Yet the fact is that these same "devices of transcendence" are still very much operative in the thinking of the various Freudian, structuralist, and behavioral science schools of our own century. It may be maintained that while nineteenth-century thinkers were aware of the fact that human consciousness is determined by various deep mechanisms, the twentieth century has discovered the actual mechanisms involved. The whole nineteenth-century experience would, however, suggest the need for extreme caution in accepting such claims.

Foucault has suggested that while nineteenth-century "discourse" was largely concerned with "constituting" or "integrating" man, twentieth-century discourse necessarily leads to the "dissolution" of man. Here again one is profoundly puzzled. It was precisely the nineteenth century which established the social and biological sciences as we now find them embedded in the conventional academic disciplines of biology, psychology, economics, sociology, anthropology, and so on. Inspired by what was taken to be the model of the natural sciences, it was the nineteenth century which set about the project of turning these disciplines into discrete, autonomous, self-enclosed "sciences." The image of man that emerges from all this is as fragmented and segmented as one can possibly imagine. Where in all this is the impulse to "constitute" or "integrate" man? To be sure, the project to divide the territory has not succeeded, and there are constantly imperialist encroachments of one discipline on another. But Foucault's claim that his project of dissolving man is new is most puzzling indeed. Even his own method of embedding men in completely discrete "archeological" layers of "discourse" does not seem in the end so radically different from the major thrust of nineteenth-century historicism. Perhaps the difference lies in his abandonment of the hope for "reintegration" that was still so much alive in nineteenth-century progressive historicism and evolutionism. If this is his message, it remains profoundly obscured by his vocabulary.

Perhaps one of the more original features of twentieth-century thought lies in its deep concern with language and the machinery of communications. It is a concern that can be found not only in Anglo-American linguistic philosophers, but in the continental thought of men such as Foucault, Derrida, and others. Levi-Strauss's concept of "structure" is, of course, very much based on the model of language as a paradigm. I shall not pretend here to know the deeper reasons for this twentieth-century preoccupation with language, but again one is led to wonder what its implications are for twentieth-century thought in general. One really wonders whether deeper "ontic commitments," to use Quine's phrase, are very much changed by being cast into the framework of a discussion of language. To the extent that language is conceived of as a kind of process of reality independent of individual consciousness, it is simply one more of those abstract structures and processes laid on top of economic, cultural, and social processes which all claim to account for our behavior.

I have here allowed myself to raise certain perhaps ill-informed questions concerning matters of the "high thought" of the century because I have a sense that some of the puzzles raised may possibly be shared by others. When one descends from these heights to what might be called the ordinary public intellectual discourse of our times, one becomes aware of the extent to which contemporary thought remains dominated by orientations that have been with us for some time. In my remaining remarks I would like to consider three of these orientations, which seem to me to illustrate the theme of immobility.

One of the dominant orientations is what might be called the ongoing technico-economic obsession. Here one might immediately object that the word *obsession* is misused, since what it refers to is a state of mind, whereas the dominant role of the technico-economic factor in our lives is not as an idea but an objective fact. Indeed, one of the most powerful ideas we have inherited from the last century is that the technico-economic sphere has, in fact, always been the dynamic sphere of human life, even when men were dominated by a false consciousness that prevented them from realizing this fact. This is a notion, incidentally, which is often attributed to Marx. It appears quite clear, however, that it represents a broad stream of thought that would no doubt have arisen if Marx had never lived.

Yet despite the constant insistence that technico-economic growth is an objective process independent of the "will of men," the entire discussion of this matter continues to waver between the language of descriptive determinism and the language of prescription. We are constantly being exhorted to promote attitudes and habits that will enhance growth and constantly being warned about irrational attitudes that will impede growth.

I use the strong word *obsession* in the hope that the attitude expressed here may not be immediately identified with a romantic antitechnologism or Luddism, although any critique of the obsession is bound to receive these labels. Men have in the mass always been concerned with economic survival and economic betterment. Even so-called traditional thought was quite aware of this fact. To the extent that the Industrial Revolution has opened up the possibility for the first time in human history of satisfying basic economic and physical needs and even of providing amenities and comforts, its results must be affirmed whatever its negative consequences.

At this point, one might be inclined to say that having made these concessions, the whole notion of "obsession" crumbles. If the goods industrialism has yielded have been genuine goods, how can there possibly be too much of them? How can one possibly draw a line between enough and too much? The answer is not easy to come by. The only possible answer—namely, that where the infinite pursuit of one good may actually negate the pursuit of other goods, it may cease to be good—does not provide concrete direction for drawing guidelines.

The concrete image that comes to my mind is that of physical exercise. Physical exercise is certainly a good, and yet when we see the results that ensue when some spend all their waking hours "building their muscles" we have a sense that it is possible to use the phrase "too much."

The whole matter is very much complicated by the fact that technico-economic growth is generally conceived of as the only way to achieve noneconomic as well as economic goods. It would indeed be unjust to say that all those obsessed with technico-economic development are concerned only with economic goods. If fact, many of them are concerned—or profess concern—with many other social values such as liberty, equality, democracy, and "careers open to talents." They are convinced that all these other values are a spin-off of infinite technico-economic growth.

Karl Marx himself was convinced that technico-economic growth would at one point make inevitable or at least possible the realization of all those values associated with socialism, while Ronald Reagan—*ceteris paribus*—seems sincerely convinced that liberty and democracy are entirely the product of an ever-advancing free enterprise economy. Even some of those who dream of the revival of community fondly hope that the next new form in technology will make possible a radical decentralization of the entire social structure. Ecologists ardently hope that the technology of solar energy will finally make it possible to remove the need for the exploitation of nonrenewable resources. The rescue of the vast masses of the poor in the "undeveloped" world from their grinding poverty cannot be achieved by the wider distribution of our present production techniques and knowhow but will be achieved by constant new breakthroughs in production technology. It would thus appear that all our aspirations, both economic and noneconomic, remain utterly dependent on the singleminded pursuit of ever-higher levels of technico-economic growth.

At the same time, all values, beliefs, and institutions which are perceived as blocking such growth will either automatically disappear in the natural course of things or should by all means be done away with. Here again one finds that constant passing back and forth between the language of confident prediction and the language of exhortation and prescription

On the level of middle-class individual life, the preoccupation with the technico-economic, with the processes of getting, spending, and worrying about security, has come to occupy a good part of our waking life. Here again, it must be emphasized that we are not here speaking of the indigent masses of the Third World or even of that very large mass in our own societies which continues to live from hand to mouth even when not faced with the specter of unemployment. We are speaking of large parts of our middle classes who spend whole stretches of their lives planning their portfolios, avoiding taxes, and planning for the future. Daniel Bell, during the hectic days of the sixties, was concerned that Western capitalism was producing a generation of total consumers completely devoted to instantaneous gratification and incapable of carrying on the culture of production. In retrospect, it appears that his fears may have been premature. We now again have a generation just as interested in money making (whether all forms of money making are equally productive is another question) as in spending. Within the more prosperous middle class, the balance between career and leisure has again been reestablished. Whether this balance in itself provides the total formula for the good life is a question I shall not consider.

In sum, one can say that the obsession with technico-economic growth as an overriding goal remains so dominant in our world that it continues to inhibit all discussion. The proposition that in pursuing these goals man has finally discovered his true nature and destiny after all the confusing and delusive gropings of the past remains difficult to challenge and yet may demand challenge.

Nevertheless, alongside this orientation one does find the vigorous survival of another orientation some might even consider contradictory—namely, the orientation to nationalism. There may be some room for argument about the present strength of nationalism in the so-called advanced industrial societies, and it may well be that within that world it has lost its aggressive potential. I would nonetheless submit that it remains an extremely vital passion. In a secular world, it continues to fill a religious need for some kind of identity with a larger reality that the technico-economic obsession fails to provide.

The nineteenth and early twentieth-century dreams of a socialist or anarchist future were capable of surrounding life with a religious aura centered on the future. The present science-fiction futurological projections of technico-economic splendor remain vacuous and meaningless. Nationalism, on the other hand, binds the members of a community by all sorts of tangible bonds and symbols to a presumed common past and a larger identity in the present.

It is curious that the notion that the nation-state as an entity and nationalism as a creed are obsolete and incompatible with the needs of the age is almost as old as nationalism itself. Early nineteenth-century liberals as well as socialists and anarchists were all convinced that the nation-state and nationalism were obsolete. Thus all the current talk of the global interlocking nature of the world economy and the irrationality of the nation-state as an economic unit is part of a long, respectable tradition. This talk may, of course, be quite correct when viewed in its own terms, but what it continues to overlook is the extent to which the vast mass of people still identify with the national societies to which they are bound by a thousand strands.

In fact, when one examines somewhat more closely the historic relationship between nationalism and the technico-economic obsession, one finds that it has in fact been extraordinarily complex. We know that national rivalry, national security, and technological breakthroughs have been closely interwoven in the past. To Japanese and Chinese statesmen and intellectuals who looked at the West from their own particular perspectives during the last hundred years, the intimate link between national power and technico-economic advance seemed patently obvious. Indeed, a candid perusal of the utterances of present-day economists about the necessity of not "falling behind" in technico-economic growth always introduces a noneconomic nationalist note into the very heart of economics itself. Considerations of national security and sheer national pride almost always figure as a leitmotif in this discourse.

Using the phrase of William James, one can say that we have yet to find the "functional equivalent" of nationalism. Events such as the Falkland Islands war or the detention of the American hostages in Iran are often sufficient to create a sense of solidarity which no other political or religious movement seems capable of creating. Whatever one may think of nationalism as a secular religion, it would appear that the impulses that lie behind its vitality have by no means disappeared.

Another orientation of twentieth-century thought which I

should like to consider briefly is what might be called the orientation to political and cultural radicalism. At the moment this heritage does not seem to be flourishing, although it was of course very much to the fore during the turbulent sixties. Within this strain of thought, which might be called the Rousseauist strain, the dominant language tends to the moral rather than technico-scientific (although in Karl Marx one can find a potent mixture of both languages). To oversimplify, radicalism operates with an image of man quite different from that of the technico-economic model. The latter seems to operate with a simple, mechanical "economic man" model; the former begins with the model of primal goodness which is blocked and distorted by the effects of a corrupt social environment. Jean Starobinski, the biographer of Rousseau, uses the image of transparency and obstacle. When the obstacle of the evil social system is removed, the human capacity for the good and the true will flow unimpeded. Out of this image there easily emerges the concept of the redemptive revolution that does not so much "construct" a utopia as remove those distorting factors which prevent the emergence of a harmonious society.

In expressing skepticism about "redemptive revolution" as an expression of moral philosophy, I do not mean to suggest hostility to all actual violent revolutions against entrenched corrupt establishments; we can readily understand why in many parts of the world "redemptive revolutionism" continues to make a strong appeal to local intellectual elites. Yet the fact remains that the concrete ideologies of radicalism which have emerged during the nineteenth and twentieth centuries have proved to be quite as disappointing to their adherents as to others. Revolutions have occurred, but the promise of redemptive revolution has failed. Within the camp of radicalism there is still wide agreement that the "obstacle" resides in an entity or process called capitalism, but the positive definitions of socialism have become ever more tenuous and misty. This does not mean that critiques of the contemporary world offered by self-styled radicals are not often cogent and penetrating, but that their proposals for redemption seem singularly unconvincing.

On the other hand, the kind of cultural radicalism that proposes a return to communities of like-minded people who reject the materialism of the modern world seems to be based on the notion that the mere fact of community life will transform the members of the community. There are in the modern world groups such as the Amish or the Hutterites which have in fact succeeded in creating a separate communal life. Yet what one finds here is not a belief in primal innocence, but a deep commitment to a rigorous and highly structured religious life. Nevertheless, political and cultural radicalism, like the technico-economic obsession and nationalism, lives on—whatever the cogency of its solutions.

These reflections are on the whole lugubrious and somber, despite the fact that we have not dwelt on gulags, holocausts, two world wars, and the threat of nuclear annihilation. If, as I have maintained, the twentieth century is in many ways a continuation of and extrapolation of tendencies already present in the previous century, it is probably the case that all these catastrophies also have earlier roots. And it thus seems to me quite wrong to oppose the irrationality and barbarism of the twentieth century to the sunny enlightment and hopeful progressivism of the nineteenth.

Despite all these catastrophies and doubts, however, at least in the United States the twentieth century continues to be enormously self-congratulatory. The need for a rethinking of the categories and metaphors that continue to dominate our thought is still not deeply felt.

THE SEARCH FOR COMMUNITY

LESZEK KOLAKOWSKI

There is no greater falsehood than to maintain that thanks to the development of communication, we now live in a giant village extending over the entire surface of the earth; that after destroying the traditional village, we have re-created it on a global scale. Rather the opposite seems to be true: There is no "dialectical spiral," there is only an irresistible process whereby any vestiges of rural communities are systematically wiped out. The most advanced areas of urban and industrial civilization are standing testimony to its effects. This monster village of which we sometimes fancy ourselves to be denizens differs from the ancient village not only in its technology (the rural economy was a perfect model of recycling; the farms produced hardly any waste and everything was reused, whereas the problem of waste disposal is one of the major worries of our civilization), and not only in the dizzy rhythm of change that is far removed from the monotonous cycle of peasant life. It differs in that it is above all an imaginary, artificial village, a badly disguised cerebral substitute which leads to increasing nostalgia, albeit concealed beneath various ideological decorations, for the "genuine" village.

This television screen on which we watch, with just a few hours' delay, riots in Paris, corpses in Iran, a speech by the American president, and a football match in Sydney, far from making us familiar with the world, seems instead to efface the difference between reality and fiction in favor of the latter. Those wars, revolutions, sufferings, and horrors are just Westerns, thrillers, interesting fantasies of film producers. Reality, instead of becoming closer and more palpable, is converted into a literary fiction; the dense mass of visual and verbal information we try in vain to digest, instead of giving us the opportunity to participate in world affairs, offers us a world with which we identify only esthetically, with some pleasure and no responsibility. The real village is a world of personal, unmediated contacts that are important in life. The global village therefore does not and cannot exist.

The destruction of the village and the mobility of life mean not only the progressive loss of that relatively stable and quasi-natural milieu, the neighborhood; they also mean an end to the human space that had once been a frame of reference on which our world built itself up step by step. The concepts of home, the family house, the links from generation to generation, and with them the very idea of childhood, seem to be on the way to extinction. Being everywhere we are nowhere; our space is purely Cartesian, without privileged points. It is perhaps difficult to grasp this loss or to define it in the categories of empirical sociology, but it is nonetheless real and really experienced. People have repeatedly depicted those new districts of great cities, which though well planned and properly equipped with all kinds of comforts, stay mysteriously dead and indifferent, producing no community, no spiritual space where anyone would like to strike roots.

As we drift in a geometrical infinity, incapable of defining ourselves by reference to an order that transcends us, without the image of such an order and thus without rules that would mark our field of natural responsibilities, our needs tend to inflate boundlessly. The subjective feeling of privation now has nothing to do with what we already have. Real resources not being inexhaustible, we often fall victim to painful hunger amid abundance; and the real, physiologically defined misery which is around us or of which we are aware has no relevance to this feeling.

And so, in both our political slogans and our philosophical speculations, we fall prey to the same vain nostalgia for the village that has haunted Western civilization for over two centuries, since the beginning of urbanization and industrialization. Vico, recently rediscovered and now attracting the attention not only of historians but also of dissatisfied young people, had already described periodical and inevitable declines of civilizations in terms that would soon become popular among post-Rousseauists and Romantic critics of modernity: the disappearance of myth and authority, the dissolution of spontaneous tribal solidarity, the exclusive absorption of everyone with private interests. Is it our fate endlessly to repeat all those pathetic clichés about "atomization," solitude in a crowd, the "mechanization" of life, the destruction of familial, tribal, and national bonds, the "depersonalization" of rootless people, "reification" and the vanishing Gemeinschaft? It seems we are indeed condemned to do this, and we invent new formulas to refresh a little the obsolete vocabulary of Rousseau, the German Romanticists, Saint-Simoniens, the young Marx.

Our spiritual life revolves around the same dreams: to revive the arcadian imagery or to drive it out and dismiss it as a puerile and reactionary folly. What is the philosophy that has fed us for decades but the neurosis of exiles from paradise—genuine or imaginary, it does not matter—the result of repeated attempts to face a life that can no longer discover an intelligible order in established mythologies or in the feeling of tribal solidarity, a life that offers no place of identification with a whole? Heidegger's early metaphysics seems to have been obsessed by the contrast between the man who tries to escape his freedom and responsibility, to dissolve himself within the ready-made convenient anonymity, and the man who looks for his roots in the ineffable Being and in this quest reasserts his own irreducible existence. The early metaphysics of Sartre, on the other hand, seemed to express an unhappy acceptance of a world that offers us only two possibilities: either we slide, disingenuously, into inauthenticity, into a universe of things, or we remain in our empty freedom, with no hope of finding roots and identifying with a real community. Now that everyone separately creates his own time from his own unlimited freedom, no common time can emerge to provide the framework for a communal existence. Therefore there *can* be no community; we can only escape, in bad faith, to the false shelter of the world of things, and our encounters with other people are mainly based on our desire to possess them.

After abandoning his philosophy of existence, Sartre tried to sketch a community that is constantly building itself within a revolutionary "project" and, without ever attaining a stable shape (remnants of his previous battles against "reification") provides the participants with a kind of identity. This seems, alas, to be another illusory return: Since revolution is, by definition, a process whereby institutionalized forms of social life are destroyed, it cannot establish itself as a permanent way of life. And though the active groups experience during the process a strong feeling of collective identity, this is possible only in the short periods of euphoria that are inevitably followed by bitter disappointment once the institutions begin to reassert themselves. Revolution conceived as a device to appease minds craving for a permanent identity cannot be but an adolescent chimera.

This need to belong to a genuinely experienced community, those dreams of a life where people communicate directly, without the intermediary of institutions, has been repeatedly described as a reactionary and desperate attempt to annihilate modern civilization and find refuge in a serene barbarity. Reactionary or not, this need persists in us more strongly than ever, and it expresses itself in a variety of ideological masks. In any event, to claim that the adjective *reactionary* is not merely descriptive (signifying a return to something which has disappeared), but that it involves a pejorative value judgment, we must admit not only that there is progress, but that there is nothing but progress: *Return* implies return to something worse. To use the adjective *reactionary* in a normative sense, we must espouse a global theory of incessant and inevitable progress, a theory which, to say the least, is not quite unshakable.

Here is an example of this confusion. When Adorno attacked Heidegger's metaphysics, he associated the idea of a return to "the roots" with the Nazi ideology of "blood and soil." Even if such an association was justified, it is no more than a third of the truth, and the other two-thirds is still to be added. First, what else could Adorno himself offer us except the global condemnation of industrial and bureaucratic civilization that imprisons us in its "reified" forms, except praise for the culture of feudal elites? And (this is the last third) once we reflect upon the spectacular success—brief as it might be in historical terms—of Nazi ideology, we are tempted to see in it a monstrously barbaric rebirth of the same romantic nostalgia, of the same search for a lost tribal community, for "organic" bonds (to use the suggestive and deceptive catchword of the post-Rousseauist tradition).

Romantic sources of National Socialism have of course been discussed and analyzed on many occasions. It is not enough to say that the undisguised cruelty of this ideology, its patent barbarity and its universal condemnation have made it impotent; the Romantic inspirations that once contributed to its emergence are still viable. One finds them frequently in both Leftist and Rightist political phraseology; one finds them in the malaise of youth in the most developed countries, even if this malaise is sometimes expressed in grotesquely naive ideas and desperately counterproductive activities. The search for new forms of religiosity, the successes of various charismatic sects, the exploration of the wisdom and legends of the eternally mysterious Orient, various techniques of collective psychotherapy—all these are symptoms of the same bizarre disease, which is intimately linked with the vague feeling of having lost the ability of so-called direct communication. Through all this, of course, a wide field has been opened to all sorts of charlatanism and deception, yet the very fact that human needs can easily be exploited by sellers of false medicine proves that the needs are genuine and urgent.

This yearning after the Eldorado of a lost conviviality, this quest for a *bei-sich-sein*, persists and develops in social and psychological conditions far different from those in which the Romantic revolt arose in Europe, and those changes have given a self-contradictory character to this entire spiritual movement.

On the one hand, the increasing influence of the state in the social and economic spheres, the inexorable process—resulting in part from demographic expansion and technological progress—of concentrating major decisions in the centers of power (and I have in mind democratic countries and not Communist or military dictatorships) lead to a widespread feeling of the impotence of the individual and unceasing complaints about "big government." Time and again the feeling is expressed that the forms of participation offered to people in representative democracies are inefficient, that all the channels of influence are blocked by an established apparatus and bound, in their own interest, to feed the Leviathan. People know this, but they can suggest no viable alternative.

On the other hand, it is thanks to us that the Leviathan flourishes—not only because it is indispensable, but because the demands we make of it unavoidably contribute to its growth. Throughout the civilized world we see society degenerating into infantilism—a reverse side of the welfare state. We become accustomed to the idea that it is the duty of the state and of its omnipotent bureaucracy to distribute happiness; whatever goes wrong, even in our private affairs, the state is to be blamed. The state should take care of all aspects of my life—my work, my health, my body, my marriage. This growing immaturity brings an obvious totalitarian threat; once the need for security with which the state is expected to supply us becomes the supreme value, we become ready to let ourselves be nationalized mind and body, at the price of devolving full responsibility for our lives onto the state. This is the central principle of totalitarianism: the nationalization of everything, including human beings; the promise of security in exchange for total submission; an end to the inevitable insecurities of personal life for the renouncing of any personal life at all.

Briefly, we are torn asunder by incompatible desires: We resent the state's interference in our affairs, for it is when faced with it that we are made aware of our own weaknesses, and thus we want less and less state control. At the same time, we want to be protected from all imaginable evils with which nature or society may threaten us; we want a guarantee of total security, a guarantee that our particular cause will be favored above all others. Thus we want more and more state control.

This schizophrenic attitude is perhaps best expressed in the Leftist ideologies which promise us that once their adherents come to power, everything will be both planned and spontaneous. Still, analogous contradictions, more or less concealed under nebulous slogans, can easily be found in the ideologies of almost all political movements except for those of the extremists. The messages of the main European parties, setting aside rhetorical differences, usually carry two promises that contradict each other. On the one hand, they tell us: All the others want to regulate your life from above, by bureaucratic decisions; we are the only ones who want you, the people, to take all the decisions that concern yourselves; briefly, we want society to be its own master! Yet they promise us, on the other hand, that the state which that same party would steer will protect all the interests of all social layers, that it will take care of the poor and of children, of schools and hospitals, that it will support the legitimate aspirations of workers and of the middle classes, that it will fight energetically against unemployment and inflation, and so on. To put it crudely, the political ideologies seem more and more to promise us a society which will blissfully and harmoniously combine an anarchist with a totalitarian paradise: The state will be nothing and, at the same time, it will be everything; it will take care of everything and it will hand over power to the people; everyone will be protected like a baby in its cradle and everyone will have perfect freedom of individual expression, of personal self-realization.

Indeed, in recent decades, political parties have ceased to be or even appear to be what they had been or appeared to be before; that is, political organs of well-defined clusters of interests and of specific social layers. All parties now make increasing claims to represent the needs of the whole of society, to be at the service of all, to favor the welfare of all groups and to incarnate all aspirations. In order to make such claims they are forced to make their language more and more blurred, their slogans increasingly vague. This applies also to the Eurocommunist parties, in which appeals to the ruthless class struggle are gradually being replaced by the concept of a national interest. As a result of those changes, all parties, except for the extremist ones—Moscow-oriented Communist parties, fundamentalist Marxist or Communist sects, explicitly racist or Fascist parties—are desperately searching for their own identity, and none of them is really sure what it is.

On the ideological level, we witness mortal battles between meaningless battle cries or shibboleths; they will do to distinguish rival groups, but have lost almost all intelligible content. Politicians are incapable of defining terms like *social justice, equality, the people, freedom of initiative, the quality of life*, and the like. Those expressions are useful as conventional signs or as colors to identify hostile regiments, but their semantic value has nearly vanished. There are, of course, differences between political orientations, but there is practically no transition from daily politics, where the struggle is real, to the empty general ideas. Many of us feel that the political divisions we inherited from the nineteenth century or from the period of World War I, divisions that still determine the structure of the parties and their language, do not correspond either to the most urgent problems of our world or to the real, though often subterranean, crystallizations of interests on a global or national scale, and that the existing political formations are ready to crumble. But they continue to live not only because by their very hostilities they support each other, but because attempts to reshuffle the existing spectrum, though frequent, have thus far been abortive. They have not been able to offer a clear alternative and, more often than not, they live in the same generalities.

But this is hardly a reproach, for reproaches in such conditions are justifiable only when a better proposal is available. In the meantime the feeling of being cornered in an intellectual cul-de-sac seems to be almost universal. Great political perturbations, revolutions, and civil wars in the Third World are of interest to us mainly because of their significance in global conflicts. Otherwise ideological symbols hardly matter: Islam or scientific socialism (or both, simultaneously), democracy or liberation, such words are to us but the symbols of political alliances. It is perhaps not so for the participants in those events, at least perhaps not for some of them; but even so, the distance between the labels and the acting forces reveals to what extent social realities have lost the means of expression. There is often talk of the "crisis" of parliamentary institutions and their inability to cope with the problem of representation. No doubt there is some truth to these criticisms; however, since the alternatives to parliamentary institutions have so far been dictatorial institutions, those strictures either remain sterile—if they do not suggest other forms that would guarantee the same civil liberties and the same protection of human rights—or they simply reinforce totalitarian dreams.

Democratic movements in despotic regimes—Communist or otherwise—are in this respect very conveniently placed: They can be unequivocal in voicing their claims. When they say "we want free elections, abolition of censorship, freedom of speech, freedom of political and trade union movements, and legal guarantees against the police," no one is in doubt as to the point and content of their claims. If instead someone says that "alienation has to be done away with" or "social justice established," he does nothing but manipulate words whose only function is to channel existing feelings of frustration and discontent for non-articulated political purposes. Where are we to find this cruel Alienation which a noble Brutus could drag out from its hiding place and stab to death? And once we try to translate such a word into well-defined and practical proposals, we immediately face a mountain of complicated and interdependent problems we do not know how to tackle.

Almost everybody knows there is no universal key to the world-wide difficulties we inefficiently try to cope with; that the old liberal opinion that everything will be arranged if everyone separately takes care of his own affairs cannot be taken seriously any longer; that the anarchist or leftist ideal of perfect self-management of productive units would, if it were feasible, inevitably lead to the economy of unlimited competition of the past century, including all its nefarious effects—extreme inequalities, crises, mass bankrupticies, mass unemployment and poverty; that the opposite ideal of a state which nationalizes everything and takes all responsibility can be implemented only in the form of totalitarian slavery. Leaving the ideals aside, we are left only with more or less clumsy compromises between incompatible demands ultimately rooted in our need to have both total security and infinite space for individual expression. And we will never have both.

Everyone seems to agree that the need for global solutions is gaining in urgency and that the greatest dangers we face can conceivably be reversed or alleviated only on a world scale, an insight that hardly needs justification. And it seems very unlikely that such solutions will be found and applied within the time we have left before some kind of apocalypse occurs. Hardly a week goes by without the press feeding us sinister prophecies made by the most competent people: There will be a new ice age and there is nothing we can do to prevent it, or the manmade increase in temperature will cause slow but inexorable flood; we will suffocate as a result of air pollution or because of the deforestation of Amazonia; famine will decimate us because of overpopulation or by the expansion of deserts.

Global war apart, there are numerous variations on possible universal catastrophes, and most people have no means of verifying them or of weighing the arguments. We both trust and fear science: We think it can save us or lead to our extermination; at the same time, we are aware of our inability to control it. Enough to think that one now has to be a highly qualified physicist to understand the obligatory international definition of a meter. In democratic countries, the population is sometimes required in referendums to make decisions on the effects of which the most competent people are in violent disagreement; no wonder then that the decisions are actually made for reasons quite irrelevent to those specialized debates. There is some comfort in thinking that the chances of a right decision (meaning a decision of which the outcome is in keeping with expectations) are the same, whether it is made by experts or the result of accidental popular emotions.

The problem is even more glaring when we think in terms of "global solutions." Who are the infallible experts to suggest them, and how can the rest of us, who do not pretend to be competent, decide on them? The most effective democratic mechanisms can often produce mediocre leaders, a fact not only borne out by experience, but implied by the very word *mediocre*; despotic mechanisms produce mediocre or criminal leaders more easily, even though the mediocrity is usually of a different kind and more dangerous. Needless to say, a pluralist and open society has more chances, albeit of course no guarantees, of making important decisions on rational grounds and, above all, of correcting its mistakes. Still, despotism, especially Communist despotism, does have its virtues: It offers security at the price of servility, it liberates us from the obligation to have ideas or opinions of our own and to take part in public affairs, it rocks us to sleep in an ocean of the optimist lie (and who has proved that one necessarily lives better in truth than in a lie?).

That social forces favoring the totalitarian tendency will not prevail, after all, is not a prediction supported by an unprejudiced calculation, but a wager based on our belief that the human will for freedom is sufficiently strong to withstand them. Clearly, some aspects of our situation favor the totalitarian tendency, while others do not. Among the former, military considerations apart, we find all the economic imperatives that are conducive to the concentration of power in the state apparatus insofar as this apparatus has to be responsible for the distribution of scarce goods (soil, raw materials, plants, sources of energy) and for the general "health" of the economy; these tasks cannot be regulated by the automatic play of market forces. There is also a powerful psychological factor, in the form of that infantilism mentioned above: our increasing readiness to rate security above all other goods and to expect from the state a prescription for happiness and a medicine against evils both collective and private; to blame the state if it cannot deliver this medicine on all occasions.

The opposing factors include not only all the repugnant aspects of totalitarianism, its oppressive, mendacious, and anticultural nature, but its incurable economic and technological inefficiency as well—weaknesses confirmed by experience and clearly linked to the political structure. They include increasing opposition against the state power, even if this opposition is sometimes expressed in childish form. They include, as an incalculable yet powerful psychological counterweight, the human need to have a large field of personal life and of individual expression, free from state-imposed regulation.

All these forces have dangers of their own. The search for the lost village, combined with the belief in the infinite possibilities of the state, produces the sinister illusion, widespread among leftist ideologists, that social techniques can be efficiently employed to create a conflictless society: in other words, that it is possible to institutionalize fraternity by violence and bureaucratic decree. Thus on the one hand, socialism has been strongly identified with the cult of bureaucracy; on the other, liberal and conservative advocates of economic and political decentralization try to cope awkwardly with increasing ecological and economic imperatives that the game of supply and demand cannot possibly fulfill. It is conceivable that in some countries radically liberal solutions resulting in gigantic unemployment could be repaid by rapid growth of productivity; however, such solutions being for obvious social and political reasons impracticable, the government must seek compromises that are always uncertain and lame. Briefly, on both sides radical solutions are worse than the disease they are supposed to cure, whereas partial and nonradical ones are necessarily provisional and cannot satisfy people in search of the definitive salvation of the world.

A similar contradiction between the quest for security and the need for freedom can be found in nationalist ideas and movements. We must distinguish, of course, truly oppressed nationalities which are prevented by a foreign power from developing their distinctive culture from their oppressors, from ethnic minorities in democratic countries, and from tribal groups that have no clearly developed historical consciousness but are nevertheless identifiable enough. There are, however, analogous tendencies in conditions that differ widely in many respects. The nation that is a cultural community is identified with the state; once national values are proclaimed to be supreme, this identification leads naturally to the cult of the state and leaves no rights to individuals. Thus we have, on the one hand, a peculiar nationalism whose focus is a state with no ethnic homogeneity, and on the other, cultural isolationism and protectionism in conditions where no real national oppression exists—as if national freedom consisted in the growth of customs posts and passport control offices. Once again we see how the mirage of "natural" and "organic" solidarity can easily be translated into the glorification of oppressive tribalisms.

Even ecological movements are prone to similar ambiguities. If they confine themselves to general slogans about the need to protect nature from destruction, they will naturally meet with little opposition. Once real choices have to be made, however, problems arise. We cannot ask both "stop the construction of nuclear power plants" and "give us unlimited amounts of cheap energy." One should rather say unambiguously: "We are ready to have less than we have—less food, less travel, less heating, less of everything." This is not exactly what one hears; it is rather: "You, the state, are obliged to supply us with all the energy we need, without incurring danger or interfering with nature." However, since here, as elsewhere, our choices must be based on a rational calculation of the risks, costs, technical possibilities, and social consequences of each solution, ecological ideologies often manifest that same infantilism which characterizes the desire both to believe in the omnipotence of the state and to get rid of it. No politician, no political movement, can afford to say to the citizens of relatively rich countries: "You have too much, you could easily be satisfied with less." Individuals, on the other hand, can and ought to say so; churches can say so and occasionally do, without great success. We have, for that matter, the convenient word *consumerism*, which we are free to use as long as it suggests a vague moral reproach and as long as we do not try to translate it into well-defined practical projects.

No one can predict what the confrontation of these powerful tendencies will bring in the coming decades. We feel that by now neither the ideologies nor the political divisions we inherited from the past apply to the challenges of modern technology and demographic conditions or to the enormous and perhaps increasing disproportions between different regions of our planet; we feel vaguely that the mechanisms of representative democracy are not properly adapted to those conditions, even though they are the best we have to protect us against despotism. Other viable forms of democratic and representative government have not been invented, let alone tested; possibly, if they should ever emerge, many of the forces involved in present conflicts will contribute to their development. If any synthesis comes about, however, we should expect it to proceed in conformity with the familiar course of human history: amid dramatic convulsions.

Discussion: Schwartz Paper

Schwartz: I would describe my state of feeling more as anxiety than as pessimism. I think this anxiety may be increased by the fact that I am coming from the United States, where there has been a revival of what I would call a kind of optimism. And one might say that things have not so far, except for the nuclear threat, turned out to be as bad as they seemed to be. But some of the impulses that led to those horrors are still present.

Maier: Schwartz uses the word *immobilism,* and the paper very skillfully goes through most of the leading categories of twentieth-century thought and shows aspects of continuity. But certainly immobilism implies a judgment about being stuck some place, which continuity would not. Why do you choose *immobilism,* and why you would reject *continuity?*

Schwartz: I used the word *immobilism* on purpose, because we have such an obsession with originality that just to speak of continuity suggests immobilism. Every Monday somebody comes up with a new vocabulary, so I meant to use a harsher word than just *continuity.*

Kyogoku: I wish to put forth a case in defense of the twentieth century. When one asserts his identity to others, one insists that there is distance. It is quite human for anyone to insist that the twentieth century is different from any other century. I think it is in line with basic human nature.

Schwartz: Certainly, as we move into the twenty-first century, there are things from the Enlightenment tradition that I would very much like to see preserved, wherever we move, such as legal protection of human rights. To that extent, I still regard myself as an old-fashioned liberal—perhaps more eighteenth-century liberal than nineteenth-century socialist. But I do think there are precious things, particularly the notion of human rights and also the notion that in the end one cannot prove the truth of any doctrine by physical coercion: in other words, the notion of intellectual freedom. So I certainly do not regard myself as an enemy of everything in the twentieth century.

169

Yamada: In the eighteenth century, science and technology were two different things. In the nineteenth century they began converging. Electrical engineering and chemical engineering were products of science and technology converging upon one another. This process was completed during World War II, when science and technology accomplished their combination, both externally and internally.

Now, what about twentieth-century technology? It is based upon implementing nineteenth-century ideas. Even today, a substantial portion of technology is based upon nineteenth-century science. Much of twentieth-century science has not yet been translated into technology, or is still in an experimental, embryonic stage. What is the likely direction of twentieth-century science developing into a future technology? In my view, it will take two directions. One as in the case of silicon: individual propensities or properties of special materials will be further elucidated and exploited. Another direction will be that, as the mechanisms and propensities of these materials become better known, technology will be advanced by making use of these things.

To give you an example: at present a great deal of scientific manpower and funds are poured into cancer research, and knowledge of the mechanisms of carcinogenic genes, the birth of cancerous genes, will do a great deal to explain the secrets of life at the molecular level. It will probably be at the molecular level that we will see the birth of a new technology to control human life. For example, the study of the cerebral mechanism will show that the generation of some particular chemical elements in our cerebrum or in our big brain will affect our sentiments—happiness, sadness, and so on.

Technology has both good and evil qualities from the value point of view. It is not that technology can be either good or bad depending on how you use it; there is both intrinsic goodness and badness in technology. A case in point is the insecticide DDT. The bulk of human beings have been freed from malaria, thanks to DDT. But DDT is also highly toxic. These two facts are inseparable. Nuclear technology is another case in point. To me, nuclear power generation has no future. For one thing, we cannot experiment with the safety of nuclear reactors. How can you reproduce a meltdown? You cannot experiment with meltdowns in the laboratory and build a safety apparatus. Second, a huge amount of radioactive waste is generated that will become safe only after several million years. Unless and until we find an effective way of waste disposal, nuclear reactors will not be safe for us, because for many millions of years reactors will keep producing dangerous materials. And of course some of these products from reactors can be used as destructive weapons.

What do you do with all these reactors when they become obsolete? When reactors have a high degree of radioactivity, how do you scrap these instruments? Nobody has produced any plausible, constructive ideas about this. So for these reasons and many others, nuclear energy to me is not safe. In terms of value judgment, this particular technology has good and evil in it, and they cannot be separated. The more advanced the technology, the greater the amount of evil, together with the amount of good.

But having said all this, is alternative technology such as that advocated by ecologists feasible? I offer my view that it does not offer solutions. True, given the present state and structure of technology, it can supplement and complement it, but it cannot be a substitute for it.

Schwartz: I do not wish to give any impression of being anti-science, but sometimes one wishes that there were not always an immediate application of scientific theory. What I would suggest is that maybe we start thinking of technological development as just a kind of personal process of history; it involves decisions. I think the time has come when there should be a dialogue with technology. In other words, I would bring technology into the question of values again.

Hersch: I think Schwartz has dared in his very natural, simple way, without being categorical, to say a thing that is always very disagreeable to say; namely, that the king is naked. The pretense of being absolutely new. The pretense of being absolutely revolutionary. The pretense of always being a radical breakthrough. I believe this pretense brings sterility with it. Now, about immobilism: Perhaps in philosophy, instead of *immobilism* we could say *sterility*.

Now I would like to say something about language. There is

a tendency that is paradoxically in contradiction with itself. Language has to be considered real in the sense of things being real. Language is as real or more real than what usually is called reality. On the other hand, language prevents us from reaching reality, or comes instead of reality. Somehow reality disappears and is disaggregated through language. I believe that theories of language are in themselves an attack upon human consciousness in its fundamental condition—that means in its relationship to something that exists and which we have to rejoin and which gives meaning to truth. It is true that we have had too simple a conception of truth. And in this sense, theories of language have brought to our consciousness something very important. But insofar as they destroyed the sense of reality and the relationship to reality, they are extremely bad. They say that no human being is thinking, that the language is thinking by itself through the human being. In French, *ça pense*, not *je pense*. So there is no responsibility for thinking, no intention, no finality. Somehow it dissolves into a meaningless technology. And I believe these are very deep and dangerous attacks against human consciousness.

Friedländer: Could we not say that from the start of industrialization, immobilities reversed themselves? That is, industrial and technological changes develop more and more rapidly, but on the other side our mental structures remain immobile; and at that level of mental structures, immobile history remains. If that is true, one of the many problems would be the growing discrepancy between more and more rapid changes at the technological, industrial level and constant immobility at the level of our mental structures—the forms of our minds, I would say. How long can this discrepancy go on? I see two logical possibilities. Either this immobility at the mental level is the anchor or the roots that allow change, or the growing tension between more and more rapid change at the technological level and the impossibility for mental structures to adapt creates the nostalgia Kolakowski speaks of. And then, obviously, technological change may be used in a rather horrendous way to bring modern society into what is a kind of dream of immobility.

Schwartz: On the business of a nostalgia for the past, I hope I was not taken as implying that there is any past period of human history I would like to go back to. I do think that in dealing with the future, we have to open ourselves to the whole of human history as far as thought is concerned. And not only to Western thought, but to non-Western thought as well.

Maier: I think that the question is choice, and this is obviously difficult. I would try and relativize or historicize the present conjunction of technology in the world. I am not sure with Friedländer that this is a question of mental structures. I am not sure I believe in mental structures so rigidly, because I do not think we are frozen into a virtual structural determinism by dealing with science. I do think we are at a point, a sort of gap where problems of collective decision are very difficult because we cannot envisage all the ramifications of choices. We are at that point where processes of decision making are slowly changing. Now I have no great solution, but I do think a certain amount of humility toward history would suggest that we not get overly pessimistic about the present conjunction, assuming that we can avert what is obviously the end of civilization—a nuclear holocaust. I think that if a conference on the twentieth century comes to the conclusion that this stuff is just beyond our capacity to cope with, it leaves a very one-sided message. In fact, examples of great civilizations show that there are choices.

Joll: I think both Schwartz and Hersch have been rather unfair to some of the Anglo-Saxon philosophers of linguistic analysis, who have taken over one aspect of Wittgenstein's thought. It seems to me that many of them—by no means all—are trying to clarify the kind of discourse we use. It is only by distinguishing levels of discourse, I think, that we can begin to see how to use words in a way that will make them really mean something.

This leads me to the second point. It seems to me that one of the great dangers of the contemporary world is the obfuscation of language in the sense that metaphors, catch phrases, are constantly used to mask the real intention of the speaker. It is a topic that has been much elaborated on by George Orwell and others. And this seems to me to be particularly important at a time when a body of universal clichés is being developed, particularly in the discussion of international relations where, for example, whatever the differences between their policies, the Americans and the Russians use the same language to defend what they are doing. Until we can purge the language in such a way as to use words to mean something quite specific, we are only liable to make our condition worse.

Structuralism originated with the study of linguistics; people began to look for the underlying structures common to many languages. They have tried to apply structuralist ideas to other branches of science, to anthropology, to history, to literature, and so on. What they are trying to do, while recognizing the differences of language, is nevertheless to find what there is in common—what is the basic structure of the human mind, what is the basic structure of the development of human history, what are the basic structures of human society—in the hope (maybe a vain one) of trying to find some sort of common ground on which we can discuss these very different phenomena. So I myself would not be too pessimistic about the application of the study of language to human society.

Mommsen: What went wrong in the development of Western societies in general in the early twentieth century was almost totally in the realm of politics and of the social organization of society. It does not seem to have been due to technological developments at all. I tend to believe, by and large, that the reason we have had these great catastrophes, in particular the so-called Fascist systems, was partly because of an unwillingness to put up with the results of modern life.

Schwartz said something about the great philosophical schemes of the nineteenth century, those of Hegel, Marx, Spencer—that they discarded the role of individual human consciousness. I myself have the feeling that they tried to develop grandiose schemes in order to prove that man is still on top of things. Hegel presupposed a sort of basic unity between the individual and the universal process of history which we nowadays would consider far too optimistic—at least we cannot buy it that easily. Marx designed great schemes for reconstructing social reality in order to get rid of *Entfremdung*, alienation, with a rather naive belief in progress as we find it most outspokenly in the philosophy of Spencer. We are much more aware of the limitations of developing general philosophical schemes today. I really think that in the twentieth century we are in a situation in which we have lost this rather naive belief in rationality as a substantive principle. We are very much aware of the relative conditions under which one can talk about rationality, and that perhaps is not so bad a position from which to cope with our problems.

Kolakowski: I think that putting together Wittgenstein and Heidegger is a reasonable approach. What they have in common is the reversal of the Cartesian hope that we might one day find or that perhaps we have already found some transcendental ground or observation point on the world which presupposes nothing—an absolute positionless standpoint. Both in Heidegger and in later Wittgenstein this Cartesian hope has been abandoned. It has been recognized that language is not transparent to reality. There is no such thing as language that presupposes nothing. On the other hand, however, this very admission involves an anti-utopian view, giving up the utopia of a transcendental philosophy. Linguistics as it developed in the nineteenth century was reputed, and with some reason, to be the only human science that achieved a kind of strict rigor and was able to formulate what might be called laws in the human sciences. Many people involved in various branches of the human sciences tried to ape linguistics in order to make their branches as good as the linguistics of de Saussure perhaps was. But there was more than that to this effort. I think that in this fascination there is a contradiction. On the one hand, there is the feeling that language is actually the only reality we have to do with. This fascination displays the same anti-utopian spirit that we find both in Heidegger and in ordinary language philosophy. On the other hand, it petrified language to such an extent that it itself started operating as a kind of absolute reality, a primordial reality which we have always to start with and which eventually gives us an insight of a metaphysical kind.

Schwartz: In a way what I have been talking about is what I call technological utopianism. There is the adage that there is no problem created by technology which technology will not cure. Well, I believe that is a lie; there are lots of problems created by technology that technology will not cure, it seems to me. So this is a utopian myth—that every problem technology creates will necessarily have a new technological fix in the future. The idea that every new theoretical advance science makes should necessarily be applied at least should be a matter of discussion.

Now it may well be that some of the movements of the twentieth century were a felt need to escape from some of the results of modern life, but I am not sure that felt need has disappeared. These irrational movements are still very much alive. So it is not so much empty technologism, but antitechnological utopianism that I mean to address.

Discussion: Kolakowski Paper

Kolakowski: In the second quarter of the nineteenth century and in particular in the 1840s, two main ideologies of which we are inheritors came to fruition, socialism and nationalism. Both can be considered antimodernist, Romantic reactions in the sense that both expressed a malaise of civilization—that as a result of industrialization and of the ruin of the traditional village, we were losing the real sense of community. Both of them, while expressing this kind of antimodernist revolt, gave birth in due course to various forms of totalitarian ideologies and movements. In this kind of antimodernist spirit, in the feeling of our malaise about the lost community, we continue the nineteenth-century tenets, even though the ghost that keeps haunting us appears in various disguises, different from the nineteenth-century forms.

I stress especially one point—namely, what I call the growing ideological infantilism that is perhaps a byproduct or to some extent the cause of the special role taken by the state and the bureaucratic structures of modern societies. We, of course, resent the growing control and supervision of the state bureaucracy and structure over various aspects of our lives, and lament so-called big government. On the other hand, we have become used to the fact that we should expect from the state the recipe for happiness. We somehow expect that the state should be the distributor of happiness, and we blame the state for all the failures of our lives, for all the unsatisfied needs, as if it were the duty of the state to distribute happiness. Therefore, we want both less state and more state at the same time.

These self-contradictory expectations are expressed in various political ideologies, both of the Left and of the Right. We are told at the same time that the state will be nothing and everything. Most ideologies (inherited either from the nineteenth century or from the period of World War I) promise us a worth that will harmoniously combine an anarchist paradise with a totalitarian paradise. We need security and we need freedom or room for individual expansion. We want to have both in unlimited form, and we will never have both. This is why I believe that the language of contemporary political ideologies is bound to become more and more obscure in order to cover the self-contradictory character of ideologies which, in fact, are ready to crumble. I perceive in this self-contradictory characteristic of our attitude a totalitarian danger. However, my paper ends with a kind of timid optimism, which again is based not on any unprejudiced analysis of existing trends, but rather on the belief that the human need for freedom is as strong as the need for security and that eventually we will not let ourselves be swallowed up and deprived of our personal existence by the omnipotent state.

Maruyama: With regard to continuity and discontinuity mentioned by Kolakowski, I cannot but question why we should or can draw so clear a line between the nineteenth and twentieth centuries, in spite of the very theme of this symposium. I see greater significance in the new trends visible in various fields, not so much in the beginning of this century as in the last decades of the nineteenth century. There was not only the rise of socialism and the labor movement, but also what A. V. Dicey called "collectivism," which became evident in the latter half of the nineteenth century. The change and turmoil is vividly described in J. S. Mills's autobiography. And the same is true of the psychological impact of mass movements which G. Le Bon describes for the first time in his *Psychologie des foules* (1895). The impact of the movement was bound to play, as we all know, a formidable role in the twentieth century. The revolt against—or, more mildly, the skepticism about—rationalism and positivism which had been hitherto prevalent became something akin to *les idées-forces* since Nietzsche, Bergson, and Kierkegaard, and I suppose it is these philosophers who continue exerting or even increasing their tremendous influence on the twentieth century, an influence that both Schwartz and Kolakowski have criticized. I wonder if the philosophical trends characterizing the twentieth century are not a parasitic outgrowth of the intellectual products of the late nineteenth century.

Our dependence on the nineteenth century is not limited to philosophical thinking alone. Look at the symbolist movement in literature represented by Charles Baudelaire and Stéphane Mallarmé, who were succeeded by Paul Valéry in the twentieth century. Take Dostoevsky's case. I think he was a prophet, far earlier than George Orwell, of what can become of the colossal bureaucratization of the whole society in which each individual is destined to be but one key on a pianoforte. Recall that Richard Wagner paved the way for atonal music in his famous Tristan's chord (*Tristan-Akkord*).

I used to say facetiously that the twentieth century's only unique contribution to civilization, an invention entirely unknown in the nineteenth century, is nuclear weapons. Nuclear weapons are qualitatively different from conventional bombs, as is painfully evident in the lasting influences of nuclear pollution and disease. My point here is simply that it may be more adquate to discuss the whole problem in terms of the continuity rather than discontinuity between the late nineteenth and the first half of the twentieth century.

Kolakowski: You certainly are right in pointing out the central inadequacy of our language in dealing with such matters as continuity and discontinuity. What kind of conceptual instruments do we have to say this or that change in such and such areas of culture marks a discontinuity, or to deny it? We have nothing remotely comparable to differential calculus in the human sciences in order to state where the continuity or discontinuity is. We are thrown upon our uncertain intuitions in dealing with such matters. Nevertheless, physicists would probably agree that the theory of relativity and the quantum theory marked a turning point in the development of the physical sciences: they introduced a new way of thinking. Did nonfigurative painting mark a discontinuity in the history of painting? I would tend to say yes. However, such statements about discontinuity can always be challenged, because we lack adequate conceptual instruments to deal with such matters.

The same can be said about centuries, because after all, what is a century? It is an arbitrary span of time, a product of the decimal system we use in counting, which has nothing transcendental in it. We have no reason to elevate the number one hundred into a kind of historical law. There is no such thing as an arbitrary counting system that can be projected onto history. Nevertheless, we cannot do without some more or less arbitrary divisions in the historical process. And I think we are right in supposing that there are points of discontinuity in history; that it is not unreasonable to think some events were more important than others; that some events in political history, in religious history, or in the history of values and cultures were really crucial. While there is no chronological parallelism in the development of various areas of culture, I do not think we can do without a belief that there is a hierarchy of importance in historical events.

Karl: My generation of Americans was raised to believe that local government was that which had to be transcended in some form, if not totally transformed, in order to produce rights for many of the citizens of the United States. So the recent movement, the recent concern with localism, with community, has a rather discordant sound for many of us who do not see local government or the sense of community as the answer to problems of development.

Kolakowski: The issue of decentralization and deregulation, the slogan of scrapping or at least enfeebling big government and centralization of decision is being heard from both the Left and the Right, in fact, in the most vocal way on the extreme Left and on the extreme Right. By extreme Left I do not mean Communist ideology, but anarchist ideology. We are in a predicament for which we can have no easy solution because, after all, on many occasions the intervention of the federal government was very important in breaking the resistance of the southern states against the legal equality of blacks. Without the federal government, those states would perhaps never have ended racial discrimination. But we cannot have the federal government settle for us issues that we like, and leave local or territorial units to deal only in issues where the solutions would be much more to our liking. We cannot have both. I am sympathetic to the idea of scrapping big government as much as possible. Nevertheless, I understand that there are many issues which cannot be dealt with except by big government.

Schwartz: What does one include within the precincts of the modern, of modernity? I have a reservation against making the whole Rousseau strain, the radical strain, something nonmodern. The quarrel between Voltaire and Rousseau was to my mind the quarrel within the Enlightenment. The whole Rousseau line does stress very much the moral side of things, and some people think that "modern" means a technological attitude and "moral" means a pretechnological attitude. It is, however, a moral attitude within the Enlightenment framework. The whole story of revolutionism is part of the dialectic of the modern world, and it is not a quarrel between the premodern world and the modern world. It is a quarrel within the modern world.

Second, the growth of reliance on the state relates to the fact that the whole mythology of the big state versus the individual—not even versus the local community—is a fiction too, it seems to me. This sharp dichotomy, either complete collectivism under state planning or the rugged individual, no longer fits the reality of our time. In some places one would like to see the growth of the state; in other places one would not like to see its growth, at least in a liberal state like America.

Yamada: At the dawn of the twentieth century, Newtonian physics was challenged when Planck came up with the quantum theory; and Einstein, the theory of relativity. What is the relationship among these three? In Newton's dynamics, in terms of scale, it was the dynamics of the solar system. The relativity theory is on the scale of the universe. The quantum theory is the dynamics of the atomistic world. In this sense, these three are discontinuous. But they are continuous in another respect, because in the law of relativity the speed of light is considered to be finite, but if you consider it infinite, then Newtonian dynamics can be explained.

Windsor: I share most of Kolakowski's pessimism, and I also, like a painting which is black and tinged with orange, put some faith in the clumsy compromises at the end of his paper. But I wonder if the pessimism might not also arise from the fact that the destruction of the village is not just a product of technological and industrial processes, but also a product of liberalism itself. In the preliberal or pre-Enlightenment era, the organic communities living in their villages were almost necessarily hostile to each other. They maintained their identity by separation from each other, and war was almost a social requirement. Belonging was therefore belonging only to one's group, not to any idea of humans more generally. To give one example of the change that came about, during the debate on the abolition of the slave trade in Britain at the end of the eighteenth century, Charles James Fox declared that slavery was based on the assumption that other people were other, and that he declared it to be inadmissible. And in this sense the liberal triumph which was embodied in the abolition of the slave trade was also the abolition of these organic communities.

From that kind of illustration and that kind of moment onward, what one can see is the attempt to create an idea of us being human. But that means, by necessity, the abolition of any kind of village. And it is this which produces the tensions you delineate, the way in which we lapse through nostalgia into infantilism or totalitarianism, or both. And we have not thought out a way of living with these tensions, which are themselves the product of the liberal Enlightenment. In that sense the liberal Enlightenment has imposed on us the need for thinking about what one means by humanity, but we have not yet thought out what it means. Liberalism has done us a lot of damage.

Maier: Kolakowski talks about those who seek community and describes this as infantile, because in a sense we cannot live without institutions. Anyone who lived through the university tumults of the last fifteen years understands that there is a great deal of truth in it. One found a student movement that really wanted to break through the crust of bureaucratic institutions and live in a type of unmediated presence with their teachers and their fellow students. Obviously, this is an impossible dream.

We have a bipolar type of political experience in the modern world. Politics as transaction: the ordinary day-to-day allocation of goods and values, symbolic goods and material goods through political discussion, voting, and such. And then politics is in a sense the creation of history. Politics is participation, one can say, in the making of history. Obviously this has problems, and yet I see no alternative in the modern world. I would argue that those who speak for politics as a transaction in a sense try and work in a little bit more of politics than infantilism.

Mommsen: My feeling is not so much that this is a pessimistic paper, but that it has a very distinct air of resignation. Weber, of course, made his gigantic onslaught on all sorts of substantive theories of social change. The rationalization he ended up with has been described as heroic pessimism. Yours is a little similar in tone perhaps, if not in substance. And I have a feeling that the paper presents variations on the theme of the alienation of man: man's having lost his original sense of community, where holistic philosophies provided answers in order to give him a secure place in a meaningful whole. Modern individuals are at home not in one community, but in peer groups of various kinds. One can perhaps say that communalized existence has been parceled out into many sections, but by and large it may not work that badly.

Perhaps I am a liberal in this sense, but I would think that the existence of controversial and even contradictory partial social philosophies is not only in itself not a bad thing, but a good thing inasmuch as that creates, I would say, a competitive pattern of social change, which makes freedom in a practical sense possible.

Nivat: Russian thought and Russian ideological quarrels all through the nineteenth century and, in a way, until now in the Soviet Union are full of the idea of the search for the community and the *sobornost*, the *conciliarity*. The idea that something will be lost definitively if the village community is destroyed has been common to two adversaries, the Slavophiles and the Occidentalists. Dostoevsky had a paradoxical answer to the kind of schizophrenia that is described in Kolakowsk's paper, schizophrenia of the man who wants both liberty and security. And his answer is given in *The Possessed*, in which Shigaliev says we'll put an end to that kind of schizophrenia, because four-fifths of humanity will have security and the other fifth will have liberty, so that schizophrenia, individually, will be transcended by a division in humanity; that was Dostoevsky's prophecy.

Kolakowski: I would be very glad to get rid of the concept of alienation altogether, because it has produced so much confusion and so many ideological catchwords with the hope of easy solutions for the entire predicament of mankind. Nevertheless, insofar as these words may be used at all, I would say that it is a vain dream, getting rid of alienation; alienation is life itself. All human efforts, all creativity inevitably include the process of alienation. Neither did I say that everything is bad in this process which I described. Whether it was resignation, I do not know. However, there are obviously areas of life which are technical or bureaucratic, and which it would be a puerile dream to get rid of. There is a distinction between these areas of communication and what we call personal communication.

It is a real distinction, and many people think that in the social processes themselves there is something that makes this personal communication less real, as it were. The medicine suggested for this malaise might be counterproductive or silly. The hippies who tried to build their own communities produced nothing. In fact, they spent their days and weeks doing nothing and not even talking to each other.

Nevertheless, the malaise I think is real, and the phenomenon itself is real. Even so, I would never say that the social processes which brought about this malaise are necessarily to be condemned, or that they brought nothing but evil: no. The simple fact is that life means tension. There is no such thing as life without tension. There is no such thing as progress that does not bring about changes we consider painful. All progress is pain, and therefore we are never in the position of opting between absolute evil and absolute good. We are doomed to clumsy compromise. It is not necessarily a tragedy, not necessarily a catastrophe. Life is simply like that.

Nevertheless, I would agree in a limited sense with what Maier said, that a little bit of utopianism might be healthy in politics. What I mean is that there are two kinds of utopianism. There is a utopianism consisting in the belief that there are technical means to bring about a society without conflict, without evil, without misfortunes—that there is a happy ending to history. There is another kind of quasi-utopianism that is Kantian, philosophically speaking, and which means that utopia is not something we can expect to be implemented by technical means, because such attempts can end only with totalitarian misery. But we have to have in mind in political activities something like a set of values, which we treat, to use Kantian idiom, as a regulative rather than a constitutive idea. And we need them indeed. In this sense, we need values that we consider not to be relative and that we want to be implemented as far as possible.

But we make fools of ourselves and others if we believe that the set of values we have at our disposal and to which we want to stick make a coherent set. Because it is, again, a simple fact of life that we share and cherish values which, if they do not directly contradict each other, at least limit each other. And we will never enjoy all those values simultaneously and in full. Again, the simple fact of life is that we are not gods. Even though we might have a society in which there is no equality and no freedom, we will never have a society where there is full freedom and full equality. Only compromises are possible, and so tensions are necessary. We should not complain about it as long as we want to stay alive. We can opt out of life, to be sure, but it is not the solution to be recommended for mankind.

MAN AT HIS FRONTIER

THE NAZI PHENOMENON IN THE LIGHT OF CONTEMPORARY CONTROVERSIES CONCERNING THE NAZI POLICIES TOWARD THE JEWS

SAUL FRIEDLÄNDER

In many ways, Nazism remains the most enigmatic upheaval of the twentieth century, in fact one of the most enigmatic and monstrous sequences of human history. When the Third Reich collapsed, it left behind a continent in ruins, tens of millions of dead—and millions of documents telling of its inner workings. But despite the immense amount of information brought together by historians, social scientists, and experts from the most varied fields, the very core of the phenomenon still seems to escape our understanding. The role of Hitler, the function of ideology, the very sources of the enthusiasm and the devotion mobilized by the movement and its leader, the complete perversion of the most basic moral norms within significant parts of the system—all this, in a way, has not found a convincing interpretation. Various explanatory frameworks have been used—German history, tyranny, fascism, totalitarianism—and various approaches attempted, from Marxist analyses to Freudian ones. The whole gamut of historical interpretations, or those drawn from sociology and political science, does not eliminate the mystery. And if one had to single out the area where most of the problems of understanding and interpretation converge, one could point, without much hesitation, to the Nazi policies toward the Jews. There, the whole impact of Hitler's role seems to appear; there, ideology played, so it seems, its crucial role; there, the basic norms of human behavior disappeared.

But precisely this kind of presentation has been questioned, more and more systematically, over the last decade. A fundamental controversy about the nature of Nazism has erupted. The presentation of this controversy and particularly of its contradic-

187

tory interpretations of Nazi policies toward the Jews may help us in reexamining some of the problems we just mentioned and in trying to assess them as they appear now.

I shall present the contending interpretations in their general form and in their application to the Jewish question first; then I shall examine the central issue of the debate, Hitler's role in the "Final Solution." Finally, on the basis of these, I shall attempt a reassessment of the various approaches and present my own evaluation of the Nazi phenomenon.

After the end of the war, the prevalent view of National Socialism established a direct link between Hitler's ideology and Nazi policies. Adolf Hitler's absolute centrality within the system was considered obvious, and the testimony of all those who had participated as actors in the party or in the state confirmed it. This centrality, the extreme "charismatic" nature of Hitler's power, created one of the problems the historian had difficulty in explaining, but there was no doubt that such a view was the only possible one. This school of thought, later tagged "intentionalist," was challenged by the end of the sixties by a new approach subsequently called "functionalist." It denied any necessary necessary relationship between the ideological dogmas of Nazism and the policies of the Third Reich, suggested that decisions are functionally linked to one another and do not follow any preestablished pattern, and established that the constant interaction and the constant pressures exercised by multiple agencies within the system necessarily limit the role of the central decision maker. His decisions take on the aspect of a planned policy with clear aims only through the artifices of propaganda or, for the historian, with hindsight.

One immediately perceives that beyond the discussion about the centrality of Adolf Hitler or the role of ideology, two essentially contradictory visions of Nazism appear: On the one hand, it is the eruption within an advanced industrial society of a movement and a system entirely dependent on the impact and role of a charismatic leader, which means in fact an astonishing fusion between archaic motives, irrational forces, and modern technology and organization within a movement seemingly unique in modern history. On the other hand, if the functionalist position is accepted, Nazism is reinserted within the known framework of bureaucratic

politics and organizational behavior; the role of the central decision maker becomes functional and secondary. The opposition
between these two positions becomes even clearer if one applies
it to a concrete issue, in this case Nazi policies toward the Jews.

For "intentionalist" historians such as Helmut Krausnick,
Ernst Nolte, Eberhard Jäckel, Karl-Dietrich Bracher, Klaus
Hildebrand, and Andreas Hillgruber, to mention only German
names in this case,[1] there is a straight line from Hilter's anti-
Semitic ideology of the twenties, as expressed in his early speeches,
in his dialogue with Dietrich Eckart, and in *Mein Kampf* to the
policies of the Third Reich, all the way to the Final Solution. To
prove their point, the intentionalists can show the clear and rapid
succession of stages in Nazi anti-Jewish policies (as well as in
other fields too, foreign policy being perhaps the most telling
example): "The National Socialist program called for the disen-
franchisement of all the Jews," writes Karl-Dietrich Bracher;
"anti-Semitic activities were part of its early history. Once in
power, the Nazis began the systematic organization of the persecution of the Jews. No tactical considerations were allowed to
interfere substantially with instituting the boycott of the Jews,
expelling them from public life, making them subject to special
laws, and finally annihilating them."[2]

It goes without saying that from the intentionalist viewpoint,
Hitler's presence is felt at each crucial stage. Doubtless it is from
him that the signal came some time in 1941, on the eve of the
attack against the Soviet Union, when the order was issued to
shoot all Red Army commissars, when the *Einsatzgruppen* got
their instructions for the extermination of the Jews in occupied
Soviet territory, and when a "certain final solution of the Jewish
problem" was mentioned in an instruction from the Central
Office for the Security of the Reich (the RSHA) forbidding further
Jewish emigration from Belgium and France in May 1941.[3] Or
it could have been given in the early summer of 1941, after the
beginning of the German attack on Russia, when Goering in-
structed Heydrich, on July 31, 1941, to prepare the "total solution
of the Jewish problem in all the territories under German control."[4] No historian would believe today that such an order was
given in writing. In its oral form, it could be either a clear instruction passed on to Goering or to Himmler, or more probably

a kind of broad hint everybody understood. In any case, for intentionalist historians, a signal must have come from Hitler himself to set the Final Solution in motion.

For the functionalists, most of the basic tenets of the position just described are unacceptable. Let us restate the common denominator of all functionalist interpretations: The Nazi system was in great part chaotic, and major decisions were often the result of the most diverse pressures, without any imperative central planning, forecasting, or clear orders from the top indicating the aim and the means of a given policy. More specifically, in relation to the plans concerning the Jews, the functionalist position can be summarized, very schematically, as follows: When the Nazis came to power, no planning existed concerning the Jewish question, and all through the thirties, up to 1941, in fact, Nazi policies relating to the Jews followed one course after another, without any clearly established aim. Extermination did not exist as an aim toward which the Nazis were striving. As Uwe Dietrich Adam puts it: "One cannot speak of a coordinated and planned policy towards the Jews . . . a global plan concerning the nature, content, and scope of the persecution of the Jews never existed; it is even highly probable that the mass extermination was not an aim which Hitler had set *a priori* and which he tried to achieve."[5]

The growing radicalization of Nazi policies, which seems by itself to indicate a clear direction, is not, according to Hans Mommsen, the result of any ideological impetus, but the consequence of organizational competition resulting from the constant infighting for the acquisition of power positions within the system. ("In each individual case, the common denominator of the competing power blocs was not a midstream compromise, but whatever in any given circumstances was the most radical solution, previously considered as beyond the realms of possibility.")[6] In any case, the persecution of the Jews was more or less haphazard according to this point of view. For some functionalist historians, it is probable that even the physical extermination, started in 1941, came as the result of a series of *ad hoc* local initiatives. (One was perhaps to solve the problem of growing overcrowding in the ghettos of eastern Poland or the Baltic countries in the fall of 1941, when further transports of deported Jews were arriving from the west, when at the same time the German advance into Russia—and therefore the possibility of pushing the Jews farther east—was coming to a halt.) The local initiatives, when they developed, were finally adopted as general policy: "It thus seems," writes Martin Broszat, "that the liquidation of the Jews began not solely as the result of an ostensible will for extermination, but also as a 'way out' of a blind alley into which the Nazis had maneouvred themselves. The practice of liquidation, once initiated and established, gained predominance and evolved in the end into a comprehensive 'programme.' "[7]

It may be tempting to keep the balance even between intentionalists and functionalists and to seek a synthesis between the two positions. In fact, functionalism, which stresses the dynamics of a system instead of concentrating on the central role of a leader, fits better in many ways within the mainstream of modern historiography. The image it offers of Nazism is more "normal," easier to explain: Any group can stumble haphazardly into the most extreme criminal behavior. Responsibility remains, obviously, but it is more diluted, more nebulous, because of the very automaticity of the process, its unforseeable outcome—and because of the absence of real premeditation. Intentionalism, on the other hand, while giving Hitler a predominant role, implies much greater awareness at various levels because of some kind of planning of the courses of action. Moreover, functionalism, pushed to its logical conclusion, gets very close to excluding Hitler from accurate knowledge of the Final Solution, leaving most of the operation to subordinate agencies—to police terror, in a nutshell.

These considerations are not to be dismissed lightly, but for the historian, the only valid test is that of documentary evidence. It appears, in my opinion, that in scanning available evidence, historians may tend to be more convinced by the traditional intentionalist position, as least as far as the crucial fields which were Hitler's obsessions are concerned: the fight against the Jews and the conquest of living space. I cannot enter here into a detailed demonstration of the case for intentionalism in the decisive area we are dealing with,[8] and will limit myself to presenting some material showing Hitler's direct involvement with the Final Solution and with the Jewish issue in general. His initial intention and his constant attention to the fight against the Jews, it seems to me, suffice to call in serious question the whole functionalist position. This will then allow me to move again from the specific issue to more general problems and finally to the Nazi phenomenon in its widest sense. But the general argument has to rest on the basis of concrete evidence.

When, in August 1941, Otto Bradfisch, head of the Einsatzkommando 8 operating in the Minsk region, asks Himmler who bears the responsibility for the executions, Himmler answers that "the orders come from Hitler and, as such, have force of law."[9] A year later, answering SS General Gottlob Berger, who in the name of the Ministry of Eastern Territories suggested a more precise definition of the term "Jew," Himmler, after rejecting the very idea of further definition that would entail only limitations, adds: "The occupied Eastern Territories will be freed of Jews *(Judenfrei)*. The Fuehrer has laid on my shoulders the execution of this very hard order. Nobody can anyhow take the responsibility away from me, and I therefore forbid any interference."[10] During the first half of 1944, Himmler refers to the very specific order of the Fuehrer concerning the Final Solution in no less than four different speeches, three of which were given in front of large audiences of senior Wehrmacht officers (January 26, May 5, May 24, and June 21, 1944).[11]

At the end of December 1941, Bernhard Lösener, the adviser on Jewish affairs at the interior ministry, tells his chief, Wilhelm Stuckart, that the extermination of the Jews in the Riga region, news of which had reached him, did not allow him to remain in his position. Stuckart answers: "Don't you know that these things happen according to the highest orders?"[12] And in May 1942, during a very heated discussion regarding the exterminations that took place in Prague between the head of the RSHA and newly appointed protector of Bohemia-Moravia, Reinhard Heydrich, and several Abwehr officers, Heydrich declared that the RSHA was not responsible for the killings; they were being done at the personal order of the Fuehrer.[13]

Not only are there many references to Hitler's orders, but there is much evidence concerning the Fuehrer's interest in the process of extermination: On August 1, 1941, Gestapo Chief Heinrich Müller sent the following order to the heads of the four *Einsatz-*

gruppen: "Regular reports have to be submitted to the Fuehrer concerning the work [sic] of the Einsatzgruppen in the East" [*Dem Führer sollen von hier aus lfd. Berichte über die Arbeit der Einsatzgruppen im Osten vorgelegt werden*].[14]

In December 1942, report No. 51 is sent by Himmler to Hitler: It deals with the *Einsatzgruppen* actions in Soviet territory for the period August to November 1942 and mentions 363,211 Jews "evacuated" (according to a note by Hitler's adjutant Pfeiffer, the report was submitted to Hitler on December 31).[15] During the same month, Himmler notes: "Conference at the Fuehrer . . . Point (3) Jews . . . to be eliminated, Jews in France 600–700,000 to be eliminated" [*Judden . . . abschaffen, Juden in Frankreich, 600–700,000, abschaffen*].[16] In fact, as far as statistics are concerned, Himmler will be better informed at the end of December, when the chief statistician of the SS, Richard Korherr, will have prepared for him a complete and precise report on the course of the Final Solution. In April 1943, the report, updated to March 31 of the same year and condensed to six pages, is ready for the Fuehrer. The report, typed on the special "Fuehrer typewriter" (a typewriter with extra-large letters), is submitted to Hitler some time before April 1943.[17] According to Eichmann's testimony, when the report was sent back to the RSHA, it bore the mention: "The Fuehrer has seen. To be destroyed. H.H." [Heinrich Himmler].[18]

Finally, some indirect evidence of Hitler's attention to the extermination process should be added. For instance, Odilo Globocnik, the Higher SS and Police Fuehrer in charge of the four extermination camps set up in the General Government during 1942, visited the Reich Chancellery in the autumn of the same year; a note by Himmler referring to a conference with Hitler on October 7, 1942, bears the following mention: "Situation in the General Government. Globus." [Globocnik bore the nickname Globus].[19] The subject of the conference is obvious. When, on April 13, 1943, the proposal to raise Christian Wirth (Globocnik's right-hand man and specialist in killing by gas) to the rank of SS Sturmbamnfuehrer is submitted to the personnel office of the SS, the file bears the mention that, since the beginning of the war, Wirth has been "on special mission by order of the Fuehrer."[20]

The evidence seems to be clear: Hitler is the source of the Final Solution, he follows its development, he is the sole reference point of the whole system, he is the unquestioned leader whom a sizable fraction of the population and of the elite follow with blind obedience, even if his orders mean mass murder. On January 26, 1944, Himmler spoke to several hundred high-ranking Wehrmacht officers at the municipal theater in Posen; nobody in the assembly, one may safely assume, thought that the Reichsfuehrer's words were empty rhetoric. Himmler said: "When the Fuehrer gave me the order to implement the total solution of the Jewish question, I wondered first if I would ask that of my brave SS men . . . but finally it was a matter of a Fuehrer order and against that, there could be no hesitation. In the meantime the task has been executed and there is no Jewish question anymore."[21]

In *Mein Kampf* Hitler declares that the roots of his anti-Semitism and of his anti-Marxism are definitely to be found in his Vienna years. But, in fact, we know practically nothing about the origins of Hitler's ideology. We recognize common themes, we can identify some sources—but beyond that, everything is pure speculation. In a recent publication of all of Hitler's early texts (from 1905 to 1924),[22] one may notice a strange paradox as far as this problem is concerned. On the one hand, not a single text written before 1919 mentions any ideological theme (except for straight nationalism) even in a single word. Take, for instance, the five-page letter written from the front line to Ernst Heift on February 15, 1915; there is not the flimsiest allusion! On November 11, 1918, Armistice Day, when the German Army got the final "stab in the back," Hitler writes a poem about the forest graveyard of Passewalk (the poem may be a fake). On the other hand, from 1919 on, a flow of political texts appears. And among those texts, the Jewish question is the dominant theme; the references to the Jews are three or four times more numerous than the references to Marxism, the theme that comes next in importance. As a matter of fact, Hitler often mentions the Jewish problem without directly linking it to Marxism, but he hardly ever mentions Marxism without alluding to its Jewish basis. One gets the impression that Hitler tirelessly depicts some multifaceted image of evil in which the Jew is the quintessential element. And if that obsession is indeed central to Hitler's world view, as it seems to be, then most of the generalizing interpretations of Nazism seem to lose much of their validity.

There are three main generalizing approaches to the explanation of National Socialism: through "German history," as "fascism," and as "totalitarianism." I shall try to show now that if Hitler is central to Nazism and if anti-Semitism is central to Hitler's world view, then these categories are insufficient.

That Nazi anti-Semitism cannot be explained with reference to the general background of European anti-Semitism and without more precise reference to German racial anti-Semitism goes without saying. But when we try to consider a more precise link, the way may be narrower than has been argued in many studies. The fact is that similar themes do appear in France and in Germany at the end of the nineteenth century.[23] Moreover, the acceptance of anti-Jewish themes within German public opinion at the end of the empire and under the Weimar Republic is not clear (wide diffusion during the eighties and the nineties, but then apparent regression; new and fierce extension at the end of the war and during the first years of Weimar, but then regression again, even during the crisis and the first years of the Third Reich). The most one can say is that German racist anti-Semitism was propagated in a continuous way through rather extreme right-wing groups and that the population was mostly passive and indifferent.

This means, in other words, that the very core of Nazi ideology was not the expression of a growing impetus coming from wide strata of the population, but rather the expression of the fanatical belief of the leader, of some of his close followers, and of a section of the Nazi party members (one-third of the SA members declared that they were convinced anti-Semites). The dynamics and results of Nazi anti-Semitism do not therefore find a sufficient explanation in the course of German history; other explanatory frameworks have to be brought into the picture.

I shall not develop here the arguments that can be brought against the two other major explanatory models, fascism and totalitarianism. Suffice it to say that both show their most obvious weakness precisely when it comes to the explanation of Nazi anti-Semitism. Proponents of the Fascist model have tried to cope with Nazi anti-Semitism by explaining it as a variety of anti-Marxism (the anti-Marxism of the Fascist radicals—Ernst Nolte), as a result of the structure of Fascist parties and of the "cumulative radicalization" of Fascist politics stemming from that structure (Hans Mommsen), or as another aspect of Fascist aggression against minorities and foreign groups (Wolfgang Schieder). All this still belongs to the liberal conception of fascism. As for the Marxist interpretation of Nazism as fascism, it tries to cope with Nazi anti-Semitism by using two major arguments: Persecution and extermination of the Jews was the ultimate result of capitalist-fascist exploitation, the Jews being robbed of their wealth and worked to death for the benefit of German capitalism, or persecution was a means of deflecting the attention of the German masses from the growing difficulties of the system.

Let us start with the end: The deflection argument falls for the very simple reason that the Final Solution was kept a close secret. The economic exploitation argument is contradicted by all we know about the course of events: The Final Solution destroyed an immense workforce, against the wishes of the Wehrmacht and even against the wishes of the heads of SS industrial concerns in the East; the orders were to exterminate, without taking any economic considerations into account. As for the arguments of the liberal proponents of the interpretation of Nazism as fascism, the equation between anti-Semitism and the anti-Bolshevism or anti-Marxism of Fascist radicals is contradicted by the fact that in Hitler's texts and speeches, for instance, the reference to Jews, as already mentioned, is much more frequent than to Bolshevism and Marxism. And what about "Jewish capitalism"? The explanation using the structure of Fascist parties and the Fascist politics of cumulative radicalization leads immediately to the question: What about Italy? What about other Fascist parties? Nothing similar seems to appear on the Fascist horizon. Comparing the Final Solution to the anti-Slav hostility of the Italians, for instance, simply does not deserve any refutation. I would therefore agree with Karl-Dietrich Bracher when he writes: "A general theory of fascism will always remain problematic when one confronts it with this problem [Nazi anti-Semitism and the extermination of the Jews,] ... while Italian fascism was centered upon the quest for a strong state, *stato totalitario*, ... Hitler's basic

notion was that of the primordial role of race, the racial foundation of the future empire, for which the organisation of a strong
state was only instrumental and not an aim in itself."24

But this very last sentence of Karl-Dietrich Bracher also shows
the difficulty in explaining Nazi anti-Semitism within the framework of totalitarianism. Totalitarian bureaucracy, the total state,
becomes in this case the instrument for the implementation of an
ideological-messianic obsession. The obsession is the core, at
Hitler's level at least: Everything else converges, ultimately,
toward that aim. In a totalitarian system, "enemies" are functionally used to tighten the grip on society; enemies therefore
change according to needs. In the case of Nazism—or more
exactly, within the framework of Hitler's ideology—the central
enemy remained the same from the very beginning to the very
end.

In summary, my argument up to this stage is the following:
In the crucial areas of the battle for "living space" and "the war
against the Jews," Hitler's role seems to be dominant. Bureaucratic and organizational politics, be it within the peculiar
context of a "fascist" movement or a "totalitarian" regime, do
not seem to offer a convincing alternative explanation. If, moreover, we admit that the war against the Jews formed the very
core of Hitler's ideology, we are faced with a contemporary
political phenomenon in which a whole system is dependent upon
the will for a decisive confrontation with the forces of ultimate
evil. The question then is this: How can one insert this obsession
within the framework of the various interpretations we have of
modern political movements; how did such an obsession "link up"
with the bureaucratic processes necessary for its implementation?

*　*　*

The easiest answer to this question would be in terms of Hitler's
"charismatic" influence creating a following of such scope and
intensity that his orders were obeyed whatever their nature. (In
Himmler's terms, ". . . it was a matter of a Fuehrer order and
against that, there could be no hesitation.") But leaving it at that
would almost mean begging the question, for one would have to
explain the possibility of charismatic power leading to such
extreme results within an advanced modern society. Let me try

therefore to approach the problem in a somewhat roundabout way, leaving the argument of Hitler's charismatic impact to the very end of the discussion.

At the beginning of this discussion, I argued that we knew nothing about the origins of Hitler's anti-Semitism. There is no difficulty, however, in analyzing the structure of his image of the Jew. First of all, there was an almost metaphysical conception of the Jew as a kind of cosmic principle of evil. This view, a manifest transformation of the extreme trends of religious anti-Semitism, appears very clearly in Hitler's conversations with Eckart and in *Mein Kampf.* A second component was simply the classic racist position pushed to its most extreme formulation: The Jews are a culture-destroying race which, throughout history, has attempted to eliminate the culture-creating efforts of the higher races and is now aiming at world domination through racial defilement, internationalism, Marxism, democracy, and pacifism. Finally— and most important—the Nazis considered the Jew a *bacillus,* a source of possibly mortal infection. This "bacterial" component of the image was quite distinct from the general racial one, and its absence from their explicit ideological framework does not diminish its importance. On the contrary, this is the part of the image that appeared first at the level of spontaneous expressions, and then at the level of extermination practices and rituals.

Now let us see how the distinction among the three components of the image allows a clearer analysis of the link between Hitler's obsessions (his pathology, one could say), those of the "true believers," and the dedication of a huge bureaucratic machine to its murderous task. We shall come back to the "blind obedience" and the "charisma"; let us consider it as a partial explanation, at this stage. A second explanation could be that Nazism constantly tended to obliterate the distinction between the symbolic plane, that of metaphors, and that of reality. This tendency allowed, by definition, the interlocking of fantasies and reality assessments; it helps to explain the penetration of the weirdest comparisons into Nazi theory and practice. If one links this second point to both the racist ideology and the microbe image, the point will become clearer.

What was considered reality at the microbe level by Hitler,

for instance, was essentially symbolic and metaphorical at the racist-ideological one. The Jew was a poisonous, disintegrating, mortal element for Adolf Hitler. These images were not necessarily part and parcel of the belief of tens of thousands of "true believers," but they were easily integrated as telling metaphors, as strong symbolic representations of evil within the framework of their world view in general. The fuzzy racial ideology was not the prime mover of the extermination process, but the "transmission belt," the mediating element between the murderous pathological drive and the bureaucratic and technological organization of the extermination. Again, not all the bureaucrats of the extermination believed in the ideology itself, and many followed more practical considerations and acted out of sheer discipline (or even fear). But a core of believers was necessary; those, in turn, were linked through the use of metaphors to what appeared as real and mortal dangers in Hitler's own mental world. "We don't want," declares Himmler in a speech to SS generals in Posen on October 4, 1943, "in the process of eradicating a bacillus, to be infected by that bacillus, to fall ill and to die ourselves." Metaphor? Reality? We don't know, but the links in the chain are clearly marked.

We have left out the first element of the image of the Jew: the Jew as a cosmic principle of evil. We are on another plane there, that of the transposition of religious beliefs, belonging both to a general apocalyptic tradition and to some aspects of medieval and postmedieval Christian anti-Semitism. Hitler's obsession with the Jewish peril is channeled into a double world of symbols and metaphors, that of racist thought and that of a deeper, more potent current: the apocalyptic tradition, the religious roots of Western imagination. Racist thinking bears the reassuring confirmation of modern science, as understood by the Nazis and many others from the second half of the nineteenth century on; the apocalyptic vision of the Jewish peril can tap the deepest layers of shared myths and religious imagery. It gives a religious dimension to political action, to police terror, and to extermination practices; it is that part of Nazism, often recognized, which makes of it the most complete *political religion* of modern times. Erich Voegelin called Nazism a "political religion" at the end of the thirties, Norman Cohn came back to this thesis in his *Pursuit of the Millennium*, and nowadays James Rhodes has tried to analyze systematically the structure of the Nazi movement and the elements of Nazi ideology in terms of a millenarian movement.

It is this double reference to the world of science and to that of myth, to biology and to religion, it is the fusion of the two into a general picture of ultimate battles channeling all possible elements of social discontent and of revolutionary hopes that creates the fertile ground on which Hitler's charismatic impact can unfold. The pathology of the leader becomes the moving element of a whole system because it seems to fit quite naturally into a world of shared symbols, deeply held beliefs, and concrete social resentment. Total obedience becomes in fact religious or secular faith; the order to kill, a sacred duty.

Notes

[1] Most non-German historians of Nazi anti-Semitism may be considered intentionalists, with the clear exception of Karl A. Schleunes; his *Twisted Road to Auschwitz: Nazi Policy towards German Jews 1933–1939* (Urbana, 1970) is perhaps the first comprehensive "functionalist" presentation of Nazi policies toward the Jews during the thirties.

[2] Karl-Dietrich Brecher, *The German Dictatorship* (London 1979), p. 252.

[3] Helmut Krausnick et al., *Anatomy of the SS State* (London 1968), pp. 60, 67.

[4] Raul Hilberg, *The Destruction of the European Jews* (Chicago, 1961), p. 262.

[5] Uwe Dietrich Adam, *Judenpolitik im Dritten Reich* (Dusseldorf, 1972), p. 357.

[6] Hans Mommsen, "National-Socialism: Continuity and Change," in Walter Laqueur, ed., *Fascism: A Reader's Guide* (London, 1979), p. 179.

[7] For this thesis, see mostly Martin Broszat, "Hitler und die Genesis der Endlösung. Auf Anlass der Thesen von David Irving," *Vierteljahrshefte für Zeitgeschichte*, 1977. The English translation used here was published in *Yad Vashem Studies*, 12 (1979), p. 93.

[8] I have dealt with it at greater length in the introduction to Gerald Fleming, *Hitler and the Final Solution* (Berkeley, 1984).

[9] Gerald Fleming, *Hitler und die Endlösung* (Munich, 1982), p. 62.

[10] *Ibid.*, p. 126. See also Krausnik et al., *Anatomy of the SS State*, p. 69.

[11] *Ibid.*, pp. 65–67. One cannot imagine that Himmler would have referred to a nonexistent order, even less so in front of such audiences.

[12] Bernhard Lösener, "Als Rassereferent im Reichsministerium des Innern," *VfZ*, 9 (1961), p. 311. See also Fleming, *Hitler und die Endlösung*.

[13] Fleming, *Hitler und die Endlösung*, p. 77.

[14] *Ibid.*, p. 58.

[15] *Ibid.*

[16] *Ibid.*, p. 78.

[17] For the text of both Korherr reports and the related correspondence, see Serge Klarsfeld, ed., *The Holocaust and the Neo-Nazi Mythomania* (New York, 1978).

[18] Fleming, *Hitler und die Endlösung*, pp. 149–152.

[19] *Ibid.*

[20] *Ibid.*, pp. 37–38.

[21] *Ibid.*, p. 65.

[22] *Hitler: Sämtliche Aufzeichnungen 1905–1924*, Eberhard Jäckel, ed., with Axel Kuhn (Stuttgart, 1980).

[23] For France, see Zeev Sternhell, *Le Droite revolutionnaire française* (Paris, 1979).

[24] Karl Dietrich Bracher, "The Role of Hitler: Perspectives of Interpretation," in Laqueur, ed., *Fascism: A Reader's Guide*, pp. 201–2.

MAN AND THE GULAG

GEORGES NIVAT

Gulag: This word, a Soviet abbreviation, was coined in 1934 when control over the forced labor camps was transferred from the People's Commissariat of Justice to the NKVD. It was at this time that the directorate of forced labor camps was set up, the acronym of which was GULAG.[1] The term subsequently passed into universal usage in 1973 with the appearance of Alexander Solzhenitsyn's "artistic inquiry" into the penitentiary system that developed as a consequence of the Russian revolution: *The Gulag Archipelago*. Solzhenitsyn's title suggests two things: the birth of a new totalitarian civilization that carries with it the seeds of the concentration camps (European civilization had its cradle in the Greek archipelago); and a generalized dissemination of the new slavery system.

I always have to overcome a number of psychological reservations whenever I deal with this subject, although this is by no means the first time. In many ways it is still very much a taboo subject, even if the word *Gulag* today has been debased and is applied to third-rate nuisances (in May 1968 the students at Nanterre University wore yellow Stars of David as they faced the police; it was the same unthinking sacrilege, or rather the perverse effect of the same unthinking *censorship*).

We have learned about life in the concentration camps through David Rousset, Leon Poliakov, Olga Wurmser, Jules Margolin, Alexander Solzhenitsyn, Varlam Shalamov, and even Pasqualini (China),[2] and yet the subject is difficult to approach for those who have not lived through the experience. The survivors themselves are affected by a form of paralyzing internal censorship, a phenomenon that has been studied by the psychiatrist Bruno Bet-

203

telheim, who was himself a prisoner in one such camp. His articles on this subject have been collected and published under the title *Surviving and Other Essays*.[3] A definition given by Bettelheim is universally applicable to all forms of concentration camps, to all camp prisoners: Completely in the dark about the reasons for his imprisonment and the length of his sentence, he finds himself in an "extreme situation," broken as an individual, reduced systematically to a state of infancy in his behavior, completely submissive to his torturers, having lost his ego. Bettelheim adds that the camp played two additional roles in the Nazi system: It generated terror in the rest of society, and it was useful to the Gestapo as a laboratory for finding out the best way to break a human being.

Bettelheim was the first to describe the survivor's resistance when it came to analyzing or even simply recounting his experience. The death drive that had invested the mind of the camp slave continued to pursue the survivor. For many survivors, the outside world, the "normal" world, had been made into something so unreal in the camps that the effect was to remain definitive. "Not one week goes by without my dreaming of the camp," Siniavsky was to declare.[4] Sarah Kofman, a French philosopher whose father, a rabbi, perished at Auschwitz, added by way of an appendix to her book on Plato's aporias a totally unexpected account of a nightmare triggered off by the sight of the words *Com mar fui née* [I was born into misfortune], the words of a French medieval heroine which conjure up the nightmare of her father's death, of the escape with her mother in February 1943 from occupied Paris. The holocaust, the camp, the Gulag are marginalized, "unclassifiable, unfathomable."

Another taboo is protected by a more generalized form of censorship. Why open up an "incurable" wound now that the misfortunes of the past have been patched up or camouflaged? The subject implicitly arouses the wrath of those who wish to lead a "normal life." The totalitarian state has managed to make the camps taboo for a long time to come. Political barriers are masked by the similarity of vocabulary. We will not go into the history of how the Soviet state was able to silence the voices of the camps. At first the camps were celebrated, then totally hushed up (during the period when their growth had made them omnipresent), then timidly denounced by Khrushchev, who threw the doors open. Solzhenitsyn writes: "He had this Christian trait in him of which he was unaware." Today the censorship has returned. And not just today; the French intelligentsia long continued to deny the very existence of the Soviet camps, as was demonstrated at the famous Kravtchenko trial against the "Lettres françaises" in 1949.[5] On January 26, 1949, Etienne Fajon wrote: "The decadent French bourgeoisie . . . is preparing to welcome Washington's repugnant little puppet with the same docility as if it were taking delivery of a cargo of chewing gum or corned-beef." The merchandise thus designated was the reality of the camps.

More generally, one encounters an almost religious barricade that surrounds the subject of the camps in that we know we are dealing with factories created systematically to dehumanize those who are drawn into them. The camps fall within the province of numen, or religious awe. In our attempt to break the taboo, we might well be overinclined to classify them in the chain of evil that exists on earth. In *Paroles d'étranger* [A Voice from Outside], Elie Wiesel tells of his anger and shame at the discovery that the Soviet monument erected in Kiev at the site of the executions of Babi-Yar bears no mention of the word *Jew*: "By what right do you deprive them of their identity? They lived as Jews, dreamt as Jews, it was because they were Jews that they were isolated and singled out by the torturers, it was as Jews that they trembled with fear and suffered torture and death. How dare you now throw them back into oblivion? In whose name do you rob them of their essence?" In much the same way we are left aghast by the decision of the Council of State of the People's Republic of Poland to award the victims of Auschwitz a military decoration "for having died fighting against Hitler's genocide."

The other way of breaking the taboo that surrounds the subject is to include it in the vast process of dehumanization which is taking place in advanced urban and industrial societies. The essence of the camp martyrs is thus watered down into a kind of generalized process that could best be described as "Kafkaiza-tion." There is a grain of truth in this analysis, and it is strange indeed that it should have been Franz Kafka, the Prague insur-ance agent, who depicted and diagnosed the depersonalization of man in the totalitarian system. In an article published in *Language and Silence*, George Steiner has perfectly captured this premonition: "The key fact about Kafka is that he was possessed of a fearful premonition, that he saw, to the point of exact detail, the horrors gathering. *The Trial* exhibits the classic model of the terror state. It prefigures the furtive sadism, the hysteria which totalitarianism insinuates into private and sexual life, the faceless boredom of the killers." But are we not putting words into Kafka's mouth?

It is as though the entire field had been struck by paralysis, subjected to excess, tetanized. There exists today a pathological condition, that of the censorship on the camps. Saul Friedländer tackles the issue in his *Reflets du nazisme* (Images of Nazism],[6] as does one of the numbers of the review *Esprit* dedicated to the memory of Auschwitz. The historian Pierre Vidal-Naquet, in an incisive article entitled "Un Eichman de papier" [A Paper Eichmann], has produced a convincing analysis of the Faurisson phenomenon—that is, the appearance of a "school of thought" which maintained that no extermination camp ever existed, and that the showers of Auschwitz were never equipped with Zyklon B. The upholders of this doctrine, checking all the available "sources" to find out what went on in the Nazi camps, attack those whom they refer to as the "mythologists of extermination." The problem goes well beyond the boundaries of a simple if obnoxious fraud. It is true that the totalitarian state covers its tracks, destroys all records. We are faced here with a kind of pathological mania. Even Vidal-Naquet is caught up in its net, since he concludes: "Come to terms with Faurisson? Why not, have we not come to terms with Giscard d'Estaing?"—which is perhaps another way of breaking the taboo, though even unconsciously, about the "incurable wound."[7]

The only way to fight against the Faurisson phenomenon is to open up museums on the camps, to print picture postcards of the crematoriums. Elie Wiesel has already described the sickness he felt on his "pilgrimage into the land of darkness," now a tourist site. We can also discover a pathology of denunciation, and George Steiner falls into the trap when he refers to the responsibility of the German language, which has been infested by bestiality: "The German language cannot be cleared of the responsibility for the horrors of Nazism." Moreover, it was Steiner once again who, in a provocative novel describing Hitler's capture (he had survived after a false suicide) by a Jewish commando in the Brazilian jungle, puts one of the most appalling paradoxes into the mouth of Hitler: "To set a race apart. To keep it from defilement. To hold before it a promised land. To scour that land of its inhabitants or place them in servitude." The Third Reich had learned all it knew from the chosen people![8] The same idea can also be found in the work of the French author Pierre Gripari.

All these taboos, all these different pathologies of the senses— which I do not put on the same level, make no mistake—lie in wait for us as we try to approach the subject. In a way, what is expected of us is that we think the unthinkable, that we come to grips with something we dare not name. We have to overcome both our pity and our hatred. Indeed, Steiner has written a splendid page at the beginning of his novel where he evokes the way that pity acts as a barrier to our attempts to apportion blame. If a "crime against humanity" (a legal notion which I think was invented at Nuremberg) was committed, is not the guilty party inevitably humanity itself? Those who have succeeded in vanquishing these obstacles—that is to say, those who have broken down the wall of silence erected by the subject—have done so, in our opinion, thanks to a soteriological approach, a new post-Auschwitz, post-Kolyma religious thinking. All the other attempts at cauterization have worked only partially. In other words, we might call all the great exponents of the concentration camp phenomenon *post-Auschwitz theologians*.

What enables me to justify my dealing with this subject is the knowledge I have of that part of Russian literature which covers the realities of the concentration camps. Today there is an impressive and magnificent body of texts in Russian on man in the camp, man under the reign of terror, man terrorized. For a long time, none of the novels or poems that had taken up this rather fearsome subject of the concentration camps had appeared convincing, less so in any case than David Rousset's inquiry, or psychoanalytical analyses such as *The Informed Heart*. For us, the crux of the matter is to determine whether or not fictional literature has been capable of reacting to the concentration camp phenomenon. But let us first remember one thing: In the case of the Nazi camps it was possible to erect memorials whose very power resides in the stark numbers, the interminable list of the victims' names they commemorate.[9] No such thing is possible, nor does it even exist for the victims of the Gulag. On the other hand, the literary production generated by the concentration camp phenomenon in Russian letters is first-rate in my opinion, and certainly more important and more universally expressive than that to be found on the Nazi camps.

Before the camps came into being, prisons had given birth to a wealth of literary production. On the documentary side, just to mention the best-known texts, we have Dostoevsky's *Memories of the House of the Dead* (1863), the author having been a convict himself; Anton Chekhov's inquiry in 1894 into the Sakhalin penal colony; and many chapters in Tolstoy's vast prison novel, *Resurrection* (1899). But the fiction writers who dealt with prison life were far more prolific. Let me refer the reader to the excellent work by Victor Brombert, *The Romantic Prison* (Princeton, 1978), which studies the *topos* of prison in French literature (Stendhal, Hugo, Nerval, Baudelaire, and so on). "Prison haunts our civilisation. Object of fear, it is also a subject of poetic reverie. The prison wish does exist. The image of immurement is essentially ambivalent in Western tradition." The Western fiction writer dreams of an elevated prison (as in *The Charterhouse of Parma*) where immurement signifies enfranchisement. The reverie brought about by confinement is connected to the appearance of defeat and the secret certitude of victory; it is romantic and Christian. Thanks to Byron, the prison cellar of the Château de Chillon has become the archetype of the prison where the ego can rise up and be sanctified:

> Chillon! Thy prison is a holy place,
> And thy sad floor an altar . . .

The words are echoed by the Russian poet Zhukovsky when his hero, freed at last, murmurs: "And up to you, prison, my sighs shall rise!"

The romantic poet is not only inclined to glorify the prisoner, he even goes so far as to identify his own creative process with the whole process of confinement. In his final chapter, Brombert outlines a fictional camp personage, someone who is both vague and *elusive*, as Jean Cayrol puts it in his *Pour un Romanesque Lazare* [To a Romanesque Lazarus]. We no longer witness the crystallization of the ego, but rather its decay, its fall into confusion. The small castle of the Spielberg of Pellico gives way to the dismal and shapeless horizontal spread of the sheds and the zone. The prison characters and the camp characters play diametrically opposed roles. In a sense, the one exacerbates and the other destroys the fundamental essence of man—nature, religion, relationships. Modern Russian "concentration camp" literature feeds on these two imaginary characters.

Anus Mundi and Utopia Come True

The expression comes from the diary of Dr. Kremer in Auschwitz, quoted by Poliakov in *Bréviaire de la haine* [Breviary of Hatred], a text upon which Faurisson based a number of his "deductions."

> 5.IX.1942. This afternoon I witnessed a special practice applied to the prisoners of the women's camps. It was worse than what I had ever seen before. Doctor Thilo was right this morning when he said to me that we were now living in the anus of the world.

The Nazi camp was "the anus of the world," the rubbish heap or cesspool of humanity. It was to establish a barrier against the impure, a genetic barrier through sterilization, a total barrier through extermination. The first step is the enslavement, the second the suppression of the other, who is perceived as the impure, the diabolic. We have the systematic production of a satanic agent whose job it is to catalyze all the antisocial tendencies that oppose the source of absolute power. Out of the fantasy of the imagination has come a destroyer who must be destroyed. The invention of this impure center of attraction wipes out all the different cultural strata: memory, history, social and emotional relations. The two elements of this mechanism are hatred and negative sacralization.

The Soviet camp seems to have hesitated between opting for

the "anus mundi" version and the utopian one. The fact is that at the outset, the camp was intended as the regime's window, the showpiece of its ambition: the regeneration of humanity. And even though there were convicts in the penal colony in the former monastery of the island of Solovki on the White Sea who were "temporarily fulfilling the tasks of a horse" (abbreviated to VRIDLO), exotic trees were also being planted at the very edge of the Arctic Circle precisely to demonstrate that the Solovkis were also "transforming the world and building a new life." The "Lettres d'un communiste" [Letters of a Communist], written by the Christian Bolshevik Pierre Pascal, describe an exemplary visit to Solovki penal colonies in 1921.[10] In 1929 it is Maxim Gorky's turn to glorify the "preparatory school" of the camp; in 1934 he sings the praises of the "work school" of the building site at Belomorkanal, where tens of thousands of convicts wear themselves out and die. The camp is a school where enthusiasm reigns, but "the year, the month, the day are not far off when remedial camps are no longer necessary, and when they are all joined together in one giant movement to build socialism."[11] Instead, it is the glorification that comes to an end, for the camps, far from making utopia come true, have turned into the "anus mundi" where enormous convoys silently jettison the victims of the purges.

The Nazi camp also has a didactic and moralistic aspect, albeit to a lesser extent. Even today, there is a certain amount of unease in trying to compare those two factories that dispensed and dispense dehumanization. "It is monstrous, but in a different way," writes Olga Wurmser. On the one hand, an entire people, including the old and the newborn, are systematically eliminated. On the other, specific social classes or groups are deported, families broken up, children brought up to hate their parents.[12] There was no Zyklon B in Stalin's camps, but they were responsible for a greater number of deaths. The two systems are closely inter-related in the totalitarian mechanisms they set up: The camp, with its negative charge, omnipresent and yet never named, acts as the driving force of terror outside the camp. Its presence-absence plays a fundamental role in the area referred to by the Russian inmates as "the great zone" (the rest of the country); the camps dull the minds of the subjects in the totalitarian state.

In his introduction to the *Memoirs* of Margarete Buber-Neumann, a German Communist who was transferred from a Soviet camp near Karaganda to the Nazi camp at Ravensbrück (she was handed over by the NKVD people to the SS on the Brest-Litovsk Bridge), the Swiss humanist Albert Bégnin wrote in 1949: "Whilst life in the camps seems to point to the fact that the Russian *people* still retain an element of humanity, one that has remained more intact than in the case of the German people, a comparison between the two police states would tend to prove that, conversely, the Soviet *regime* has succeeded more than Hitler's in ridding itself of the last vestiges of Christianity."[13] These words were prompted by the totally arbitrary nature of the deportations in 1937. Many commentators were left reeling from the shock when confronted with the many cases of prisoners being handed over by one system to the other. For many Russians, the path led in the opposite direction. Solzhenitsyn, in *A Day in the Life of Ivan Denisovitch* (1962), mentions Senka Klevshin, who has come straight from Buchenwald. And it was Senka who was to trigger off Jorge Semprun's political reverie in his book *Quel beau dimanche!* [What a Lovely Sunday] (he also wrote *Grand Voyage*). Solzhenitsyn writes: "Senka hardly ever talks (Lord knows, he must have seen a lot!). He does not hear and he never joins in conversations. So much so that nobody really knows much about him except that he was in Buchenwald." Semprun adds: "It was not as if the Russians felt that they were on a foreign planet in Buchenwald; it was just like at home."

I think that Hannah Arendt covered most of the essential points as early as 1951 in her work *The Origins of Totalitarianism* (1951).[14] The concentration and extermination camps in totalitarian regimes act, in her opinion, as laboratories to verify one of the fundamental tenets of totalitarianism—after all, nothing is impossible. Arendt then goes on to analyze the different elements involved in this attempt to obtain total domination over and degradation of human beings. These elements can be found, of course, in a more concrete form in all Russian literature on the camps. Our reflections might be halted at this point by the living testimony of men such as Semprun who, as survivors of the Nazi camps, as ex-Communists, were forced little by little, after much reticence and many regrets, to accept what Hannah Arendt

describes so brilliantly, so clinically, as the common nature of the
two systems. This painful discovery sustains the whole fabric and
the somber energy of *Quel beau dimanche*!: "I thought that Stalin
wanted to destroy the potential innocence of our memory." And
this leads him to thoughts of this hue: "I have thought that the
authentic mausoleum of the Revolution was to be found in the
far North, in Kolyma. That we could dig tunnels through the
mass graves or rather the construction sites of Socialism. That we
would parade in front of the thousands of naked, imputrescible
corpses of the deportees caught in the permafrost of eternal death."

Degradation achieved by making criminals the masters of the
others, the crucial problem of getting rid of informers, and one
common ethnography for the *zek* tribe (those who were called
Muslims in Dachau are rebaptized "the goners" in Kolyma):
Daix, Semprun, and many others soon realize to their dismay
that they share a whole set of memories with the Soviet *zek*. This
discovery, coupled with Solzhenitsyn's revelations, is perceived
as "an unsettling, unpleasant, almost inadmissible truth by left-
wing intellectuals" (the others do not interest Semprun "in this
particular context"). Many others before them were to live the
same experience, not to mention those whom the SS handed over
directly to Stalin. We would do well here to remember the
case of the Polish writer Tadeusz Borowski, a survivor of the German camps, who became the eulogist of the Polish "people's"
regime and who committed suicide in 1951. The author of *Kamienny
Świat* [The Stone World], a terse and cynical acknowledgment of
a new cannibalistic world,[15] can accept neither his survival
nor his new allegiance. The author of the terrible story "Ladies
and Gentlemen, to the Gas Chambers, Please!" was himself
to open the gas tap on July 1, 1951. The attempt at cauterization
had failed.

The difficulty in understanding Auschwitz is compounded by
that of overcoming utopia. Total domination can be achieved
only if all human spontaneity is wiped out. Here I should like to
invoke the French philosopher René Girard, who sees man
throughout his entire history as a prisoner of the myth of the
sacrificial victim—first sacrificed, then deified. The "victimiza-
tion" process made a strong comeback in the twentieth century,
although it was less embedded in the mythological, since Chris-

tianity had put a stop to the process by unmasking it. The better we comprehend the process, the more violence is needed to re-suscitate the myth, to "get the human community to turn in on itself." The scapegoat, in our "rational" era, has become an im-mense crowd. Girard writes: "All the virulent ideologies that have been developed and been locked in battle with one another throughout the XX century have always been exposed to a kind of monstrous, and in the last resort ineffective, rationalisation of the mechanisms of victimisation."

Totalitarianism is not a form of personal power; it acts in the name of science, of history, or of nature. It is obliged to conceal the totally arbitrary nature of the "scientifically" selected victim. Once designated, the victim is loaded into a wagon and dispatched toward the "anus mundi." In a sense, totalitarianism abolishes the tragedy of the situation; it splits, degrades, annihilates, but never with any ostentation. There is no executioner to hold up the head for the people to see.

The dissident Soviet sociologist Alexander Zinoviev imagines in his satirico-fictional work a totalitarian world where the Gulag is superfluous: In his "communitarian" society, the ends of the scientific Gulag are attained without any recourse to constraint in the old meaning. In this world bereft of any authentic alter-native, where everyone is degraded and constantly exposed to the view of others, any nonconformist is caught up in the large social melting pot, a kind of gigantic socialist barracks where the whole group is responsible for surveillance. The archipelago has grown to such an extent that it has become a continent unto itself; society is now composed of one single element, the utopian dream. We are in utopia. Zinoviev's paradoxical thinking uni-versalizes the barracks principle, the society of expendables. But above all it shows that the principle of pleasure is at work.

The Eclipse of God

It became necessary to rethink both Jewish and Christian theology after Auschwitz. We have all heard of Martin Buber's phrase "the eclipse of God." After Kolyma, there was also a need to rethink the tenets of socialism, the idea of "progress," and even the idea of "man." Literature on the "anus mundi" is only superficially vast; in reality, it is quite small. The unrealness of the extermination camps is such that not only did the future victims refuse to believe in their existence, but even afterward the survivors wanted but one thing, and that was to stop believing what had happened. "The revulsion of our common sense against believing that monstrous things are being perpetrated is something that the totalitarian power-brokers never cease to encourage" (Hannah Arendt). The "incommunicability" of such subjects is encouraged by totalitarianism's systematic perversion of the truth. And even if this were not so, the normal person is so taken aback that he allows himself to be seized "like a rabbit" (Solzhenitsyn). We know of the paradoxical retrospective "indictment" brought by Bruno Bettelheim against Anne Frank's family, who did nothing to avert the danger since they almost religiously refused to see it. Arendt's summary of the Eichmann trial also caused an uproar. Semprun, for his part, suspects Bettelheim of refusing to forgive himself for having survived. Borowski had leveled this charge forcefully against himself as early as 1946. Survival, then, is tantamount to self-laceration.

To accept Auschwitz or Kolyma implies one of two possible courses: One can attempt to find room for them in some ancient rationale, or one can desperately try to reformulate God. To my mind, Schwartz-Bart in his admirable book *Le Dernier des justes* [The Last of the Just][16] belongs to the former (and more numerous) family of post-Auschwitz thought. Schwartz-Bart solves the dilemma by considering Auschwitz as one in a whole series of ordeals, as a part of the cycle of salvation through ordeal. The "last of the just," Ernie Lévy, a volunteer for the Zyklon B showers, leads the children off to Paradise: "We shall enter the Kingdom together, in a moment we shall go in, hand in hand, and there a great feast of succulent dishes awaits us. . . ." Sublimation is achieved through familiarity with the pain suffered by the Jews over the centuries. "Praise be to Auschwitz. Let it be so." Auschwitz mysteriously rounds off the earthly wanderings of Israel "which for two thousand years had no sword," and the letters of its name are "carried away," like those of the Torah wrapped around the rabbi who was tortured to death by the Romans.

But there can be another reaction, that of those who refuse to accept that Auschwitz was yet another evil set within a whole chain of evil. The catastrophe which must be associated with the divine presence this time goes beyond the simple crossing of the Red Sea or the two destructions of the Temple; it is enough to make anyone lose his mind. In his novelistic work, Elie Wiesel uses madness to a new end. The theologian Emil Fackenheim claims that the "Voice of Auschwitz" orders the believing and the nonbelieving Jews not to despair and not to escape their destiny, otherwise Hitler would be proved right posthumously. Wiesel, for his part, has written a magnificent description of the "twilight" of the souls who had to face the camp: "We were incapable of thinking anything at all. Our senses were blunted; everything was blurred as in a fog. It was no longer possible to grasp anything. The instincts of self-preservation, of self-defence, of pride had all deserted us. In one ultimate moment of lucidity it seemed to me that we were damned souls wandering in the half-world, souls condemned to wander through space till the generations of man come to an end, seeking their redemption, seeking oblivion—without hope of finding it."[17] Wiesel has expressed the situation better than all those who reject a God who can tolerate an Auschwitz, but what he proposes is more than just silence; there is another path toward salvation—laughter. A new jester must be invented to fight evil. "Hush, Jews! Don't pray so loud! God might hear you. And then he would find out that there are still a few Jews around in Europe who have survived!"[18]

The camps of the twentieth century certainly call God to account once more. The old argument according to which "nothing has changed" is no longer sufficient. How can we escape here the question of the "death of God" which preceded all the grandiose totalitarian visions of the nineteenth century? The major exponents of the downfall of rationalism, Kierkegaard and Nietzsche, spring to mind. It was Nietzsche who argued the "death of God" with the greatest vehemence in the episode of the madman who sought God: " 'I am looking for God! I am looking for God!' But as there were many people there who did not believe in God, his cries were greeted with great laughter. 'Is He lost, like a child?', asked one! 'Is He hiding? Is He afraid of us? Has He embarked? Has He emigrated?' So their laughter and shouts rang out. The madman rushed into their midst and gave them a piercing look. 'Where has God disappeared to?' he cried, 'I shall tell you. We have killed Him, . . . you and I' " (*Joyful Wisdom*, § 125). These reflections of Nietzsche's are linked to his thoughts on European nihilism and the collapse of Christian illusions.

For his "master," Dostoevsky, the "death of God" is linked with terrorism and with the secret contagion of the disease of terrorism that marks the novelist's whole body of work from *Crime and Punishment* onward. The "decomposition" of God lies at the heart of Dostoevsky's intuitions; in his *Diary of a Writer*, he recounts the trivial event of a man taking a shot at an icon. And from there he develops his prophetic vision of the establishment of a totalitarian power, of a new and all-embracing form of bondage that is imposed in the name of equality and is the doing of a particular type of weak and fine-talking intellectual: "The strange thing is that all the executioners I have ever met have always given the impression of being intelligent individuals, glib talkers, imbued with an excessive amount of self-esteem." The death of God, the weakening of others, enslavement carried out in the name of liberty—what strange mirrors Dostoevsky held up for us in which to view our era. He truly foresaw that the "death of God" would unleash a generalized process of terror which would place the power of total domination in the hands of a particular type of fanatic, and he was convinced that there was an element of the fanatic in every "intellectual."

The mirror thus held up is a source of problems for us. Dostoevsky's mirror reflected the desire for a totalitarian state. Perhaps his greatest intuition was to have perceived to what extent reality could change its color—how, in certain psychological situations, reality could vanish entirely, to be replaced by sham. That is the great discovery of his "underground." Hannah Arendt has written some unforgettable pages precisely on the debasement of reality in a totalitarian system. Aliocha Karamazov says to his brother Ivan, "Can one live with so much hell in one's heart and in one's head?" The problem after Auschwitz was that there was a shift from the idea of "everything is possible" to the realization that "all is indeed possible." In fact, it would appear that this transition can take place only if a group of fanatics seizes upon a utopian idea, the idea of a unique City, and then tries to set up its "secret society in practice."

This vision of total social uniformity, and the portrait of the sentimental fanatic, lend an extraordinary depth to Dostoevsky's writing. The dialogue between Verkhovensky and Stavrogin already contains all the elements: terror, the fascination of terror, the need for a deified gang leader (whom Claude Lefort names the Egocrat, so as to set him apart from all preceding despots).[19] Finally, another of Dostoevsky's foresights was the link he created between the transformation of reality into "unreality" and the death wish which is incarnated by Kirilov in *The Possessed* and which, according to the mathematician and philosopher Igor Chafarevitch, appears as a leitmotif throughout the entire history of socialism.[20] "One belongs to all, and all belong to one" (Dostoevsky).

The pre-Auschwitz era can help us to find some answers. But what about after Auschwitz? Come 1984, Orwell's fateful date, will we have understood the meaning of Auschwitz? Is it enough for the Polish bishops to have suggested to the German Christians that there be a "mutual pardon"? Are the visits by heads of state (and that includes John Paul II) to Auschwitz an adequate answer? And then, where is the monument to the dead of Kolyma? Christianity is trying to redefine itself in terms of a "dissident" force within society. Israel claims it is an answer to the "prescriptive voice" of Auschwitz. The revolution is breaking up into thousands of revolts in the West, while in the East it has kept its stony face. "Anti-utopias" appear at regular intervals: Zamiatin wrote his "We" very soon after the October Revolution, followed by Orwell and Huxley, and today Alexander Zinoviev has completed what Zamiatin began. However, these attempts at mockery have not really had a major impact. The peculiarity of the anti-utopian lesson is that it has to be repeated time and time again, simply because utopia continues to be the driving hope of history. Very few are able to believe that they are now in the "post-utopian era." "What you need is to remember from time to time that you are now living in the society of the future" (Alexander Zinoviev).

That is not the way Elie Wiesel sees the solution to the "death of God." In the epigraph to *The Town Beyond the Wall*, he quotes Dostoevsky: "I have an idea: I shall become mad. . . ." Wiesel's heroes ask the others, ask us, by what right we are not mad. "These days honest men can do only one thing: go mad! Spit on logic, intelligence, sacrosanct reason! That's what you have to do, that's the way to stay human, to keep your wholeness. But look at them: they're cowards, all of them. They never say, 'I'm crazy and I am proud of it.'" But, paradoxically, Wiesel saves man *at the last minute*, just as God *at the last minute* saved the man "who will laugh," Isaac. God loves the mad. Death and madness are both liberating forces. Strangely, voluntary death is rare in the camp. But that still leaves madness. And that madness will continue to return when the ordeal is long past. Reconciliation through madness is basically what Elie Wiesel's demented laughter and the prayer of his character Pedro are all about: "Suddenly he stopped in front of me and shouted his anger to my face: 'I don't like your prayer! It's humiliating! It gives God what he doesn't deserve, unconditional allegiance. I have a personal prayer, too, made just for me. This one: Oh God, give me the strength to sin against you, to oppose your will! Give me the strength to deny you, imprison you, ridicule you!—That's my prayer.'"

In *Night*, Wiesel has lent extraordinary expression to the rejection of God (addressed to God, and therefore quite different from the "death of God"). On the day of Yom Kippur, the Jewish prisoners are locked in a bitter discussion on whether to fast or not. "I did not fast . . . there was no longer any reason why I should fast. I no longer accepted God's silence. As I swallowed my bowl of soup, I saw in the gesture an act of rebellion and protest against Him."

Face to Face with the Gulag

Dissident Russian literature, as said, provides us with an immense and remarkable body of texts on man before, in, and after the camp. Indeed, we have a greater wealth of texts, and of a more varied nature, than ever came out of the Nazi camps. There are a number of reasons for this. First of all, the Soviet camps are still in existence; they serve as a constant reminder; and they handle enormous numbers of people from all social categories. Second, with the thaw the camps were weakened, and "miraculously" released millions of survivors. This weakening has prompted a few to reveal their experiences. Finally, Khrushchev ushered in a new era in which recognition was given to the harm done by the concentration camps. All these different causes were thus combined and added to one basic premise: a heritage of classical Russian literature based on the demanding primacy of ethics.

There are clearly two different generations of Gulag writers. The survivors of Stalin's camps, Alexander Solzhenitsyn (imprisoned from 1945 to 1955), Evgenia Ginzburg (from 1937 to 1955), Yuri Dombrovsky (a total of more than twenty years), and Varlam Shalamov (more than twenty-five years), are all people who were marked by the Stalinist era. Andrei Siniavsky, Vladimir Bukovsky, and Edward Kuznetsov came into contact with the camps after the thaw, and although the camp was less hard, sometimes the prison was that much more refined. They went to prison having already heard tales of the experiences, real or imagined, of their elders. Siniavsky, in his *Fantastičeskie Povesti* [Tales of the Fantastic], described his future arrest down to the smallest detail. They are the second generation, for whom the Gulag was already a cultural notion long before it actually became an existential experience.

It would seem to me that the former are more concerned with unleashing their "cry from the depths" on behalf of the victims, while the latter are more involved with the defense and reconstruction of their egos. For the former, the essential experience of their lives is the camp, and surviving the camp. The others have long been acquainted with prison life; in fact, the prison experience outweighs that of the camp, and occasionally their texts carry the mark of an imagined prison world, as Brombert points out. Vladimir Bukovsky, for example, left alone to fight against "the element of isolation," builds in his mind an immense fortified castle with "spiral staircases, turrets and passageways." In Bukovsky's surprising and stimulating book, the title of which comes from Ecclesiastes, a lot of thought is devoted to the lack of "consistency" of human beings caught in extreme situations; it is also a major lesson on the prison world, which makes it very similar to "classical" prison literature: "You have to learn not to see any of the things that surround you, not to think of your home, and not to wait to be freed. You have to allow life to go on alongside you, in parallel, as if it did not concern you."[21]

There is no room here to provide a complete historical survey of post-Gulag literature. The problem is compounded by the necessity of having to include important texts that do not describe the Gulag directly, but rather its impact on society. Such works include the *Requiem* by Anna Akhmatova,[22] *Sophia Petrovna* by Lydia Chukovskaya, the extraordinary dialogue of the two women in *Zapiski ob Anne Akhmatovoj* [Conversations with Anna Akhmatova] by the same author, or Nadejda Mandelstam's *Memoirs*. It might not be amiss to point out that these accounts of fear and the overcoming of fear have been written by women. The compost of totalitarianism is fear, and the area covered by fear is the "great zone," everything that is not yet Gulag. As for the Gulag itself, either man is broken definitively, or else he learns to conquer fear definitively. Women, who have seen their husbands, sons, or brothers taken from them, have experienced fear to a greater degree than anybody else.

"In 1938, a man said to me, 'You are a courageous woman. You are frightened of nothing.'—'What are you talking about?' I answered, 'I never cease to be afraid.' There was no way of avoiding it. You were arrested, and before they liquidated you, they forced you to betray others."[23] Akhmatova adds: "Fear stays in your blood, just like a disease," and she goes on to consider Joan of Arc, who recanted at her third interrogation; "Because I was afraid of the fire," Joan declared. The fear of ceasing to be oneself, the fear of being frightened, that's what holds it all together. When the arrest finally comes, it is felt as a relief.

Once arrested, the subject of the totalitarian power, after a long spell in prison, becomes a member of the *zek* nation. *Gulag Archipelago* by Solzhenitsyn is an attempt to embrace the existence of this *zek* nation. The objective of the Gulag machine is to turn a man into a totally flexible object, a hunk of meat (it is symbolic that the prison van which crosses the last page of the *First Cycle* bears the inscription, written in all languages, *Miaso, Fleisch, Meat, Viande*). Solzhenitsyn paints an immense picture of the birth, the growth, and the legal and geographical development of the Gulag. His method is that of an anthropologist who is intent on making a detailed record of concealed or submerged civilization. The metaphor of the *archipelago* irrigates the entire work, from Eos with her roselike fingers to the interminable convoys (the "transfers"), the establishment of commercial channels, of crossroads, of departure and arrival ports for this slave civilization.

Gulag Archipelago is a book apart because it combines the scope of the epic, the violence of mockery, and an immense amount of information, which it proceeds to classify, with personal elements: fragments of memories, avowals of weaknesses, the dialogue with his little hero Ivan Denisovitch (in a way, Solzhenitsyn's Virgil). At the same time, the virulence, the verve, and the anger of the author are joined by an enormous chorus of voices: the voices of the 227 witnesses who "collaborated" in the writing of *Archipelago*, the voices of the tortured and the dead toward whom the author feels an obligation. Throughout this immense work, every single detail is picked out; after all, the Gulag planet is entirely barren, so every detail is indeed worth noting. After her encounter with Solzhenitsyn, Akhmatova said: "He is like a beacon.... We had forgotten that people like him even existed. His eyes are like precious stones. *He weighs each individual word.*"

The "weighing" of words, a new thrift in writing and recounting, are inseparable from this way of handling the history of man. The immensity of the path followed by this inquiry should not be interpreted as a means of kindling pathos; each word has been carefully and purposefully chosen. The survivors have all lived through silence. The fourth part of the book, "The Soul and the Barbed Wire," is its very core. "Of course, in comparison with prison, our camps are harmful, even poisonous. Of course it was not for the good of our souls that the hypertrophic growth of the archipelago was permitted. And yet, is there really no hope of being able to preserve one's integrity in the camps? Or, more importantly, is the elevation of the soul truly impossible there?"

The *zek* has a clear conscience: He does not commit suicide; at worst, he mutilates his body ("the arithmetics are simple: the sacrifice of one part to save the whole"). From the very moment he sets foot in the Gulag, he must learn to abide by its rules: survival (doing the "richer" inmates some small turns), doing one's job (Ivan Denisovitch's famous wall), and *keeping one's integrity* (not to inform on others, not to beg for favors, not to "lick the bottom of the bowl"). "Your eyes are the reflection of a conscience that is as pure as a mountain lake. And your eyes that have been purified through suffering will not fail to detect the slightest opacity in the look of others."

For Solzhenitsyn, it would seem that it is the virtues of purity and liberty that find refuge in the camp in a totalitarian regime. His entire *First Cycle* is built around this paradox: the enslavement of the "free" in the "great zone" and the enfranchisement of the prisoners in the "small zone." None of the oppressive ritual of the great zone, none of the stultifying ideology can affect you. The camp can thus, in a totalitarian country, become a Socratic refuge. "Of the years spent in prison with my back bent, almost broken, I learnt one thing: how man can become good or bad." As a unique area of social *concentration*, the camp reveals more things about a person's character than does war. Throughout the entire book, Solzhenitsyn can be seen fighting against another school of thought, that of Shalamov, for whom the camp inevitably becomes a place where you learn depravation. With the gloomy voice of a prophet, Solzhenitsyn admits, "How scabby become the souls of prisoners when they are systematically encouraged to clash with one another!" But then he continues, "Just as in nature, where oxidation cannot take place without a gain in electrons (When one atom becomes oxidised,—another atom is reduced), depravation and elevation go side by side."

Evgenia Ginzburg shares Solzhenitsyn's approach here. In an admirable book entitled *Krutoj Maršrut* [An Abrupt Itinerary],[24] she manages to take us with her on a spiritual ascension. From solitary confinement, where she spent two years and survived only through reciting verses, to a camp where things could not have been worse, a prison colony for women, where murder and rape were done for fun ("these humanoids live a fantastic life, where the constraints of day and night have been abolished"), this admirable woman reaches a quasi-mystical elevation. She has just come rushing out of the barracks where a monstrous and fetid orgy is going on. "Above me stretched an immense black sky dotted with large, brilliant stars. I did not cry. I prayed. Passionately, desperately. Lord, may I be struck by fever and lose consciousness, may I forget, and may death come!" Then, little by little, an amazing resurrection takes place, the landscape, the cosmos, the stars all return. Thanks to an encounter with one of the prisoners, Dr. Walter, who is a saint, she finds herself "in paradise." "I feel the birth within me of a feeling of reconciliation, of acceptance. . . ." One summer evening, as they stand facing the bay of Nagayevo, she and the doctor exclaim, "But it is as beautiful as the bay of Naples!"

On the other hand, the movement is not always upward, debasement also exists. This theme is found in Shalamov, the author of about a hundred well-known short stories that describe horrifying things in the style of Pushkin's elliptic beginnings, such as in "Queen of Spades": "We were playing at Narumov's," which Shalamov quotes in one of his stories (crooks play cards and other *zeks'* lives are at stake). In contrast to the Solzhenitsyn type of construction, here one has these terrifying closeups, with a unity of time and place that could not be more classical. Put together, they re-create the very universe of human *concentration*. But the logic of this universe is radically different from the normal "human comedy," with its criminals who act like lords, its doctors-cum-torturers, its informers who are assassinated at night, its down-and-outs curled up on some horrible bit of filth they have just discovered. The baths, for example, represent a catastrophe for the *zek* which he will fight against tooth and nail because they will mean the loss of the personal rags that serve as clothes. The time span of one day has an eschatological dimension to it, and nobody can even think in terms of more than one week. First everything shrivels up inside, then everything becomes frozen: "The very same frost that can transform spittle into ice in midair reaches right into the human soul."

Shalamov's short fables are in the style of "the marchioness went out at five o'clock," set in a universe of survivors and human wrecks. The criminals have but to say a word and the life of one of the "others" is immediately at stake. And what about shame? Yes, there is such a thing as shame, but it becomes distorted by the laws of degradation that govern the Gulag. An additional meal granted a prisoner might give him the strength to commit suicide. A former clergyman, who has gone mad and who has succeeded in keeping the picture of his daughter on him, receives a letter from her informing him that she has officially disowned him. The hand of a friend throws the document into the fire so that the unfortunate man can continue to cherish the photograph. "The worst thing," Shalamov writes, "is when a man begins to feel that the dregs with whom he lives have become a part of his own life and will always remain so, and when he bases all his moral values on his experience of camp, when the ethics of the criminals apply to his life . . . once all this has happened, is he then still a man or not?"

In Shalamov's tale "Pervyj zub" [The First Tooth], the narrator, a "new recruit," spits out his first tooth, having had it knocked out trying to protect one of the "politicals." Three possible outcomes are offered. In the first, the narrator has learned the "law" of the camp; in the second, his assailant later comes up to him to make peace, for fear of retaliation; in the third, after several months have gone by, a specter is seen walking past: "The young giant had disappeared. In his place, there was an old man with white hair who limped and spat blood. He didn't recognise me, and, when I took him by the hand and called him by his name, he tore himself away and continued on his way." None of these variations is satisfactory but, as the narrator concludes, "You write and you can forget." This triple dénouement simply goes to show how amazingly quickly things can become reality in camp.

In a remarkably pithy literary style, Shalamov describes all the things that become detached from man. Once the brain starts to freeze, the process is irreversible; even the imagination cannot escape. It is the human material which freezes, which cracks and allows itself to be debased in a series of successive stages, like trap doors that are thrown open under the reader's feet. For Shalamov, there is no "elevation" of the soul in camp. He talks about human waste, man like a piece of timber being cut up, *man without companions*, left alone to face the human wolves. The Shalamovian world is in the hands of a cruel child who has lost the use of his senses and his humanity, but still has some violent colors left, like those found in polar landscapes. Siniavsky, in a preface to one of Shalamov's works, wonders whether one can or should read it to the end. "Yes, but then how can one live without having read to the end? Like a traitor?"

Many survivors feel ill at ease with Shalamov and accuse him of pathological exaggeration. They suspect that he trades in horror. Nevertheless, the purity of his fables about man debased is the best proof of Shalamov's authenticity. He has given the short story genre a new lease on life by endowing it with a form of suspense it had never known. Where does the dehumanization of the humanoid end? Where does *human death* begin? The "suspense" of the short story in this case is the *suspension* of life in its strictest sense.

We should also have to analyze the evidence submitted by someone like Marchenko on self-mutilation, the ultimate language of communication in a system characterized by total social deafness. It is the "body art" of man in a situation of incommunicability. Russian literature offers us some extremely important works on the imaginary world of the deportees, the tortured, people who are subjected to the arbitrariness of prison *unreality*— for example Edward Kuznetsov, Andrei Siniavsky, or Yuri Dombrovsky's novel *Fakul'tet nenužnyh veščej* [The Faculty of the Useless].[25]

*   *   *

Real-life experiences overlap with the imaginary. Dreams slip into other dreams. With no compass to guide it, memory can but scratch its head and stutter. This is not due to the passing of time: everything that exists on the other side of those watchtowers belongs to another planet. . . . But sometimes I catch myself red-handed engaged in slightly schizophrenic mental games: the camp and all things linked with it become a unique reality, the rest being nothing more than a mirage, one provoked by the incredible action of the watery soup. Or else I suddenly realise that on that unforgettable New Year's Eve 1971, when I was carted off to be tormented, what happened in reality was that I was shot. After I had been riddled with holes like a sieve in the real world, I continued to function mechanically in an imaginary dimension which was the fruit of my earnest prayers at the moment when the salvo was fired (E. Kuznetsov, *Diary*).

When he read these lines, Jorge Semprun recognized that "this dream was the dream of a dead man." He had experienced the very same thing in the German camp.

Dombrovsky too is fascinated by the "cadaverous mystique,"

since in his own way the *zek* corrupts his warders and the outside world. "These corpses are diabolically cunning zombies: they pretend to be alive and yet they stink of death." Caught in the stranglehold of "conveyor" interrogations,[26] the tortured feel an abyssal sea rise up toward them out of which comes an enormous crab, the symbol of life at any cost, an irrational, uncertain life that hails from the depths of the mind. Betrayal eats away at man, the noxious atmosphere of death destroys interrogators and guards alike. But the vital crab continues to wriggle in the vise of the imagination, in the depths of the human soul.

Once again, Siniavsky brings us back to the imaginary world of camp in *Golos v hore* [A Voice in the Chorus]: Restricted to the enclosure of the camp, a human being enters a new world, where his imagination is unleashed. The smaller his part of the cosmos, the stronger his perception of the cosmos in its entirety. In much the same way, Avvakum, leader of the schismatic Old Believers in the nineteenth century, when thrown into a hole in the ice in Pustozersk before being burned alive, had the impression of space opening up and coming toward him—just like in the inverted perspectives of the icons, where nothing disappears over the horizon; rather it converges toward the center. Life in camp (a "Brezhevian" camp which does not kill) seems to the *zek* Siniavsky like a life "on the screen," a life that is continually being acted out, or even, as he says himself, life as an artistic representation: the constant musical background from the radios, the men under constant surveillance, and the constant workings of the imagination, which feeds on the smallest nuggets of landscape and space to reconstitute the whole of space, the entire cosmos. Language reduced to dialogue, the syncopated structure of intercommunication characterized by curses, obscenities, anecdotes, and the uneven rhythm of popular language, are all much a part of this place where everything is exacerbated, everything is acted out. For Siniavsky, the camp is the literary *topos* par excellence today. It has replaced family, travel, the theater. It is humanity on show, portrayed in terms of art and death, akin to art precisely because so close to death.

*   *   *

A dream of culture Europeanized had marked the 1920s.

Pasternak and Mandelstam, in their own original ways, are good examples of this. What the great Russian poets of this period have to tell us is, as Nadejda Mandelstam has said, mostly concerned with the question of memory and the loss of memory, of reason and the loss of reason.

> O dearly beloved leaven of the world,
> Sounds, tears and labours—
> The heavy accents of the rain
> of adversity swirling,
> Sounds dying away—
> In what mine shall I find you?
>
> In my beggar's memory
> Suddenly I feel the wounds
> Filled with water the colour of rust—
> I stumble after them
> Hating myself, without a guide,
> I am the blind man and his guide.

This poem by Mandelstam, written between two arrests[27] in Voronèje, in January 1937, tells us about the loss of sound and of senses. The old Europe, brimming over with sounds and senses, had given way to a blinded Europe, now unsteady on its feet. After Kolyma, how was one to renew the links with others, with sounds and senses? After Auschwitz and Kolyma, what meaning could one give to the noble philosophical construction of a symbolist poet like Viacheslav Ivanov, whose famous formula "Thou art"[28] was intended in 1907 to overcome the "crisis of individualism"?

Shalamov and Dombrovsky set out to prove that "Thou art" no longer has any significance. Solzhenitsyn and Evgenia Ginzburg attempt to recreate a "Thou art" on a different basis, on the basis of the indescribable fraternity of the camps, one that has precious little to do with the fraternity of the esthetes in 1907. Dombrovsky writes: "Do you underestimate the human person? Do you believe that people are incapable of throwing themselves into the mud? Of becoming as grotesque as a dog with a tin of food tied to its tail? Man is capable of anything.

But do you know what the worst thing is? It is that we continue to maintain an appearance of culture, to churn out nice turns of phrase, to have our little vanities, to be erudite, braggarts. Are we not the salt of the earth?" Faced with such merciless derision, Solzhenitsyn answers with great conviction: "Your soul, which had dried up, is now irrigated by suffering. If you can no longer love your neighbour, as Christianity teaches, at least learn to love those who are close to you."

In fact, the disagreement is about the "contents" of man. Once man finds himself in an "extreme" situation, torn from his family, deprived of all his possessions, subjected to the will of criminals, placed in the quasi-abstract space of the camp, has he still a means of communication? Is he still a man, is he still a companion to his "neighbors"? Or has this life-giving capacity become frozen? The Shalamov-Solzhenitsyn debate touches upon the very heart of our problem. In the final analysis, we are forced to agree with both answers: Human communication ceases (Shalamov), a new form of communication is born (Solzhenitsyn).

On This Side or Beyond

There are many of us who continue to think, to write, and to live on this side of Auschwitz and Kolyma. Are these books "obligatory" reading, and do we have to go through the ordeal they represent? Do all roads today pass necessarily through Shalamov? Can one or should one impugn the progressive Panglosses who continue to believe in a radiant and normative future? Or rather, should one allow oneself to become paralyzed by the "eclipse of God," to be walled up in that unnamed place from which no communication passes?

The survivors themselves have not managed to agree on the answers to these questions, but they are all a lesson in strength and energy to us. After Solzhenitsyn's appearance on television on April 11, 1975, Semprun realized that "there we had it, the immense truth, the larger-than-life portrayal of that truth by Alexander Solzhenitsyn." Sheer size, overpowering realism, and cathartic laughter are all recurring elements in Solzhenitsyn's works. Everything has to be *created anew*. The old values are dead.

In conclusion, let us take the example of a Soviet writer, Vassili

Grossman. Grossman was never sent to camp. He was a "normal" Soviet writer, that is to say committed and a good Communist. It was not his own suffering that "irrigated his soul." Grossman, a Soviet writer of Jewish origin who felt nevertheless that he was first and foremost a Soviet man living in the "light haze of the official myth," glorifying "the fortifying virtues of work"[29] along the lines of the *production-oriented* literature of the Stalinist era, is doubly interesting to us here. First of all is his "conversion" to the "truth" of Auschwitz: Standing by the victims of the gas chambers of Auschwitz, Grossman belongs to that category of people for whom the holocaust is something that cannot be bypassed, *an obligatory staging post* for the twentieth century. Grossman felt bound to continue his "conversion" and to draw a parallel between Auschwitz and Kolyma. In other words, alone and in an extremely risky situation, he was forced to think through the key problem of the relationship between the two systems that had bred the world of the concentration camp.

It was during his investigations into the genocide of the Jews at Treblinka and Auschwitz[30] that Grossman felt the first inklings of his "conversion." Together with Ehrenburg, he wrote the famous "Black Book" on the Nazi genocide of Jews. But the work, which had already been completed, was banned: The Jews were not supposed "to stand apart." Not long afterward, state anti-Semitism, which went under the label of "anticosmopolitanism," was to come into full swing, deporting and shooting, exiling and terrorizing. At the time Grossman was working on a major novel on war centered around a family from Stalingrad. It appeared in 1952 and was immediately brought down by the critics, although it was completely orthodox. Then Grossman decided to write a second part, to which he gave the title *Žizn' i sud'ba* [Life and Destiny].[31] It was confiscated by the KGB and only appeared abroad, by a miracle, some twenty years after its completion, in 1980—long after the death of its author. The book is of vital importance for our subject.

Life and Destiny is written in a somewhat heavy style and concerns itself with the "destinies" of hundreds of people. A Jewish mother writes a final letter to her son from the ghetto in which she has been imprisoned, saying that she is about to be massacred (this takes place in occupied Ukraine): "Do you know,

Vitia, what I felt behind the barbed wire? I thought it would be horror. But would you believe it that, in this park for animals, I felt relieved? Do not think that I have a servile nature. No, no. All around me stood *people with the same destiny*." A young woman adopts and consoles a small boy during the transfer to Auschwitz and cradles him in her warmth, even into the fatal shower: "The noise of footsteps ceased, all that could be heard were unintelligible words, people moaning, stifled cries. There was no longer any sense in talking, actions had become pointless, actions are directed towards the future and in the gas chamber there was no such thing as the future." Grossman describes a Soviet camp, portrays both Hitler and Stalin, takes us off to an "islet of liberty" right in the middle of the inferno of Stalingrad, an islet of Russian resistance fighters who have reconquered freedom. The Jewish scientist Strum, while he awaits his imminent arrest, goes to see his old teacher Chapyzhin, who has refused to work on the fission of the atom, and who explains his philosophy: A living being grows in the universe at the expense of inert matter, freedom prevails over slavery. Strum's answer is Grossman's: "Won't man change the world into a gigantic concentration camp?"

Even before Solzhenitsyn, Grossman had already committed to paper this living encyclopedia of the camp with its different classes—the crooks, the "bitches," the "noncriminals," the "goners." He already knew how people committed suicide in Magadan: "In the marshes of Kolyma, you just stop eating, and for a few days you drink water—you die of an edema, of hydrocephalus. People call that 'drinking the water.'" The heart of the book is the interrogation of the old Communist Mostovsky by an SS Obersturmbannfuehrer, Liess. Liess speaks in the name of evil, but at the same time he proves to Mostovsky that they are in fact joined in solidarity: "Yes, we are your declared enemies. But our victory is also your victory. Do you understand that? And if it is you who win, we shall bask in your victory." And he goes on to demonstrate that Stalin and Hitler are like "surgical mirrors" for one another, the massacres of the one inspiring those of the other. "We are a form of the same structure: the State and the Party." Mostovsky feels an abyss open up beneath him. The exchange of victims, the rivalry between Hitler and Stalin in massacring their own partisans—Liess was right.

Grossman paints a portrait of one of the Communist fanatics, the real "hardliners" (like the terrorists at the beginning of the century), who had become torturers. "Their hatred stemmed from love." Grossman's lesson is both terrifying and yet very modest. It is necessary, he thinks, to remove the capital letter from *good*, and to trust in "impulsive acts of goodness" whose favors are distributed sparingly and at random. But that other force, *goodness*, has been responsible for too much harm.

The readers of this book, which has quite miraculously been rediscovered today, will probably reel from the shock of the monumentality of the diagnosis, as well as be moved by the naiveté of this philosophy of salvation. We ought to pay tribute to the courage of those who had to endure the experience of terror in the twentieth century. Most of the time, there are only two possible reactions to this type of experience: Either you choose to ignore it, or you throw yourself into it body and soul. I am thinking here of a writer such as the Pole Kosinski who wrote his violent *The Painted Bird* in English, or the Russian emigré Aleškovsky who wrote *Ruka, dnevnik palača* [Rouka, the Account of a Torturer]. Sadism and dementia can be exploited to excess, even to the point of immodesty. It is far more difficult to stick to the concision and density of *A Day in the Life of Ivan Denisovitch*. It is precisely in the grayness, in the absolute routine of a day as imposed by the concentration camp system, that Solzhenitsyn has succeeded best in exposing this new being, adapted to the *topos* of the camp, but still resolutely human—Ivan Denisovitch.

"At five this morning, like every morning, we were given the signal to get up: a hammer banged against the rail in front of the administration hut." This simple, trivial sentence was responsible for setting into motion the flood of Russian literature that has attempted to tell us about the camp.

This side or beyond.... What part of ourselves must we give to this reflection? Should we go along with Alexander Zinoviev, and maintain that the whole of the human species is already totalitarian and the Gulag is superfluous, since the totalitarian exists and fulfils all our needs? Should we, like the Polish producer Grotowski, get actors who perform the refined plays of the beginning of the century to put on the clothes of deportees? Should we give our fantasies free reign to the point of nausea, like Aleškovsky? Should we join Mandelstam in his silence, or laugh with Elie Wiesel?

Solzhenitsyn and Grossman, who wrote their major works, each completely unaware of what the other was doing, who have virtually nothing in common, the one a *zek*, the other a "Soviet writer"; the one a Jew, the other an orthodox close to the Old Believers, have some amazing and magnificent points of encounter, which I shall draw upon for my conclusion. Both attempted to determine whether the notion of a "people" could serve as a sheet anchor. Both realized that the answer was "no," since in this case the individual turns out to be stronger than the people. (Under totalitarianism the only cement of a true people is a common death: the *people of Auschwitz*, the *people of Kolyma*.) Both need to make their own *mea culpas* heard: We remained silent, we did not see the evil that was at work behind the utopian mask, we were caught in its snare. Both are concerned with the problem of serving a bad country—or, to put it another way, with the modern problem of medieval tyrannicide. For Grossman, the only solution possible is the rebirth of individual, even insignificant "impulsive acts of goodness." Solzhenitsyn, on the other hand, advocates individual martyrdom, the refusal to submit any longer. Basically, they are united by their common biblical roots, their biblical heritage. To that extent they are very close to Elie Wiesel, who never ceases to rethink the Book of Job. And indeed it might well be that only the great prophets of Israel can help us to come to terms with the deportation of man out of his life as a man, which is precisely what the concentration camp experience represents.

Notes

1 See Michel Heller, *Le monde concentrationnaire et la littérature soviétique* (Lausanne, 1974). For all literature on the Gulag, see Heller's excellent selected bibliography.
2 David Rousset, *L'Univers concentrationnaire* (Paris, 1969). Leo Poliakov, *Bréviaire de la haine* (Paris, 1951). Olga Wormser Migot, *L'Ere des camps* (Paris, 1973). Jules Margolin, *Putešestvie v stranu Z/K* (New York, 1952). Alexander Solzhenitsyn, *Gulag Archipelago* (in Russian, 3 vols.) (Paris, 1973, 1974, 1975). Varlam Shalamov, *Kolymskie rasskazy* (in Russian) (London, 1978). J. Pasqualini, *Prisonnier de Mao* (Geneva, 1977).
3 Bruno Bettelheim, *Surviving and Other Essays* (New York, 1976).
4 *Journal de Genève*, 9 (July 1983).
5 See Natacha Dioujeva and Francois George, *Staline à Paris* (Paris, 1982).
6 Saül Friedländer, *Reflets du nazisme* (Paris, 1982).

[7] See *Esprit*, September 1980.

[8] George Steiner, "The Portage to San Christobel of A. H.," *The Kenyon Review*, Spring 1979.

[9] The Yad Vashem in Jerusalem, a memorial museum for the victims of Nazism.

[10] Pierre Pascal, *En Russie rouge* (Paris 1920, new edition 1921).

[11] *Belomorsko—Baltijskij kanal im. Stalina* (Moscow, 1934).

[12] There is a poignant example of this in Wolfgang Leonhart's book *Die Revolution entlässt ihre Kinder* (Cologne, 1956).

[13] Margarete Buber-Neumann, *Déporté en Sibérie* (Paris, 1949).

[14] Hannah Arendt, *The Origins of Totalitarianism* (New York, 1951).

[15] *Kamienny Swiat* (Warsaw, 1948; translated into French, Paris, 1972).

[16] André Schwartz-Bart, *Le Dernier des justes* (Paris, 1959).

[17] Elie Wiesel, *La nuit* (Paris, 1958).

[18] See Joe Friedemann, *Le Rire dans l'univers tragique d'Elie Wiesel* (Paris, 1981).

[19] According to Lefort, the autocrat takes care to govern at a distance from society. The egocrat, although hidden in his bunker, claims to be "at one with the whole of society." See Claude Lefort, *Un homme en trop, réflexions sur l'Archipel du Goulag* (Paris, 1976).

[20] Igor Chafarevitch, *Le socialisme comme phénomène de l'histoire mondiale* (Paris, 1973).

[21] Vladimir Bukovsky, *Et le vent reprend ses tours* (Paris, 1978).

[22] Anna Akhmatova, *Requiem* (the poem was written in 1939 and is as yet unpublished in the USSR).

[23] Lydia Tchoukovskaia, *Zapiski ob Anne Akhmatovoj* (Paris, 1970).

[24] Evgenia Ginzburg, *Krutoj maršrut* (Milan, 1970).

[25] Edward Kuznetsov, *Dnevniki* (Paris, 1973). André Siniavsky, *Golos v hore* London, 1973). Yuri Dombrovsky, *Fakultet nenužnyh veščej* (Paris, 1978).

[26] In other words, uninterrupted: For days and nights on end, the interrogators relay each other, exactly like a "conveyor" system.

[27] Osip Mandelstam, *Sobranie Sočinenij*, vol. I (Washington, 1964), p. 224.

[28] Vjačeslav Ivanov, *Sobranie Sočinenij*, vol. III (Brussels, 1979), pp. 262–68.

[29] See Shimon Markish, *Le cas Vassili Grossman* (Paris, 1983).

[30] V. Grossman, "L'Enfer de Treblinka," in *Znamja*, 11 (Moscow 1944).

[31] V. Grossman, *Zizn' i sud'ba* (Lausanne, 1980).

Discussion: Friedländer Paper

Friedländer: I chose what is apparently a rather limited topic, but I feel that this apparently limited topic is related to our general concerns at different levels. First of all, this is perhaps the most extreme instance of systematic inhumanity of man to man, carried out in a planned manner, and the twentieth century was the framework for this series of events. I chose to present those events in a roundabout way, dwelling on the controversy between two schools of thought, intentionalists and functionalists, which allowed me to move from the level of the events to the level of interpretation of National Socialism as such. That led me to a third level of discussion at the end of the paper: that we are facing something which cannot be explained only within the much-discussed frameworks of the course of German history or fascism or totalitarianism or the three mixed together, but something which I chose to call a political religion with very specific characteristics. The central characteristic was the faith in the leader, the absolute obedience he managed to create around him, and the complete change of norms which the movement and this leadership managed to achieve in a very brief span of time. Is it a unique phenomenon, which we have seen once in the twentieth century? Or is there something in our present civilization that may allow for the resurgence under different circumstances of movements of this type, the conjunction of millenarian or utopian ideas brought forth by a charismatic leader, using all the potential of modern organization and technology for aims of eventual total destruction?

Mommsen: The functionalists tend to argue that though Hitler was a particular phenomenon and though we have to deal with a political movement of charismatic character with a very strong ideological appeal, it was structural conditions that explain why the majority of the German people, or at any rate its leading elites, were drawn into that system and into the extinction of the Jews. I do not believe that the success of a nationalist social system can be put down to the attraction of its ideology; I tend to

235

think that it has been successful in spite of its ideology, and in spite of its anti-Semitic element.

Functionalists have been blamed for reducing responsibility by putting it down to mechanisms. I think it is rather the other way round. By not putting the main responsibility on Hitler himself, but rather on a great many people, especially on the middle ranks of the machinery, the real responsibility is spread to very many people. And of course by now, much to the irritation of many in the Federal Republic, it has been discovered that the army was deeply involved in the whole thing, that the extinction of about one-third of the Russian prisoners of war was the so-called trial for the extinction of the Jews. That makes things appear in another light. And given that, I must admit I have some reservations about the paper.

No functionalist would argue that Hitler was not necessary; he instigated anti-Semitic policies in the first place. But the question is whether and how the process could move on from the initial policy (elimination of the Jews from public life), which was carried out more by the party and the SS than by Hitler. The next stage was the policy of emigration on a grand scale. The third stage was emigration to the East European territories under conditions of forced labor—which was already tantamount to deaths in very great numbers. The final stage was the policy of extinction.

The functionalists argue that such acceleration cannot be attributed to the Fuehrer's orders, or at any rate not in the first place. There is a strong indication that in some ways the real initiatives for the extreme solution came from the middle echelon of the machinery and not from Hitler. The fatal document that comes nearest to the Hitler order, Goering's order of July 31, 1941, was, according to Raul Hilberg, drawn up by Eichmann. He produced that document and made Goering sign it. From that point of view, the situation looks very different. Then there are the technicians who say it is quite impossible to send more and more Jews to the East; that they will perish. Then orderly extinction may be more humane (excuse me for putting it that way).

It is extreme, it is unbelievable, it is incomprehensible. And I myself have great sympathy with those who say that Hitler must have given an order, because an event of such enormous dimensions becomes even less understandable if responsibilities appear to be blurred. But the railway officials somewhere in France or somewhere in Germany who took care of those trains never heard anything of a Fuehrer order, and that is the sort of thing that has got to be explained. From that point of view the functionalist interpretation carries more weight, because it is not just a small elite that somehow convinced the German people that the Jews had to be eliminated. One has of course to admit that the whole thing cannot be explained without taking into consideration the extremely outrageous way in which the war against Russia was conducted. I do not think that before that stage any sort of extinction policy was thinkable, or could have been maintained.

Friedländer: I see things differently from Mommsen, but not because of the problem of responsibility. I certainly would disagree with the thrust of some arguments presented today in Germany that functionalist historians tend to dilute responsibility and that intentionalists keep the weight of responsibility as it should be kept. I switched to a more determined intentionalist—that is, traditional—position after reading new material. I am aware of the fact that taking that line makes the historical interpretation more difficult, because the structural interpretation fits our historiography better—if one may say this about such events. The process of dehumanization and extermination certainly needs a whole structure, needs the dynamics of bureaucracies. But it needs to be pushed ahead against the growing difficulties of total war, the more so that the German Reich was losing that war, certainly after Stalingrad. Nonetheless the process was precipitated and even brought as far as possible to its conclusion in the very last stages of the war. And there, in the case of the Jews of Hungary, you see a determined will at the top— that is, Adolf Hitler's—even against his closest advisers, like Himmler, who were trying to equivocate and maybe stop the process in 1944. So the last stage would very much confirm the intentionalist position, though again, the whole thing is inexplicable on any count.

Maier: I think that one need not polarize a will at the center and set it in opposition to a type of system that functioned around this core of Eichmanns and the like, whether some of them disagreed with each other at the end or not. That does not mean that Hitler did not have some central conception of getting rid of the Jews. I think that system was not inscribed in the Hitler Nazi vision at the very beginning, largely because the Nazis never imagined they might achieve so fantastic a degree of success. Thus, I have a certain sympathy for arguments about a step-by-step capacity to radicalize and approach this goal from one reason or another.

Now, in what sense is this central to the twentieth century? It seems to me an act that is almost arbitrary and of almost meaningless noncentrality, while at the same time it is very central to our personal experience—it is crucial to what we think about the first half of this century.

Hersch: It seems to me necessary to make a distinction between the will to do something and the possibility of actually doing it. In the field of the will, one cannot avoid being an intentionalist. And here Hitler is the central figure, to be understood as such. I believe that maybe this element is the least representative of the twentieth century. But what seems to me very important and perhaps most important is the question of how it was possible to turn the opportunities into realities. Would the circumstances have been there in another century? Here we come to the functionalist interpretation and explanation. What was specific in the twentieth century which paralyzed to such a degree so many people's ability to say "no"?

Friedländer: We have here the conjunction of the will, the will of a type of leader who appears very seldom—the still incomprehensible charismatic aspect of Hitler's personality, the Weberian type of rule and power which goes under that name and which we have great difficulties in comprehending in industrial societies, and the structure of modern industrial bureaucratic society to implement that will. That will. That is the phenomenon which is unique: Somebody at the top has such power and such influence on his nearest followers and on those who follow the nearest circle that if he hints, if he winks, letting all those around understand that they can now proceed to exterminate to the last person millions of people, the machine will start. This kind of influence that mobilizes all the possibilities of industrial technological society is hitherto unique.

But the point is really that somebody at some stage can say, "Go ahead." And those who have to implement it feel it is a burden, and Himmler says many times, "It is a burden. It is something I hesitated to ask my brave SS people to do." But against the Fuehrer's order there is no hesitation. He says, "It was difficult," and he says it in four speeches to the officers of the Wehrmacht. It was terrible. But it was a Fuehrer order. For me, one incomprehensible aspect, among others, is that it was a Fuehrer order, and one must therefore obey. That is the point of the phenomenon which nobody has yet succeeded in really penetrating.

Mommsen: Jews were exterminated in tens of thousands in the context of the extermination of prisoners in the Russian prisoner-of-war camps. So in some ways extermination was already going on long before it was ever named. That is one of the arguments of the structuralists. I also think the guilt starts much earlier. It starts at the stage when the German population lets the segregation of the Jewish population happen, so that it begins to disappear from their daily lives, to be downgraded into nothingness, and can then be treated as the bureaucracy chooses. That, I think, is the decisive step. The guilt starts here. People did not know anything much about extermination as such. But they allowed others to be treated as less qualified human beings.

Karl: It appears that one American public response to what was going on in Germany, particularly from 1938 on, was an increase in open anti-Semitism, rather than a decrease.

Nivat: Friedländer says that Nazism constantly tended to obliterate the distinction between the symbolic plane, that of metaphors, and that of reality. And indeed, in the totalitarian state, and state of mind, the metaphorical plane pervades all other planes, and the plane of reality begins to disappear. Reality is something that is submitted to cross-examination, to dialogue, to guilt; but the metaphorical plane that has invaded the two main totalitarian regimes we know was univocal, and that sort of univocal reception of the outer world was the main phenomenon for millions of people. And without that univocal, metaphorical level, things such as one man's order or hint being obeyed could not have happened.

Schwartz: One should introduce another category—namely,

opportunity. For instance, in China Chairman Mao was quite cautious when he first came to power in 1949. But then the whole experience from about 1949 to about 1956 appeared to be a great success; China was really unified. At least in Chairman Mao's mind, the view that even his greatest hopes might be realized became very credible suddenly. This is the Mao of the Great Leap Forward and the Mao of the Cultural Revolution—the Mao who really begins to think that he can change man. The emergence of unlimited opportunities that seem to appear once there is an initial response to the leader ought to be introduced as yet another category. There is nothing more maddening than to have unlimited opportunities.

Friedländer: Indeed, opportunity, yes, but I think the key word is *indifference*. There have been many studies on German public opinion, using all kinds of methods, to assess how it responded to the segregation of Jews. It was not against it. It was sometimes mildly in favor of it, but mostly it was rather indifferent. The problem could be generalized. That is, hostility can exist, but the hostility even of small groups can expand immensely if the majority do not care at all about other groups being segregated or destroyed. So I would say the key word is opportunity *because* of the indifference of man to man. Or the indifference of the majority to what is considered a group of outsiders. If the group is singularized, and the Jews obviously were, increasingly as outsiders, then the others turn their backs, and the process that will lead to their annihilation begins.

This leads to Nivat's intervention about metaphor and reality and the univocal character of metaphors. Totalitarian ideologies use a few images. They have the strength of dogma; they are not discussable; they do not allow this testing that the reality of politics in liberal societies asks for. So it becomes difficult for people to distinguish between metaphor and reality. When Nazi functionaries, or people at the level of Himmler or Hitler himself, allude to the Jews as microbes, do they mean it, or do they mean it symbolically?

Kolakowski: One cannot reasonably argue that the Nazis invented genocide; of course they did not. Or anti-Semitism, for that matter. Even ideological genocide was not invented by the Nazis. One might argue, for instance, that the massacre of the

Cathars in the twelfth century was an example of ideological genocide. So what was new, what was peculiar about this experience? One can argue that in massacres of genocidal proportions perpetrated in the name of religious ideas, there was, to put it somewhat crudely, a redeeming side in the sense that it was supposed to be done for the sake and on the order of God, whose order not only cannot be questioned, but who also is omniscient. What is characteristic of the ideological genocides of the twentieth century is that they were perpetrated in the name of secular global ideologies. All religions—at least universal religions—are in a sense global ideologies, which means that they are supposed to encompass all areas of human life. But the global ideologies of the twentieth century are secular, and perhaps the ideological genocide of our century is characteristic in this sense—an example of how global ideologies function once they take secular form, and once their leaders take the place of gods.

Friedländer: How is it that millenarian or even classical religious trends were transposed into the modern political context as secular religions, but with all the trappings and even the dynamics of deeply felt religious movements? Functionalism does not allow one to approach this point, since in this type of religious movement you need a kind of messianic figure. Hitler certainly was that for the true believers. You also need some kind of dogma, at least believed in by the core of believers, the group of dedicated followers. And you need some kind of blind obedience and belief in the ultimate aims of the movement that gives it its dynamics. It is structured as a religious movement, but uses all the potential of industrial society. Can one speak of *eine politische Religion*, with all this means, for our century and the results it can bring about? And can one say that Stalinism was the same thing? I am not sure. Are these both political religions? I am not sure. Nazism was, in my view; perhaps Stalinism was not.

Hagihara: At the Tokyo war crimes tribunal, the prosecutors were, by and large, intentionalists. They were convinced that there must be some basic documents directing Japan to invade China. But all that their search uncovered turned out to be the so-called Tanaka Memorandum. What they discovered in the end was that it was a fake. In that process, the intentionalist position taken by the prosecutors of the Tokyo war tribunal collapsed. Could such things as Nazism occur in a non-Christian society, or are they confined to Christian civilization, and maybe not in another civilization?

Friedländer: Is this type of messianic political faith something which is linked deeply to Western civilization, to Christian civilization, or to Judeo-Christian civilization? Or is it something that may be universal? Would the skepticism and less centrist religious structures of East Asia make something like it in fact impossible? Is this a Western phenomenon, which would be something not of the twentieth century, but of the West? Or is it generalizable?

Iriye: The empirical problem is this: While so many countries have gone through democratization and technological development and conformism, not all countries have experienced or committed genocide. Genocide seems to be more specific—specific to certain countries, and specific in terms of time. Thinking about all this, I come back to the observation that all this must have something to do with the brutalization brought about by war, war preparedness, or war psychosis, or the blurring of the distinction between peace and war. That is, societies in a mental state of war preparedness, when everything is looked at in terms of militarization, tend to seek out internal as well as external enemies. There is a psychological readiness to accept mass murder as a necessity brought about by military preparedness, war planning, or war execution. Even non-Western, non-Christian societies practice genocide. One has to remember Japan's rape of Nanking. It does not take a Christian country to do that. In a wartime situation such as has characterized so many decades of the twentieth century, this kind of brutalization tends to be tolerated.

Friedländer: The Final Solution was never linked to a military necessity. On Soviet territory, you find in some documents a link between the killing of the Jews and the killing of the commissars. But documents also exist advising no links between military necessities and the extermination of the Jews, because it was simply in another realm.

Second, one cannot argue that it was functionally necessary to exterminate internal enemies in order to provide cohesion in a state of war, because it was kept secret from the population. Or at least the perpetrators attempted to keep it secret. The action was parallel to the war—against war necessities during the last years, in terms of rolling stock and logistics, and kept secret. So I come back to my initial idea: this was considered a sacred mission.

Discussion: Nivat Paper

Nivat: In his novel *August 1914*, Alexander Solzhenitsyn says: "There was a concentration camp" (he shows a concentration camp of prisoners), "and there was the beginning of the twentieth century." This definition of the twentieth century is the reason for my paper. I am always astonished when I hear scholars or historians speaking of there being no discontinuity between previous centuries and this one.

My paper is on man and the Gulag, but I have extended the meaning of *Gulag*. It is a Soviet word, a Soviet aberration, but I include the German concentration camp. This forms part of my intellectual biography. Only two details: I visited the Auschwitz camp in 1958 with a very great Polish friend who had been in Auschwitz for one year, and this made a very deep impression on me when I was twenty. And I read *One Day in the Life of Ivan Denisovitch* when it came out. From that time on, I read Russian literature on that subject. And then I found out that I could not limit myself to Russian literature, that I had to move also to the literature on the German camp, and not only historical literature, but also just literature. I became aware that Russian literature distinguishes itself now by the fact that it has become the richest literature on the bare fact of the concentration camp from all points of view: the history of the concentration camp, the ethnography of people—millions, dozens of millions—kept in concentration camps, and so on. Another discovery in that study of this theme was the pathology, the pathology of the literature on the concentration camp and the postcamp pathology.

Since all archives and documents on, say, the Kolyma camps are hidden and forbidden, I suppose that historians must read the testimonies of people who have been in the camps and who are either writers or, as often happens with some kind of terrible trauma, become writers because of their experience.

So the role of literature is very prominent. That is why Solzhenitsyn's subtitle for his *Gulag Archipelago* is "an artistic inquiry." And that is why Siniavsky says that in his eyes the camp is now, and will be, the literary *topos*, which replaces, say, the bourgeois family life of nineteenth-century European literature. There is a book by an American historian, Victor Brombert, on the imagination of the prison. He has a chapter on the imagination derived from the camp, but he does not take it further.

There is a huge literature on the prison, and the prison has become a sort of metaphor of the ego. There is very little literature on the camp. The imaginative canvas of the prison is verticality, and for that reason it fits with the imagination of our self, whereas the main definition of the camp is horizontality. It is the Siberian plain with small, lost barracks on it, with nothing theatrical. There is no camp metaphor so far, and the camp has not been interiorized in our imaginations. But in literature one meets some texts that seem beforehand to give a sort of interiorization not of the concentration camp, but of what led to the concentration camp. That is to say, the complete horizontality of society. I feel that there has been more of *anus mundi* and secrecy in the German camps, and more of didactic exhibitionism in the Soviet camps. At least this was true at the beginning of the Soviet camps. But then, at some time in the mid-thirties, they also become secret, as secret as the Final Solution. If documents were left by the Nazis after their annihilation, there are no documents from the other side.

Another point is that you cannot speak of the concentration camp, which is called the small zone by the *zeks*, without speaking of the great zone. The link between the small zone and the great zone is absolutely essential. This is where we meet the mythical level and the work of a philosopher I respect, René Girard, and his ideas on the need for a victim in a myth.

Also I had to come to an idea that I call the eclipse of God, after Martin Buber, which recalls Dostoevsky and his prophecies. He said that everything is possible when God is dead. Today this has come about, and the reality means that humanity, in my view, is no longer confronted with the sheer idea that everything *may* become possible, because everything *has* become possible. Also, in comparing the literatures on the two camps, I found some particular testimonies that struck me very much, such as Buber-Neumann's book, the testimony of one who was first a Communist woman in the Soviet camp and then was handed over to the SS on the Brest Bridge to go to the Gestapo camp. She is a contemporary of ours. Or the books of Semprun, a Spanish-French writer who was so astonished to discover the similarity between the two systems of camps—the similarity in details, the similarity in what we might call the civilization, the concrete physical civilization. Even the words, even the vocabulary is the same, and for Semprun and many others it was extremely difficult to come to terms with, in a way to formalize, this discovery. This discovery is still active and still not digested by most of us.

In Solzhenitsyn we find that he needs a tool to speak of that. This tool is first of all a kind of enormous irony, and I was struck by the fact that in Elie Wiesel's books you have a similar tool for dealing with the impossibility of describing and thinking about what the extermination concentration camp was. Laughter in Wiesel and irony in Solzhenitsyn seem to me to be, in a way, parallel.

I also met Shalamov, whose thesis that the concentration camp is a factory of complete dehumanization contrasts completely with Solzhenitsyn's thesis that the concentration camp may be the salvation of humanity.

The third great Russian writer in my paper is Grossman. He made extremely strange discoveries that coincide with what can be said now. He died in 1962, and he wrote his book in complete solitude. Kolakowski has remarked on the religious genocide which preceded that of Kolyma or Auschwitz. I think there is a difference in that when the Cathars were dying, they knew why they were dying. It was a religious war, and many of them were perhaps deeply happy to die for their faith. The point in secular genocide is that millions of people were taken to the camps on criteria, at least in the Stalinist era, that were haphazard. First it was the class enemy who was taken, but later it was a sort of percentage of the population.

I think this theme of the concentration camp is not about violence, of course, because violence is bound up with the history of humanity. It is about some link between violence and utopia. This link is really a part of European culture; it happened and could happen only in de-Christianized societies, societies that were deeply Christian and that have lost their Christianity, as Russia had, quite suddenly.

Hagihara: I have two questions. First, in China too are there concentration camps? Second, with regard to Auschwitz and Kolyma, in the Soviet case the camps began as a sort of reeducation school. "Idealistic" may not be the right descriptive term for them, but in the case of Auschwitz there was no "idealism." Nazi concentration camps had a different specific purpose, and this made them different. Am I right?

Schwartz: After all, Marxism-Leninism is a European heresy that has come to China. China, of course, has a long history, and there has been much killing over the centuries, as well as political imprisonment. I suppose a lot depends on how one chooses to define genocide. But today there are such camps in China. Of course, they do claim to have an educational function, but it is a rather severe education, sometimes lasting thirty years.

Nivat: What is written at the entrance to the Auschwitz camp, Arbeit Macht Frei, is didactic. There was an element of reeducation in the Nazi camps, at least at the beginning. As for the marked differences between the camps, when you read the testimonies you find out, first of all, that Socialists were in camps, that Communists were in camps, and that people taken by haphazard ratio or percentage ratio were in camps. And when you read the description of some of the camps in the Kolyma region, you find out that reeducation was completely secondary, although I agree that from the testimony, say, of Evgenia Ginzburg, even in the worst camps you would have newspapers—the *Kolyma Pravda*, and so on. What that meant for people who were struggling for life by looking for a little bit of frozen garbage is not at all certain. But anyway, I offer Semprun as an example of those who spent years fighting for the meaning of reeducation, for the meaning of socialism. He, and others, found out that the actual result, at least at some stage, was exactly the same.

Maier: I am willing to accept, in a sense, the unity of the camp experience, apart from those camps that were just designed to eliminate people as they came. I would like to draw attention, though, to something about terror in these societies and how it relates to the camps. It seems to me that in the Nazi system terror, because it was more predictable, in a sense, drew a circle around the community within and the community to be cast out. That is, outside the circumference, those who were to be deported were, early on, political opponents, Communists, Social Democrats, outspoken liberals, and then racial enemies of the regime: Jews, Slavs, gypsies. But an Aryan or a political conformist, by and large, was a person who could count on the perimeter holding, unless someone had a grudge against him. The terror, in a sense, circumscribed a society and achieved control, precisely by separating the nonelect and the elect. Whereas the Soviet terror, at least after the purges began in the second stage of these camps, achieved its type of control precisely by making it absolutely unpredictable whether you might or might not be sent away.

Friedländer: Obviously, there are some basic facts that are similar. Those who died in Soviet camps or in Nazi camps, *died*. The mass murder is similar in both camps; be it several millions more here or there, it is mass death. And that is a twentieth-century phenomenon. But I would consider the difference between concentration camps and extermination camps. A key word here is *haphazardness*. From the mid-thirties on, haphazardness in the Soviet process of putting people into camps made it terrifying. Anybody could be taken, which gives a functional aspect to the Soviet camp. It really terrorized everybody, because nobody knew if they would be taken to a camp tomorrow morning or not, or tonight. If you landed in a camp, in the Soviet system you may have had a chance to survive if you managed somehow, because there was no systematic extermination process. On the other hand, in the Nazi camp if you belonged to a certain group— Jews, gypsies, mostly—you had to assume that you would die. It would be pure chance if you didn't.

Nivat: The camp is central in a system of organizing social malleability. There were many degrees in the Soviet camps, as shown by Solzhenitsyn's title, *The First Circle*. You may be in the first, the second, the fifth, the eighth, or the ninth circle. The organization of the circle was such that if you did not behave well in the first circle, you would go to the second, and so on. You moved from one circle to the other and from the reeducation camp to the extermination camp.

Mommsen: One study of life in concentration camps by Pingel, a young German scholar, describes the rules of social conduct and the strategies of survival. Of necessity, they included a certain degree of collaboration in the subhuman system of a concentration camp. And that matches the sort of problems Nivat is speaking of. Equally, it is technically not quite correct to distinguish between extermination camps and others; there was extermination through work in German camps at different times. Camps, technically speaking, were at various times extermination camps and at other times not. On the German territory of the time there were, technically speaking, no extermination camps. It is difficult to make the distinction quite categorical. Socially and ideologically, both were work camps; but at Auschwitz the intent was not education, but camouflage.

Kolakowski: What is really new in the concentration camp as a specific experience of our century is of course not violence, extermination, even mass extermination. It is not utopia as such, because utopia as such is nothing more than a literary genre. It is rather the belief, profoundly un-Christian, that you can make of people anything you wish. Human beings become plastic material which you can, with the appropriate technology, remake in any shape you wish. This is important, both in Soviet and in Nazi ideology. You can reforge the human soul to any desirable shape by using the proper technique. To be sure, there are categories of people—like Jews in the Nazi system—that are unredeemable. So were Polish officers in the Soviet case; they had to be exterminated. And there were categories which were redeemable—the Germans, obviously, even when they were wrong. A Soviet man could be formed.

But there is more to it than that. In the Soviet system people who were destined to be killed were still, in a sense, supposed to be reeducated. In this sense, the Soviet camps were reeducation camps even for those who were to die, even for those who were sentenced to death. People had to be morally annihilated, and the victims were to become collaborators, accomplices of the hangman. In this sense, the system was educational in both cases.

The ideological foundation of this idea was precisely the belief that there is nothing in the human person that could not be remade. In other words, there is no such thing as the human person. In this sense, Nivat is right in saying that it is characteristically a de-Christianized society, because in Christian terms people could be killed for their errors or heresy or apostasy or whatever, but the implication was that they were sentenced as human beings, either to be saved or in order to protect other people from the disease heretics might spread. In all cases, the assumption was that they were human beings, whereas in the case of the twentieth-century concentration camp, the ideological assumption was the opposite: that you can remake the human person into anything you wish. Therefore, to me the most important literary testimonies of camps are those which concentrate not on the perversity of the hangman, but on the moral degradation of the victims—like Borowski's books from Auschwitz or Shalamov's tales from Kolyma.

Nivat: Today, the ninth, eighth, seventh, sixth, fifth levels of the camps probably no longer exist. The earlier levels do still exist. But we must not forget that this huge amount of material on human deprivation does exist, is somewhere in the archives, and still is an active factor in the inner life of Soviet society.

Hersch: In what sense is it still an active element? Because to me it seems that there is something completely crazy in the whole story. Crazy in the sense that after so many years of existence of these camps and these millions and millions of people who have passed through these camps, they have not reeducated people. They have not remade them. To justify the system, they should be able to show us people who have become decent Communists in the camps and through the camps. Then it would have some meaning. I quite believe what you say about what they say or think. But there is something completely crazy about that. It is an education of nobody, because nobody comes out of this education. There are no results in the end. And then I wonder.

Since it is crazy, we should look for a crazy explanation. Would it be possible to think that in a way the camps exist in order to convey the impression that the world outside the camps is the free world? Because if there were no camps, everybody would know that the whole country is a camp. Because there are camps, you can be outside of the camps. I would also like to ask if we should not ask ourselves why there is a disease in these totalitarian states—emptiness, spiritual emptiness. Where there is emptiness, anything can fill it. Nivat said de-Christianization; that is one aspect of emptiness, but not the only one. The lack of substance, a loss of motivation, loss of values, loss of meaning—these would be important to study, perhaps even more than the camps themselves.

Friedländer: The Soviet system uses terror to rework personality, to "educate." That, in my opinion, is the aim of the confessions. There is a kind of "dialogue" up to death, up to the most vicious use of torture and death; but it is a "dialogue" between the torturer and the victim: The victim will admit in the end that the system is right. There is a "didactic" intention even if millions and millions have to die. There I see a basic difference between Soviet inhumanity and the Nazi inhumanity, which had no dialogue with those who were to die. Because they were to die on account of totally uncontrollable factors, there was no attempt to reeducate them. These are two schools of totalitarian thought. In one, there is reshuffling of the personality or changing it into some kind of object, but the victim has to admit that he dies within the justness of the system. In the other one, the human being is refuse, biological refuse.

Nivat: If we speak of the Nazi camps, we speak mainly of a historical fact, "local in time and space." Of course, that fact has left deep traces in all of us. When we speak of the Soviet concentration camps, as far as extermination camps are concerned, we speak of camps that no longer exist. But the function of the camp still exists, for two reasons. First, the same regime is there. Second, the camps do exist and are filled by a vast population.

At the beginning of the sixties, when de-Stalinization had gone quite far, they wanted a memorial to the millions who died in the camps. There is a kind of literary memorial, the fact that *One Day in the Life of Ivan Denisovitch* was published, along with some other things. So I cannot agree with Hersch's contention that the camp exists to prevent the rest of the country from feeling that it is itself a camp. These people do not live in a camp; this metaphor does not, in my view, exactly describe the situation in the

Soviet Union. But I do not think that people were really reeducated by confessions. I meant in the mind of the torturers, because when we read the memoirs, and again this is the only source we have, we see that the torturers would give up if the person was too tough. This is shown clearly in a beautiful novel by Dombrovsky, *The Faculty of Useless Things*. His hero does not confess. At last he is broken, of course; but he is not broken in the sense that he is degraded. The novel, by the way, ends with a photograph in a square, a while later, of these people, sitting on the same bench: the traitor who denounced the victim; the tortured man who resisted the denunciation, was broken, was in prison, and is now temporarily free; and the torturer, who has been dismissed and is also broken. All three sit sadly on the bench, silent.

TECHNOLOGY AND UTOPIA

"MODERNIZATION" AND JAPAN

KYOGOKU JUN-ICHI

"What *was* the twentieth century?" In the 2030s or 2050s, following their own interests, which are shaped and determined by the
society and culture in which they live, historians will try to answer
this question by proposing various images of this century, many
features of which will be alien and unimaginable to us today.
Many other answers will be supplied by historians of subsequent
centuries. Historians are those who monopolize the privilege of
dividing the past into eras both long and short, of constructing
learned historical images of these eras, and of distributing these
images for consumption by their contemporaries.

In contradistinction, "What *is* the twentieth century?", the
main theme of the symposium, is an entirely different question.
We are now living in the twentieth century, which still has seven-
teen years to go. It is a question being posed by people who are
now alive and who are looking for self-knowledge and self-orientation. One of the motives prompting people to ask this question is
the experience of frustration and failure for more than eighty
years. The twentieth century inherited from the nineteenth
century a firm belief that mankind would continue progressing
until it reached perfection. This optimistic belief was undermined
by the miserable experiences of the twentieth century. The twentieth century had given us a glimpse into the abyss of the evil that
is part of human nature. Today the rumor of an Armageddon
brought on by thermonuclear weapons constantly haunts us. In
their search for self-knowledge and self-orientation, it is natural
for people to ask, "What is the twentieth century?"

The Characteristics of the Twentieth Century

The characteristics of the twentieth century can be most conveniently illustrated by contrasting them with those of the nineteenth. One of the prominent features of the previous century was the completion of world domination by the West through its advanced military technology. When seen from the standpoint of the non-Western peoples living in the areas or countries that were colonized or that barely escaped the fate of colonization, the nineteenth century was nothing more than a century of Western rule and Western civilization, best represented by advanced military technology, as well as by the advanced industrial technology on which it rested.

The most representative characteristics of nineteenth-century Western civilization are to be found in Great Britain, which was the first "advanced" country in the world in the present-day sense. Foremost among these were constitutionalism and parliamentary government. The system was common practice in Britain and was regarded as the ideal political system not only in Europe, but also in the whole world. A nation's having the political maturity to be capable of national self-government by means of a parliamentary system was the criterion for distinguishing (and also discriminating) between civilized countries and colonies and legitimizing the colonial system. Constitutionalism and parliamentary government were the political symbols of the "advanced" status of Western civilization.

The second characteristic of nineteenth-century Western civilization was the industrial technology first developed in Great Britain, which the Industrial Revolution had turned into the world's factory. The soot and smoke produced from coal, the main source of energy in those days, blackening the skies of new industrial cities, were the symbol of advanced industrial technology. The organization in the factories was strongly paternalistic and depended upon the master-apprentice system. Concurrently, political movements advocated the establishment of an ideal social order on earth through socialism, which was to put an end to the class conflict between capitalists and workers.

The third characteristic of nineteenth-century Western civilization was the emergence of huge colonial empires. Great Britain, which maintained the Pax Britannica with the aid of strong naval forces, boasted a colonial empire on which "the sun never set." Subsequently, France, Holland, Belgium, and Germany also established colonial empires. Colonialism in the nineteenth century appeared to belong to "the nature of things." It was the colonial system that supported economically what was the "century of enlightenment, progress, and prosperity" to the people of the West.

The twentieth century experienced the decline and fall of these ideals and institutions. First, the colonial empires were dissolved amid the turmoil of national self-determination and independence movements during and after the two world wars. The number of independent countries, both large and small, rapidly increased, reaching 160. Colonial empires have now been replaced by satellite state systems or allied state systems based on a network of international treaties.

Second, among these multitudinous countries, very few practice constitutionalism and the parliamentary system in their domestic governments. The Socialist movements became one-party dictatorship by the Communist Party in the USSR and in those countries under Soviet control or influence. The Nazi dictatorship in Germany was also modeled after that of the USSR. And the political system of one-party dictatorship, military dictatorship, and government that combines a façade of popular elections with martial law rule prevails among many countries, including newly independent countries facing severe economic difficulties. In many countries, constitutionalism and parliamentary government are no longer accorded the status of political ideals.

Third, industrial technology has become a secular religion of the twentieth century, guaranteeing the salvation of mankind both in the United States, where the American way of life has been continuously advanced, and in the USSR, where heavy industrialization has been pursued under Lenin's slogan, "Socialism is electrification." The most conspicuous characteristic of twentieth-century industrial techonology is the mass-production system typical of the United States. These large-scale plants adopted a military-type organization composed of three strata—officers, noncommissioned officers, and soldiers. The officers, who are the engineers of the factory, draw up the manuals for standardized operations to be executed by the soldiers or workers. The noncommissioned officers, who correspond to foremen, oversee workers' assignments and behavior. The soldiers, or workers, are required to carry out the standardized operations "mechanically." And in order to raise productivity, human workers, who are prone to absenteeism and erroneous behavior, are constantly regarded as replaceable, whenever and wherever feasible, by robots. (Such films as Charlie Chaplin's *Modern Times* depict workers as slaves in large-scale plants.)

The amateur inventors who characterized the industrial technology of the nineteenth century are being replaced by Ph.D.'s at research institutes owned by big businesses, and basic scientific research is now directly connected with the development of industrial technology. The promotion system whereby apprentices gradually acquire enough experience and proficiency to become masters has disappeared. Upward mobility in factories, as well as in management, now usually depends on one's school and diploma. Such a stratified organization has naturally given rise to labor union and political party activities that aim to realize ever higher levels of both wages and social welfare. Also, the low morale of workers, which is unavoidable with such an organization, has come to be considered the weakest link in the production process and thus a symptom of some basic defect in the industrial system itself.

The Driving Force of the Twentieth Century

The driving forces that led the people of the twentieth century to turn against the nineteenth century's "promise of hope" that mankind could progress infinitely are nationalism, the desire for power, and "politics"—that is, power politics. In terms of these driving forces there is little difference between the nineteenth and the twentieth centuries. What makes a difference is the great number, the intensity of psychological involvement, and the methodical ruthlessness of the participants in the game of power politics.

The Western civilization of the nineteenth century has been diffused over the whole world—both the cognitive institution, in which every country of the world is graded on a one-dimensional scale of "development" and assigned a relative (relative to other countries) position ranging from "developing" to "advanced," and the institution of evaluation, in which the advanced countries are more highly assessed and given more prestige. Nationalist political leaders, through fervent national self-determination and independence movements, first achieved their countries' independence. Then they adopted policies to import, copy, and assimilate advanced military and industrial technologies in order to achieve the survival, security, and prosperity of their newly independent countries.

Modernization, industrialization, development, five-year plans, the Great Leap Forward—all became catchwords symbolizing the twentieth century, particularly the period after World War II. The gigantic steel mill became the symbol of a country's prestige and a nation's pride. France in the days of the French Revolution and Napoleon I and Germany under the leadership of Prussia found themselves "underdeveloped" countries compared with Great Britain, but they became the nineteenth-century pioneers of the "catch up and overtake" policy. In the twentieth century, the USSR after the Russian Revolution and later Japan after World War II followed the same line. Today a host of countries have joined the long procession trying to import, copy, and assimilate industrial technologies from the United States and other advanced Western countries, giving birth to the South-North problem.

The advanced Western countries and the developing countries therefore take a contrasting stance in cognition, evaluation, and preference. The former have a great economic advantage over the latter, owing to their superior industrial technology. In the nineteenth century the international division of labor and free trade were strongly advocated by Great Britain, which predominated over all other nations, on the basis of British one-state capitalism. Today the international division of labor and free trade form the core of those policies in international relations that are supported mainly by the advanced capitalist countries. Those countries, supported by their economic superiority over developing countries, have achieved domestic prosperity, affluence, and extensive social welfare through constitutionalism and parliamentary government. Democracy, prosperity, economic rationalism, and a nonmilitaristic peace orientation characterize the cognition, evaluation, and preference of the advanced Western countries of the twentieth century.

The developing countries, by contrast, try hard to assimilate and nurture imported industrial technology. They adopt economic systems that are more or less guided, planned, controlled, or directly operated by the government, the strictest form being the Socialist economy. And in international trade they practice a protectionist or controlled foreign trade system, more or less restricting free trade. The most rigid system is the government-run foreign trade system. In those countries the survival, security, prestige, and glory of the country depend upon the success of importing and assimilating industrial and military technologies. Consequently, autocracy or dictatorship to consolidate the political leadership, austerity for national defense and economic development, and a frame of reference oriented toward power politics and military considerations in international relations characterize the cognition, evaluation, and preference of the developing countries.

The efforts of the developing countries to catch up with the advanced nations presuppose the universality of military and industrial technologies. Efforts to catch up with the advanced countries are, through imitation and the learning process, accompanied by the influx of Western civilization, the increased influence of Western civilization, and eventually by the contamination of these countries' own traditions. Nationalist leaders therefore have to try very hard to establish and then repeatedly to reestablish a national identity so that they may maintain their own power as well as national integration. Starting with education in the vernacular language, they set up educational institutions to teach both children and adults the content and glory of the national tradition, the mission of contemporary nationalism, and Western science and technology, three items that are not always compatible. (Exceptions are such nationalist leaders as Mahatma Gandhi, who espoused both nonviolent resistance and the revival of traditional handicrafts while rejecting Western military and industrial technologies.)

Thus, political education and the international political environment diffuse, among a certain portion of the people of developing countries in particular, nationalism, the desire for power, and a frame of reference oriented toward power politics and military considerations in regard to domestic politics and international relations. These people support voluntarily and—at least for a certain period—enthusiastically the military actions of their countries. Man is corrupted by both the possession of and the thirst for power. The twentieth century witnessed not only two world wars, but also numerous military encounters between and after these two wars. Moreover, advanced industrial technology begets advanced military technology, and the destructiveness of weaponry has become extremely high. It is natural that the twentieth century came to have the image of emerging chaos annihilating "civilization and nomos," the image of an emerging force of destruction and death.

The Experience of "Modern" Japan

It is by no means easy for developing countries first to import, copy, and assimilate advanced military and its underlying industrial technology, and then to attain the level of industrial growth at which they can develop those technologies on their own. It is, however, not so difficult to import a machine system or a weapons system, which are products of those technologies, and learn how to operate those machines and weapons. The method of operating machines and weapons is universal; it is a combination of the flow of human behavior, which is observable from the outside and therefore possible to instruct and train, if such is desired. The adoption by many developing countries of the railway systems, airport and air traffic systems, jet air service systems, and such weapons and combat systems as jet fighters and missiles are the fruit of importation and learning.

The Russo-Japanese War of 1904–5, especially the naval battle of the Japan Sea won by Admiral Togo, was impressive and shocking in that it demonstrated that a non-Western developing country was capable of importing and successfully learning how to use the weapons and combat systems of the advanced West. It suggested to the West the emergence of the power of chaos, and hence apprehension about the "Yellow Peril." It was "a sign of the times" to the national self-determination and independence movements of those days, showing that colonialism was not in the "nature of things" and that it could be changed by human effort.

The experiences of Japan over the 130 years since the visit of Commodore Matthew Perry's fleet in 1853 may be divided into three periods: (1) the fifty years up to the end of the Russo-Japanese War in 1905, (2) the forty years up to the defeat in World War II in 1945, and (3) the forty years thereafter until the present. The second period, the first part of the Japanese experience in the twentieth century, was marked by the Japanese invasion of mainland China with the aim of expanding its colonies, Japan's clash with the advanced Western countries and the international legal order laid down by them, the military alliance with Nazi Germany and Fascist Italy, and participation and total defeat in World War II. It was a period in which a developing country tried to imitate the colonial imperialism of the advanced Western countries belatedly, in a rough and violent way, and in vain.

The third period, the forty years since 1945, first saw Japan's political institutions remodeled by the occupation forces and the consequent establishment of constitutionalism and parliamentary government. After the 1951 peace treaty came into force the Japanese economy, based on nonmilitary industries and foreign trade, registered steady growth. Japan concentrated its energies not in military industry, but in civilian industries. Eventually Japan came to export to the advanced Western countries of the United States and the European Economic Community large volumes of industrial products for daily use by the general public—that is, such high-performance and high-quality mass-produced goods as medium-sized cars and electronic appliances. Hence the "friction" between Japan and its American and EEC trading partners.

Japanese industries imported the original findings of basic scientific research from the West, concentrated their efforts on the development of applications and of plant production technologies, and at times succeeded in organizing mass-production systems capable of producing inexpensive, high-quality goods. Today, it is said both in Japan and abroad that basic inventions are made in Great Britain, pilot plants are built in the United

States, and the mass-production system is completed in Japan. This saying does not praise Japan alone. In any event, it seems to have been proved that a developing country can not only import machine and weapons systems from the advanced countries and learn how to operate them, but also import and assimilate industrial technology systems and attain a level of industrial growth at which it can develop them as a system. Thus, the success of Japanese industrialization proved the universality of the industrial technologies that originated in the West.

Can the experiences of Japan be a model for the modernization and industrialization of all developing countries? The answer is both yes and no. The experiences of Japan cannot be copied, for they are unique historical experiences. The conditions under which the political leaders of today's developing countries design systems for modernization, industrialization, and development are not the same as those Japan faced in the past. Such environmental conditions as the structure and characteristics of world politics and the world economy and the state of science and technology, and conditions unique to each country, such as the size of the population and economy, the level of economic and technological development, the level of literacy and education, and the degree of national cohesion and integration—these conditions are all different. Nevertheless, there are a few aspects of Japan's 130 years of experience that might be helpful to the developing countries.

The first aspect is related to the political leadership. In the first period of modernization Japan faced the task of building an integrated nation. At that time, the Meiji emperor played an important role as a charismatic symbol in building and integrating the nation. He was both a model for an austere and ascetic life as grand marshal of Japan's Western-style army and navy and a poet who, composing traditional *waka* verse in quantity, represented an aspect of traditional national culture. Japan also imported a legal system based on a written constitution and Western jurisprudence. Thus Japan set up a government that operated according to Western-style laws and a precisely organized bureaucracy relatively free from corruption. Since the seventeenth century most Japanese families had been small, the members limited to two or three generations of direct lineage. The family system was not the "Oriental" or "East Asian" large-scale extended family system where very remote members were expected to support each other. Japanese society did not have the traditional inducement to bureaucratic corruption found in the large-scale family system. On the other hand, the lack of security provided by the large-scale extended family system led the members of the bureaucracy to pecuniary and psychological dependence on the bureaucracy itself, resulting in a quest for security by "playing it safe" and leading to bureaucratic conservatism and "trained inefficiency."

The second aspect is related to the policy of protection and development of industries particularly prominent after World War II. When a department or a ministry of the Japanese government decided on a policy of developing a certain industry, that industry was often provided with facilities for importing related advanced technology and with a domestic market guaranteed by some import restrictions and by various government subsidies to help create domestic demand. The industry was also provided with necessary funding through a government-endorsed investment and loan system. There were also some special tax breaks. The growth of competitive power in the international market was rewarded by extending export bounties. These policies of protection and development, carried out effectively in the 1950s and 1960s, came to be well known internationally owing to the "trade friction." The policies aimed gradually to improve the living standards of the people, who suffered greatly from the devastation of World War II and were on the verge of starvation, by importing energy and raw materials and exporting industrial products.

Japan's economic system was under the supervision and control of the government for more than thirty years, from the late 1930s through World War II, the occupation by the Allied forces, economic reconstruction, and the rapid economic growth period. Many business people, who firmly believed in the institution of the free market, vigorously objected when the Japanese army began to control the economy in the late 1930s. But the close relationship between the government and business over the following thirty years made both aware of the convenience of having close ties. The government ministries obtained the power, competence, and organization to plan, control, and guide business activities. Business, while subject to supervision and intervention, gained protection, aid, and guarantees against risks unavoidable in their operations.

The third aspect of Japan's experiences concerns social egalitarianism. One hundred thirty years ago, when Japan embarked upon modernization, the previous social system of four "estates" was officially abolished, and the door to upward social mobility was opened wide. The newly established political hierarchy, with the emperor at the apex, indicated the path of upward mobility and the terminus of social ascent. Equality of opportunity released the psychological energy for upward mobility, which had long been dammed up under the feudal estate system. As a result, the culture of the warrior (*samurai*) estate, which had been the ruling class, came to be imitated by the former farmer and merchant estates, and this led to the building of the national "middle class" culture. At the same time, the entire nation was given the freedom to learn and to model itself after the West. The spread of the school system and the continuous rise in the number of students going on to higher levels of education contributed not only to the diffusion of nationalism, but also to the spread of Western science, technology, learning, and culture. (Japanese universities had faculties of technology and engineering from the beginning.) Moreover, as it became clear that the diploma was favorably related to social mobility, more people came to acquire diplomas. School life taught people the discipline to work according to the clock, not the sun, knowledge essential for the transfer of Western industrial technology.

The Cosmos of Meaning

Technology is one of the constituent elements of the industrial civilization, but it is not the civilization itself. The constituent elements of Western industrial, technological civilization are not limited to the institution of technology, the system of crafts techniques, and technologies developed before, in, and after the Industrial Revolution. The institution of society, which facilitates the operation of the institution of technology, and the institution of knowledge, which enables the operation of both the institution of technology and the institution of society, are constituent elements of every civilization, including the industrial civilization. And what are called "culture," the "value system," and the "cosmos of meaning" in anthropology and sociology are very important parts of the institution of knowledge, since they form the foundation for the ideals, aspirations, objectives, motives, and desires of human beings. Since, according to the Polish philosopher Leszek Kolakowski, "the language of the Sacred is not universal," so the cosmos of meaning is not universal.

The Japanese success in importing and assimilating Western technology demonstrated the universality of industrial technology itself, but at the same time it demonstrated that Western civilization, although an industrial technological civilization, is not global but local. (Both *global* and *local* are used here in the same sense as in calculus.) The industrialization of Japan has been possible only by "grafting" industrial technology onto the traditional institution of society, institution of knowledge, and thus the cosmos of meaning.

In the first and second periods of Japan's modernization, the national middle-class culture based on the culture of the warrior estate covered the surface of Japanese society like a hard shell. In the third period of the last forty years this hard shell was shattered, and people learned to live more informally and freely, if in a less ordered manner. In addition, the mass culture of the West, particularly of the United States, flowed in and has had a great influence on the daily life of the people. The more people were freed of the old middle-class culture, the more dependent they became on the common traditional culture. It is true that the so-called democratization of Japan initiated by the Allied forces introduced the Western-type cosmos of meaning to the populace. But the new cosmos of meaning did not succeed in replacing or eradicating the influence of the traditional one. Rather, democratization itself was naturalized.

The traditional Japanese cosmos of meaning is based on the following articles of faith. The first is that the eternal being is the being that pulsates rhythmically from eternity to eternity. Although some religious sects adopt personalized statues, there is no personal god who had dialogue directly with human beings as in the Judaic, Christian, and Islamic traditions. The second article is that nothing in the cosmos has been "created" *ex nihilo* by a personal god; everything comes into being through the pulsation or self-development of the eternal being. The third article is that in the ontological sense the eternal being inheres, at the same time and as it is, in everything in the cosmos—organic and inorganic substances, plants and animals, human individuals and groups, various events and phenomena—though different, distinct, and separate, or that everything in cosmos is the embodiment of the eternal being or is the eternal being itself. (The eternal being is variously defined as Eternal Life, Reason, the Law, the Way (*tao*) of the cosmos, and so forth by the different religious sects. And in spite of doctrinal differences, these basic articles of faith are common to most religious sects.) The fourth article is that man does not hold a special position in the cosmos as the master of nature. He is merely *primus inter pares* in nature. Therefore man has a strong feeling of ontological solidarity toward everything in nature. He also has a strong sense of ontological equality toward his fellow man. (These two features may be useful to explain, at least partially, the traditional sensibilities to nature characteristic of Japanese literature and fine arts and the social system that prevails in Japanese organizations and gives, in organizational promotion, priority to seniority rather than to ability.)

In this secular world of daily experiences, every individual is far removed from the eternal being. In this world of daily experience, the road to ontological union with the eternal being and hence religious rebirth lies, for people of religious profession, in meditation, asceticism, or a combination of both. For people of nonreligious, secular professions, there are at least two roads to ontological union with the eternal being. The first is to realize the Way (*tao*) by attaining skill and expertise in one's vocation. In this case, work is not manual labor in exchange for wages, nor punitive toil that one wishes to finish as quickly as possible. To improve one's skill in one's work and profession is a "pilgrim's progress" on the road to self-improvement. Hence professional activities are accompanied not only by the work ethic of diligence, but also by innovative proposals to improve the production process so that productivity may rise and product quality may improve. The second road by which people of secular professions may realize ontological union with the eternal being starts from their "place," "position," or "locus" in the cosmos. One can progress on this road by performing the role, function, and duty that has been assigned by the group, organization, and collectivity to which one belongs, expending as much energy as available. Thus cooperation in group life, active dedication and self-sacrifice to the organization, and collectivity become the means to realize one's "true self." The very fact that such a cosmos of meaning underlies the common knowledge shared by the engineers, foremen, and workers in many of Japan's factories is one of the reasons for Japan's success in assimilating industrial technology.

Now, if everything in the cosmos is, ontologically speaking, an embodiment of the eternal being, then wealth and power in glory and opulence are manifestations of the favor of the eternal being. Wealth and power are accepted as such by the Japanese people uncritically and unconditionally. Rich and influential people are, by definition, people the gods chose to favor. Thus, secular and "modern" pragmatism, which uncritically affirms, approves, and accepts whatever profits are realized in this life and which chooses these profits as the objectives of activity and as the criteria of preference, forms the core of the frame of reference in the cosmos of meaning. It is a world where Max Weber's "theodicy of happiness" prevails.

So the military and industrial technology of the West, as well as advanced Western civilization, has been affirmed, approved, and accepted from the viewpoint of secular usefulness. And it is a time-honored tradition to invite an alien, efficacious, numinous power that operates effectively in the outside world into the collectivity in which people live. Lacking the self-restraint and self-limitations imposed by the Middle Kingdom type of thinking that originated in China, Japan indiscriminately invited in, copied, and assimilated many elements of foreign civilizations, the most outstanding exception being the Western cosmos of meaning. It is a matter of course that, insofar as everything in the cosmos is, ontologically speaking, an embodiment of the eternal being, conservatism that adheres to tradition, such as the "expel the barbarians" movement, always comes into being. However, the progressivism that aspires after that which is "advanced" also materializes. It was through the coexistence of and the conflict between conservatism and progressivism, and through the alternation of politically influential groups advocating these two approaches, that Japanese history unfolded.

The traditional cosmos of meaning has other consequences. First, setting aside the political considerations based on secular pragmatism, there is no moral restraint against the corruption of power. There is no ethic based on moral commandments laid down by a transcendent creator-god, nor is there the tradition of prophets who transmit the words of reprimand of the creator-god to those in power. Apart from the mandarin morality of Confucianism, there is no justification in the traditional cosmos of meaning for demanding that those in power practice self-reflection and self-restraint. Hence, the arrogance of power, the hubris that does not have to be afraid of the nemesis of the gods, and the boundless corruption and evil of power become a matter of course. The arrogance of power prevails also in the ministries and departments of the government. These ministries and departments are justified in their existence by the very fact they exist and are characterized by conservatism that adheres to tradition. The characteristics of their behavior are found in their following a "carry on" policy instead of a thorough and fundamental reexamination of their policies and setup. (Incidentally, the lack of commandment ethics in Japanese tradition does not mean a lack of discipline and morality based on mores and tradition in the daily life of the Japanese people.)

Second, in the traditional cosmos of meaning, aside from secular pragmatism there is no inducement to develop sensibilities toward "heterogeneous others" and the political skill to coexist with them. Almost by definition there are no "heterogeneous others," such as a transcendent creator-god or the "end of time." There is no "intellectual" orientation aimed at rising above the level of daily experience in order to control nature and inquire into the divine design of a creator-god. Instead, a general and diffuse feeling of "homogeneous" continuity and solidarity toward man and nature is the keynote of life, and unity and harmony between and among individuals and social groups are required. The structures and boundaries of "meaningful" social groups, organizations, and collectivities are defined by tradition or by stipulation. The feeling of "homogeneous solidarity" does not extend beyond the boundaries of these groups, organizations, and collectivities. Beyond these boundaries lies the battlefield of competition where *homo homini lupus*. Also, social unity and harmony are usually called for by influential people "above."

So in daily life and real politics, oppression and tyranny by the strong, and willing submission by the weak, or backlashes and severance of relations on the part of the weak, take place very often. With regard to the people beyond the boundary of "homogeneous solidarity," the people of the out-groups, there is a strong tendency to avoid much contact and exchange, to retire into one's own in-group, and to lead a self-contained, complacent life. There are very few incentives for developing and training sensibilities toward and the political skill to live with "heterogeneous others."

The modernization of Japan was successful in importing, copying, and assimilating industrial technology. But Japan cannot be said to have always had a successful political coexistence with the advanced countries and other nations. As is evident from the experiences of Japan and other countries in modernization, industrialization, and development, although it is possible to transfer technology, it is not possible to transfer an entire civilization.

Modernization, industrialization, and development in the twentieth century promoted technology transfer. As a result, mutually heterogeneous civilizations, civilizations that share a common institution of technology but do not always share a common institution of society, institution of knowledge, and especially cosmos of meaning, came to face the task of coexisting. And it is precisely the cosmos of meaning that forms the basis of nationalism, the desire for power, and "politics"—that is, power politics. The twentieth century witnessed the difficulty of political coexistence of various civilizations that, while sharing the common institution of technology, including military technology, cherished their own cosmos of meaning, and observed many a military clash between and among these civilizations, including two world wars.

The self-knowledge of the twentieth century will be expressed in many of its aspects, only two of which will be mentioned here.

The first is the knowledge of the structure of civilization. It is erroneous and at times fatally dangerous to conclude hastily that other countries share with one's own the same institution of society, the same institution of knowledge, and particularly the same cosmos of meaning, simply on the grounds that they share a common institution of technology. It is useful to study objectively and from a distance the institution of society, institution of knowledge, and especially the cosmos of meaning of other countries and try to contact, exchange, and coexist with those countries on the basis of that knowledge.

The second item is the knowledge of, or belief in, man's ability to do evil and the imperfection of man. It is also a long tradition in the humanities to say that although progress belongs to science and technology, there is no progress in morality, art, and politics. The twentieth century has witnessed the fact that power—be it of oneself or of others, of one's country or of other countries, in domestic politics or in international relations, in the effort to keep it or in the effort to acquire it—has always corrupted man and developed man's capability to commit evil. It is morally imperative to some people and pragmatically useful to others to begin at once, whenever it is noticed, to make a deliberate effort to arrest the growth of evil, both in oneself and in others, on the basis of that knowledge.

HISTORY AND SOCIAL SCIENCE: THE PARADOX OF AMERICAN UTOPIANISM

BARRY D. KARL

It might be useful to explain by way of preface that the argument of this paper rests on a use of two terms that have a long and complex history for Americans. The first is *utopia,* and the second is *elite.* Both are terms Americans have used from time to time to describe their society's aims—or to lament its defects. Their relation to one another as terms in the American social lexicon is also a confusing one that requires some explanation.

American society is essentially a utopian society in several significant respects. It was, first of all, a society created in a dramatically new landscape that generations of settlers insisted on considering uninhabited, and therefore unowned by any other people and essentially without prior sovereignty. In the colonizing process, efforts to negotiate with the native Indians ultimately became artificial and gradually disappeared. American society rapidly became a society intellectually committed to the establishment of some kind of perfect state in a geographical setting that would be accepted not simply as the New World it had been for almost three centuries, but as a "Virgin Land."

Although the term *elite* is relatively new in modern discourse, the question of the roles played by citizens especially qualified to govern was raised early in American history—even, it could be argued, by the Puritans themselves. Although every generation has debated the existence and function of such groups in the management of the nation, at times as part of the debate about the ideal state, their presence has never been acknowledged for long without the arousing of some sense of threat to democracy. Thus, the relation between *utopia* and *elite* is itself part of an important problem to which this paper must address itself.

Utopian thought is generally associated with a literature of fiction that various generations of American reform writers have used to characterize what they have believed to be the unique elements of American government and society. Those elements have centered around a commitment to equality of opportunity and individual freedom. That both are believed to be guaranteed by the Constitution of 1787 has served as the basis for either laudatory or critical accounts of American society rendered in the form of fiction. Edward Bellamy's novel *Looking Backward* was one of his generation's notable examples, but there have been others. Americans, obsessed at times with the limitations reality has imposed on the promises Americans have always claimed for their society's place in world history, have taken numerous such occasions to criticize the present and to demand a renewal of the crusade.

Utopianism has also played an important role in the American definition of cultural uniqueness. Even before the Declaration of Independence, Americans had sought to mark their independence from their European origins by pointing to the role played by the physical and geographical conditions of the New World as the source of historically unique opportunities for cultural advance. Such arguments were perfectly consistent with the history of utopian literature from Plato to Thomas More. Classical utopias seemed to require a geographical distance from known lands and an important innocence of the political and social practices of the "real" places they served to contrast, if not to satirize. It is particularly significant for our purposes that such utopianism depended on the creation of whole cultures and states *de novo* rather than on revolutions against existing governments. By aligning themselves with the utopian tradition of state building once they had completed what was in fact a revolution against an existing government, Americans came to perceive themselves as possessed of a unique opportunity to operate without the revolutionary ideology destined to be developed by other modern states seeking to justify revolutionary new orders. As a new culture in a new geography, they had no need of revolution.

Thus, as Louis Hartz pointed out many years ago now, the Americans had no *ancien régime* to overthrow or to restore. Hartz's thesis does, however, raise two issues made important by his use of the concept *ancien régime* and his use of Tocqueville's observations of the importance of Jacksonian egalitarianism. *Ancien régime* is a metaphor that may inadvertently obscure the fact that American colonials of every generation had rejected the idea of an indigenous aristocracy. While there may have been those in the early national period who were prepared to play with John Adams's ideas about titles for the nation's leaders, the concept of a born aristocracy was not part of the game. At the same time, implicit in the Jacksonian emphasis on equality is the belief that Americans rejected the idea of governing elites. "Rotation in office," before it was renamed "the spoils system" by its critics, became the American version of the Benthamite idea of representative government. While the Jacksonian era did see a partial revolution against the ideas of limited participation in government assumed by American colonial leaders and written into the constitution of 1787 by that document's drafters, the earlier experience with leadership by local elites is much more persistent in later history than the celebrations of the Jacksonian transformation suggest.

The framers of the constitution appeared to accept without argument the need for an elite that would both govern and select those who would govern. They assumed that deference politics and the role of notables characteristic of the colonial period would continue. They built their conception of republicanism into the constitution by prescribing methods of selection of the president and the Senate that relied on the power of local elites to supply electors for the Electoral College and local notables for state legislatures charged with the responsibility of selecting senators. Property qualifications for voting in local elections provided further assurance that the voting public itself would reflect at least one fundamental proof of stability.

While the method of selecting presidents was transformed early in the history of American government, the conditions that led to the change had more to do with the unanticipated rise of political parties than anything else. The Electoral College may seem empty to us because we have forgotten why it was put there in the first place. More important, perhaps, direct election of senators did not come about until early in the twentieth century. Underneath the rhetoric of participatory democracy was a set of practices that assured limits and controls on access to office.

Washington and Jefferson both looked toward some kind of system of education that would lead to the training of natural leaders for the nation, but that was not destined to come about. Nonetheless, if we assume that a national elite was not formed, we are apt to raise many more questions than we can answer easily. For Americans have coped uncomfortably at times with the recognition of a political leadership that is drawn significantly from groups whose social, economic, and educational backgrounds distinguish them from the so-called common man of the Jacksonian era. Certain families, from the Adamses through the Kennedys, have provided particular eras with leaders. More important perhaps, certain educational institutions have trained a disproportionate number of political leaders and administrative managers of public and private affairs. While pointing to such circumstances can lead to arguments about the existence of an "establishment" or "invisible government," let alone a secret elite, the truth of the matter is that there is nothing secret about the political system that sought two Roosevelts or three generations of Stevensons to run for office, or the educational system that trained Dulleses for important administrative appointments. They are perfectly visible; and for anything worthy of the name "establishment," their careers have been remarkably subject to the vagaries of chance and the pressures of public scrutiny that have shaped all such careers in American political history.

Thus, utopianism and elitism have potential significance for any interpretation of American intellectual developments, among which certainly one must place the growth of the social sciences. For it was in the United States that "social science" took on the program of reform-oriented research that has stood so uncomfortably, at times, at the edge of the ground other societies reserve for religion and moral philosophy.

I

Although American social scientists have been reluctant to admit it, their conception of social science shares with social philosophy in general a potential commitment to reform that always threatens to assume revolutionary proportions. Periodic calls for objectivity in social research, like the periodic uses of research models drawn from biology and physics, have been used to counter the aims of scientifically oriented social reformers, but never enough to change the basic direction of social science research in America. How far back in the history of social philosophy one wishes to push that phenomenon depends on one's sense of the meaning of revolution. Plato's *Republic* has obviously served as a recurrent vehicle for such debates. The relation between modern philosophers from Locke and Rousseau to Marx and the revolutionaries who either implicitly or explicitly utilized their theories would also provide cases in point. The idea of progress or human perfectability has been a factor in many religious movements that sought to affect the operations of the state, so the notion itself, at least, has no uniquely American roots. Indeed, many American historians have traced the origins of the American Revolution to its roots in European religious conflicts of the seventeenth century.

What may distinguish the American case in one obvious sense is the difficulty Americans have had in connecting modern American social science with the traditions of social philosophy, and in accepting the relation between social science and social reform. When the University of Chicago began making plans to celebrate the fiftieth anniversary of the opening of its Social Science Research Building several years ago, the committee planning the celebration took the relation between social science research and public policy as its theme. One department threatened to withdraw from the event because its members believed that such a relationship was inappropriate to the purposes of social science. The argument that ensued was itself characteristic of attitudes toward social science in the present decade, to be sure, but as I shall argue, it is characteristic as well of a much longer series of debates in American social thought.

While it is clear that recent arguments are still related to the conflicts in the American academic community's response to the Vietnam war, the problem itself is much older. That response was an angry reaction to the advisory, even participatory, role in government policymaking American academics had been seeking for more than a century. Their periodic successes in the Progressive era, World War I, the 1920s, and the New Deal had all been followed by varying degrees of repudiation, as professors from "Dr. Wilson" to "Dr. Kissinger" were subjected to critical attacks not only from populist political critics but from former academic colleagues. The episode that began with the Kennedy administration and its repudiation of the Eisenhower administration's supposed anti-intellectualism ended in the Vietnam experience's exposure of the so-called best and the brightest. But it was an episode in a much longer history. The American conception of democracy has always held intellectual elites in suspicion, even while Americans were working to produce such elites and to use them effectively in government policymaking.

The relation between American social science and American social reform has been a complex one that has always appeared easier to understand than, in fact, it may be. Interestingly enough, critics of American social science have been just as willing to attack its periodic reform commitments as they have its periodic rejections of a moral or value content, as though the relation between a commitment to reform and a commitment to moral principle were based on a sharp distinction that made one possible without the other. To be sure, the history of American social science over the last century supports a belief in such a distinction on the part of those who established the various phases of modern social science methodology as a rebellion against some previous phase.

The modern disciplines represented by the creation of the national academic associations, which began in the mid-1880s, were often viewed by their creators as the replacing of the previous generation's gentlemanly amateur by the new era's professional, by which they meant the replacement of an interested but ignorant subjectivity by a trained, scientific objectivity. The new professional generation produced the social sciences on which Progressive-era reforms were to be based. Economists like Thorstein Veblen, John R. Commons, and Richard T. Ely represented different positions in economics, but a new view of the economist as an educated and responsible commentator, independently reviewing economic events in order to interpret and to influence the direction of public affairs. Woodrow Wilson could distinguish himself from devoted amateurs in the writing of history, like

Theodore Roosevelt and Henry Cabot Lodge, by the fact that he was a professional historian and political scientist with a doctorate and a publication record that rested on academic scholarship.

If the successors of that first generation of professionals saw them as thinly disguised reformers more committed to influencing policy than to furthering scientific investigation, they did not often say so. There are exceptions—Arthur F. Bentley's attack on Albion Small in *The Process of Government*—but they are treated as professional scandals to be quietly ignored, rather than as occasions for rebuttal. The new academics, particularly those in the rapidly expanding state universities of the Midwest and the West, were not themselves members of older elites likely to produce the professoriats of the eastern schools, but the products of the small towns and farming communities of the settled agrarian states. They adopted the manners of older academic groups and looked with selective envy on the habits of British and European universities. But they were inclined to confine their imitation to architecture, costume, even social occasions, rather than to the intense professional infighting and complex controls of intellectual development that were part of Old World academic tradition.

The social scientists of the 1920s and 1930s thus looked on their claims for scientific objectivity as an odd kind of revolution *de novo* rather than against past enemies. There was a rather tattered *ancien régime* made up of faculties of the nation's oldest institutions, old-line donors to those institutions and the new donors to the newer research institutions, but it operated with little effect—or, perhaps more accurately, at cross purposes that negated effect. The newer donors, particularly among the staffs of American philanthropic foundations, were attracted to new research methods, even if they didn't always understand them. They saw social research, for example, as an alternative to partisan politics; and they could be convinced of the utility of social research not because it was objective, but because it was a more acceptable form of subjectivity. Those who worked to convince them were mediating a dispute they preferred to suppress, and they manipulated the meaning of science to suit their own purposes.

The introduction of research in human behavior was accompanied by new methods of gathering and analyzing data based on new discoveries in statistical method and opinion research, quantification, and psychological testing. With the aid of interested donors, such schools of thought could take over whole disciplines in what were virtually bloodless coups. Academic departments in particular institutions could decide to emphasize one method rather than another, competing in the national marketplace for new faculty and bright students. But the dispersion of institutions across the country and the availability of resources kept the national structure weak and the level of competition relatively low.

Throughout the 1920s Herbert Hoover, first as secretary of commerce, then as president, pioneered in the use of social scientists as advisers; but they remained outside government, as commentators and sources of data and ideas rather than as policymakers. The relation between policy and social science remained an uneasy one, as Hoover learned that he could not control the advice he sought. His social scientists, too, puzzled over criticisms from some of their colleagues and contemporaries that they were being too optimistic in their predictions of the future. As the Depression deepened, many social scientists saw in the crisis a portent of permanent stagnation, rather than a dip in a more familiar cyclical pattern, and began looking toward revolutionary changes in government as a means of adapting traditional methods to new conditions.

The Depression and the New Deal helped revive the older Progressive commitment to utility as the growing state and federal bureaucracies, hungry for trained staff to organize programs and administer them, employed academicians as advisers and administrators. The experience kept alive a process begun in World War I by the necessity of staffing a wartime state machine with part-time citizen help. The coming of World War II tended to reinforce the process again, and the expansion of universities and the college-educated in the years of the GI Bill of Rights strengthened the system even more, but in an odd way. Americans were building a network of social science supports for government programs, but by a series of accidents and ad hoc responses to events, not by any perceivable design.

World War II and the two decades that followed it produced a transformation in American social sciences as dramatic as anything that had happened previously, but again the lines of change are not easy to trace, because the relationships among the various elements seem so accidental.

First, the Atlantic migrations of the war years produced an intellectual revolution that introduced Americans in all fields to European thought that previously had been understood only dimly, and in many instances not at all. Translation and widespread publication of the writings of Max Weber, Roberto Michels, Georges Sorel, and numerous others—in addition to the migration to the United States of scholars like Paul Tillich and Friedrich von Hayek—broadened the range of social theory available to Americans, producing along the way a new set of intellectual divisions.

Second, the predictions of a return to prewar stagnation, elegantly argued by writers as diverse in their beliefs as Karl Polanyi, Joseph Schumpeter, and Karl Mannheim, did not prove to be correct in the decades that followed. Western fears of the collapse of capitalism were eclipsed by the rise of Keynesian economics. It became not simply an answer some economists were proposing to a condition all economists recognized, but a varied program of policy adapted for use even by former enemies of Western capitalist democracies, and with a success that American policymakers were destined to find as threatening as the previous ideological attacks.

Third, American perceptions of the nation's obligation to the new states created in the aftermath of the breakup of colonial empires generated an American nationalism in the social sciences that took a variety of forms, from so-called consensus history among historians, to studies of nation building in political science, economics, and public administration that based at least part of their argument on theories of the historical origins of American government, now referred to as "the first new nation." Developing countries, first called "underdeveloped," and "modernization" became subjects of concern and objects of transformation.

Fourth, the confrontation between the United States and the Soviet Union sparked periodic outbursts of suspicion of the social sciences. Echoes of the criticisms made of the social sciences in the New Deal years—that they were repositories of radical thought—surfaced in new forms. At the same time, increased federal funding of the social sciences marked an acceptance by the federal government of social science as an element in the nation's defense. The growing sophistication of quantification and the machinery for handling it also helped breach barriers between the social and the natural sciences.

Fifth, the development of the civil rights movement as a youth movement, and the youth movement as a political movement centered in the nation's colleges and universities helped provide a confrontation between the generation of the young and those who taught them and managed their educational institutions. The very meaning of education became an issue, from the governance of universities to the design of curriculum and requirements. In the process, the view of objectivity and science changed as terms like "relevance" and "commitment" were introduced to define the educational needs of the young, but from their own youthful perspective.

The decade between 1965 and 1975 was a decade of confrontation as the five factors I have described briefly established their shifting relations with one another. While one can see the shape of what happens particularly after one adds to it some of the events that gave it its intensity—the series of assassinations, beginning with John Kennedy in 1963, the Vietnam war, and the urban riots—it is nonetheless difficult to describe in an orderly fashion. Similar upheavals were taking place in other societies. Youth movements, embattled universities, and sharpened ideological conflicts were by no means an American monopoly. Yet the fact that Americans had produced their problems seemingly without program or purpose makes them somewhat more difficult to explain. Other societies were much more conscious of the necessary relationship between universities and government in the continuing production of the managerial elites needed to run industrial societies. By not acknowledging that relationship, Americans were able to pretend it did not exist—even to believe that they were protecting themselves against elitism—despite the fact that their inventions since the end of the nineteenth century had been producing a startling facsimile. The nation's intellectual elites were committed to arguing a conception of democratic government that denied their existence.

II

What I am trying to describe for you is something I believe to be a genuine American dilemma. American democratic theory has always required an intellectual leveling that transcends class lines, whether those classes be defined economically, socially, racially, or sexually. The anti-intellectualism to which historians have periodically addressed themselves is a profoundly held belief that democratic judgment depends more on talent and education than it does on money or station in life. Generations of disputes over immigration restriction and literacy tests for voters have all tried to deal with the issue. But the intellectual modernizing of America, so to speak, has brought them to an end. Our political system has required that we obliterate all tests for the right to vote or to hold the nation's highest offices beyond the test of citizenship itself.

At the same time, the demands of industry and technology have required of our society the same things they have required of all societies—namely, an educated managerial elite trained not only to run the system, but to maintain its growth and development. The stakes for entry into that elite have had to keep pace with developments in the sciences. Those stakes have increasingly come to depend on the availability of native talent, an educational system capable of training it, and professional structures geared toward recognizing and advancing trained talent.

American society has thus a special difficulty in relating the meritocratic demands of modern industrial society to the traditional democratic requirements of the American political system. For the changes in the political system over the past century have all, by and large, been toward an increase in political participation and a decrease in the restrictions once used, however unfairly, to maintain the dominance of those who considered themselves superior. At the same time, debates over the quality of the education the American system is able to provide have increased as Americans now find themselves comparing the educations they provide their young with those provided by societies like Japan and the Soviet Union.

The fact that these are old and recurrent battles for Americans tends to be obscured by the immediate circumstances that produce them. Again, as in the case of the reponse to the Vietnam war, the more shocking the events that raise the questions, the more difficult it may be to see the questions in their appropriate historical context. For American history has been a history of constant striving toward utopian goals that require shaping historical reality to fit ideals which from time to time appear unreachable. The process produces periodic collapses into states of depression and remorse which, because we are unable to change the goals, may become angry attacks on one another for the perceived failure. We are in such a period now, perhaps the most profound one in more than a generation. I should like to trace some of the intellectual history which, it seems to me, underlies that sense of collapse.

There is a certain historical logic to the fact that an American social science would have an intensely reformist streak right down its center. The same had been true of American government in the years after the revolution. There is a logic, too, to the fact that American social science would, again like American religions and American government, reflect a rebellion against the past that sought in the present a release from the traditions that inhibited change. The essential principle of pragmatism as an American school of philosophy—perhaps the only one that tied together such diverse minds as Charles Saunders Pierce, William James, and John Dewey—was the commitment to an ideal of research that made scientific examination not only a method for investigating reality, but an ideal that assumed the existence of previous wrongs which scientific research could correct. From the Progressive era onward, then, the tie between scientific research and reform invoked an aura of rebellion that in turn recalled the utopian ideals of the nation's revolutionary past.

The fact that that rebellion was also a rebellion against history is the paradox on which this paper rests. More precisely, the belief that science was a method of escaping the past represented by world history itself was central to the American belief that American science, combined now with America's utopian history, could rescue the world from its own history. Such beliefs have infused twentieth-century American policymaking with its characteristic crusading spirit.

Initially, Progressive-era reform was in part a response to a remarkable expansion in knowledge in biology and medical treatment, knowledge that suggested that each human disease had a cause which could be discovered and eradicated. The rapidity with which medicine became the model for social reform can be seen in the private wealth that flowed into the creation of universities not only as medical centers, but as centers for higher learning. Americans were in a peculiarly advantageous position to benefit from such expansion. They had few traditional educational systems to have to transform. The histories that in Europe had tied education and research, as well as medical care, to royal patronage, religious orders, and universities with professional traditions that reached back to the Middle Ages did not exist here. Critics could assail the quality of the education that did exist without having to dismantle the professional hierarchies and national institutions that served them.

Equally important, they had available financial resources of an unprecedented kind. The post-Civil War millionaires who funded research through the creation of the nation's major research universities were, by and large, middle-class Victorian entrepreneurs whose access to new financial resources in oil, steel, railroads, and the like made them enormously wealthy. When they moved to New York City from home bases as varied as Cleveland, Pittsburgh, and upper New York State, it was to take advantage of the centralization of the country's financial institutions there, not because New York represented a social mecca. They did not generally choose to join that city's society, and they married their children to the children of other entrepreneurs, not to European royalty. Insofar as we understand their motives, they were a combination of the tradition of religious tithing they had followed before they had become wealthy and a very hard view of the way intelligent investors should invest vast resources for the greatest public profit.

It would be simplistic to suggest that the sources of funding governed the particular combination of utility and optimism that developed in American social thought. While one could argue that they were the originators of the persistent American belief that money could solve any and all problems, no matter how intransigent, that belief emerged naturally, perhaps, out of the older conviction that American material abundance was a universal panacea. The very character of their wealth, arising as it so often did from the exploitation of natural resources like oil and iron whose myriad and changing uses gave ample evidence of the magic of technology, suggested the sense of gift that gave their money an almost religious mystique. Andrew Carnegie's use of the term "Gospel of Wealth" was not the blasphemy some of his critics could take it to be.

Equally important was the shared middle-class ethic that tied the newly rich to a new generation of academics moving now into a rapidly expanding, talent-hungry educational system. Their patrons were often products of the same small-town backgrounds and religious traditions. The terms on which they manipulated one another had developed out of a common heritage. The system of institutions through which they moved in the course of their careers encompassed both state universities and private ones, both of which could trace their origins, for the most part, to the small sectarian colleges and academies of the eighteenth and nineteenth centuries. The creation of larger research institutions did not mean a separation from those origins in any social sense. The first generation of modern academics moved freely through a system that seemed to have little structure and no systematic political control over it nationally because the social and economic order on which it was built had its own implicit structure.

American Protestantism had that character. A collection of loosely structured national religious associations that encompassed a variety of forms of national governance capable of accommodating to local constituencies, they had gone through national divisions over slavery, various fundamentalist commitments, and the rise of modern science. These convulsions left the system more or less intact, but subject to regional and local pressures. The national academic system had a similar looseness of structure that seemed visible only through the movements of leading figures who carried their careers from one leading institution to another, thereby establishing a sense of a national profession.

Those careers are now being traced by American social scientists who have been developing a new interest in the history of their disciplines over the last decade or so. Biographies of leading social scientists of the last century have joined histories of the academic associations, a small number of them approaching their centennials, to suggest an interest in an accurate documenting of the social sciences. It's important to put it in precisely that form, for this is certainly not the first historical interest as such. Like many of our American institutions, the social sciences have celebrated their birthdays and anniversaries like newlyweds and children— that is to say, at every interval considered minimally decent, without regard for the accuracy with which what was being celebrated had to be described by the celebrants, and with more of an eye to the promise of the future than a critical discussion of the past.

The creation of the various disciplinary associations and the subsequent building of paper halls of fame to house the listings of the yearly presidents of those associations were in part at least a series of acts of intellectual institution building that Americans have engaged in over the past two centuries as they transformed for themselves a sense of professionalism that began with the classical ministerial, medical, and legal triumvirate and came to include virtually every endeavor for which formal education and some form of certification could be required. Celebrations served an important purpose by calling attention to the new professions and justifying the definition of limits and the routes of access.

The recent interest is something else again. While the heated arguments of the Vietnam era focused attention on splits within the various professional disciplines, some of them generational, others ideological, the seemingly specific attention to one historical event ought not to obscure a general transformation in the social sciences which the more recent historical interest helps recount. The interest in the past is no longer simply celebratory, if it is still that at all. It is analytic, sometimes critical, and sometimes nostalgic. It is becoming increasingly possible now to recount the disputes between alternative methodological approaches, between leaders competing for available resources for research, and among institutions vying for "star" professors. The American social sciences have become internationalized too in ways only now beginning to be examined, even by scholars abroad. We are accustomed to reading about British and European influence on American social science in the years before World War I. We are beginning to be made aware of the impact that American social science had on other countries where disciplines like political science were significantly reshaped in the years after World War II.

It is possible, too, that in a general sense the fundamental character of American social science has been undergoing its most important transformation in more than a century, which may account in part for the recent historical interest. Some of that interest, certainly, reflects a serious critical doubt about the meaning of the past, and the role played by American social science in attempting to transform governmental policies in other parts of the world. The possibility that these attempts were undertaken in the belief that American ideas were transferable rather than unique products of American social development itself is now being seriously reconsidered.

III

The special character of American social science grew out of historical conditions peculiar to the development of American society itself. The first of these was a consciousness, characteristic even of the Puritan period but dramatized more generally in the early national era, of the shortage of domestically available knowledge which, like the labor supply and capital for investment, hobbled the quality but not the pace of expansion. The hardships Americans seem to bear with more pride than realism were often the product of a mobility that outran the supplies of modern resources, among them the knowledge of how to manage those resources most effectively.

The second condition was an emphasis on utility that ordered the sciences, giving priority to those that could transform the sometimes new and unfamiliar resources in usable ways and reshape social and governmental institutions to deal with them. For much of the nineteenth century, Old World distinctions between pure and applied science, like the developing concerns with laboratory experiment and scientific theory, reflected a stability in the interest and location of a scientific community that Americans could not really imitate. One of pragmatism's major sources as a unique American philosophy was the seeming boundlessness of the laboratory lands in which nature would be studied and the limited institutional controls over the roving explorers who studied it. The institutional structures for research that

European science had developed in the wake of the great scientific revolution were places American scientists visited for the advanced training they knew they needed.

For a large part of the nineteenth century, they took that training back with them to the open reaches of western lands to explore its meaning, while they spent their careers in institutions only beginning to meet their research needs, however much they may have come to require their experience. The gap between respect for their eminence as trained scientists and the demand for their services as teachers of fundamentals to the young—few of whom were planning to follow them in their scientific careers—reflected the awkward growth of American universities in the nineteenth century. It also represents a fundamental issue in the social sciences, where an acceptance of pure research developed even more slowly than it did in the natural sciences. The point to be made is that both partook of an enveloping sense of utility that was a product of the urgency produced by expansion, not the pragmatic ideal it would later be glorified as being.

Finally, although to put it last should not be allowed to obscure the fact that it is just as important as the others—many might think even more so—American social science began as an escape from, even a rejection of, history as the fundamental social science. In the Old World where the development of natural science had first to be freed of the oldest of histories—the religious doctrines that dominated conceptions not only of human society, but of nature as well—social science had begun as part of the reshaping of the political and social structures of government. Political theories like those of Hobbes, Locke, and Rousseau began in analysis of the nature of man, his dependent physiology, his perceptions, his natural condition, and proceeded from there to define the role of the state. That too required an escape from history, in a sense, but it was an escape that did not require or even make possible a repudiation of the whole of the historical past.

The historical or antihistorical nature of American social science stems from two different but related sources. The American sense that it was a nation without a history was part of that early religious commitment to a new beginning, a new Eden, if you will, or a model city on a hill freed of the corruptions of

Europe. The two commitments came to be different, however identical their origins, for Eden suggested a new beginning based on the discovery of a new innocence, while the rejection of Europe suggested an experience with sin that could stand as a permanent model of what was to be avoided. The latter commitment had a strong historic base, an awareness of the European experience that could be rejected. The former had no historic base, the history replaced by an inward-looking self-examination that made the forests and the plains of the new lands the basis for a genuinely new beginning. In useful but simplistic terms, the battle between Hamilton and Jefferson reflected the early national restatement of an older American issue. The choice seemed clear: on the one hand the building of a new competitor in the world of international trade, one destined to develop a superiority among nations by utilizing its resources and skills to transcend the nations of the Old World, the other the creation of a genuine alternative, freed from the Old World by its distinctive cultural opportunities.

The Hamiltonian view, in that sense, was a call for a new manipulation of an old and valid history. The Jeffersonian was a rejection of that history—indeed, it called for periodic revolutions to make certain that history might never again have the opportunity to inhibit intelligent responses to scientifically perceived needs. The attraction of the French Revolution for Jefferson, like the attraction of the American Revolution, was in part the dramatic liberation from the past. The fear of the French Revolution, like the fears that led those who gathered in Philadelphia in 1787 to frame the American constitution, was a fear that so total a rejection of the stable frameworks of the past would lead to anarchy. Although historians have disagreed on how they perceived those frameworks, a degree of consensus on the need to preserve property ownership helped frame their larger agreements. That Jefferson still suspected the need may suggest the persistence of his own sense of difference.

The two positions, nonetheless, can help us define in broad terms a basic distinction in American social science on the role to be played by history in the development of the disciplines. To see the past as an experience to be rejected and replaced or to see the past as irrelevant are points of view that have affected the way American social science has developed, particularly with regard to its use of history. For both have been responsible for a distinctly reformist mode of social science, but from two rather different perspectives.

The first is an essentially moral mode of social reform, a mode that connects firmly with the history of American religion and philanthropy. The second is an essentially scientific mode that fits with stages in the nation's industrial and technological development. To the extent that a reformist social science may be based on utopian concepts of the future, each implies a different utopian ideal. In the context of American reform history, a reformist social science is always devoted to correcting deviations from what are perceived as the intentions of the founding generation. Every reform battle from the Federalist era to the present has based its arguments on a perception of the original revolutionary intention, whether that be the creation of the strong national government John Marshall believed he saw in the constitution, the egalitarianism the Jacksonians committed themselves to, the control of wealth argued by the Progressives, or the preservation of opportunity and the American dream of success championed by the New Deal. Each has taken the era previous to it as an era of usurpation by some presumably "invisible" oligarchy, although the individuals who make it up are generally visible enough: robber barons, malefactors of great wealth, political bosses, and the like.

What also emerged in the Progressive era and reached its peak in the 1920s and 1930s was a new utopianism based not on an image of a lost or threatened past, but on a supposedly scientific and objective analysis of the present that obviated the necessity of appealing to past models and made application of the most immediate standards of equity and justice the real standard. In law the Brandeis brief had already begun to replace older appeals to statutory practice with what purported to be objective tests of present conditions in industry and in the government of public services. Rates, appropriate profits, conditions of labor, concepts like "a living wage" became objective and persistent standards by which to measure the quality of life in an industrial society. The meaning of an idea like "social justice" rested on the substitution of newly created legal definitions of the social order for traditional definitions of the economic order. Such definitions would enable the courts to define social rights as explicitly as they had been defining economic rights.

The approach of the new social sciences to history was not simply a rejection of it, in a sense, but a use of it that made it a manipulating instrument in the fulfillment of reform aims. In the years between the two world wars the positivist rejection of traditional patterns of thinking and the search for a radical empiricism that examined a real world of facts became part of a whole variety of philosophical positions which gave history a manipulative role to play in the development of new senses of nationalism everywhere. Such manipulation could be useful without pretending to be scientific, unless one chose to call the creation of myth an exercise of the scientific method, as indeed many technicians of propaganda did. While Americans were not inclined to think of their efforts in that regard as comparable, say, to the Italian revival of ancient Rome or the German attraction to a Wagnerian image of a mythical past, Americans were engaged in a revival of their own pioneer roots.

The revival ranged in style and profundity from cowboy movies and school contests funded by the Daughters of the American Revolution to the systematic reconstruction of Williamsburg, Virginia, the beginnings of a new school of American archeology. A new social history championed by Arthur Schlesinger, Sr., called for a similar investigation of the past to determine how Americans actually lived, not what they believed about the way they lived. John Dewey provided his Japanese audiences in 1919 with a similar depiction of the restrictions traditional cultural commitments placed on our efforts to understand and cope with the present. The lectures that became his *Reconstruction in Philosophy* provide the ultimate statement of the threat to utopia posed by adherence to traditional ideas no longer useful in solving human problems.

At the same time, the need to create a usable past, as one historian put it, made history a tool of science without making it a science in itself. A scientific history that could describe the past as reality was not deemed even possible by some. But a history that could be used to sustain patriotism, citizenship, respect for leadership and authority, even the willingness to sacrifice life in the interest of the state was essential to the manipulative aims of the new social sciences. The past had either a stabilizing or a revolutionary role to play, depending on the aims of the state the social sciences were committed to supporting. In the years between the world wars, the issues of national power and cultural homogeneity were to be supported by the national histories of countries as opposed in their conceptions of national interest as Germany and the new Soviet Union, as well as by historians in the United States.

Nonetheless, the cultural identity of the American South posed problems for the New Deal that bear striking resemblance to the problems some regions of Germany posed for the Third Reich and the complex of Slavic, Middle Eastern, and Asian enclaves posed for the Soviet Union. Some argued that distinctive cultural enclaves had to be integrated with the new industrial states, but not in ways that threatened traditionally stabilizing senses of identity. Yet others were bound to see the possibility of disruption and hostility in the maintenance of such traditions, even to the point of seeking to obliterate them entirely. While comparisons tend to be risky, Hitler's absorption in German *Volk* culture, Stalin's problem with the Kulaks, and Roosevelt's efforts to include Negroes in New Deal programs reflected similarly troublesome problems.

The conflict between a scientific history and a usefully mythical history emerged in an odd way in the opening decades of the Social Science Research Council. The American Council of Learned Societies had been organized just after World War I to serve as a clearinghouse for nonscientific academic societies similar to the older National Science Academy. The officers of the ACLS objected to the efforts on the part of social scientists to form an organization of their own, yet it was clear that some in the social science community felt hampered by their association with humanists and were unwilling to join the natural scientists. Their effort to identify themselves as an independent group required an organization of their own.

The problem of where the historians properly fitted was undoubtedly exacerbated by the fact that historians had been prominent in the founding and running of the ACLS, but the issue had really been there for many years. American academic associations had reproduced initially by a kind of cell division that began with the American Philosophical Society. The American Social Science Association had been the parent body for the late nineteenth-century "separatists" who formed the American Historical Association and the American Economic Association. Those separations were in part a response to a new distinction between amateur practitioners and the growing number of academic professionals, many of them with the now necessary German university degrees and American Ph.D.'s. The amateur practitioners had been, by and large, gentlemen philanthropists who not only helped support the initial organizations financially, but tended to emphasize the utility of their intellectual endeavors for social reform. They saw little need to distinguish between their interests in civil service reform, conservation, and the condition of life for American industrial workers, and their interest in political science, economic geography, and sociology. The new academicians saw the need for such distinctions, but they recognized their financial dependence on interested amateurs until the years just before World War I, when the development of the modern foundation and the creation of the professional philanthropists gave them alternative sources of funding—sources they could perceive as being professional and oriented toward their research aims. The ACLS and the SSRC, both of which were created with funding from the new foundations, were an acknowledgement of the new independence.

The relation between financial independence and their roles as reformers was a complex one for the new social scientists. The wealthy amateur donors had had no reason to conceal their aim: the improvement of society. American Victorians, they combined an American utopianism that called for infinite perfectability with a Victorian certitude that blamed failure on a refusal to accept the right pathways to perfection. Their successors in American social science, as well as in the new philanthropy, inherited their conviction that there were no inherent characteristics in human nature that prevented the achievement of their aims, that human beings were capable of infinite improvement, and that research would provide the methodological and educational routes to success. Defects in past behavior were based, therefore, on the absence of the kind of useful knowledge their research could supply. The alliance of foundation managers and social science academics was bound to exclude those who doubted man's capacity to be improved by research; analytic methods that suggested otherwise could scarcely be encouraged.

IV

The creation of a modern national history based on social science research was thus related to the development of the new social sciences in America. Few among the Progressive-era historians really were prepared to face the problem of basing a national history on a social science that rejected historical analysis. The result was a history that looked, for all intents and purposes, like a traditional Whig history in that it followed a progressivist commitment to the improvement of the conditions of American life. Where it differed from Whig history was in its selection of a scattered and ideologically disorganized collection of enemies internal to the American political and economic structure who were nonetheless constant threats to progress. Trusts, robber barons, corrupt politicians, even parts of the federal constitution all were subjects of criticism and targets for attack by historians who otherwise lauded Americanism, the constitution of 1787, and a careful selection of political leaders they were prepared to define as "great." To be sure, their reform counterparts in their much-adored Great Britain were looking to reforms in the House of Lords, the monarchy, and even Fabian socialism. American reformers, even those attacking the U.S. Senate and its method of selection, were not inclined to see themselves as engaged in so fundamental a rebellion.

Charles Beard was virtually alone in his generation in recognizing the paradox posed for historians by a social science that rejected history. Yet he was unable to articulate that recognition in ways that spoke either to his colleagues or to the new social scientists. Part of his problem lay in his own refusal to write a genuinely critical American history—that is, a history that acknowledged fundamental flaws in American historical development and institutions that might not be correctable by amending the constitution, electing better leaders, or controlling those who wanted to manipulate the political system in their own interests. Even he persisted in seeing Madison's use of "interests" in *The Federalist* No. 10 as a recognition of some kind of suprarational system of beliefs that Americans had embedded in their economic institutions, rather than as the Hobbesian idea of a basic irrationality that required strong sovereignty.

For American utopianism required a mystical faith in human rationality that made evil an anomaly rather than the source of an equally rational opposition. Generations of American commentators on American politics would point to the fact, as they saw it, that the American political structure had never brought a dishonest man, let alone an evil one, to the presidency. Even Bryce, like Tocqueville before him, feared mediocrity in American politics far more than the threat of tyranny. The adjectives that modified corruption—petty, local—all pointed to the belief that at the very top of the political structure a fundamental honesty prevailed. Our most corrupt president until Nixon was Harding, a sweet but honest dupe, and many of Nixon's defenders were not inclined to see him in much darker terms.

It is quite possible that the breakdown in that two-centuries-old faith may be one of the most profound phenomena of twentieth-century American history and that we ought to look at it more closely. Much of the writing by American historians over the past two decades has had a revelatory quality that suggests a design to attack not simply the consensus history of the 1950s, but the very conceptual base of American nationalism itself. To the extent that the writings of Daniel Boorstin, Louis Hartz, David Potter, and Richard Hofstadter constitute a single school of writing—and it is a very limited extent, to be sure—it is based on the belief that there is a fundamental American character that leads to a commitment to American government and American society in nonrevolutionary terms. The belief that Americans had their revolution in the eighteenth century and that the Constitution of 1787 is sufficient to ensure continuing change does not deny the need for change. It does suggest a certain degree of virtue, however, in a world seemingly beset by revolution as the only method of achieving progress. And it has made the threat of revolution elsewhere in the world peculiarly difficult for Americans to deal with. To have achieved one's national utopia would be inhibiting enough in a utopian world; but to be uncertain about whether or not one has achieved it may be even worse.

The Vietnam era has done more to shake American utopianism than any era since the Civil War. The changes it has produced in American attitudes toward social science and reform are just as profound. The Great Society and its efforts to organize social change systematically are all subjected now to serious questioning not only on the part of government managers faced with the cost of sustaining those programs, but on the part of analysts examining their actual effects. Equally important, the power of money in the attack on social problems—the ending of poverty, to put it in its most dramatic terms—is being questioned more seriously than it has been since the turn of the century. If a new national history stands somewhere on the historiographic horizon, it is difficult to see what it would look like. For it seems likely that the utopianism which has fueled American nationalism for over two centuries now is at its lowest ebb in living memory.

The basic relationships that established an American nationalism in the twentieth century were built on a social science that believed the past to be irrelevant to the future of reform, a history which accepted that irrelevance and sought to create a unique American historical experience out of it, and a commitment to utopianism that glorified the rationality of the autonomous individual acting out of self-interest. It is quite likely that the three are in a state of collapse they have never before suffered all at the same time. It is not possible yet to see the consequences of that state of affairs, but they will be significant.

Discussion: Kyogoku Paper

Kyogoku: First, I should explain the theoretical framework. My own specialization is the study of government and politics, so it follows that the concept of institution is central. I would like to use it as a criterion for considering three aspects of civilization. The first institution is that of technology, the second that of society, and the third the institution of knowledge. These three I would like to consider separately, but I should emphasize that within the institution of knowledge, the cosmos of meaning is to be included. Modernization as commonly understood starts with the institution of knowledge. In the nineteenth century there was a global institution of knowledge which specified how to judge between the civilized and uncivilized or, in today's terms, the developed and underdeveloped. Thus, people's cognitions, evaluations, and preferences were institutionalized.

Now in Japan's case, the samurai class had the power in the mid-nineteenth century. When they faced the institution of knowledge, they could not bear to be categorized as uncivilized. In the secular sense, it would have been inconvenient for the samurai, but it was also unbearable for them in the sense of the cosmos of meaning. Thus, Japan took off toward modernization. Technology transfer is possible through the institution of technology, for the industrial technology that began in the West is universal in character. Japan began its modernization, and today, as we all know, it has reached the stage of trade frictions with the Western nations.

After World War II, the idea of the American century seemed to come true, and the United States showed some inclination to overhaul the world on the American pattern. Japanese modernization came to be seen as a classic example of modernization *à l'américaine*. Why have many other countries not succeeded in modernization as Japan did? It might be a matter of leadership, as the Meiji emperor recognized. It might be the role of the bureaucracy. It might also be a matter of governmental protection of economic growth and expansion. Finally, there is the

299

importance of social equality. In the interest of self-realization, individuals tried to realize an upward social mobility. They also enjoyed a psychological security in terms of belonging to the nation. This combination of initiative and security has not obtained in many other developing countries.

When Japan surrendered, the political reconstruction of the country was undertaken. It was a remarkably utopian enterprise. In terms of the legal system, a parliamentary government was instituted. At the same time, American occupying authorities considered that the Japanese cosmos of meaning was to be remade on the American model. There were utopian New Dealers among high-ranking officers of the American occupation. But the institution of society and the institution of human relationships are not exportable or importable like the institution of technology. Even when Americans drafted the constitution and gave us Japanese the draft ordinances and laws, they included nontransferable aspects. For anyone to tell other people not to commit themselves to tradition is almost like saying, "You can't live." Only through traditions can one gain knowledge and inherit the cosmos of meaning.

So, this American-style social utopianism, when it was implanted in Japan, succeeded in changing the legal and political system, as far as technology transfer was concerned, but not the cosmos of meaning. But this is not to suggest that Japan is monolithic. We have our own varieties and diversities. Some changes in the cosmos of meaning do come about. For example, in the Meiji period, women missionaries from America succeeded in bringing about the education of women against the often stubborn and fearful resistance of the authorities. So within the cosmos there is some room for diversity.

Schwartz: Utopianism, to my mind, is a holistic state of affairs. One goes from the good whole to the good parts, and might say it is one big package. This corresponds also in the social sciences to the fashionable current concept of the total system in which everything fits together. I wonder, when dealing with the twentieth century, whether the whole notion of systems in which the parts all necessarily go together must not be abandoned.

Karl: My sense of utopia is not holistic. It is based on an idea of an expectation of success: that individuals by taking certain actions will achieve certain aims; if that is built into the argument and into the society, the people will have this expectation. But when obstacles are also built into the society, what you have is a utopian conception with, in fact, dystopian elements in it.

Kyogoku: In the seventeenth and eighteenth centuries a clock was an example of a system. Everywhere, every part of a system could be made artificially by men. I think a legacy of this model survives today. The social scientist, very much like the watchmaker, can construct or reconstruct a social system artificially, as is expected in Japan. But there is an alternative model: a system comprising loosely connected components. Take an octopus. Every part moves very loosely, very flexibly. It is still a system. Whether an octopus would use an artificial leg or tentacle I do not know, but it may borrow a leg or tentacle from another civilization. But you have to find a meaning and a legitimacy for such importation from other bodies. So within the system that is given, one must be able to attach meaning of some sort to everything that we borrow from outside. Japan has a hedonistic, pragmatic culture, so we can borrow anything that is useful and pragmatic to us.

Iriye: The discussion so far may serve to set the two countries, Japan and the United States, in a larger context, and not in exceptionalist terms; that is, not from the viewpoint that the United States is exceptional and Japan is unique, but from that of twentieth-century history. When we discuss European utopias and what they led to in the twentieth century, there is a contrasting sense that in the case of the United States and Japan, utopianism has achieved some successes and has not led to disaster and calamity.

Maruyama has pointed out that American utopianism goes back to the constitution or to the Declaration of Independence— written documents. Those are specific in defining what is meant by an American utopia. Because of American influence, one could also argue that the postwar Japanese constitution serves as a definition of postwar Japanese utopianism. The American creed of racial equality, civil rights, and so on, is missing in the Japanese case. Kyogoku's paper refers to the phenomenon of Japanese exclusiveness, the unitary national homogeneity, to the exclusion of other alien elements. How Japanese conceptions of utopia can cope with that is a very important problem.

Karl: The constitution was not the kind of religious document in the nineteenth century that it became in the twentieth century, partly because of the role of the federal government. The constitution became a central document as a national government became a central element in the United States. It really is not until the Progressive period and then dramatically in the New Deal that the constitution became what it has become today.

Kyogoku: About the Japanese constitution, the rulings of the Supreme Court say that many articles are declaratory programs, which do not necessarily give rights. Such articles as refer to social security and welfare are ideals inscribed in the constitution. In other words, the constitution gives us goals for our efforts, provides the utopian direction. Now on the definition of "others." Unlike the Christian tradition, where the definition of "others" is simple and uniform, we do not have a simple definition of self and others.

Nivat: The problem of Russian civilization is to take European technology, but not to get involved in the things of European society. This kind of Slavophile thought is still alive in Solzhenitsyn and other people. He lives in America and he has looked at America and at Japan. In the case of America he came to a moral condemnation, delivered in his Harvard speech, in which he declared that Americans have lost their virility, in all the meanings of that word. In Japan he delivered this message: You are a model because you are a homogeneous nation. You must, of course, be aware that you can lose that homogeneity, but what is superior in your nation is the ethical primacy in each of your deeds.

Kyogoku: Let me borrow Kierkegaard's words. In personal relationships, first you have the stage of esthetics; then you move to the ethical stage; then up to the religious stage. Now in the Japanese case, the esthetic aspect is markedly strong. Commandment ethics—like the ethics regulated by the Ten Commandments—are not the Japanese form of ethics. If ethics is to be defined as observance of such commandments, the Japanese system is not ethical. And with respect to homogeneity, it may be a virtue, it may not. Within Japan we really have diversities living in myriad different cells or groups. Within each cell or group, we live and experience some homogeneity. Outside the group, there is a sort of common battleground of fierce competition between and among heterogeneous groups.

Yamada: Individual things can be imitated, but not the whole pattern of development. In Japan the pattern of development after Meiji—scientific and technological development—is remarkably similar to the pattern of development in Europe and America. Our departure lagged behind the West by fifty years. Japan took full advantage of being a late starter. But Japan did not derive any momentum from World War I. There we differ from Western nations. But then came World War II, and we began assuming patterns identical to those in the West. Bureaus were created for science and technology; many scientists were mobilized to develop military and industrial products. People were engaged in research and development, and tremendous sums were spent. The technical foundation for industrial growth after World War II was all created during wartime. Japan's industrial prowess after World War II was based upon the wartime government policy of channeling funds and efforts into military-related technology. True, the direct fruits of scientific and technological endeavors were much fewer than in America and in Britain; but insofar as the *patterns* of growth and development are concerned, you see remarkable similarities.

Umesao: Needless to say, Japan has emerged as an important factor in the history of the World. This is perhaps the meaning of the twentieth century to Japan. But what was Japan to the twentieth century? Japan was a trigger in shattering the nineteenth-century world. The Russo-Japanese War helped to trigger World War I. But this also caused a chain reaction leading from World War I to World War II, both involving the collapse of empires and the birth of new nations.

Japan cannot be a model. Rather, for developing countries, we have been spreading an illusion. In Japanese terms, we have done something wrong by spreading the illusion that Japan could be a model. For even before the Russo-Japanese War, Japan had assumed the role of an imperialist power. It was certainly not a developing country. Why did modernization take place so rapidly in Japan? I think the question itself is wrongly based. Why did

Germany succeed? Why did France succeed? We should also ask these questions, because their historical backgrounds are quite similar, in some ways almost identical: the consequences of a long feudal age that began in the thirteenth century. Japan, in a way, must be considered a European nation. It is only others who group Japan wrongly into an Asian family to which it really does not belong, and for whom it cannot serve as a model.

Hersch: I am struck more by the common features of our fate in the twentieth century than by the differences. It was said before that the impossibility of tragedy now is not only an American matter, but a technology matter. Because technology is the contrary of tragedy. Technology is a movement of means toward ends. And the relation, means to ends, is exactly the opposite of tragedy, because in tragedy something is done, whatever the result. This naked and absolute character of tragedy is completely foreign to a civilization based on technology. I think that is true everywhere—not only in America, but also in Europe and probably also in Japan. Now I believe the rejection of tragedy has certain consequences, because tragedy has a unifying effect. Its rejection, implied in technology or in the technology-shaped world, leaves behind not tragedy, but a specific loneliness and sadness we all experience in our different countries.

The second instance of our similarity is related to Kyogoku's discussion of the different cosmos of technology, knowledge, and meaning. It is not true that in Europe it is possible to have a continuity between the cosmos of meaning and the cosmos of technology and knowledge. We Europeans are just like others, in a different way, perhaps to a different degree; but we are also faced with a gap, a lack of unity, of continuity. We have not culturally digested science and technology.

Kyogoku: The Japanese people do not usually show interest in what happens in other parts of the world. We do not share the same pain as people afflicted by unfortunate things elsewhere. There are plenty of exceptions, but by and large, the Japanese people do not feel affected by or associated with events outside Japan.

Karl: There is a persistent thread in American thought that has always considered American society successfully isolated from the rest of the world—the escape, the haven from the rest of the world. On the other hand, the citizens who constitute that haven are all of them themselves immigrants. And that attachment to some sense of traditional home or former home somewhere else has played havoc with American politics historically.

Mommsen: To what extent can we learn from the Japanese experience in order to assist other countries in the developing world? In this context, what is the particular role of a cosmos of meaning? From the paper, it would appear that the Japanese cosmos of meaning must have been singularly adapted to the pragmatic absorption of technology.

Hagihara: In the summer of 1863, the Chōshū batteries attacked Dutch, French, and American merchant ships. So the next year a combined American, British, Dutch, and French fleet went to destroy the batteries. The marines landed, expecting to meet with severe resistance. To their great surprise, they were treated well by the peasants and merchants. Even at the height of the expel-the-barbarians movement, anti-foreign sentiments were confined to samurai classes. This example may show that the less educated, or less indoctrinated, are more receptive to what Kyogoku calls "heterogeneous others."

Umesao: May I offer a few observations? Japan is a unitary nation, one single people. But prewar Japan consisted of some twenty ethnic groups. For a long time, Japan had had the experience of being a compound, mixed nation. After the war, we suddenly made up our minds to become a homogeneous, unified nation. But we do have a lot of experience in failing to accommodate different peoples. There were miserable failures, too, in administering colonies, trying to rule different races, different nations. We suffered many failures, and because of those experiences, the Japanese can benefit from the past. But what about America? In the twentieth century, what is the meaning of America? I think, for one thing, that America has collapsed as a utopian image. America accepts all sorts of races and a free and an equal society is a possibility: This is the utopia of America. That was an opportunity which the Americans had. The opportunity has been lost, and friction is rampant between ethnic groups within American society today. The "melting pot" has failed. I think this is the meaning of America in the twentieth century. In other words, they cannot transcend ethnic or racial barriers. A haven was mentioned. People may have gone to this haven, but they find the same fate.

Discussion: Karl Paper

Karl: The constitution of 1787 in my argument very clearly assumed the existence of a managerial elite in American society. It was an elite defined by property qualifications for voting. And the provisions in the constitution for the selection of the Senate through the state legislature were a method of assuring that the local elites in the former colonies would continue to manage the Senate. To the extent that they had any democratic conceptions of it, those conceptions were, in part at least, defined by Washington, Jefferson, and Adams in their concern for the education of this elite, a kind of meritocratic system, in their first hopes for a national university or a national educational system which would provide that continuity. And then with the Jacksonian revolution by the 1820s you had a genuine transformation of this conception of elites and the destruction of it, in many respects, through the creation of expanded suffrage and primarily the expansion of an educational system. The decisions that Americans made between 1840 and 1860 were those that forbade the federal government from establishing a national educational system. There was a very real attempt to create a national educational system, but Congress vociferously rejected it. The decentralization of American higher education provided more opportunities for experiment, for provision of all kinds of alternatives. Underneath there was a national system being built by the end of the nineteenth century, a system held together by the creation of professional associations. Indeed, they were counterfactors to the university system. The professoriat in the United States achieved independence from the university structure and created a network of its own. The professionals did it by going to private philanthropy, to the major foundations—Rockefeller, Carnegie—to get the funding they needed to provide this kind of independence.

American utopianism is, I would also argue, a peculiar form of utopianism, and in some respects a rather dangerous or deceptively unstable one. It begins in the Puritan migrations, which were unlike other colonial migrations primarily because the Puritans wanted to build a society that was a rejection of previous societies. They were middle-class business entrepreneurs who knew exactly what they were doing in the management of the economic system they were also forced to deal with. So you get this kind of backhanded utopianism being formed. The Declaration of Independence reads much more like a list of union grievances against an incompetent management. The Bill of Rights is an after-the-fact attachment, not a major declaration of principle that leads to a constitution. The rights of man were really not that central to the establishment of the constitution in the first place. So what you have is this odd kind of pragmatic businessman's utopia, if you will, that has been very, very characteristic of American utopian history.

It is an opportunistic history and it sits uneasily in a utopian world—or in the world of utopian history. It also lacks the sense of tragedy that is essential to an understanding—in my own philosophical sense, at least—of what utopia means. Americans have difficulty producing a sense of tragedy out of the failures of their utopias. Arthur Miller's *Death of a Salesman* is a typical example. The result is not a classical conception of tragedy in which you have fundamental human failures being the source of the problem, but a sense of tragedy in which the system really does not achieve what it promised in the first place.

Maier: The advent of industrial society and mass male suffrage in the late nineteenth century in Europe—and perhaps in Japan—required an ideology that justified an elite. What is interesting in the twentieth century is how expertise is claimed. American social science is one way. In business, engineering ideologies from the turn of the century through 1920 or so—such as Taylorism, Henry Ford's notion of industrial prosperity, and various sorts of technological administrative fixes, become very important. I think these change by the 1930s into psychological types of justification. The American manager is much more a manipulator of minds, a practitioner of human relations—such as Elton Mayo. You see this in European ideologies too, so that we have successive types of legitimation principles for elites. Each of these principles invokes a type of justification which supposedly no rational man can object to. Each involves a certain search for harmony, whether in terms of productivity or of psychological harmony within a factory. Probably the high point of the quest for legitimation principles is reached after World War II, when American social science models—modernization, growth, and so on—are exported to re-create a generation of social scientists in postwar Europe and postwar Japan.

Karl: Americans rejected Taylorism as a consistent ideology, whereas Europeans looking at Taylor found it a much more acceptable point of view.

Schwartz: In America many things tend to be regarded as quite readily compromisable that in Europe seem to have a greater sense of tragic confrontation. I have always felt that democracy and social science have a great tension in them. But when you read John Dewey, he says that science is something that can be easily democratized; his definition of the word "science," a sort of Baconian definition, assumes that we can all learn science in high school.

Karl: It is not simply that things go well; it is that there is a particular way in which things have to go well that is part of what I see as American utopianism. The concern with it at the end of the twentieth century and the problem in the twenty-first century is that we have over the last twenty-five years gone through an enormous revolution of inclusion, of bringing into the system people who continue to demand more and more of it, more than the system can possibly supply as it becomes more technologically complex. Can you really educate all these people, particularly the large underclass that exists now in the United States? It is going to be extremely difficult to fulfill this utopian aim.

Schwartz: One sees how American Dewey is when one tries to apply him to China. But it was not just his individualism; in a way, as in Marx's utopia, in Dewey somehow complete individual fulfillment and social harmony will necessarily go together.

Mommsen: I am of course a product of American reeducation at some stage, and I think this connects me with the Japanese. I would say that this sort of message of how society should be constructed, which surely is—or was—utopian to a very high degree, was a major constituent in my intellectual development. From that point of view, of course, after 1945 America went out to form societies according to the American mold. This is very important: It leads us right to the center of our theme, because if the second part of the twentieth century means anything, then it is formed by the fact that a great portion of the world has been remodeled according to American ideas, with a substantial element of British traditions as well. We have had this influx of an American ideology which says you can reconstruct the world according to scientific principles in line with the basic elements of democracy as outlined in the American pattern. There must be something in it; otherwise it would never have been so successful. To some degree and surely after 1945, one would have thought the twentieth century was the American century. Weber heralded that as early as 1916. In some ways your paper sounds to me almost too self-critical.

Karl: The problem with American utopianism has been the disillusion that sets in when the specific aims set up by the utopian planners do not work out. Then what you get are recurrent periods of criticism. I think the American response to World War I is certainly the most dramatic modern example.

One of the classic examples of American utopianism is that of the political scientist who argued in a major journal that we were really improving Vietnam because we were forcing all these peasants into the cities, and this was part of our great modernization program. There is almost a Platonic notion that there is an internal something in human beings which will make them behave like Americans if only they are given the opportunity to do so. All we needed was to give people a two-party system. Once we give these new countries two parties, instantly they will set up some kind of democratic framework and start behaving like democrats. American utopianism requires, unfortunately, very specific forms of behavior which may even have to do with how many automobiles one country sells to another. It is not simply a problem of trade restrictions or trade barriers. There is a sense of loss of faith somehow: a sense that the American triumph did not really succeed that is so deeply ingrained in these arguments. Even what you would characterize as success is not viewed by Americans as success.

Friedländer: Would you say that the whole determining influence of German philosophy and German universities, which had such an impact on American thinkers in the nineteenth century, was systematically turned the American way? After all, most American intellectuals got a lot of their training or their inspiration from German universities during the second half of the nineteenth century. So how would that dimension of "tragedy" have disappeared? Would it have been systematically sifted through the American vision, and transformed and changed? Much more fundamental, where is the second part, that part I think Harry Levin has called "the power of blackness," and where is the Puritan question of sin—Poe, Hawthorne, Melville—which came so strongly through American literature and which is a strain in American thinking from the beginning to our day? Has that disappeared from the view of politics, political science, political reality?

Karl: American writers about American education have vastly overstated the nineteenth-century impact of the German university. I have read through some of the course notes taken by those Americans, at least three of them, in German classrooms. Their German was often limited, at least at first. What they were actually learning in Germany was also limited. The impact of Germany does not hit the United States, I would say, until 1935. At that point, it hits it with a bang. The migratory influence, particularly in American social science, on American university development is absolutely extraordinary.

The question about what happens to evil is probably the roughest question. Obviously it is there; it is there in literature. The question of what happens to it in politics—in political thought—is a much more complicated issue. It certainly disappears for periods of time. For example, poverty had been in existence—literary existence—in the literature of the 1920s; Herbert Hoover was moving to stamp out poverty. Then it disappears during the war, though a few people keep trying to raise the issue. It really is not until you get funding sources willing to support this interest that you begin to get a vast expansion of studies of poverty and of the real problems, perhaps the intractable problems. But if you look at the Moynihan Report on the black family, you get a statement that raises all kinds of issues about whether we do take seriously how long it takes us to understand what it is that we are supposed to be engaged in examining. But the darkness is still there, with the aim of using funding to reach the light.

Windsor: It seems to me that there is from the history of seventeenth-century America a strong tradition of the sense of sin, of the sense of evil. But equally I think a very important theme in Karl's paper is the absence of tragedy. There is a peculiar combination here of the sense of evil and the absence of tragedy. It is not a question of purely American development; it is a question of the historical moment at which the United States came into being. The United States was a child of the Enlightenment, and the Enlightenment itself was lethal to tragedy. Eric Heller's *Disinherited Mind* begins with a chapter called "Goethe and the Avoidance of Tragedy."

The avoidance of tragedy, I think, has been characteristic of much of modern Western thought and Western attitudes. I think what is unique in America is that the absence of tragedy has not led to the developments we have discussed and has, in a sense, reinforced the utopianism you discuss, but at the same time has left this sort of tremendous dissatisfaction, this sense of inability to grapple with things except on a very practical level, the level of funding, the level of problem solving, and so on. But I think that is also part of the American impact on Europe and other countries after World War II. There the absence of tragedy— or the death of tragedy—led to particular kinds of horrors and made them extremely receptive to American ideas, American techniques, American influence—and not just to American money.

Karl: The major religious movements in the twentieth century that are popular religious movements—from Billy Sunday to Billy Graham—have all been movements that have argued for the possibility of immediate salvation. That form of Protestantism fits much more in the American conception of problem solving than does Calvinism. There is a neo-Calvinist revival after World War II that is extraordinarily important and that involves Reinhold Niebuhr's *The Children of Light and the Children of Darkness*. But it then moves into another kind of ecumenism with *Life* magazine. There is a *Life* magazine series on religion which argues that really they are all the same; you just change the pictures once a week and you can leave the text pretty much untouched. That religious movement starts in a Calvinist mode, but moves rapidly into the Arminian sense that you really can use religion to stamp out evil.

Kolakowski: Certainly one of the most powerful works of social criticism in American literature is Dreiser's *An American Tragedy*. Nevertheless, it is not tragedy in the sense we normally use in literary works; it is really social criticism. And you mention *Death of a Salesman*; that is a similar case. What struck me in my first contact with the American Left was this terrible American self-aggression—ideological self-aggression—which in conceptual terms was often expressed with the help of German anti-Americanism, of the *Massen geselschaft* theory the German emigrés of the thirties brought to the United States.

My speculation in answering the problem brought up by Friedländer and Windsor is that America was a society founded by people of profound Protestant background and therefore with a deeply rooted idea of sin and the corruption of human nature; subsequently, however, it produced a society with predominantly hedonistic values. So, Americans, ingenious people, invented a device for coping with this clash. The feeling of sinfulness and of guilt was projected onto the society in such a way that the predominant attitude became this: Everybody is individually perfect, but the society is terrible. And so society itself, like Jesus Christ, took on all our sins—individual sins—and we could be happy. That kind of social criticism became very popular in America, perhaps not without a certain contribution from the Freudian ideology which is so widespread in American culture.

Karl: That is an extremely good idea. In 1941, Archibald MacLeish wrote a marvelous essay called "The Irresponsibles," in which he castigated a whole generation of intellectuals of the 1920s for not taking responsibility for what they were doing. The question of the personal responsibility of the intellectual, of the individual, for events is part of an American argument.

Maier: That is why I think that the sense of sin, the sense of conversion or inadequacy in sin, can be localized in different ways. It can be localized in provinces such as Appalachia and in Baptist culture. And it can be localized in a culture of opposition, the "irresponsibles," our version of a sort of Parisian Left. It can be localized regionally. We are the country in which the Civil War had two states each claiming—and with some legitimacy—the legacy of the Declaration of Independence. But not by and large a civil war in the sense of the Spanish Civil War.

The sense of sin and tragedy and Protestantism still does thrive in certain aspects of America. And the sense of optimism can thrive at certain times and be transmuted into these social science elites. One of the paradigmatic examples of the revenge of one against the other is the Oppenheimer trials, when you had a whole generation of scientific assumptions connected vaguely with the Left being publicly put on trial in the United States.

Maruyama: Just a remark about the influence of John Dewey on Japan. Insofar as I know, there have been two periods. The first is the prewar period, when there was a movement among educators and private citizens to encourage students to write compositions based on their daily lives. This was an attempt at departure from the formalistic school education, which since the Meiji era had been based on a conventional body of knowledge that pupils were forced to memorize. Unfortunately, the promoters of this movement were suspected as dangerous elements, and some were arrested during the war.

The second period started immediately after the war and came about as a result of the collapse of nationalistic education. The Ministry of Education had an influx of new administrators and advisers who had been strongly influenced by Dewey. And these people opposed the handing down of knowledge—including, in the very broad sense of the term, ethical education—from higher authorities. They formed the starting line of postwar education in Japan, but unfortunately, their influence was shortlived.

Karl: The point about objectivity and policymaking: The American system as it developed from 1900 on—and it is a twentieth-century phenomenon—is a system that until 1965 separated policymaking from government by utilizing the system of private foundations that had been created, and universities, to fund the policymaking developments. In the 1960s that situation changed as the federal government began to organize its own policy research. My argument is that foundation groups in the United States serve a terribly important purpose, primarily because, as Tocqueville pointed out many years ago, the American political system turns everything into very short-range politics. It is necessary for the government in the United States to limit itself to what is publicly and politically acceptable, or to lie about what it is doing. And therefore long-range policy research cannot be undertaken by the federal government with a large degree of safety.

John Dewey is a fascinating phenomenon. As many of you may know, a similar thing happened in the Soviet Union after World War I. American educators—George Counts, the whole faculty of the Columbia School of Education—moved to Moscow for a period of time to try to reorganize the educational process in the Soviet Union, and did so with some success. Dewey presented in *Reconstruction in Philosophy* the basic argument that a commitment to tradition was dangerous to education. That by teaching traditional stories and traditional practices, you were inhibiting educational development not only for the child, but for the philosophy of the community as a whole. And that a community whose philosophy depended on tradition was a community doomed to an inability to solve any of its problems. I could see how the Soviets could find it useful, because that after all was in part what they were trying to do, so there was a certain attractiveness to it there. But I could not understand how he could be a success in Japan.

HISTORY AND MEANING

THE CONDITIONS OF MEANING AND THEIR DESTRUCTION AT THE END OF THE TWENTIETH CENTURY

JEANNE HERSCH

The Sense for Meaning

In the term "meaning" there is an immediacy which, at first, confounds thought. It is certainly for this reason that in a relatively old dictionary, such as the *Littré*, we do not as yet find, among the many meanings listed for this word, the one which interests us here and which relates to the raison d'être, the justification, the ultimate purpose of anything. Here we will be concerned with human life and what gives it its value.

Some believe that the meaning of life is questioned only when everything is going badly and life itself becomes too difficult. Rather, we should like to suggest that the contrary is the case. When the question is one of escaping privations and facing menaces, we usually content ourselves with a prereflective state: Survival is sufficient. Survival constitutes in and of itself purpose and meaning. The question of the meaning of life is raised only when survival is easy and, as it were, goes without saying, when the pressure of needs and of threats to life, is not suppressed—it never is—but, in some sense, relaxed and kept at bay. By the same token, the question concerning the meaning of history can be posed with great force. It would seem that the struggle for life maintains, as it were, a state of moral and social health: in such situations, life finds its value in itself and its meaning in its daily victory over death.

When the urgency diminishes, man seeks to give to his life a meaning which is external to it, a finality or *telos* to which it can be subordinated. The more unconditional his commitment to

317

this ultimate end, the more vigorously and independently does what he recognizes as his "sense for meaning" affirm itself within him. At that point, the question is raised: What is "meaning"? What do we mean by "to have a meaning"?

Those who complain that "life has no meaning" and point to the fiasco of our society, or even of our entire civilization, are speaking of meaning as of a thing, almost as if it were a piece of merchandise. One ought to be able to find it ready-made and be able to buy it like everything else. They claim a sort of "right to meaning" the way the World Health Organization postulates a "right to health" (a right difficult to conceive for mortal beings).

The idea of an objectively given meaning is, by the way, a contradiction in terms. Facts in themselves never have meaning. It is up to us to give them one, it is a responsibility with which we are saddled. Meaning exists only for and by free beings. We must therefore strengthen in ourselves "our sense for meaning." If our lives and the entire world seem divested of meaning, it is because our liberty, the source of meaning in us, has exhausted itself.

The word *meaning* is linked to the representation of a movement going in a certain *direction*. It implies the *sighting* of a goal, a finality which gives to life its *orientation*. The image which corresponds to it is that of the flight of an arrow directed toward a clearly defined *target*. One must immediately note that it is not the goal, target, or purpose which is the source of meaning— quite the contrary is the case. It is because the subject *lives* according to the schema of a certain aim that he adopts a given finality. It is his commitment which establishes the result aimed at as a goal, thanks to the "sense for meaning" which lives in him.

Conditions for Meaning

What are *the implications which make possible such a finalistic or teleological and sense-giving "structure,"* implications which elicit and animate the subject's "sense for meaning"?

The first condition, from the subject's point of view, is the capacity *to recognize the real datum,* as it is given to him or imposed upon him. This recognition is so much a matter of habit that we are unaware of it. But all it takes is a mental disturbance, a loss of the sense of reality, the substitution of an imaginary datum for a real one, or simply a hesitation between a real experience and a dream, for the decisive importance of the recognition of the real to become manifest. Without it, it becomes impossible, through lack of a datum, to conceive or imagine a different datum at which we can aim and in so doing give birth to a *meaning*.

In order for the subject to be able to modify his situation he must first be able to recognize himself as being "in a situation," that is, in a situation which is determinate, which is real and which offers resistance.

The second condition concerns the subject's consciousness. Although aware of his situation, the subject must not be completely overwhelmed by or subject to it and thereby incapable of imagining or conceiving something beyond it, a different situation. Such is the dimension, or opening, of *the possible*. Without it, meaning is inconceivable: Only the massiveness of fact exists. All we can say is: What is, is.

The third condition is that the subject be able to *compare* what constitutes his real situation with the possible one he imagines beyond it. He must be able to *prefer* or *fear* the imaginary situation by comparing it to the given real situation. This implies that his real situation, although recognized as such, must not be experienced as ultimate or definitive. For example, the subject must recognize its lacks or insufficiencies in comparison to an imaginary one to which he gives value by his desire.

But this act of valuation, this preference as a source of meaning, implies a *fourth condition*: The subject must be capable of distinguishing between the possible and the impossible. For, in a situation where nothing is possible, or else where everything is possible, valuation has no meaning. If all that is, is necessary, a yes or a no takes on an absolute and transcendent value from which time is excluded. (Such would be the perfection of the Spinozan universe.) If, on the other hand, all is possible, if nothing prevents anything and everything from happening, taking aim is impossible for lack of resistance. The magic wand, being all-powerful, overwhelms and annihilates meaning. It is the distinction between the possible and the impossible (it is not important for our purposes that this distinction be correctly established), between a utopia and a project, which introduces the notion of a *limit*, indispensable for the concept of meaning. It is by the notion of the limit that the possible presence of a meaning is linked to human finitude.

It should already be clear, in terms of what we have said, that the *most important condition* for a meaning, for a raison d'être, for a justification, for an aim, finality or *telos* is *the life of consciousness in time*. We are speaking here of its *temporality*.

The temporal condition of man is usually conceived as being essentially constituted by the inevitability of death, an inevitability which denies to life an infinite duration. Although this is true, it is quite insufficient. Neither birth nor death exhausts the meaning of the temporal condition. The temporality of human existence differs, in each of its instants, from the structure and nature of physical and biological temporality. It is composed of the three heterogeneous dimensions of time, all coexisting and interdependent: past, present, and future.

The past is the dimension of *that which must be recognized* as it was, of that which is only subject to appear in a different light, a different interpretation, and the light itself, at a certain period, was of a certain kind and must be recognized as such. Everything that is now *given* as past—or should be given but is now lost to us—belongs to this definitive past.

The future is the dimension of the *possible*, of what the subject conceives or imagines through or beyond what is given, and which it is the subject's responsibility to realize or to prevent from coming into being. Thanks to the future, to the dimension of the possible, the comparison between what is given and what is imagined allows affectivity or the emotive life to unfold in terms of the experience of lack or insufficiency, valuation or devaluation, preference or refusal. The given (as past) appears simultaneously as susceptible to elimination (as future) and as capable of bringing into being another given. By the same token, as the means and the condition for the future, this given *limits* the possible. The subject envisages the future and has a tendency to "realize" it within the possibilities delineated by the given.

The *present*, as the limit of the two other dimensions, is not of itself a genuine dimension. It is the unimaginable bond/separation which articulates time as past and future, which simultaneously opposes, constitutes, and unites them through the active consciousness of the subject. The lived present is absent from physical time. And it is this absence which renders the latter, although seemingly more familiar in experience, literally unthinkable. It is the moment in which the world is present to consciousness and consciousness to the world, the moment of the emotive wound, of the subject's decision and intervention. It is here that all "meaning" finds its roots and its object. It is here that we find the interest or the stakes, whatever they may be. Even if the result lies in the future, it can be imagined, in terms of the interest or the stakes, only as a present.

The three dimensions of lived time are indispensable for meaning, and the "sense for meaning" will be all the more vigorous the more the three dimensions reinforce the divergencies of their natures and their functions. Meaning requires that the subject have faith in the reality of the past (even if poorly known or still to be discovered), that the subject rely upon it and seek there his means of action. Meaning also requires that the subject have faith in a certain malleability of the future, in the plurality of future possibles and in his capacity to influence them. "I can still do something"—in other words, meaning requires that the subject, when faced with a given which is recognized and explored as such, be capable of continuing to hope and to believe in the possibilities—not infinite ones—of his freedom. This implies, for the present, not only the opposition-conjunction of past and future, but also a relation of another kind, according to a vertical dimension, with that which, though not foreign to time as are triangles, nevertheless transcends it.

The Destruction of the Conditions of Meaning

It would first of all be necessary to make a study, difficult but indispensable, of the way in which the modalities of scientific thought, and usually of pseudoscientific thought, have imposed themselves upon the everyday representations of mankind. Many examples show that great scientific minds have been capable of using the schemata and concepts of science without thereby losing the ability to think, to believe, and to live in other domains, according to very different models and "symbols." In contrast, those lesser scientists, or even pseudoscientists who are incapable of a vision reaching beyond or beneath their own discipline, have rushed, often with arrogance, into a univocal and exclusive dogmatism which they have propagated through intimidation. They were incapable of realizing that they themselves, in other aspects of their lives, were applying other schemata and were making other demands, and that they were thereby settling into a form of incoherence where their scientific dogmatism was nothing but a rather narrow superstition, albeit one with devastating effects.

This simplification and popularization of the schemata of pseudoscience has had in no domain an influence more penetrating than in that of the representation of time and the manner in which we must relate to it and live it. For the natural sciences, and especially for that science which I take as a paradigm, physics, time is not articulated in several dimensions; it ignores the present. In physics there is no *hic et nunc*, no genuine "now" except that constituted by the lived act of the researcher. But that is no longer physics. The time employed by physics is therefore *continuous* and *one-dimensional*. From the temporal point of view, the physicist only distinguishes and compares moments situated on the same continuum: a *before* and an *after* whose distance he measures and whose terms he compares in his attempt to discover a constant relation.

The so-called human sciences have always sought to imitate the so-called exact sciences in the hope of attaining, like the latter, objectivity, verifiability, and universal validity in their methods and results. As can be seen from the examples of sociology, psychology, and history, the human sciences thus extended the one-dimensional and continuous representation of the time of physics to human realities. But because they were less certain of their scientific status than the exact sciences, the human sciences were less adaptable to experience and maintained more rigidly their schemes of intelligibility, mostly causal relations, for which they sometimes substituted structural variants or relations borrowed from computer science.

Ordinary consciousness thus gradually subjected itself to a representation of time from which the present—the only point at which the subject meets the world and the only occasion for a genuine decision—had disappeared. Simultaneously the distinction disappeared between the past as having taken place once and for all and the future as something which still depends, though to a limited degree, on the decision of the subject. Henceforth there is no longer room for decision, nor for action, nor for responsibility. The unfolding of facts constituting the flow of time is from now on just as it is and nothing more.

We therefore find that the conditions for meaning listed at the beginning of this paper are all simultaneously abolished. To the degree that they are consistent with themselves, the "human sciences" lose their humanity, and probably their rigor as well.

Scientific ways of thinking are not the only factors which influenced, to the point of transformation, the thought processes of people living in industrialized countries. *The development of technology* modifies man's private and collective life at all levels—to the extent that he often forgets the constants of his condition and even finds his relation to reality radically altered. Let us examine a few examples of this alteration.

The success of scientific research and its technological repercussions has surpassed all expectation. In many areas the descriptions found in fairy tales have been eclipsed by reality. More and more victories of different kinds have been won over all forms of human toil. In order to live much better and much longer, we now need to work less, for fewer years, with infinitely less effort, pain, and risk. The most diverse pleasures are available to a great number of human beings. Nature and culture become generally accessible. Long years of training, this former luxury of the privileged few, have now become available to young people of all classes. Absence and separation—these situations of despair from which human beings have endlessly suffered over the course of millennia—were almost defeated by the speed, or even the instantaneous quality, of the means of communication. The epidemics and plagues that decimated entire populations, and infant mortality, are also on the verge of being eliminated. Men's ambitions, developing from a given which was known and studied, were realized so effectively that success was finally taken for granted. Success was claimed as one's due. Confronted with the evils that remained or with new threats, men were shocked and scandalized.

From the human point of view, meaning implies dissatisfaction, lack, finitude. There exists neither nostalgia, nor hope, nor ambition for the one who lives in plenitude. Adam and Eve in Paradise knew neither lack, nor aspiration, nor work. They were ignorant of time, they had no use for a meaning which plenitude excludes. The human condition, with all it entails, was engendered by the creative fault. Man never ceases to dream of an overflowing plenitude which at the same time would be full of meaning and desire. Meaning requires that we expose ourselves to suffering by attaching ourselves to the irreplaceable which can always be destroyed. It is for this reason that the need for meaning does not coincide with the demand for happiness. If we wish to live the human life, it is *this* we must understand and learn, and even learn to bear with and to love.

And yet, progress in scientific and technical civilization was so considerable that the very meaning of work and human research seems today to be foundering, submerged in the superabundance of results. It is as if we were witnessing the beginning of a new, previously unknown, misfortune.

Consequences

Technological achievements, by shortening the amount of time one needed to devote to life-sustaining work, and by increasing— in ways one had never imagined—the proportion of culture, narration, images, and fiction in everyone's daily life, *blurred*, in the individual and collective consciousness, *the clear distinction* between *reality as given* and the *realm of the imaginary*. Since the surest sign of the real is its resistance to variations of affectivity and desire, and since precisely such cases of resistance have become rare, the sense of unavoidable reality and the choices it demands has been lost. We attempt to live as in a dream. We even demand of reality the malleability of the dream world. Reality as such gradually becomes intolerable. The electronic media surround and conceal this new confusion.

For lack of resistance, for lack of reality, meaning gets lost: It is replaced by *excessive demands.* Men forget or reject their mortal condition and their finitude. They demand, as a birthright, the immediate satisfaction of all their desires—as if desire were the basis of right. "Everything, all at once!" they proclaim. They want heaven on earth, without understanding that if all desires are satisfied, there can no longer be any meaning, for want of a lack, for want of aspiration toward that which is other. They fail to understand that, for human beings, Paradise is necessarily projected beyond time and temporality; otherwise, even if it were materially realizable, it would collapse, for lack of meaning, into deadly *boredom.*

Benefiting, as if by right, from the achievements of technology, living in the confusion propagated by the invasion of words and images, suspended between reality and fiction, man finds himself unaware of resistance as such. Not only *is everything permitted* in a world over which we have achieved complete mastery, but *everything is possible.* Man feels himself and wants himself to resemble God—or, rather, to be superior to that Being whom history and science have overthrown.

"Master of oneself as he is master of the universe?" No. It is no longer necessary to be master of oneself; we only require a mastery of the universe sufficient to annul the natural consequences of our acts. Thus, for example, we guarantee by techniques the sterility of the sexual act, thereby snatching pleasure away from the chain of cause and effect. From this technical mastery men demand not only that it nullify the effects of their acts, but also that it *guarantee their innocence.* How burdensome to be a man, this limited being, always in a state of desire and always guilty. His guilt is rooted in his double allegiance: to nature through the needs of his body, vulnerable and mortal; to freedom through his capacity to prefer, to judge, to decide, and to act. To assure his innocence, man will thus attempt to break up this double allegiance, to exclude one of the two terms, to reduce himself *either* to pure body *or* to pure spirit.

It is for this reason that, under all sorts of cultural guises, men of this era prefer, to all other sins, those which seem to deliver them from their human condition: the reduction to pure animality or to pure spirituality, *the sin of bestiality* or *the sin of angelicism.*

Furthermore, at least insofar as we can ascertain, the dimension of meaning cannot exist in a purely animal world. This is because of the animal's absolute subordination to the necessary order of nature. It is a subordination which is absolute because it is without consciousness, a state of which the human being is quite incapable. When he attempts to achieve it, thereby betraying the double reality which constitutes his being, he is not obeying nature, he gets stuck in it.

Conversely, when he claims to forget his mortal body and his needs in order to transmute himself into pure, disinterested freedom and to conceive the community to which he belongs on the angelic model, he is obviously rejecting everything which belongs to the realm of constraint—values, rules, institutions, laws. But has he not here relieved himself of what is real, of everything which has weight, which poses an obstacle and offers support? He pretends to have emerged from time and its dimensions. He forgoes all the conditions of human meaning and everything which allows a man to have in himself "a sense for meaning."

One should not be surprised, then, when such a man refuses to acknowledge his mortality. Everything that might involve a *risk* or a *threat of death* appears scandalous. Until recently, the repeated experience of all kinds of catastrophes, or merely the risks involved in satisfying basic needs, had followed like a shadow, like a constant menace, human enterprises and innovations. It is despite this shadow and in its company that human history has always unfolded. Without it, nothing was possible, no action, no meaning.

And people knew—even if they placed their hope and their faith in the supernatural, in the eternal—that on our planet not only men, but everything was, in actual fact, destined to die. One day the planet would become too cold or too hot, or else it would collide with another celestial body, or else there would be a universal flood or drought. The history of man, and of life itself, would end, because at one time it had begun. Eternity was not yet conceived as an empirically unending duration. The meaning of actions and of events requires, certainly, the dimensions of past and future, but not of an infinite future. Rather, it takes root in the knot of the present which articulates, slices, and transcends time.

The Refusal of Finitude

Today, however, we are witnessing a massive and all-pervasive refusal of risk and of the threat of death. It is true that the record of conquests by science and technology is contradictory. On the one hand, in the technically developed countries an unheard-of security has been attained. In these countries one lives twice as long and ages much more slowly. One is less exposed to physical suffering, for most epidemics and a large number of diseases have been eradicated. Famines are nonexistent; infant mortality is minimal. Nevertheless, the armaments man now has at his disposal have made the threat of generalized death a concrete and pressing reality. The manner in which he uses and abuses the resources of the planet raises further fears. He is now capable of intervening in the very processes of the transmission of life, and this also is frightening.

Fear is a healthy signal as long as it does not paralyze the sources of meaning or drag men into blind submission to some superstition or other. For not a few human beings today, fear has destroyed the conditions for "a sense for meaning." They have lost the meaning of the present between the given of the past and the possible of the future. Besides terror, all they have left is an attitude both defensive and passive, a vague refusal of everything, motivated only by the concern not to die, to *persist*. Thereby exposed without protection to various kinds of propaganda, they reject the achievements of research and invention which were attained with such efforts and condemn ahead of time future conquests. Their present shrivels up. For fear of absorbing harmful or impure substances, they no longer dare to eat, to drink, or to breathe. They are ready to let themselves die in order to increase their chances of living, thus smothering the dimension of the possible which is indispensable to meaning.

Stimulating excessive demands through the desire to be "like God" or "like the angels," submitting oneself to physical nature in order to be "like an animal," refusing guilt, refusing risk, and death—all these involve giving up room for the possible and support for the real, as well as a misreading or a denial of the limits of the worldly condition. The conditions for meaning are destroyed, as are the conditions for freedom, or at least for freedom such as man can know it.

Contemporary Ideologies

Contemporary ideologies are too often accused of direct responsibility for the attitudes and commitments people have regarding the great problems of our time. I am inclined to believe that these ideologies are often themselves only the effects or the explicit translation of attitudes obscurely generated by the profound changes which have occurred in our life patterns and our environment. One would not have guessed some of the characteristics they have in common.

Whatever they are—liberal, progressive, or Communist ideologies, "professions of faith," either religious or atheistic—they are all at one in condemning the contemporary world, as much from the moral point of view as from a look at the future which awaits us. They are just about unanimous in denouncing our civilization as "materialistic," as one whose only purpose is that of accumulating "profits" and which finds itself completely submerged under an ocean of "things" produced or slated for production. They all also predict the outbreak of universally destructive wars that will eliminate life from the face of the earth. These predictions are not really warnings, since they do not suggest any plausible methods for avoiding such an end. At most, they serve to spread a preventive paralysis: perhaps it is best not to do anything at all.

These ideologies take great relish in producing facts and estimates so exaggerated as to exclude any reasonable response. Starting from real ills and dangers, we suddenly find ourselves caught in the net of total helplessness. The result is not far to seek: a universalized sense of the loss of meaning which, in spreading over all that has been accomplished in the past and affecting any action that might be attempted in the present, completely blocks the future. All possibility is extinguished.

This state of mind is reinforced by the invasive popularizing of the sciences—or rather, by the superstitions to which this popularizing has given birth. Teleology is replaced by determinism or by the mechanism of programming. People insist that science proves the absence of freedom. Bowing to the "necessities" of natural mechanisms passes for a new way to innocence. People have recourse to psychotherapeutic techniques to rid themselves of guilt feelings. One surrenders with relief to the constraint of the "genetic code" which determines our nature and whose "alphabet" has not been deciphered. We are delighted that biologists and data processors are using the same vocabulary and look forward to machines that are at least as "thinking" and "creative" as men, and men as innocent and programmed as machines. Perhaps we will soon celebrate the marriage of a man and a machine or a robot and a woman. Clearly, one can no longer speak of meaning, or of a "sense for meaning," or of "conditions for meaning." Only objectivity remains.

The human sciences can rejoice. In theory, nothing separates them any longer from the rigor of the exact sciences nor requires them to consider human beings and their societies as a "different" field of research. Their development is supported and sustained by hypotheses and methods that maximize the reduction of the human being to his bare objectivity, to what can be ascertained from the outside, measured, and derived. It should come as no surprise, therefore, that the exclusion of meaning encourages, in all sorts of ways and in all sorts of areas, the development of a universal sense of the ominous. What is thus excluded is not merely "the meaning of life" indispensable to thinking beings. The sense of reality itself, of being, is equally affected. For the different sciences only reach, each according to the particularity of its point of view, its aims and its methods, some aspect or other of being. This restriction is the very condition of their rigor.

Interdisciplinary research, much discussed but little practiced, could only do damage by confusing or attenuating the specificity of each scientific approach. On the contrary, such research must combine and confront, as clearly as possible, approaches that are discontinuous and mutually irreducible. It is for this reason that it has value only when practiced by researchers who have prior training in *one* discipline; it cannot be elaborated in contexts that precede all specialized training. It is for this reason that great scientists do not lose the sense of being, nor the sense of meaning. They know that their science grasps only a certain discontinuous aspect of being, never being itself.

It seems to me, therefore, that complacency regarding a feeling of impending doom, extending to all the domains and all the dimensions of the human condition, arises much more from the destruction of the conditions of meaning than from the external changes occurring at the end of the twentieth century. Even the horrors of history during this century cannot account for the destruction of our sense of being, of the real, of the possible, and of hope.

Human life loses its meaning, and the conditions for meaning evaporate or disintegrate to the degree that men no longer accept their condition. When they want to be like gods, angels, or animals, when they refuse to accept human time and its irreducible dimensions, when they demand paradisaical happiness, total knowledge, perfect innocence, and unlimited power, they can no longer even be men. They no longer harbor within themselves a sense for meaning, and their life becomes meaningless. For human beings, the meaning of life implies the acknowledgment of finitude.

The Great Events of the Twentieth Century

I could, of course, have treated my subject in an entirely different way. I could have—perhaps I ought to have—since the subject is the twentieth century, started with the unprecedented events which have convulsed history and the possibilities of the future, in order to discover there the loss of meaning men are experiencing today. The twentieth century: two world wars, more extended, more destructive, more violent than any the world has ever known. Totalitarian regimes devoting themselves to the planned and scientifically executed extermination of millions of men and women and of entire peoples. The invention, toward the end of the second of these wars, of nuclear arms, so deadly, with effects so dreadful that until now they have succeeded, on several occasions, in stopping a new world war which was about to break out —without, however, preventing numerous local conflicts from flaring up over the years.

We have witnessed violently contradictory historical processes. On the one hand, decolonization has allowed numerous peoples to claim their personal and national autonomy. The Universal

Declaration of Human Rights has in a way become, at the international level, at least in theory, the common charter to which any justification, any accusation, any demand can refer. On the other hand, more and more countries have been subject to powers that are not only totalitarian but also "logocratic," which means that these powers are not content with an external domination based on force, but also require, under the threat of persecution, personal adherence to the ruling doctrine. The rights of man are recognized by everyone, but it has become impossible to defend them by force when they are violated behind the protection of atomic armaments.

The universalization of the rights of man has been strangely paralleled by a reverse phenomenon: their raison d'être, their root, this vital nerve where human beings experience themselves in their responsible and irreducible freedom, seems afflicted, in the normal circumstances of life, with a kind of necrosis. Except when confronted with extreme circumstances or tragic alternatives, man no longer cares to believe in what he believes, because he hardly believes it at all. He no longer cares to will unconditionally what he wills, because he has reached the point of no longer caring, of simply subjecting himself to external stimuli. He is even willing to accept the attempt, thanks to progress in biological engineering, to remake man, to program him in any way one may wish, "made to order" for "good" collective functioning.

In truth, is there still a "meaning," or are there "conditions for meaning" still to be defended, after so many years during which so many men have lived under criminal powers, under criminal laws, while all decency has sought refuge in illegality? Can we still understand Socrates, who died in order that a sentence pronounced against him unjustly, but according to the laws, be executed? Indeed, one is tempted to interpret the destruction of meaning, during these final years of the twentieth century, as the the result of the great monstrosities of history rather than as the consequence of the way in which man rejects and flees his own humanity.

I wonder, however, whether these great monstrosities were not themselves rendered possible by man's failure to be responsible before himself. This failure is probably not the cause, but it has suppressed that which, from within, opposes and uncompromisingly resists the inhuman. It has excluded all recourse to that which is unconditional.

When man loses this recourse he does not simply fall, like the creatures of nature, into the relativity of causes and effects. He clings to any sort of imitation of an absolute, to which he subordinates everything else, with all the more fanaticism because there persists within him the vague feeling of substitution and nullity, a feeling fostered by the memory of an absolute which would have saved him from arbitrary absolutizations by making full allowance for what is relative, but allowing it only its proper place.

What I have just said can be specifically verified in the manner in which man deciphers—or believes he deciphers—the sense or the non-sense of history.

To say that history has no meaning is like saying that life has none: In withdrawing oneself from history, one gives up the attempt of making it meaningful. But to say that one has in hand *the* unique meaning of history in its totality is to allege that one can tear oneself away from it and hold it up in its entirety as an objective reality, continuous and totalized, of which we can know the outcome. Such history is no longer man's history, experienced in and through human temporality. History possessed and dominated in this fashion no longer has a present. It unfolds, like physical reality, in a time where the after flows from the before. Decisions can have no grip upon it. An objective science pretends to reign over it, allowing the engineers of history to impose the realization of their designs for a future known with supreme clarity and held up as an absolute end for all humanity.

We thus lose the conditions for human history and destroy the meaning it can have for man. "The meaning" of human history still depends now upon every actual moment, freely and resolutely experienced. It is not situated in the future. It is contemporaneous with each present and it transcends each present toward what we attempt, as we feel our way through our finitude, to call "eternity."

THE TWENTIETH CENTURY
AS SELF-CONSCIOUS HISTORY

PHILIP WINDSOR

I

There are three twentieth centuries. The first is continuous with a kind of past. The second breaks consciously with the past. The third is discontinuous with itself. Yet they all meet in certain crucial forms of experience; and these forms are vital (or fateful) to the question of what it is to be human, perhaps even to that of whether the human race will survive. Unless humanity can be recovered from these twentieth centuries, it is doubtful that the species has a future.

I shall consider these different centuries, their meetings, and the implications; but it might be useful to begin with an example.

In 1963, the American psychologist Stanley Milgram conducted an experiment designed to observe the readiness of people to inflict pain on others in obedience to authority. The results were startling. It should be borne in mind that those concerned were volunteers, chosen through their response to advertisements in "respectable," even "intellectual," newspapers and journals. They were under no compulsion to obey orders, they faced no punishment or other consequences for themselves or their families if they refused, they did not even have an economic incentive. They were told that the object of the experiment was to determine how far pain was conducive to learning, and were provided with the apparatus to inflict electric shocks on other people, the "subjects," who were being tested for their ability to absorb information. If the subject proved backward or recalcitrant, the voltage was increased on the supervisor's orders and could not thereafter be reduced. It mounted through specific gradations from one inflicting pain, to the level of severe injury, to that of death.

The subjects were in fact actors concealed by screens. Their reactions could be heard but not observed, and they were skilled in screaming. No real shock was administered, but they could read the selected voltage and had been rehearsed in the appropriate reactions. The volunteers pulling the switches were moreover guided by a chart, in which they also had been thoroughly rehearsed, outlining the consequences of their decisions. Not one of them (by definition, perhaps) objected to inflicting pain; some balked at the idea of severe injury, but a sizable proportion was prepared to kill. This was the America of the New Frontier in which, a few months earlier, President Kennedy had proclaimed that his country would "bear any burden, fight any foe" to uphold the cause of freedom.

The observations made in the experiment are startling enough in such a context. But the experiment was by no means unique. There have been others, in which groups of students, assigned to play roles in prison situations, rapidly became so submissive as prisoners and so sadistic as warders that the experiments were called off. Perhaps the ultimate demonstration of what was at stake here was not an experiment at all, but a training program: the "compounds" to which selected American officers were sent to learn resistance to interrogation techniques before going to Vietnam. These were so brutal that, in the words of one veteran: "They taught us that, however long we held out, most of us would crack in the end."[1]

It is already possible to discern a shadowy outline of the issues and implications of what it is to question humans as humans in such examples. But that outline changes line, is smudged, and becomes even more startling in the reaction of Milgram's psychological colleagues. He was criticized for a breach of professional ethics.

The enterprise in which experimental psychologists are engaged is to inquire into the *sources*, as distinct from any conceptions of the *nature*, of human behavior. The inquiry is conducted through an inductive-deductive relationship which depends upon hypothesis and experiment—though in this case, as opposed to that of the "natural sciences," the hypothesis still represents the attempt to establish a category within which it can itself be tested by experiment. But in such a framework it is impossible, indeed treasonable to his discipline, for the psychologist to make general propositions about ethics: the idea "human" is subsequent to the category "behavior."

The normal idea of professional ethics, on the other hand, is rooted in a certain established tradition, in which any such moral or intellectual category could not exist *in vacuo*, divorced from assumptions of "common humanity" or "common good." It was itself, indeed, the *shadow* of an idea, Platonic in form, antirepublican in content, which determined that gubernatorial power (as in the medical or legal professions) should not be exercised at the expense of human relations or obligations.

Such a view, however, derives from assumptions that one is human prior to one's functions as a lawyer or doctor, or indeed a soldier: It reflects an agreement (usually prearticulate, except in the case of Just War doctrine) about the nature of the obligations and relations involved in defining oneself as a human being. In other words, such an assumption raises ontological questions. When they criticized him, Professor Milgram's colleagues raised questions that took no cognizance of such ontological concerns, but that had no meaning outside their framework. Yet the real rub is that if they accepted the empirical nature of his inquiry, they also cut the ground from under their own feet; because in doing so they accepted that empirical findings about human behavior were antecedent to the conception of what was, or could be, human.

In the confusion which this example helps to illustrate lies an interesting conjunction of the continuity and discontinuities of the twentieth century.

II

The continuity lies in the experiment itself. It is continuous with a kind of past, a relatively modern past, which is that of progress. From its beginnings, the idea of progress was associated with scientific experiment. Harking back to an eighteenth-century struggle between reason and the passions, progress harnessed the very notion of humanity to a set of experiments in space and time.

It claimed, in doing so, the status of a myth; but the method of experiment also translated the *myth* into a set of practical, not to say banal, *aspirations*. The nature of these aspirations might be roughly summarized by the proposition "The more we know, the nicer we become." The history of the twentieth century offers conclusive evidence that there is no such connection; but nonetheless, if one disregards its central experiences, it is possible to perceive that the myth retains its status because of what it represents as an aspiration.[2] The idea of the American century embodies this takeover bid to perfection.[3] Within a framework such as that, human beings are experimenting *on* themselves, in their society, in time, in their relations with themselves, in order to define what constitutes them as human beings at all.

So reason became experimental knowledge, moral inquiry and scientific inquiry became coterminous, and fact, uninterpreted fact, came to be regarded as logically anterior to value. The absence of a framework of interpretation was not, within the terms of nineteenth- and twentieth-century positivism, regarded as a particular difficulty, since it was assumed that the scientific method of *a posteriori* interpretation provided in itself the criteria of judgment. ("Value judgment" being, of course, the dirtiest word in the positivist's vocabulary.) Progress, the bastard offspring of eighteenth-century reason, became the legitimizing godfather of twentieth-century experiment.

We determine our own nature by experimenting upon ourselves. The expansion in human self-awareness that seemed to follow from the Enlightenment was transformed, first slowly and then rapidly, into a contraction: from progress to positivism, and in turn from positivism to pragmatic experiment. But there was also a growing difficulty that kept pace with this process of contraction. The experimental method, when applied to the exploration of human behavior, makes it impossible to distinguish between legitimate and illegitimate undertakings, except in the narrowest intellectual sense. The growth of this narrowly based method, a parody of Nietzsche's *Umwertung aller Werte*, created the arena for the triumph of his detested Apollo: the concentration camp. Milgram's undertaking was part and parcel of the liberal, progressive, recent past—and so his findings went to demonstrate a continuity between "ordinary" human beings and the behavior of the camp.

III

The continuity with the kind of past the experiment illustrates can also be seen as part of the context which enabled humans to break consciously with the past. Yet that break also had different antecedents. These derive not from nineteenth-century positivism, but from nineteenth-century idealism. The work of Hegel provided the framework for a self-conscious attempt to have done with what Marx subsequently termed prehistory, and in the future to create history in an autonomous manner rather than merely respond to it. Attempts to achieve autonomy in this way provided the basis for the ideologies of the twentieth century, and the impetus for its most powerful political movements—from fascism and Nazism on the one hand to Stalinism on the other. But why did they assume a totalitarian form?

The answer lies perhaps in part in the sheer ambition of the Hegelian-to-Marxist tradition. The "objectivication of the Absolute," or even the achievement of "species being," represents a pretty formidable historical task, especially if men determine deliberately to bring it about. In this sense, one might argue that Nietzsche was not (in 1876) so much an uncannily accurate prophet when he wrote that the wars of societies which had characterized earlier history would be replaced by wars of the spirits, and that "there shall be wars as never before on earth," as a man who had understood the implications of earlier philosophy. But there is perhaps a more fundamental explanation. The goal of this earlier philosophy was the achievement of a common humanity. The traditions of a twentieth-century society are those of collective humanity. The difference is total.

One can exemplify the transformation at length, especially by reference to the phenomena of mass society. But what is at stake is not only the "revolt of the masses"—which implies a torrential vulgarization in the twentieth century of nineteenth-century philosophical thought—but also a self-conscious definition of the masses, as such, as the standard-bearers of the historical creation of the future. (Fascism might be defined as the realization of mass elitism; in terms of Marxism-Leninism, the terms of reference are obvious.) But, at the same time, a similar cast of mind can be observed in the statements of that self-conscious elite which reacted against the mass definition of history—for example in the case of architecture. Mies van der Rohe, before his school despoiled the cities of the world, proclaimed: "The individual is losing significance. His destiny is no longer what interests us." Who is this "us"? The arrogant confusion such usage represents is a world away from the teleological process of the self-realization in terms of consciousness which informed the writing of Hegel, and which implied the development of a common humanity. It comes instead very close to the propaganda of the Third Reich. But the confusion goes further than that between common humanity and collective humanity. Its extent can be seen in the words of another architect. Le Corbusier, in commenting upon his design for the building of l'Unité in Marseilles, drew upon the ideal of the Acropolis. The Greeks, he said, were "drawing the desolate landscape around them and gathering it into a single thought." But l'Unité is not the Acropolis, which is noumenal in style and purpose; it has achieved a desolation of its own in the purely phenomenal world of Corbusier's "modular man."

The breakdown of the distinction between the noumenal and the phenomenal represents a further twentieth-century characteristic, one which ignores the work of Kant as the earlier confusion between common humanity and collective humanity did that of Hegel. And here indeed one can appreciate the propaganda of the Thousand Year Reich, of New Soviet Man, and other such claims to have transcended the past. They were substitutes, in time, for the timeless world of the noumenal. And to acquire control over the constant threat represented by the noumenal in the form of religion or in the form of art, they had to impose totalitarian control and create the concentration camp.

Now what is argued here is that there is more continuity between the assumptions of the liberal West and those of totalitarian systems than might appear at first sight, and that in a context in which fundamental distinctions are ignored, it is not very surprising that the subjects of an experiment in a psychological laboratory in New York should act in a manner reminiscent of the guards in concentration camps.

IV

The third twentieth century is in consequence discontinuous with itself. That is to say, it has no relations either with the past or with the future. This is most clearly exemplified in the Soviet Union, where attempts at "reform," acknowledged as necessary at the highest levels of Party leadership, are constantly blocked by the inability to face up to the entrenched legacy of Stalinism, and where, on the other hand, without reform the society has lost all meaning and all direction. But it is equally true that the alienated masses of Western industrial society have very few connections, and tenuous shorthand ones at that, with their cultural past—while their articulate consciousness is largely dominated by fear of the future. The traditions of positivism have now produced results which have led people to define the future in terms of what they wish to avoid—nuclear war, genetic engineering, or a symbolic and electronic 1984 controlled by data processing. Ecological movements and nuclear disarmers are interesting in this respect. Journalists have constantly been at pains to emphasize the heterogenous nature of the Greens in Germany or the Greenham Common women in Britain. Yet it is precisely their heterogeneity which provides their commitment. Groups of Christians, Marxists, feminists overcome divisions of belief and attempt to realize a common humanity in a shared fear of the future. Such, by now, has become almost the criterion for being human.

One would not wish to devalue such preoccupations or to argue that there is nothing to worry about in a world which bases the security of the international system on the threat to exterminate humanity. But to rediscover humanity, as it were, purely in opposition to menacing futures, even in a sense of helplessness before them, indicates a collapse of moral authority within individuals and within society. It is this collapse of authority that has become perhaps the distinguishing characteristic of the century discontinuous with itself, and the final product of the first two, combining as they did in what Solzhenitsyn has called "the systematic dehumanization of man."

V

The experiences of the twentieth century might appear at first sight to be divided into two very different kinds. The first half of the century was dominated by the vast historical forces unleashed into mass societies by nineteenth-century ideas. Nietzsche's wars of the spirits became total wars, conducted with the utmost ferocity on all sides. To give two instances: the communiqué issued by the United States Army Air Force and the Royal Air Force after the Dresden bombing read in part: "The raid on Dresden was undertaken in order to impede German military movement. The fact that between 300,000 and 500,000 civilian refugees were in the city at the time *must be regarded as a bonus*." The second instance comes from China, where the biggest battle in history was fought in December 1948 at Chu Chow. The casualties on the Nationalist side alone equaled the entire number of casualties in the American Civil War. The century of total war had become one in which war was frequently fought for the sake of war itself, but also one in which political leaders were fighting out their claims on the future, based on preconceived ideas of history and of consciousness. War became the center of experience of two generations in most parts of the globe.

Total war *between* nations and societies was paralleled by the totalitarian control *of* societies. Concentration camps were established in the name of the triumph of the will, and of the overthrow of tyranny by revolution. Humanity revealed itself to itself in the concentration camp as never before. This is not to say that such atrocities were unprecedented. It has been estimated[4] that 7 million Africans died on the slave ships of the Middle Passage between the seventeenth and nineteenth centuries. Their deaths were the ghastly byproducts of greed and cruelty. The twentieth century is not unique in terms of the atrocities committed in a particular period. What defines its specificity, however, is that these have not been carried out for the sake of power or profit, but *justified*, even decreed in terms of moral obligation, in the name of fulfilling a historical task. The 6 million Jews who were exterminated in three and a half years were sought out (at great expense and at the price of detracting from the "war effort"), rounded up, transported, and killed in specially created centers of industrial design. The millions who perished in Soviet concentration camps were sent there to die as part of a deliberately constructed system of political and social control. If there is one monument which enshrines the transformation of humanity in this century, it is the concentration camp.

VI

Yet it might appear that the historical experiences are over. Triumphant liberalism created a global system of economic stability, technological innovation, and political and social management at the end of World War II. For millions of people in the subsequent generations, the central experience has been one of economic growth, social security, and scientific progress. The conflicts of ideology, though persisting in most Western societies, were nonetheless subdued. The banality of successful management took their place. It appeared, indeed, that the century had after all become American.

"The end of ideology" was a fashionable phrase in Western salons and in the new universities of the 1950s and 1960s—so very short a time after War II! It was expected that "modernization" would solve the problems of the world. The structural demands of technological change, the social convergence of different countries engaged in modernizing, were expected by economic planners and such influential political advisers as Walt Rostow to bring about a truly global system that would blend cultural assumptions as effectively as it exchanged industrial and agricultural products.

To be sure, a power struggle was going on between the superpowers, and was expected to continue. The struggle was ideologically based: emphatically, the Soviet Union had not reached "the end of ideology." But even so, this new struggle was no longer a war of the spirits, for here too technology had come to the rescue. The culminating act of World War II, the nuclear bombardment of Hiroshima and Nagasaki, appeared to have ensured that no such wars could ever be fought again. The conflict *could* not be resolved by war, and took instead the form of a competition in nuclear deterrence. The implicit threats of such a system were obvious enough, but the explicit activities—designing ingenious missiles and multiple warheads—were relatively harmless. They were tucked away in submarines and silos, seldom to be seen and never to be used, since their whole purpose was to meet the requirements of increasingly arcane but equally abstract formulations of "strategic stability." Such competitions in technology were far removed from the hideous realities of the earlier total wars.

Western society was therefore dominated by a whole set of assumptions which indicated that the central experiences of the first half of the century were now comfortably behind, and that the world would be able, provided it escaped from the domination of totalitarian communism, to achieve order, stability, and progress. But all these assumptions were heavily flawed.

At one level, it could be argued that the system has stood up remarkably well. In spite of economic uncertainties, and such unexpected shocks as the "petrodollar revolution," most industrial societies have continued to enjoy high standards of living and persistent, if modest, economic growth. Western technology, especially as developed in the United States and Japan, is in demand throughout the world; and it is so far in advance of that of the Soviet Union that the latter now openly acknowledges its own dependence on it. But at another level, the techniques of management have not proved very successful after all. The cost of economic prosperity in Western Europe and the United States is a high degree of unemployment. Social tensions have been reflected in a reawakened interest in ideological questions in many countries. Neither technology nor management has solved the problems of society.

It is this which raises a more fundamental question. The lure of the positivistic tradition is still strong, but its inability to raise, let alone answer, the questions of what it is to be, or become, human has never been more patently exposed than by the very successes it enjoyed in the postwar period. The Milgram experiment is important not only because of its findings, but also because of its date. Equally, the bankruptcy of the aspirations attached to modernization has been thoroughly exposed by events in, for example, Iran. Modernization does not create cultural bonds, it breaks up societies and attacks their beliefs without having anything to offer in their place. It can produce a violent and factitious cultural assertiveness, and a new form of nationalism assuming messianic proportions. Belief in modernization was in the end a form of behaviorism—the belief that the behavior produces the human. As such, it reflects the discontinuous twentieth century, the one which has no relations either to its past or to its future, and which lacks any center of ethical discourse.

VII

In this more fundamental sense, one can see that the postwar period has not solved the problems of the first half of the twentieth century. Precisely because they were not problems amenable to problem solving, but transformations in humanity's experience of itself. Indeed, the whole apparatus of planning techniques, technological innovation, and economic fine-tuning only helped to aggravate the underlying condition by encouraging a false belief that human beings no longer had to concern themselves with the questions they had so recently discovered.

These questions have emerged in two forms—doubtless among many others. The first lies in the history of decolonization, with concomitant demonstrations of the failures of Western liberal thought. The second lies in the system of nuclear deterrence.

VIII

In terms of earlier liberal assumptions, it might be argued that imperialism was an obligation. Belief in progress also implied a duty to share the fruits of discovery, the benefits of education, and the wisdom of impartially administered law. Such a sense of duty implied in turn that imperialism was a revolt against colonialism. It lay behind Sir Roger Casement's denunciation of King Leopold's rule in the Congo, which represented colonial exploitation, not imperial administration. Nor was it narrowly confined. Gandhi himself, at a famous moment in his confrontation with white rule in South Africa, exclaimed: "We are all subjects of the King-

Emperor, and equally entitled to his protection." And the assumptions are not dead, even today. For they enshrined a view of human potential—one which could be stifled (but not denied) by systems of injustice, either socially derived or externally imposed; and it is precisely this view which provides the basis for contemporary denunciations of South Africa.

It is plain that the moral criticism leveled against that country is directed at the *failure* of its white rulers to become imperialist. They refuse to invite the black population into the scheme of Western education or Western values. They insist on the separateness of different cultural identities. They enjoin blacks to remain blacks not only in terms of the mask on the face, but also in terms of the brain behind it. It was even notable that at the time of the 200th anniversary of Beethoven's birth, they actually forbade black orchestras to play Beethoven's music. This was clearly not because blacks could not play Beethoven, but because whites knew that they could.

But criticism of South Africa is now leveled in an intellectually and morally uncomfortable context. The liberal tradition changed its spots. The same criterion of human potentiality, when applied to the actual politics of imperialism, had provided no adequate basis for challenging the contradiction between liberal freedoms on the one hand and imperial coercion on the other. Such notions as those of Lugard about "indirect rule" were at best an unhappy compromise. Such ambiguous forms of rejection as that of Casement's Ireland, which questioned the right of an imperial power to hold sway in an area of common civilization, or that of the Yishuv in Palestine, imperialist in terms of accepted standards of civilization and anti-imperialist in terms of their political application, only emphasized the difficulties.

In the face of such problems, the liberal forms of thought became anti-imperialist (André Gide, George Orwell, Leonard Woolf, and so on) partly because their representatives had observed the failures of imperialism at first hand, and sometimes because they were inclined to ground their liberal aspirations in a more universal form of immediately realizable humanity based on socialism. In a sense, socialist-liberal polemics provided the staple of political discussion in the 1930s. But in the end, it was the liberal view which won—and transformed itself in the process.

The sources of this change are obscure. In part it was no doubt a response to the tensions within the liberal-imperialist tradition itself; in part the reaction to the direct experience already suggested; but also in part a reconsideration of the human potential in a new context—that of the impact of the Russian Revolution. The series of earthquakes which composed the revolution seemed simultaneously to mean that human beings did not depend on the course of history or progress to achieve their potential (the "backward" Russians could do it) and that a new civilization could also arise from history, whatever its catastrophes.[5] The historical and ahistorical reactions were obviously contradictory, but they combined to shake the faith of Western progressives in the validity of the imperial mission.

In any event, the most interesting feature of the transformation was that whereas the ideals of imperialism had been dedicated to belief in a common humanity based on human potential and validated by progress, the new forms of anti-imperialist liberalism adopted an entirely contrary course. The direct experience of imperialism in its authoritarian manifestations prompted a reaction in terms of respect for other civilizations. The historical experience of the Russian Revolution meant that it was no longer possible to vest belief in the mission of advanced societies. In consequence, the earlier liberal ideas of progress became the more progressive ideas of relativism. In this context, civilizations became cultures, and all cultures became equal. The idea of the potential of a common humanity gave way to the notion that all humans were *already* human—not in terms of a possible realization of their potential or in terms of arguing with one another, but in terms of their *being* human anyway.

Progress had now stood itself on its head. What had previously been criteria for judgment now became criteria for tolerance. Relativism had become absolute (except, of course, in the case of South Africa). In doing so, it had ensured that the earlier attempts to distinguish what constituted the achievement of a commonly understood response to the condition of being human should now give way to the mere condition of a collective humanity. But whereas in the earlier part of the century such collective humanity had provided the framework for totalitarian regimes, for a false representation of the noumenal which exacted the tribute of millions upon millions of human lives, the new forms of collective humanity now existed purely at the phenomenal level—most notably, and on a global scale, in the United Nations.

The rhetoric of the United Nations reflects this condition well. Its insistent rejection of any form of imperialism is based on the assumption of the equal validity of all cultures. Women are forbidden to drive cars in Saudi Arabia on the same basis that blacks were forbidden to play Beethoven in South Africa—but that arouses no indignation because in this case it is accepted simply as a manifestation of Saudi culture. At the same time, the member states of the UN are pledged to a Universal Declaration of Human Rights, the embodiment of an ideal which derives from the Enlightenment and from the earlier insistence of Christianity on the individual responsibility of the human soul. Human rights and cultural tolerance are bound to be at variance with each other, but the incoherence of the United Nations merely demonstrates that it is not a center for ethical discourse and that the history of decolonization has failed to live up to the hopes latter-day liberalism invested in it.

But the issue goes further, and its nature can be seen in the attitude toward one another of the developing world and of the Western countries. In the case of most developing nations, it is the question of identity, not the question of human freedom, which is at stake. The validity of their grievances and their views of their own history raise questions that would need separate discussion; but in their reaction against their encounter with the West, many societies produced by decolonization have laid enormous emphasis on the need for violence as a means to achieving authenticity, winning of course Western admirers in the process,[6] but without being able to advance beyond a sense of authenticity rooted in a prehistorical and assertive identity.[7] This is the opposite of what was meant in Western philosophical terms by the relationship between developing consciousness and authenticity. Moreover, such societies have come to treat the idea of state sovereignty as identical with that of freedom. There is seldom any relationship between the two, and certainly not in a society which defends the freedom of the *state* against external forces, without any notion of extending the freedom of the individual, the group, the idea, against the power of the state.

Indeed, at this point, the emancipated countries do after all join hands with the positivistic tradition: freedom is regarded merely as an attribute, and not a criterion, of being or becoming. Furthermore, these failures are adulterated by a willing emulation in many Third World countries of the ideological authoritarianism of either the Soviet Union or China. The confluence of an indigenous tradition, hierarchical in nature but by now lacking in the social and psychological support it once offered people, and of the political despotism imported from the disastrous experiments of the USSR and elsewhere, is now the hallmark of many Third World countries. Even in the Nonaligned Movement, riven as it is by disputes about the legitimacy of supporting the "socialist cause" in international affairs, there is no evidence of concern about human freedom or the workings of society. The imperfect and frequently abused freedoms of the Western press are attacked and circumscribed in Unesco not because of imperfections or abuse, but because they, so it is argued, undermine the identity of Third World countries themselves.

This attitude finds its own image in the way many people in the West regard the developing world. To give one example: Between Athens and Tokyo, only two countries have anything remotely resembling a free press, even by Western standards— Israel and India. Yet this huge arc of the globe contains nearly two-thirds of the world's inhabitants. Among the rest of the majority of the global population, there are perhaps half a dozen countries that also enjoy freedom of the press. But Third World representatives claim, and the newborn relativists of the West agree, that such notions as freedom and democracy are "inappropriate" to the conditions and requirements of developing societies. The idea that freedom might itself be a requirement for effective development is generally accepted when applied to the history of the West. It is dismissed in terms of the Third World— or worse, regarded as a manifestation of "cultural imperialism" and therefore condemned. But the historical context demands examination. For were not the countries of Western Europe themselves undergoing the pains of development when they put forward the ideas of free speech and freedom of the press? Was it not Karl Marx who said that without freedom of the press there is no freedom at all? In stressing the requirements of development and demonstrating that they regard freedom purely as an irksome incidental, the liberal relativists discount and devalue the dignity of other human beings.

Prevailing Western attitudes to the Third World demonstrate an utter lack of criteria for moral and ethical judgment. They also demonstrate that beneath the mask of tolerance there hides a callous unconcern. These considerations suggest that the developing world has in many ways become an arena of the experience of the three kinds of twentieth century. Conflict and violence were in most cases the distinguishing hallmark of decolonization. States that are not nations become theaters for wars fought out at a lower level of intensity than earlier total wars, but conducted with merciless ferocity nonetheless. Their conflicts have themselves drawn in the great powers who, by their very intervention, endow them with global significance. The struggle between the superpowers is conducted not only through the hidden technology of missile systems, but also through the liberal use of napalm, white phosphorous, and various forms of chemicals against the wretched inhabitants of one country after another. Massacres are a routine occurrence. The security services of regimes in place are trained by one superpower and its friends; when such regimes are toppled, their substitutes learn the techniques of interrogation from the long experience acquired by the KGB or the East Germans. Perhaps this is the true face of modernization. There is one further consideration, which involves a reaction against both the prevailing ideas of positivistic relativism and the mindless assertions of identity which have come so contentedly together in the United Nations. The reaction lies in the fact that the "wars of the spirits" are not dead: they have merely been driven underground. Today, the battle for the definition of an emergent humanity takes the form of terrorism—at all levels.

A terrorist ethos has arisen distinct from, but encompassing, the ostensible causes for which terrorists "struggle." The very concept of the (now etiolated) historical struggle has meant that fanaticism has taken the place of ethical judgment—and even of historical purpose—among self-styled revolutionaries like Carlos the Jackal or their self-appointed opponents like Roberto d'Aubuisson. Just as war seemed to become an end in itself in the earlier part of the century, so terrorism provides its own justification today. The vileness of the means adopted provides, in this terrorist ethos, a measure of the importance of the ends. It does not call the relationship into question: instead, the relationship legitimizes itself. Whatever the nature of their original grievances and aspirations, terrorists are now more distinguishable as terrorists than as those who dream of a united Ireland, a return to the Palestinian homeland, or the austere observation of Islam. In many parts of the world, the rulers rule by terror and their opponents challenge them by terror. The official values that provide the ostensible ends to justify such means are dealt out indiscriminately from one situation to another, as if by a monkey playing with a pack of cards.

Now, it is sometimes revealingly suggested that the conflicts which determine the experience of so many people in the developing world are important because they threaten the stability of the international order, and risk turning North-South tensions into East-West hostilities. This is one of the themes of the Brandt Commission's Report. That report argued, indeed, that it was in the self-interest of the West to restructure the global economy and redistribute the global wealth in order to avoid such an eventuality. Yet what was notably lacking from its pages was any suggestion of moral obligation, and it says much for Western democratic leaders' views of their own societies that they deliberately chose to present the report in the language of self-interest rather than in that of obligation, because they considered it would attract more support that way.[8] But such dangers appear remote. The truly incredible aspect of the ferocity which engulfs so much of the world today is its remoteness from any set of central concerns and its inability to attract attention or reaction except as a *proxy* means of conducting superpower conflict. This might help to account for the fact that the wars of Asia, Africa, and Latin America are at the same time wars of the spirits *and* random in cause and outcome.

IX

Even so, however, there are certain kinds of nexus—of interest, commitment, and strategic location—which could at given moments bring about major confrontations and the risk of East-West hostilities. The most obvious case in point is that of the many conflicts in the Middle East. Here, it is worth recalling the words of a distinguished European politician who implicitly recognized the continuities of the twentieth century when contemplating the Middle East in 1980. "It reminds me of 1914," said Helmut Schmidt. The crises of 1980 were in part resolved without dragging the great powers into war, but one reason for this minimal success was precisely the threat to re-invoke nuclear weapons not merely as part of an abstract system of deterrence, but for the actual purposes of battlefield use. The reemergence of the nuclear weapon as an instrument that could really be used in time of crisis has been a pronounced feature of recent years. And it is this danger that provides the central meeting point for the three kinds of twentieth century.

In order to appreciate the present workings of nuclear deterrence and its applicability to the spate of potential conflicts between the superpowers, it is worth an excursus into the system of nuclear deterrence itself as it has developed in the recent past. That system might be described as one of stabilized irrationality— a comprehensive form of irrationality which in itself helps to summarize the experience of the century. In its earlier stages the system encompassed a mutual threat, directed against each other by the superpowers, of actually winning a war—the Soviet Union by conquering "hostage Europe," the United States through the nuclear bombardment of the USSR. In other words, the strategy of deterrence, and its credibility, depended upon each being able to demonstrate to the other that victory was possible, that going to war would in some sense be rational. This "credibility" was the criterion of deterrence. But by the mid-1960s it was generally acknowledged that neither side could hope to win a general nuclear war, or even expect to survive it.

And yet, the stability of the international order, and therewith perhaps the survival of the world, had come to rest upon the threat of nuclear war. In that case it was no longer the rationality of war but the irrationality of the warmaker which became the criterion of credibility. Clearly, such irrationality had to be selective. Otherwise neither adversary would be able to judge the reactions of the other in any circumstances at all, and the world would have been doomed to a knife-edge existence. But the irrationality did become selective, and its codification became "commitment." Commitment, as practised by the United States toward Western Europe, Japan, and Israel, and by the Soviet Union toward the Socialist Commonwealth, became ultimately a declaration that in certain circumstances one would be prepared to act irrationally in the name of certain values. Suicide then became the ultimate form of the wars of the spirits, even though moral authority and ethical criteria no longer existed—more fundamentally, *because* they no longer exist.

This comprehensive form of irrationality encompassed both policy and situation. The common understanding of the workings of nuclear deterrence had created, or so it appeared, a subtle and complex dialogue, one in which each party played two roles. In respect of its own commitments, it was prepared to demonstrate its irrationality. In respect of the caution it showed in the face of the other's commitments, it demonstrated its rationality. The dialogue was thus a four-way process: the irrational talking to the rational both ways round.

These were the conditions of strategic détente. But détente itself raised new difficulties. On the one hand, to the extent that the overriding importance of a stable superpower relationship was accepted, which in turn implied (as suggested earlier) the avoidance of conflict over values, détente became *value-free*: the avoidance of nuclear war made it obvious. On the other hand, the stabilized irrationality I have tried to indicate necessarily implied a commitment to values—for example, in the American undertakings on behalf of Western Europe. In this sense, the apparent stability of détente could prove its own undoing. For a détente which was value-free could diminish the credibility of that value commitment on which the stability was based in the first place. Hence, the pattern of East-West relations over the past twenty years has signaled what one might call a negative dialectic. That is to say, that the greater the interest in détente, the lower the value of the commitment, and vice versa. But it was a dialectic that was incapable of reaching a synthesis, and that in consequence remained extremely vulnerable to the interacting pattern of crises which reminded Helmut Schmidt of 1914.

The only possibility of breaking this pattern seemed to lie in the implication of a *realizable* nuclear threat directed not toward the irrational commitment to value, but toward the "rational" protection of interests. This has been an intermittent but increasingly emphatic feature of superpower, but perhaps particularly American, policy since 1974 (when the Secretary of Defense drew up new targeting lists) and continuing into the period of Jimmy Carter's Presidential Directive 59 and the "countervailing strategy" of the present day. The very notion that one could threaten nuclear war not in terms of value after all but in terms of interest, serving a pseudorational end in the name of a victory one could only *hope* to keep limited, seemed to illustrate to perfection the three meeting points of the century. A positivistic view of the purposes of war, leading to a vacuity in the wars of the spirits, leading to a definition of the future as that which humanity must fear if it is to remain human. A conflict arose between the determination to stand by the values that make life endurable and the willingness to commit genocide in the name of those values. Perhaps it is easier to think of people allowing themselves to be killed by the million in the name of value than of people killing by the million in that name. Yet both have happened—as in the holocaust of European Jewry. Strategy in the nuclear age implies that a society has to assume the roles, simultaneously, of the Nazis and the Jews.

At present, the only way of thinking about such questions appears to be probabilistic, which is a legacy of the earlier years in which the system of nuclear deterrence appeared to be decently abstract, and the prospect of the actual use of nuclear weapons comfortably remote. The result has been that the future of humanity is now determined by a kind of inversion of Pascal's bet. For the unhappy Jansenist of Port-Royal, eternal salvation was an extremely remote possibility, but one worth living for, since if it was achieved there was everything to gain, and if not nothing to lose anyway. In terms of nuclear deterrence, the extinction of the human race has also appeared extremely remote, but worth betting on for the sake of preserving society. But if the prospect becomes less remote, the nature of the wager changes. The understanding of ourselves as human is now pitted against a mechanical calculation of whether any particular pattern of interacting crisis can lead to the use of nuclear weapons and whether, if it does, a pattern of escalation will set in and lead, in a world whose accumulated nuclear stockpile is now roughly equivalent to the explosive power of one million Hiroshimas, to the unleashing of uncontrollable nuclear war.

If the nuclear wind does blow, it will be a wind blowing from, and sucking us into, the narrowest confines of our historical existence. It has been pointed out[9] that, since World War I, the word "dawn" has irrevocably changed its meaning in English literature. Equally the word "wind" can never be the same again since the invention of thermonuclear weapons. The wind in the Gospels represented the free play of the Spirit: "For the Spirit bloweth where it listeth." Throughout European literature, the wind has symbolized the noumenal, playing upon our day-to-day existence, the breath of an unattainable but nonetheless ultimate and defining freedom of what it is to be human. Today, the ultimate and defining wind constitutes the agent, and the symbol of recognition, of our failure to transcend a positivistic existence: our determination to define ourselves in terms of what we can declare to be finite rather than in terms of what we can apprehend and join ourselves into, outside the conditions of what we actually are. The twentieth centuries have joined hands in a form of experience whereby humans might only be able to define themselves by destroying themselves.

X

This is the continuity of the kind of past which I have tried to indicate, coming together with that cutoff from the past which categorizes humanity as self-sufficient and self-referring and then exposes its pretensions of historical fulfillment to the scientific method: so as to validate its own terms of reference in the first place. The warring parties that rationalize their own historical and conceptual position vis-à-vis themselves, but can do so only *because* they are warring with each other in their alienation from their own past and the incompleteness of their own consciousness of themselves, resort to the ultimate threat of total destruction, the unleashing of the wind, in order to destroy the spirit.

I have been suggesting that the human experience of what it is to be human has undergone a fundamental transformation in the twentieth century. I have also suggested that the shock of this experience has not been absorbed by the techniques of management and the global modernization which has been characteristic of the period since World War II. It is because of this that the fear of the future has come to equal the threat to inflict the future in the name of competing ideals. But has the human race itself, let alone the concept and the realization of humanity, any possibility of surviving when based upon that threat? It would seem that this is unlikely without a fundamental reconsideration of our assumptions, and without an attempt to engage in a sustained dialogue between the conflicting cultures of the present world. Conflicting interpretations of the past will in all probability otherwise enjoin a very short future.

Any dialogue between conflicting cultures must, however, entail a more specific form of self-conscious history than that of the universalizing undertakings of the past. It demands a consciousness from particular kinds of human being of how they have come to be who they are, and an answerability to this understanding once they have achieved it. The canons of relativistic tolerance emphasize the purely circumstantial attributes of human lives. In doing so, they not only reduce freedom itself to an attribute, they also deprive humans of their answerability: and that is to deprive them, especially in the knowledge of what history has wrought, also of their dignity.

The workings of responsibility and specificity demand a discussion that goes far beyond this one, but the criteria are not opaque. I have emphasized—too much—that it is possible to understand more about human potential as a result of the experiences of this century than ever before. Certainly, humans have revealed themselves to themselves both in their capacity to create hell and in a greater continuity between that hell and the liberal laboratories of the Western world than might be expected at first sight. But it is also true that other forms of human potential have been made demonstrable. Blacks can play a Beethoven concerto. Women, who in certain cultures are virtually condemned to lifelong house arrest on account of their sex, can not only drive cars but lead energetic and creative lives. The knowledge of such already realized potential does create a basis by which cultures can bring judgment to bear on each other. Moreover, it is not only possible, it is also imperative that they should. On that depends the ability to reinterpret those wars of the spirits which have created Hell in the recent past, and whose subterranean conduct threatens to annihilate the world in the near future.

These considerations suggest further that it is possible to understand the distinction between common humanity and collective humanity, and to ensure that the ontological criteria of becoming human are not simply caught up in the teleological criteria of historical becoming—indeed, that it is even possible to interpret the interaction of the two. The crimes and monuments of the twentieth century arose from their confusion; its discoveries can help to reconstitute the criteria of ethical responsibility.

But the tools at hand are very small. They do not consist in political programs, in legislation for the control of the arms race, or even in the discourse of conferences and seminars. If such larger enterprises are to succeed, it will be because they reflect changes that have already come about through the work of men and women making the most of the scope available to them. Some examples can already be discerned. In Poland, a transformation of society took place when an alliance of workers, priests, and intellectuals declared that the politically enacted measures of earlier reforming legislation were not enough, and that they were not enough because they were also politically reversible. In concentrating on such apparently mundane measures as insistence on fair meat rationing or the republication in Polish of the Helsinki Final Act, they succeeded in challenging the power of an authoritarian party. Obviously, this alliance has subsequently suffered defeats, but the status quo ante can never be restored; and the language of Polish politics has been changed for good.

More generally in Europe, many kinds of people from both East and West are attempting to draw together in a common effort to make the security confrontation, which divides each side and governs them separately, less and less relevant to the concerns, and the language of those concerns, which can draw them together. On occasion, small groups of Palestinians and Israelis are able and willing to meet and to engage in discussion, criticism, and debate about the historical identities that doom them to conflict and the possibility of a commonly undertaken transformation of those identities that might make reconciliation possible. There is clearly no guarantee that such meetings will bring peace to the Middle East, but what is certain is that the aspirations they express provide the only framework for peace. The interaction of the security considerations of the states concerned with the wars of the spirits which they also embody rule out any such possibility.

Working with such small tools, it is also possible to devise a new language—one in which the possibility of ethical judgment drawn from historical experience can be restored, and one in which, at last, it can be understood that the noumenal world cannot be realized in collective phenomena. Unless that language is heard, it seems very likely that the wind will blow.

Notes

[1] Personal conversation. Since then, it has also been discovered that in the 1950s the CIA persuaded Canadian psychiatrists to practise "brainwashing" techniques on patients in hospitals.

[2] President Carter's Notre Dame University commencement speech, 1977.

[3] It is interesting that, even at the height of their assumptions about the validity of their undertakings, the European nations never claimed dominion over time. The Pax Britannica, the white man's burden, the *mission civilisatrice*, represented a view of a historical *task*, no doubt, that of conjoining less conscious societies with the values established by Western reason, but they did not claim to rule the emergent future. In this respect, the difference between the British Empire and the American century is total—and the latter is very much more akin to Soviet aspirations than it is to British myth. Are the United States and the USSR the last two countries to believe in progress?

[4] V. S. Naipaul, *The Middle Passage* (London, 1962).

[5] Perhaps it is worth recalling here that John Stuart Mill, in many ways the positivist liberal imperialist par excellence, had addressed his *A Few Words on Non-Intervention* specifically to the case of when it might be justified to intervene when considering barbaric Russia.

[6] See Sartre's treatment of Fanon. Sartre, though heroic compared with Mies van der Rohe, was not able to provide the criteria for ethical judgments, and in spite of "totalization" became instead the contingent victim of such figures as Genet and Fanon.

[7] For example, at a conference in Copenhagen, held under the auspices of the UN International Women's Year, a number of women delegates from African countries defended the practice of cliterodectomy on the ground that it was an expression of cultural identity.

[8] Personal conversation.

[9] Paul Fussell, *The Great War and Modern Memory* (New York, 1977).

Discussion: Hersch Paper

Hersch: My intention was the following. It came from an everyday experience of mine in the last years; that is, that many people around us of all kinds, in life, in literature, in philosophy, in politics, in propaganda, and so on are saying as if it were a fact that there is no meaning any more in life, in our history, and even in our civilization. And we are in the strange situation where we are asked to make the greatest effort to spread technical civilization around the world, and feel guilty if we don't do so. At the same time, it is explained to us that it is a civilization that has no meaning, no value, no humanity, and that is pure materialism. I think this is creating a kind of schizophrenic situation.

Somehow men are tired of being men, of being a human being. And it is true that after all the terrible things that happened in this century, one can get tired of being human. There is a desire to not be human any more, to become either innocent angels or innocent cows, to get rid of our condition. Human beings, helped by the great, unbelievable successes of technical civilization, ask now to come out of this condition and to have a new one where there would be no risk, no death, no lack. I tried to suggest that the way to a meaning, or to finding our way back to a meaning, would be first to accept the conditions that are the ones of being a human being. You cannot take half of it and leave half of it. You cannot cut out what is painful in order to keep what is agreeable. And this should condition the education of our children, of our young people. We should stop telling them that they are all geniuses who have to create masterpieces from morning to night; that we are human beings who, step by step, succeeded in developing what we have developed, that science made its huge successes when it stopped asking questions about the wholeness and looked for something partial. I think we are at home in the partial and not in the whole. This kind of modesty seems to me indispensable to finding again the way to meaning—that is to say, to freedom, to being human.

Yamada: We are entrusting man's destiny to the hands of

science and technology. It is a big gamble because technological innovations are products of coincidences. They are not something we can intentionally discover. Discoveries are byproducts of coincidence. But then, technology also belongs in the domain of values. What we judge as desirable may be due to the economic values of a person, or the esthetics of a person, or the values of one societal group. But to select a product of coincidence gives way to a technological structure or an industrial structure. Thus, ultimately speaking, we can say this is a big gamble. In Kant's terms, science is in the domain of pure reason, and technology is in the world of judgment. When science and technology come together, a lot of power has been demonstrated. I think this is the marriage of the domains of pure reason and judgment.

Hersch: Of course, technology is based on science. But on the other side, technology belongs to practical reason because we are aiming at something when we are realizing something in technology; it is a result of a choice. On the other hand, when you are studying pure reason, it is also a choice. When you are studying the atom, when you are dealing with physics, you are not dealing with your intentions, but you have an intention. And that is something I believe is very important. Some people say that science is proving there is no such thing as freedom because of scientific determinism. I believe that the very existence of science is a monument to the glory of freedom; it would never have existed if people had not been able to choose the aim of knowledge. In that sense, the mere fact of doing research is an action, and it is in the field of practical reason: Pure reason also has roots in practical reason, practical reason has conditions that are imposed by pure reason. You cannot separate them.

Kolakowski: Of great interest to me is what the Germans call *Entzauberung* or the *entzauberte Welt*; a world deprived of meaning. In Hersch's paper we read that the facts in themselves have no meaning, and it is up to us to give them one; that this is our responsibility. If we make such an assumption, it appears that the meaning-giving act is, as it were, our free decision, so that we freely decide whether or not the world has a meaning, whether life has a meaning, and what this meaning might be. If I am able to decide that there is, say, one particular goal I am going to try to achieve in my life, I can certainly get the feeling of meaningfulness of life. On the other hand, it is possible to have a sense of meaning without having one such single goal to which everything is subordinated. It might be enough to believe that one's own life somehow contributes to the enrichment of society, even on a very modest scale, or for that matter, to the enrichment of one's own life. This does not imply any hierarchiy of values. I might get a feeling of satisfaction in being a successful rascal, a successful robber, or doing whatever gives me satisfaction. Now, if we speak of the meaning of life which is freely decided by an individual, then everything Hersch is saying about freedom, possibility, and time is valid.

But I do perceive a certain ambiguity in Hersch's analysis. On the one hand she suggests that meaning is something freely decreed by ourselves; the world has no value in itself. The facts offer no values; the world is not a cosmos in the traditional sense. Therefore, meaning has to be imposed upon the world by our free decision. On the other hand, once we are conscious of the fact that we endow the world with meaning by freely deciding what it is, we cannot subsequently believe—at least we cannot believe *bona fide*—that the world has a meaning, because we know that it is we who are the authors of this meaning, and that this meaning is not perceived in the world itself. Hersch wonders whether the monstrosities of the twentieth century were not themselves rendered possible by man's failure to be responsible before himself. She writes: "This failure is probably not the cause, but it has suppressed that which, from within, opposes and uncompromisingly resists the inhuman. It has excluded all recourse to that which is unconditional." This seems to suggest that the unconditional, *das Unbedingte*, is the condition of meaning.

Perhaps it is so. But if it is so, then we should admit that the meaning is not given by us, but rather is found in the world. If it requires the reference to the unconditional, there is a metaphysical foundation of the world and of values. I do not see how we can reconcile these two perspectives. It is true that science is not meaning-generating in the sense that no meaning can spring out of scientific effort. On the contrary, the world described by science is essentially a world in which no meaning can be perceived. However, one of the most important confusions of our century is the confusion of science with scientism, or science with scientific rationalism. Scientific rationalism is not a logical conclusion, a logical consequence of science. Scientism, or scientific rationalism, is an ideological attitude implying that the cognitive value is defined by procedures established in written or unwritten codes of science as they have been set up during the development of modern science since the seventeenth century.

Science itself cannot establish this definition. Nothing in science itself implies or gives a foundation to the conclusion that the procedures which establish validity in scientific effort define, at the same time, what is or is not cognitively valid—what has or has not cognitive value. This latter definition is an ideological one; it is not a logical consequence of science. We can therefore oppose the spirit of scientific rationalism without questioning anything in science itself. We do not need to deny anything in science by denying the scientistic or rationalistic philosophy or scientistic ideology; it is not in itself the road toward a meaningful world. It might be a necessary, but not a sufficient condition of it. What we need in addition is precisely the belief, which is not legal within the code of scientific method, that we do not produce the meaning but we find it somehow ready-made, that a meaning comes from the unconditional, from *das Unbedingte*. And certainly no metaphysical assumptions of this kind can be produced by scientific methods. They are metaphysical in the proper sense, and we should admit that.

We cannot convert metaphysical presuppositions into scientific statements. But once we admit them, we admit as well that the meaning is not something we freely declare. Therefore, we deny what is said at the very beginning of Hersch's paper, at least if I understand it properly: that the meaning is something we produce. If we produce it, we can always deny it. If we refuse to believe that there is a meaning which is there before we discover it, then it is something we can cancel at any moment—or at least we cannot challenge anybody who denies it. I wonder how you can reconcile these two perspectives.

Hersch: You are asking the fundamental metaphysical question of the origin of freedom. It is not only the origin of meaning; it is the origin of freedom. You say, either it exists metaphysically and you are neither free to decree the meaning nor responsible for it, or you are responsible for it, and then there is no metaphysical foundation and you are in the field of arbitrary choice. How can I reconcile this?

I am not going to reconcile it, but I would say that the whole human condition is grounded on the impossibility of reconciling it. And this is the only authentic way of living these things. I do not know if in English you can say "to live these things." I mean to experience it in the deepest sense. The question is, is a man free to be free? Is he responsible for being a free being? Is he created as a free being or not?

You have the same question about faith. Is faith given, or is anybody responsible for his faith? If it is given, it is like a fact. And if the human being is responsible for his faith, then you have a kind of arbitrary choice if you look at that from outside and if you state it like an experiential thing. I believe that the unconditional, the recourse to unconditionality, to the absolute, belongs to the same structure through which somebody makes himself into a free being—these are two aspects of the same reality, of the same act. I would not derive the one from the other. I would not say the unconditional allows a human being to have meaning. I would not say the unconditional allows the human being to be free. Either it is given together, given through a fundamental metaphysical decision of the subject, or it is not.

And I do not see how you can reconcile these things and these problems through a priority given to the absolute in relation to meaning. I think there is a little confusion. It does not mean that any meaning is good; that any value can be decreed; that I can decree freely and with just as much right that one race is superior, let us say, or something like that. No, there is no arbitrariness of that kind. It is not a question of having *a* meaning; it is a question of admitting meaning as such and taking a position in life within the relation of meaning, with which the relation with the unconditional is always given.

Schwartz: I feel that in much of what has been said, a very simple question is implicit that rises to the surface after all the efforts of the nineteenth and twentieth centuries: What is a human being? I think we face that question very starkly. One of the feelings I have about both these centuries is that people have found meanings—they have found meanings and they are still finding meanings. One can live a quite meaningful life as a technologist, as it were. But I think the question of good meanings is a very real, old question. What is good and what is bad is still there. I also feel with Kolakowski that to some extent the answer has some relationship to the unconditional; it cannot be avoided. What role would freedom then play in that? I think some people have very, very clear moral codes. Where does freedom exist in such a case? It exists either in acting according to the moral code or in not acting according to the moral code. It is the old freedom to be good or evil.

I think that what is a scandal from the scientific point of view is that the human being emerges as a very queer creature, with this whole moral dimension. And one of the ways social scientistic philosophies have of avoiding this is to take this question out of the living human being and project it onto historical or developmental processes. In other words, the individual human being no longer has to make such decisions. One of the scandals about the ordinary perception of human morality—and I think it exists in East Asian culture too, at least in the Confucian tradition—is that the human being has this sort of queer power of trying to improve himself, making himself good.

Who in the modern world asks this question: What can I do to make myself good? It is such a naive and preposterous question in terms of many modern historicist and scientistic philosophies. But I think that this very naive question—after Freud, after the behaviorists—What is a human being? has to be raised again. Then the whole question of what role technology should play in our lives becomes again indeed a question of judgment. I was very struck by Yamada's willingness to put the question of technology as a question of judgment, to say that it ought to be put back into the realm of moral judgment so that one weighs the value of a given technological development against other values. So I end with this question: Is it possible to revive the question of what is a human being?

Hersch: To the question what is a human being, I would try to answer that a human being is a being that has at least two allegiances: toward nature on one side and toward freedom on the other. It is on the frontier of at least two worlds. And because of that, the question of what is a good and bad meaning implies a previous question: Do we have sense for meaning? Therefore, the question that you ask, how can I make myself good, is not at all naive, because it implies already that the one who says that wants to be good. He already wants to be good: and that is the whole problem.

Karl: What Hersch does is certainly extend beautifully and brilliantly a kind of plea for life that has become, in American society and particularly among the young, a major issue that runs the full gamut of questions from concern for the environment to the willingness or the circumstances under which one sacrifices life for or to the state. The increasing refusal of young Americans to be willing to sacrifice life seems to me to be, whether one agrees with it or not as a moral principle, a rather important transformation. We all come from cultures in which the tradition of heroism, the tradition of the identity of cultural meaning, has been closely tied to sacrifice. The students that I teach, when they read Patrick Henry's statement "Give me liberty or give me death," no longer believe that he meant it, as my generation did. What are the consequences for historical continuity if this glorification of life at all costs becomes the fundamental of Western, Eastern—whatever—philosophy?

Hersch: The question is that when you speak of life—and it is the life of a human being—life keeps the double allegiance of which I was talking before. For a human being, life is not only a biological life. You have to understand what it means: life for a human being. You have in human language expressions like "there is no more life." It does not mean that the person is dead; the person himself feels that being alive is not a life for him.

There is an attempt nowadays, because of the great dangers that are about us, to simplify the matter through an objective God, through scientific knowledge of society, through objective foundations, and sometimes through an objectivized religion. It is an attempt to rescue collective human life. I believe this is an inadequate answer, and a dangerous path. It only seems to be easy. If we go that way—that is to say, if we lose this fundamental contradiction at the bottom that cannot be resolved except *hic et nunc* in the given situation by a specific person—then we take a path where we shall be lost. I think this is one of the great dangers we face.

Discussion: Windsor Paper

Windsor: My paper is addressed to the criterion of what it means to be human, in terms of humanity rather than in terms of what it is to be a man. But it is in part addressed to the kinds of questions that have been raised before: whether, for example, we can adapt technology to humanity in the realm of moral judgment, or whether we are the slaves of historical developments.

First, I have dwelt upon a positivistic past that continues into the present from the nineteenth century, one that denies ontological concerns and leads instead to value-free experiments by which it becomes impossible to establish moral boundaries. But I was also suggesting that the nineteenth century has come into the twentieth in a different way, that idealistic philosophy, whatever its transmutations, provided a starting point for a self-conscious discontinuity—a break with history. This discontinuity also provides a new framework for the positivistic forms of experiment. Hence, in the totalitarian forms taken by the discontinuity, you can get a positivistic activity—such as in the experiments of the camps.

The third element I was trying to distinguish is the phenomenon of collective humanity, obviously closely related to the ideas of totalitarianism as they provide a context for the breakdown of a distinction between the world of phenomena and the noumenal world. The breakdown of this distinction is what enabled the totalitarian systems of the twentieth century to emerge. They were substitutes in time for the timeless world of the noumenal, and this happened to be very much in line with what Friedländer was arguing in talking about political religion.

Therefore it seems that one matter which has to be addressed in thinking about ourselves and the twentieth century is a certain continuity between the liberal West and the world of the camps. I was interested that Kyogoku compared factories to military organizations. One could also say that the concentration camps were a concentrated form of production. In an earlier conversation, Nivat pointed out that the Tupolev bomber was designed in a *sharashka*, a scientific concentration camp of the type in Solzhenitsyn's *The First Circle*.

These considerations led me to think about the century discontinuous with itself; that is to say, having no relationship with the past or the future. This absence of relationship with the past and future also leads to an absence of responsibility. It is striking that attempts to realize what it is to be human apart from specific and circumstantial affairs are now found very largely in a fear of the future. And that in very many ways is the relationship we now have to the future.

Some here have argued that even if we are not going for some technological fix, the experience of the first half of the twentieth century is now behind us. I do not agree. My position is that the question of what it is to be or to become human has been asked in the most monstrous of forms; and that social engineering and modernization in general not only ignore but positively obscure this question. So what I have tried to concentrate on is two forms of experience, which in my view demonstrate the ignoring and the obscuring of the question of what it is to be a human.

The first is the failure of decolonization to bring about a framework for development—and I do not mean economic development, but intellectual and moral development—of the newly liberated lands and of how we see ourselves through them.

The second question is that of nuclear deterrence. In this context I also had in mind some of Iriye's considerations: peace is war and war is peace. Hersch, I remember, challenged Iriye on this point when she remarked that you could not treat a war as a single phenomenon; that wars took different forms for different reasons. But in the end, I still agree with Iriye. It seems to me that states make wars, but man makes war.

On the question of decolonization I argue that it seems to represent a global extension of the failure of Western liberalism. And I further suggest that independence has become in many countries positively regressive. One can think, for example, of the role of women in the Algerian struggle for independence, which was important and at times crucial. At that time, women were part of a revolutionary heroism. Given Algerian independence, women have by and large been locked up again. Within this context of apparent liberation but of failure to develop, of occasional regression, a generalized state of mind, expressed by Dostoevsky and cited by Maruyama, has also meant a state of mind involving terrorism. This affects not only international terrorists as such, but also many governments. In this sense "the end of objectivity" is not a phenomenon at a purely individual or social level; it is a phenomenon carried out in terroristic forms at the governmental level, and by the idealistic destruction of idealism at the other.

As to the system of nuclear deterrence, part of what I suggest is that nuclear deterrence is not a simple structure of superpower relationships. It is increasingly drawn into Third World conflicts and is no longer decently arcane and abstract. Until fairly recently, I did assume that strategic structures could be kept in stable order; that arms control had a function and a purpose; and that it was possible to achieve control of the nuclear arms race. I am now very much more pessimistic about this. The drift here is that the need to answer the questions humans have experienced about themselves, as humans, has been turned by nuclear deterrence into a probabilistic bet. And the bet is being increasingly stacked against us.

Finally, I would suggest that the historical and conceptual position of the warring parties in the world depends on the fact that they *are* warring. Again, I do regard war either at the level of thermonuclear destruction or of guerrilla warfare as part of that "war of the spirits" Nietzsche evoked in 1876. These wars, which have become random in many parts of the world, are still parts of the continuum, a state of mind.

Maier: I think the problem of meaninglessness is a relative one. Certainly, the world of private meaning, I do not believe, has drastically changed in the twentieth century. This is a historical judgment, but I accept the conditions of meaning that Hersch poses, but that I do not think have vanished. In the sense of private fulfillment—falling in love, raising children, sharing in their joy, grieving at people's deaths, and the acceptance of illness and death—I do think we still accept these. The world of private meaning keeps its richness through the twentieth century and will keep it.

In the world of public meaning I am more sympathetic to the implications of these papers. There is a tendency for science to become scientism. Real physics keeps indeterminacy. Socio-biology, on the other hand, seems to me to have dimensions of quackery and control mechanisms and pseudoscience that are immensely dangerous. I think that is a failure of historical consciousness, that our awareness of time past, which is the conditioning for acting in the present, is eroded.

Let us accept that the public world has been subject to elements of banalization and dehumanization. I think we are passing through a critical period in which we have enlarged communities at the same time that we have banalized communities. We are willing to water down standards and no longer to have the confidence that what we thought was decent behavior should apply to nine-tenths of the people of the world. But let's put this in the context of twentieth-century experience. One of its positive aspects has been the tremendous enlargement of community. We have made tribes into nations. And the nation-state is still the repository of value and of historical action. Not all nations are yet perfect nations. But we have to bear in mind that this is an effort of enlargment. I would mention some other enlargements. In the United States, one of the things we can count as an accomplishment is that of enlargement in terms of race. Everyone who travels in the United States must realize that despite the continuing poverty, the legal and the public and civic world of black Americans is immensely different from what it was.

Finally, I would mention women. The whole movement to make women into citizens has been an immense one. I think that effort at public enlargment of a community is also one in which some of these banalizations are bound to appear as a byproduct. Negative aspects can be seen, but I do think we must put them in context. It was, I believe, the eighteenth and nineteenth centuries that gave us such an acute consciousness of time as future, of time as possibility, as progress. I think in that sense there is a great continuity.

Hersch: When you say that the conditions of meaning were always those of human life—acceptance of death and so on—it is true only to a certain extent. For instance, the World Health Organization has a principle, the first principle, which is the right to health. That on an international level physicians have gathered together and adopted such a statement is a portent.

How can a mortal being who knows that he is mortal admit that there is a right to health? What they meant is a right to have physicians, to have medicine, to have hygienic conditions, and so on. But this is not the right to health.

As for science and scientism, I believe that the indeterminacy of physics is not the answer. But it is quite true that scientism is dangerous; science is not at all dangerous for the possibility of thinking, for meaning, and for freedom.

Windsor: Two points. The first is about whether in the private realm we really accept death. We all know we are going to die; that is one thing. But the acceptance of death is something quite different. Walter Benjamin has a passage where he talks about the look of indefinable authority on the faces of the dying in pictures where people died at home surrounded by friends and relations. It is very rare that people die at home now in the liberal West. They are shunted away and they die in hospital. It is equally rare that people actually accept death.

The second point is that the distinction between the public and the private realm is something which can be taken for granted only under certain political and social conditions. To give you one example: when the Soviet Union entered Riga after the Nazi-Soviet pact, the students of the University of Riga came down the steps out of a lecture and found Soviet soldiers standing outside. They were divided quite arbitrarily into two groups. One was sent to Siberia and the other was allowed to stay. It did not matter whether they were holding hands, whether they were in love, or anything. That is how it was. And one can repeat that experience ad infinitum in all parts of the world. It is a luxurious perspective which allows one still to distinguish between the public and the private realm. The public realm has invaded the private.

Friedländer: Are we discussing a general existential problem, or one of people in the twentieth century? Each paper tries to link the general problem to the twentieth century, but I find the evidence much too superficial. The answers are also very general, and necessarily so; it is more a problem of meaning in the modern world (rationalism, enlightenment, positivism, and so on), which is a very general problem of modernity and not a problem distinctly tied to the twentieth century.

Second, the social critique implied in both papers is dangerous. I agree with most of what is said, but the critique goes both ways. It goes against the evils of liberalism and positivism and scientism, but at the same time it is done too broadly, and therefore one has the impression that the whole of liberalism has led to this result. Be very careful with this kind of criticism—criticizing good and evil indiscriminately so that suddenly you are left in a kind of desert, where precisely totalitarian tendencies can then rush in. Some types of liberalism or positivism and scientism lead to totalitarianism, but there is also another way of looking at liberal society.

And third, the answers; these are, I think, crucial. Hersch actually, if one reduces her answer to something I may pin down, provides the Camusian answer. Her philosophy is Camus more or less, but that is a twentieth-century answer. Sartre's was a real attempt to grapple with the problem of freedom without transcendance, though he then went into explanations of history. But Camus—that is pure Camus.

I wonder what Windsor's answer really is, and I would be grateful if he would tell us more. How does he envision—more concretely—the kind of world where something of an answer could be given? A return to pre-eighteenth-century structures?

Hersch: Well, I am not too unhappy to be criticized for having written something that could be dangerous for a liberal society, because I am sure that there can be no liberal society without danger. And I believe that the tendencies we have, to say we must be content with liberalism as such, and to consider anything against it as being an attack that might lead to something which is the opposite of what one wants, is unavoidable. Now, when you say I am making a critique of the whole liberal world, that it has collapsed as such—that is not exactly my position. I cannot bear the general condemnation passed upon science, upon technology, upon the technological world. I acknowledge the unbelievable conquests and advantages which have been earned by the liberal world and by science and by technology. That my answer is pure Camusian, I do not believe, but it is closer to Camus and I consider it rather agreeable.

Windsor: Two small observations. I do not think I talked about the failure, but about the failures, of liberalism, and there is a very fundamental distinction between the two. The framework within which I would think would still be that of the liberal framework. But there also has to be a postliberal framework, and that brings me to the question you raised about the answers. I use the phrase "devise a language" at the end because we must try to think about these questions anew.

Nivat: I want to mention a name, the name of Andrei Sakharov. In her paper Hersch has a statement about Socrates and why Socrates accepted death under unjust law. Probably he accepted it because he could die surrounded by his friends, and his friends could maintain the dialogue with him until the end. There is no such dialogue in a concentration camp. And today the camp is not even necessary for totalitarianism once it has played its role in silencing people. Nothing very drastic is necessary to silence a man like Sakharov. I think that the real meaning comes out of dialogue, and the real dialogue comes when you have a dialogue between *convinced* people. For me, for example, the two best novels which are dialogues would be *The Brothers Karamazov* and *The Magic Mountain*. I am very much struck that on the one hand fanaticism and terrorism in a way have replaced conviction, and that on the other, conviction is considered in the pseudodialogue we get in Western media as equivalent to fanaticism. In my eyes it is the opposite.

And this brings me to another question: the word "religion." It is strange to see that many people who come from the former secular belief of socialism turn to religion and say to religion, "You should function, you should be, you should develop"; but they will not enter into religion. And even I would say that when a man like the present pope speaks, he is accepted as long as he speaks in the language of our media—let us say, about human rights. But he is immediately not opposed, but not heard, when he speaks of belief.

Hersch: Socrates does not mean that he is dying under an unjust law, because an unjust law would not be a law; but under a law that is unjustly applied. This distinction matters, because there were times recently when the whole law was criminal, and therefore Socrates would probably not have obeyed it or submitted to it. What he meant is that you cannot live without law, and the law as such is respected, but not its false or unjust application.

Now I am quite of your opinion that there is only dialogue between convinced people, and that you have an apparently easier dialogue between people who are not very convinced. Equally, it is becoming much more difficult among convinced people, so that people in our time think it is very agreeable, socially speaking, to have people lacking in conviction. It makes for an easier togetherness in the society. But it is not dialogue. Fanaticism and terrorism are not a discussion, a dialogue between convinced people, but a substitution of facts and force for dialogue.

But now you ask, what is the place of religion in my paper? You move me when you say that we ask religion to function without adhering to it. That has much to do with what my philosophical teacher, Jaspers, calls the philosophical faith. Many people think that philosophical faith means *une fois tiède* (a tepid faith). It is not. It has to be accepted with its radicality and its depth. I think there are people now who cannot find the right word or voice to speak about religion. And it would be false if they did speak. The pope can; but I cannot, for instance. I think that is something characteristic of our time. But it is honest to speak of philosophical faith in this case, and it is not a path that leads nowhere. Because you then can speak to people, to everybody, and not only to believers.

Mommsen: In a way, I have a feeling that if one is presented with arguments about the past, the present, and the future of the twentieth century in the rhetoric of doom, one is unable to take any alternative position. Posing problems using such a rhetoric has the advantage of being nearly always right and the disadvantage of being not constructive, inasmuch as it takes away the tools of fighting those tendencies and turning them from self-fulfilling prophecies into self-denying prophecies.

Now, I agree about the failure of liberal decolonization and the theories of modernization that go with it, because they did not pay attention to the indigenous historical preconditions. But I would not take away the moral obligation that goes with this Western philosophy, not even at the present moment. And perhaps at some points, the picture may not be as dark. You refer to the fact that violence and war are the reality in many cases of the process of decolonization. That is an unwanted consequence of the Pax Britannica or the imperialist peace that we had, which suppressed conflicts and let them accumulate over long periods. This must be seen as a corollary, and perhaps it is not quite a hopeless task to control it.

One last remark that perhaps refers to both papers. If we can do anything to overcome the problems we face, we will have to strike a balance between moral engagement, which is in the last resort a very personal decision (nowadays I would say there is no fundamental on which we can operate), and accepting modernity. For me at least, the phenomenon of fascism can be explained as a last desperate attempt to avoid the consequences of modernization, especially the egalitarian consequences that go with it. On the other hand, I see the Soviet phenomenon as quite different, as an attempt to enforce modernity by any means, whatever happens.

In some ways neither takes into account the real situation, though I would admit that the concentration camp and the Gulag do condition what is left of liberalism in the present age. But perhaps not only negatively. I think the very fact that we saw totalitarian doctrines collapse in total chaos, or create inhuman conditions on a grand scale, helped give new life to an ideological position that was presumed dead. I myself would say, having nothing better, I would rather stick to it than to have it undermined by the prophets of doom, whatever may come. For me, I think, there is in this sort of decision a meaning in life. I do not think that meaning has disappeared.

Windsor: On the point of the rhetoric of doom: the task was to say something about the character of the twentieth century as one saw it, in whatever dimensions one chose. It was not to be prescriptive about the twenty-first or to pretend that one could come up with answers. I'm all in favor of self-denying prophecies; and in fact I was trying to conclude with a self-denying prophecy. I think that we live in a very dangerous world and that it arises very largely out of mental confusions which it is important to clarify. But that is as far as I would be prescriptive at the moment.

On modernity. Well, it is a bit like the lady in conversation with Carlyle who said: "Mr. Carlyle, I accept the universe." He replied, "Madame, you had better." There is obviously no choice about modernity. It is the *kind* of modernity that one has to think about. There I agree absolutely that not everything is hopeless;

but things are dangerous unless we think more clearly, that is all.

In terms of the Third World and moral obligations, the point I was making was that the issue of moral obligation seems to me to be central. The Brandt report skirts the issue because it does not consider that moral obligation has political appeal in the contemporary West. That struck me as very important.

Schwartz: The totalitarian project I think has really proved to be a failure. The whole notion of an omnipotent state that can make men over in its own image really is not true. You can have totalitarian regimes, but it has been proved that they cannot do what they claim they do. To the extent that liberalism represents a rejection of that, liberalism has proved to be—if one adds to liberalism some elements of welfare socialism—much more successful. So you have there two cheers for liberalism. I would not make a total indictment of the whole Enlightenment heritage. It is a question of breaking it down and examining it point by point, it seems to me. There has been this whole industry of either attacking or accepting the Enlightenment. I think the time has come to break it down and ask what we expect even of what we want to preserve. It does not have to be a total cure for all human problems.

Windsor: I agree. It is these distinctions one has to draw.

Hagihara: Perhaps Maruyama would have some comments now.

Maruyama: In relation to the subjects touched upon in these two papers, let me refer again to the problems I raised in our discussion of the Hagihara paper. I think it is necessary to reexamine the historical process from which the present world order emerged. In a word, it was a globalization process of the so-called Western state system. All concepts of international law and politics—sovereignty, the principle of non-intervention in domestic affairs, the legal distinction between combatants and non-combatants, freedom of the open sea, and so on—were born and bred in the West. The globalization of liberalism, however, important it may be, is only one aspect of the whole concept of world order that developed through the eighteenth and nineteenth centuries in the West. One cannot neglect that the concepts of independence and sovereignty emerged from nation-states with common historical and cultural backgrounds, such as the Greco-Roman classical legacy, the system of Roman law, and last, but not least, Christianity. These factors were the common denominator which each sovereign state shared. Thus you could speak of international law in wartime, in which war was seen as something like a duel fought between sovereign states according to certain rules and tacit understandings. Only actions violating the rules were regarded as unjust; the duel itself was neither just nor unjust but simply something that was there. This form of international order lasted without losing its validity until the end of World War I.

It was in the latter half of the nineteenth century that Japan literally "opened" itself (*kaikoku*) to the West. A journalist of the Meiji era heralded his country's emergence as the first modern state in Asia in a symbolic expression: "Japan entering Europe" (*nyūō*). But, ironically enough, when Japan joined the "international" community, various contradictions inherent in the traditional concepts of world order began to surface. Putting aside the question whether and to what extent Japan really "entered Europe," what I want to stress here is that once the Western state system was extended beyond the West, its globalization was bound to bring about the atomization in a world order lacking any of the cultural and religious ties that bind together nation-states or territorial states (Schwartz). Iriye suggests that the distinction between war and peace became blurred in the twentieth century. But I wonder if it is a new phenomenon. I am inclined to think the period in which such a distinction was possible was rather brief in the long history of mankind and its validity limited in space.

As far as Western Europe is concerned, the very development of sovereign nation-states meant the split of "one world." From the standpoint of cultural history, the European Community is not so much a new creation as a rebirth of old Europe. But what about the present-day world in which one hundred sixty-odd states coexist with equal sovereign rights? During the sessions, we talked much about peace, freedom, and justice. Frankly speaking, however, so little has been discussed on the structural relationship of such concepts with that of world order. One example of the contradictions we are faced with is the emergence of the idea of war criminals in the international military tribunals of Tokyo and Nuremberg. I do not mean the so-called B- or C-class criminals, because problems concerning the treatment of POWs have already been dealt with at the Hague conferences. I mean the epoch-making fact that top *political* leaders of the state were prosecuted and given verdicts in the name of "civilization." This is unbelievable unless we presuppose that there exists one world order transcending every sovereign state and that those who violate this order are subject to legal punishment, as in the case of order within a nation. Since a judiciary of this world order did not exist, the judges of the tribunal were composed of representatives of "peace-loving nations," which actually meant that the victors judged the defeated—yet in a form entirely different from the case of duels between states.

The assumption of one world order had already appeared in Article 16 of the Covenant of the League of Nations: "Should any Member of the League resort to war in disregard of its convenants . . . it shall *ipso facto* be deemed to have committed an act of war against all other Members of the League." And everyone knows this ideal was inherited by the United Nations. It is easy to ridicule the impotence of either the League of Nations or the United Nations; but I do not share the opinion of some scholars that too legalistic a thinking is responsible for the impotence of such international organizations. The contradictions underlying the assumption of one world order are revealed in many other cases.

I cannot help seeing some invisible thread linking the indiscriminate bombings of small and large cities, killing millions of non-combatant civilians, during World War II to the terrorism taking place in the world today, which indiscriminately involves any person on the street. Superpowers today act as world police, thus justifying intervention in disputes and "peripheral violence" (Maier) anywhere in the world. This does not necessarily mean superpowers are omnipotent. On the contrary, they have revealed their weakness vis-à-vis guerrilla warfare, despite their overwhelming superiority in terms of weapons and transport. In this sense, the Japanese military invasion of China or of southeast Asia in the 1930s and 1940s may be seen as a forerunner of what happened in Vietnam and Afghanistan. Japan's joining the international community was called "entering Europe." However, it is improbable that the many states established after decolonization would conceive of their independence in terms of "entering Europe" or "Euro-America." Rather, it seems to me very ironical that the Third World has, in the process of state formation, borrowed uncritically from the West almost all concepts regarding territory and sovereignty while bitterly—and quite naturally—attacking the domination of the West. Even odder is the case of socialist countries based on Marxism-Leninism referring to "our *sacred* territory."

In short, what I would like to stress here is simply that contradictions underlying the globalization of the Western state system might be much greater than are generally perceived, the more so if one looks at what expressions should be used, for the problem of terminology is often located at the subconscious level. To what extent are prevailing concepts of law, politics, and social organization culture-bound to Western civilization, and to what extent to they have really universal validity? I would be the last to deny the necessity for non-Western peoples to continue learning from the vast cultural heritage of the West. My remarks thus far may sound cynical or pessimistic, but I must confess at present I feel, even more keenly than upon my "emancipation" from the militarist regime of prewar Japan, that mankind is now faced with the difficult task of finding a new common denominator on which different cultures and value-systems, each with their long historical backgrounds, can not only coexist but also interact effectively and peacefully.

Afterthought Sent by Jeanne Hersch

I feel guilty in retrospect. We have all, in my opinion, yielded too easily to the excessive pessimistic view of the twentieth century which is fashionable nowadays. What was said was true. But very much has been omitted. For instance:

In spite of two terrible wars and of the constant costs of the threats of war which never stopped, Europe has succeeded, through hard work, in raising the standards of living in most states to a level never known before, and in improving all social conditions of life; so has Japan.

In spite of tragedies and difficulties, the twentieth century has been the century of decolonization, even if most problems are far from being solved.

In spite of the Nazi conquests and victories, in spite of complicity and cowardice, the Western democracies have recovered because they had in themselves a source of tough resistance. The *tissu social* has not been destroyed. English people, civilians, did not yield during a year of resistance alone under bombing. The French Resistance contributed to the victory of the Allies, even if the men and women engaged in it were not very numerous in the beginning; but those who were offered their lives. These considerations should not be left out of our view of the century. Nor should the German "resistants."

We spoke of the Gulag, and we were right to do so. But then we should not forget, because they belong to the face of this century, the heroic dissidents who fought, who died, who survived and fought again—even without hope.

In spite of the fact that the political federation of Europe has not succeeded so far, much has been achieved during a relatively short period. Nobody has even mentioned the beginnings of this huge and difficult enterprise, which also belongs to the twentieth century—especially the extraordinary reconciliation of France and Germany.

And it is also part of any verdict on this century that, in spite of all the promises, lies, and threats, even the threat of nuclear weapons, the Western democracies have not yielded so far. Nobody knows what will happen, but so far their societies resist. Maybe that is, in the face of the actual conditions, our first and most difficult duty: to resist, as long as it will be necessary; to hold fast, with patience and stubbornness.

INDEX